SING WITH UNDERSTANDING

"I will sing with the spirit, and I will sing with the understanding also" (1 Cor. 14:15).

AN INTRODUCTION TO CHRISTIAN HYMNOLOGY

Harry Eskew
Hugh T. McElrath

Illustrations Prepared by Charles Massey, Jr.

BROADMAN PRESS
Nashville, Tennessee

To Margaret
and
to Ruth

© Copyright 1980 • Broadman Press
All rights reserved.
Illustrations © 1980 • Charles Massey, Jr,
Item code: 4268-09
ISBN: 0-8054-6809-9
Printed in the United States of America.

Foreword

Hymnology is both a derived and an applied science—derived from the disciplines of theology, Bible, poetry and literature, biography, music, and liturgy; applied in the church's worship and educational life. In our time the two most popular published forms of hymnology are the denominational handbook or companion and the hymnal itself. *Sing with Understanding* is neither a commentary nor a hymnal, but rather a textbook (really two textbooks) which deals with hymnology as both derived from tradition and as applied in the church's continuing mission. I believe it to be a significant contribution to hymnic bibliography.

The writers *understand* the problems of comparative hymnic criticism; they *understand* the vast hymnological bibliography and then set out to *organize* it. They *comprehend* the fixed geographic and linguistic boundaries, both ancient and modern, of the Western Church's song, and they *translate* descriptions of those old divisions into *understandings* of our contemporary situation.

But most important, they have heard and they have experienced the contemporary church with its widely divergent yet locally accepted hymnic performance practices and repertoire. They *speak a discerning word* amid the *glossolalia* of prideful false claims and uninformed opinions which have sounded forth not only from the predictable "electric church" but more vexatiously from some of this country's most influential pulpits, choirlofts, and seminaries.

Reading this book will not transform today's cacophony into yesterday's plainsong! But its study will go a long way toward providing aid and comfort to those teachers, musicians, pastors, and others who hold reason and reflection above the seductive ways of an all-pervasive-pop-folk religion—a religion characterized and acted out in the gnostic nonsense of much of today's parish worship life. In this respect, this book also will be helpful in the radical reconstruction of seminary and parish education, so necessary if we are to train church leaders to worship and in turn to lead others to worship the God that Jesus Christ worshiped and obeyed.

The book's title is drawn from St. Paul, 1 Cor. 14:15. A little further in the letter the apostle in characteristic hyperbole comes down on the side of *understanding* as prerequisite to effective church leadership:

Yet in the church I had rather speak five words with my understanding, that by my voice I might teach others also, than ten thousand words in an unknown tongue (14:19, KJV).

That's why this is an important book. Now let's hear it big for these five words of *understanding!*

CARLTON R. YOUNG
Professor of Church Music
Candler School of Theology

Emory University
Atlanta, Georgia

Acknowledgments

The authors acknowledge their indebtedness to the numerous scholars whose research has furnished the groundwork upon which this textbook rests. The mentioning of a few names—Julian, Patrick, Benson, Frost, Jackson, Bailey, Routley, Reynolds—must stand as representative of many others from whose hymnological writings information has been drawn.

We are particularly grateful to Dr. Scotty Gray, associate professor of church music at Southwestern Baptist Theological Seminary, Fort Worth, Texas, the Reverend Louis G. Nuechterlein, pastor of the Cheshire Lutheran Church, Cheshire, Connecticut, and Dr. Carlton R. Young, professor of church music at the Candler School of Theology of Emory University, Atlanta, Georgia, for reading all or parts of the manuscript and giving helpful advice and suggestions.

Special appreciation is also due Dr. Young for his writing the Foreword. To Professor Charles Massey, Jr., of the art faculty at Ohio State University, Columbus, Ohio, we are indebted for preparing the illustrations for this volume. We also are grateful for the help of several individuals for supplying specific points of unwritten information. These are indicated by footnotes at various points throughout the text. The various publishers and individuals who have permitted copyrighted materials to be used are hereby acknowledged with gratitude (those giving permission free of charge being indicated with an asterisk [*] at the appropriate places in the book).

Finally, we wish to express appreciation to the administrations of the New Orleans Baptist Theological Seminary and the Southern Baptist Theological Seminary, Louisville, Kentucky, for granting the sabbatic leaves, making possible the work on major portions of this study.

While recognizing the help of others, the authors take sole responsibility for the work's inevitable errors, omissions, and infelicities. However, from all who have occasion to use this volume we would welcome collaboration in the form of corrections and suggestions for improvement.

HARRY ESKEW
HUGH T. MCELRATH

SOURCES TO WHICH ABBREVIATIONS REFER*

BAILEY   Bailey, Albert Edward. *The Gospel in Hymns.* New York: Charles Scribner's Sons, 1950.

BENSON-E   Benson, Louis F. *The English Hymn.* Richmond: John Knox Press, 1962. (reprint of original 1915 ed. of George H. Doran Co., New York)

BENSON-H   _____. *The Hymnody of the Christian Church.* Richmond: John Knox Press, 1956. (reprint of the original 1927 ed. of George H. Doran Co.)

BLUME   Blume, Friedrich (ed). *Protestant Church Music.* New York: W. W. Norton & Co., 1974.

CHASE   Chase, Gilbert. *America's Music.* 2nd ed. New York: McGraw-Hill, 1966.

DAVIDSON   Davidson, James R. *A Dictionary of Protestant Church Music.* Metuchen, N. J.: The Scarecrow Press, 1975.

DOUGLAS   Douglas, Winfred. *Church Music in History and Practice.* Rev. with additional material by Leonard Ellinwood. New York: Charles Scribner's Sons, 1961.

ELLINWOOD   Ellinwood, Leonard. *The History of American Church Music.* New York: Morehouse-Gorham Co., 1953.

FOOTE   Foote, Henry W. *Three Centuries of American Hymnody.* Hamden, Conn.: The Shoe String Press, 1961. (reprint of the original 1940 ed. of Harvard University Press, Cambridge, Mass.)

JULIAN   Julian, John. *A Dictionary of Hymnology.* 2 vols. New York: Dover Publications, 1957. (reprint of 2nd rev. ed., 1907, of John Murray, London)

PATRICK   Patrick, Millar. *The Story of the Church's Song.* Rev. ed. by James R. Sydnor. Richmond: John Knox Press, 1962.

REYNOLDS   Reynolds, William J., revised by Milburn Price. *A Joyful Sound.* 2nd ed. of *A Survey of Christian Hymnody.* New York: Holt, Rinehart and Winston, 1978.

ROUTLEY-H   Routley, Erik. *Hymns and Human Life.* London: John Murray, 1952.

ROUTLEY-M   _____. *The Music of Christian Hymnody.* London: Independent Press, 1957.

RYDEN   Ryden, *The Story of Christian Hymnody.* Rock Island, Ill.: Augustana Press, 1959.

SCHALK   Schalk, Carl (ed.) *Key Words in Church Music.* St. Louis: Concordia Publishing House, 1978.

STEVENSON-PA   Stevenson, Robert. *Patterns of Protestant Church Music.* Durham, N. C.: Duke University Press, 1953.

STEVENSON-PR   _____. *Protestant Church Music in America.* New York: W. W. Norton & Co., 1966.

*See pages 10-12, The Hymn in History: Suggested Readings for Supplementary Study.

Contents

Illustrations

Introduction

The basic purpose of *Sing with Understanding* is to contribute to more meaningful congregational singing of hymns. It seeks to address the needs of those who lead in corporate worship—clergy and musicians—and also attempts to bring others, including lay persons, to a greater appreciation of their hymnals and the fascinating heritage of church song. Its primary use, however, is as a textbook for college and seminary classes in hymnology and related areas. Along with increased understanding, it is hoped that this book will contribute to helping persons "sing with the spirit"—with true inspiration and enthusiasm.

Singing with the spirit and the understanding implies some acquaintance with the nature of the vehicle used—the hymn itself. The word *hymn* in present-day understanding is a generic term for any kind of song suited to congregational expression in worship. Its treatment throughout this volume assumes a Christian context and content; yet historically the Christian hymn has not been subject to narrow definition.

In a now-famous commentary on Psalm 148, Augustine of Hippo set forth his conception of the hymn as "praises to God with singing." It is an excellent definition; but it is incomplete. Not all hymns used today are concerned with praise nor are they all addressed to God. The apostle Paul refers to "speaking *to one another*" as well as to "making melody . . . *to the Lord*" in hymns (Eph. 5:19), thus recognizing for singing a social as well as a divine direction. Hymns may therefore be expressions of prayer, of belief, of personal experience, and of exhortation to one another, as well as of praise to God.

To serve adequately these various functions, good hymns possess certain qualities. Some of these desirable qualities were included in an "official" definition by the Hymn Society of America:

> *A Christian Hymn is a lyric poem, reverently and devotionally conceived, which is designed to be sung and which expresses the worshipper's attitude toward God or God's purposes in human life. It should be simple and metrical in form, genuinely emotional, poetic and literary in style, spiritual in quality, and in its ideas so direct and so immediately apparent as to unify a congregation while singing it.*[1]

The chapters that follow seek to examine the implications of these hymnic characteristics; but the one incontestable facet of Augustine's earlier definition, alluded to twice in the above definition, is that a hymn is to be *sung*. Therefore, realizing that the definition of the hymn claiming the least

---

[1] Carl F. Price, *What Is a Hymn?* Paper VI of the Hymn Society of America, 1937, p. 8.

best defines it, the Hymn Society, through a recent action of its research committee, concluded "that for a working definition, the hymn may be regarded as a congregational song."[2]

Considered in this broad sense, songs of many kinds would be expected to comprise the great body of hymnody herein treated. However, "congregational song" is too vast a subject to be totally treated in one introductory volume. We recognize that today congregations are singing forms of psalmody (those of Gelineau, for example) and informal scriptural songs which would rightfully come under the broad definition of hymn. However, since these types of song are not represented in the hymnals to which this book is keyed,[3] they are omitted in this study.

Hymnody is the collective term for all this song literature. It is the subject matter for our study. The term is also used to refer to specific branches of the total hymnic corpus (e.g., German hymnody, Methodist hymnody).

Hymnology is the comprehensive study of this hymnody. It is concerned not only with the origins and development of hymns but also with their appreciation and use. As *An Introduction to Christian Hymnology* this volume seeks to introduce such a total study of hymns, viewing them from several perspectives.

Part I, The Hymn in Perspective (chapters 1-4) examines hymns as poetry, music, biblical truth, and theology.

Part II, The Hymn in History and Culture (chapters 5-9) is a chronological survey, concentrating attention on hymn texts and tunes available and currently used. It is particularly concerned with those hymns that may be found in three widely used American hymnals and one ecumenical hymnal supplement: *Baptist Hymnal,* 1975; *Lutheran Book of Worship,* 1978; *The Methodist Hymnal,* 1964 (later retitled *The Book of Hymns: Official Hymnal of the United Methodist Church*); and *Ecumenical Praise,* 1977.[4] Hymns mentioned in the text are keyed to these four hymnals using the letters B, L, M, and E.

The historical survey focuses attention on the texts and tunes. Biographical information is minimal since each of the three major hymnals have companion volumes[5] which can provide background data for the hymns and information about their authors and composers. The reader is also encouraged to supplement the study of this book with the suggestions found in the Table of Readings.

One's understanding of hymns is enhanced by moving beyond the mere consideration of words and music to a consideration of cultural and historic contexts. Chapter 9 seeks to explore the cultural diversity which characterizes congregational song.

Part III, The Hymn in Practice (chapters 10-13) explores the practical uses of hymns in the mission of the church: *Proclamation* and the sharing of the Good News; *Worship* and the hymn's place in corporate devotion; *Education* and the teaching values of hymns; and *Ministry* and the hymn as a medium of social concern.

The questions for thought and discussion at the close of the chapters in Parts I and III are given as aids for study and teaching. Also suggested in Part III are some projects for action. In addition, bibliographies by chapter (in addition to general works and sources for American denominational hymnody) are provided for more extensive study.

Hymnology is a rewarding field of investigation. It has captivated the interest of numerous Christians who want to know more about the hymns they sing and to learn more of the content of their hymnals. It is our hope that readers of this volume will also find hymnology a discipline that brings an increased understanding of the purpose of hymns and an enthusiasm to work for more vital and meaningful congregational singing wherever they may worship and serve.

[2]*The Hymn,* the quarterly publication of the Hymn Society of America, 29 (January 1978), 37. Information on this organization is available from the Hymn Society of America, National Headquarters, Wittenburg University, Springfield, OH.

[3]In *Ecumenical Praise* (E5) may be found one psalm setting by Joseph Gelineau. See footnote 4.

[4]*Baptist Hymnal,* ed. William J. Reynolds (Nashville: Convention Press, 1975); *Lutheran Book of Worship* (Minneapolis: Augsburg Publishing House; Philadelphia: Fortress Press, 1978); *The Book of Hymns (The Methodist Hymnal): Official Hymnal of the United Methodist Church,* ed. Carlton R. Young (Nashville: United Methodist Publishing House, 1966); and *Ecumenical Praise* (Carol Stream, IL: Agape, a Division of Hope Publishing Co., 1977).

[5]William J. Reynolds, *Companion to Baptist Hymnal* (Nashville: Broadman Press, 1976); Marilyn Stulken-Ekwo, *Hymnal Companion to the Lutheran Book of Worship* (Philadelphia: Fortress Press, 1979); and Fred D. Gealy, Austin C. Lovelace, Carlton R. Young, and Emory Stevens Bucke (ed.), *Companion to the Hymnal: A Handbook to the 1966 Methodist Hymnal* (Nashville: Abingdon Press, 1970).

THE HYMN IN HISTORY: SUGGESTED READINGS FOR SUPPLEMENTARY STUDY

SECTION	BAILEY	BENSON-E	BENSON-H	BLUME	CHASE
1. Old Testament Backgrounds			232-3[1]		
2. New Testament Backgrounds			25-53, 233-6		
3. Greek Hymnody	*10*		57-67		
4. Latin Hymnody	*9*		67-75, 99-100, 236-40		
5. German Hymnody	*11*		75-9, 240-2	3-51, 63-72, 127-48, 236-45, 251-62, 336-47, 378-82	
6. Metrical Psalmody	*1, 2,* 478-482		79-86, 100-5, 243-54	509-32, 549-52, 565-6, 575-86, 611-30, 639-48, 700-1, 722-3	*1, 2*
7. British: Pre-Watts	*3*	*1, 2*	105-10		
8. British: 18th Century	*4, 5, 6*	*3,* 205-16, *5,* 262-79, *7*	86-95, 110-24	725-7	
9. British: 19th Century	*7, 8, 12, 13, 14, 15*	435-60, 493-543	125-32, 262-65	727-8	
10. British: 20th Century	*16*	*11*	270-77	732	
11. American: Singing School and Folk		285-98	254-6	648-74, 678-84	*7, 10, 11, 12*
12. American: 19th Century Northern	484-95, 496-500, 502-3, 505-10, 511-52, 565-8	161-204, 280-4, 298-314, *8,* 460-81, 543-63	256-62	674-8	*8*
13. American: Gospel	482-4, 495-6 500-1, 503-4	484-92	265-70	685-6, 690	
14. American: 20th Century	552-65, 568-77	*11*		690	

[1]All numerals refer to *page* numbers, unless they are in italics in which case they indicate *chapter*

#	Davidson	Douglas	Ellinwood	Foote	Julian
1.	Antiphon, Psalm Tones	124-6			
2.	Canticle, Anglican Chant	126-8			
3.		128			Greek Hymnody
4.	Office Hymn Plainsong, Sarum Breviary, Te Deum laudamus	76-97; 128-72			Antiphon, Breviaries, Hymnarium, Latin Hymnody; Latin, Translations from the; Sequences, Te Deum Laudamus
5.	*Ausbund, Achtlieder-Buch,* Chorale, Leise	173-8 189-94			German Hymnody, Scandinavian Hymnody
6.	*Ainsworth Psalter, Bay Psalm Book, Dwight's Watts, Este's Psalter,* Proper Tune, Psalmody, Metrical; Psalters, *Ravenscroft Psalter,* Scottish Psalters, *Souterliedekens*	178-84	*2*	*1, 2*	*New Version, Old Version;* Psalters, English; Psalters, French, Scottish Hymnody
7.	Carol	185-8			Carol, English Hymnody, Early
8.		188-89; 194-8			Watts, Isaac; Wesley Family, The; *Olney Hymns*
9.	*Gymanfu ganu, Hymns Ancient and Modern,* Oxford Movement	199-211; 214-9			
10.		220; 226-41			
11.	Camp Meeting, Fa-Sol-La, Fuging Tune, Lining-Out, Seven-Shaped Notation, Spiritual		*3, 4, 5, 6,* 101-104	*3, 4, 5* 271-276	American Hymnody
12.		211-4	*13*	*6, 7,* 276-306	
13.	Gospel Song, Invitation Hymn, "Pop," Gospel		105, 232	263-71	
14.	Other Readings: Congregational Singing, Christian Year, Evangelistic Music, Folk Song, Hymn, Hymnal, Hymnody, Hymn Meter, Hymn Tune Precentor, Song Leader	222-3; 226-41	*19*	*9, 10*	

	Patrick	Reynolds	Routley-H	Routley-M	Ryden	Schalk	Stevenson-Pa	Stevenson-Pr
1.	11-16	1-2	13-6		3-7	Hymnody, Old Testament		
2.	17-23	2-3	16-7		3-7	Hymnody, New Testament; Canticle		
3.	24-6, 28-37	4-6	17-21		8-15	Hymnody, Greek		
4.	26-8, 38-69	6-11	21-32	155-8	16-54	Chant, Gregorian; Office Hymn; Hymnody, Latin; Sequence; Psalmody, Gregorian		
5.	70-85	12-25	33-7, 41-51	*2, 3, 10, 11, 14*, 152-4	56-246	Hymnody, German; Chorale; Hymnody, Scandinavian; Leisen		
6.	86-107, 166-7	23-36, 71-5	37-9, 52-62	*4, 5, 6, 7*,	248-53, 466-9	Metrical, Psalmody	2	*1, 2*
7.	108-20	37-42		*9*, 85-87,	254-67	Carol; Hymnody, English; Chant, Anglican		
8.	121-41	42-55	63-80, 88-99	87-90, *13*	268-309	Hymnody, English; Chant, Anglican	*8, 9, 10*	
9.	142-65	56-66	80-7, 101-4	*15, 16, 17, 18*, 160-4	310-429, 442-9	Hymnody, English Chant, Anglican	*10, 11*	
10.	174-80	66-70		*19, 20*, 158-9, *24*	430-41, 450-64	Hymnody, English		
11.		75-85		165				*3, 7, 9,* 87-91
12.	167-70	85-93, 98-101	99-100	166	470-537, 544-51, 566-85, 590-4, 608-13	Hymnody, American; Hymnody, American Lutheran		74-87
13.	170-3	93-8, 101-5	131-3		538-43, 552-65	Gospel Song	*12*	109-12, 126-7
14.	181-92	105-17	166-7		586-9, 594-607, 613-38	Hymnody, American; Hymnody, American Lutheran		124-6

1

The Hymn and Literature

A prominent hymnologist once wrote that "the hymn is the most popular kind of English poetry."[1] He is one of many who have focused attention on the wide interest in hymns among all classes of folk in contrast to the comparatively limited appreciation for other kinds of poetry. The significant point in the above statement is not the great popularity of hymns, for this is self-evident, but the fact that they, in a very real and technical sense, are *poems*.

Mention the word *hymn* to almost anyone and the first image that comes to mind is a hymn-*tune*. It is quite natural for the concept *hymn* to conjure up some kind of music because hymns are for singing. However, hymnologically speaking, the *hymn* as a term refers to the text. The point to be emphasized is that the text of a hymn possesses those qualities and characteristics associated with poetry.

Form and Structure

One of the most obvious characteristics of a poem, unless it be in free verse, is that it is organized into sections of equal and regular structure usually known as stanzas. A *stanza* is a division of a hymn consisting of a series of lines arranged together in a recurring pattern of meter and rhyme.

Stanza, as a technical term, is often confused with *verse*. Possibly this is because *verse*, when one has the Bible in mind, does indeed refer to one of the short divisions into which the Scriptures are traditionally divided. However, although one of the secondary definitions of *verse* makes it synonymous with *stanza*, its first and more precise meaning is that of *one line of poetry*.

One of the reasons the idea of the hymn as poetry is overlooked may be the usual placement of the hymn text between the staves of musical notation found in most American hymnals. This kind of arrangement made in the interest of facilitating the matching of words to music for singing, is a comparatively recent development in the history of hymnbook publishing. Even today in most hymnals published outside the United States, words and music are separated.[2]

In earlier times a hymnal looked like most other collections of poetry with

---

[1]Jeremiah Bascom Reeves, *The Hymn in History and Literature* (New York: The Century Company, 1924), p. 3.
[2]See Erik Routley, "On the Display of Hymn Texts," *The Hymn*, 30, 1 (January, 1979), 16-20.

the words neatly placed on the pages in stanzas. If there were any references to tunes at all, they would simply consist of the listing of the names of tunes that could be found elsewhere. In the eighteenth and nineteenth centuries small pocket-sized hymnals were in vogue and, like small Bibles or Testaments, they were personally owned and brought by individuals to worship when the church gathered. The music for the hymn was published separately in tunebooks which often would provide only one stanza of hymn text for each tune.

Hymn stanzas usually consist of four, six, or eight lines each. Occasionally a hymn can be seen with five, ten, or various other numbers of lines per stanza. The varieties of stanza length in hymns can be readily surveyed by looking at the number of digits in the metrical index of standard hymnals.[3]

Rhyme Scheme

Another obvious feature of poetry is rhyme. *Rhyme* pertains to the terminal sounds of poetic lines. There must be a correspondence in the sound of the last word or syllable of each poetic line for rhyme to be present. It is rhyme (along with meter) that enables poetry to be remembered more easily than prose.

Poetry usually makes use of uniform schemes for its rhymes and these may be quite varied. In hymnody they tend to be comparatively simple. In four-line hymns poets may have rhyming in pairs (i.e., rhyming couplets):

Holy Spirit, Light *divine.*	a
Shine upon this heart of *mine;*	a
Chase the shades of night *away,*	b
Turn my darkness into *day.*	b
(B135, Andrew Reed)	

Or one can find the inner lines paired in rhyme, framed similarly by the outer two which rhyme:

Strong Son of God, immortal *love,*	a
Whom we, that have not seen thy *face,*	b
By faith, and faith alone, *embrace,*	b
Believing where we cannot *prove.*	a
(M146, Alfred Tennyson)	

[3]See the metrical index of tunes in the three major hymnals to which this text is keyed: *Baptist Hymnal* (B) (Nashville: Convention Press, 1975), pp. 554-557; *Lutheran Book of Worship* (L) (Philadelphia and Minneapolis: Fortress and Augsburg Presses, 1978), pp. 949-955; and *The Methodist Hymnal* (M) (Nashville: The Methodist Publishing House, 1966), pp. 850-855. Also referred to on occasion is the supplementary hymnal, *Ecumenical Praise* (E) (Carol Stream, IL.: Agape, 1977).

More often, an alternating pattern known as *cross rhyme* is found:

The head that once was crowned with *thorns*	a
Is crowned with glory *now*;	b
A royal diadem *adorns*	a
The mighty Victor's *brow.*	b
(B125, L173, M458, Thomas Kelly)	

Many hymnists do not choose to rhyme all lines:

Just as I am, thine own to *be*	a
Friend of the young, who lovest *me,*	a
To consecrate myself to *thee,*	a
O Jesus Christ, I come.	b
(B243, M169, Marianne Hearn)	

Rise up, O men of God:	a
Have done with lesser *things;*	b
Give heart and mind and soul and strength	c
To serve the King of *Kings.*	b
(B268, M174, William P. Merrill)	

Five-line stanzas can have a variety of rhyme schemes:

Dear Lord and Father of man*kind,*	a
Forgive our foolish *ways;*	b
Reclothe us in our rightful *mind;*	a
In purer lives thy service *find,*	a
In deeper reverence, *praise.*	b
(B270, L506, M235, John G. Whittier)	

Ask ye what great thing I *know*	a
That delights and stirs me *so?*	a
What the high reward I *win?*	b
Whose the name I glory *in?*	b
Jesus Christ, the crucified.	c
(B60, M124, Johann C. Schwedler; tr. Benjamin H. Kennedy)	

One could make an interesting study of the various rhyming possibilities in hymns of six, seven, eight, and more lines. Such study would reveal the better hymns to have comparatively simple rhyme patterns, thus aiding in the retention of their content by singers.

Metrical Pattern

As indicated above, *meter* is another important feature of poetry. *Meter* refers to a systematically arranged and measured rhythm of accent in verse (i.e., rhythm that consistently repeats a single basic pattern). Like all verse, hymns are organized into poetic "feet." Each "foot" consists of either two or three syllables, only one of which is accented.

We have inherited our poetic nomenclature from the ancient Greeks. Thus, Greek classical poetry has bequeathed us our metrical patterns, the most common of which is the *iambic* foot. This consists of an unaccented or unstressed syllable (upbeat) followed by an accented one (downbeat). A line of verse having four of this kind of foot is known technically as *iambic tetrameter*. (Tetra = four; a 3-foot line of poetry is designated *trimeter*, etc.)

In hymnals the number of syllables of a line of poetry are counted rather than the number of feet. *Meter* is therefore indicated in the group of numbers denoting the number of syllables in the lines of a stanza. So, a four-line stanza, each line having the iambic tetrameter arrangement, is indicated by four digits as 8.8.8.8. This is commonly known as Long Meter (LM). "The Doxology"[4] has this pattern, and so in hymnological parlance it is known as Thomas Ken's Long Meter Doxology. (B6, 7, E40, L564, 565, M809)

The *iambic* foot is the basis for the three most used meters in English hymnody which include, in addition to Long Meter, Common Meter—8.6.8.6. (CM) and Short Meter—6.6.8.6. (SM). Note again that the abbreviations used for the above meters are respectively LM, CM, and SM. An added D indicates "Double" or repetition of the pattern for hymns having eight-line stanzas.

Reference to a hymnal will lead one to discover that many familiar hymns are set in one of these "common" meters[5] and by consulting the metrical index one is made aware of the importance of meter for classifying hymn tunes. By proper use of this index one can mate tunes with texts that have both the correct number of lines and syllables and also the suitable kind of poetic feet.

Besides the *iambic* another frequently used pattern is the *trochaic* (the

---

[4]There are many praise formulas known as doxologies but "The Doxology" is the familiar designation for the following lines which constituted the final stanza of Thomas Ken's three hymns written for Winchester College:

Praise **God** from **whom** all **bless**-ings **flow**;	8
Praise **him** all **crea**-tures **here** be-**low**;	8
Praise **him** a-**bove**, ye **heavn**-ly **host**;	8
Praise **Fa**-ther, **Son**, and **Ho**-ly **Ghost**.	8

[5]Note, for example: LM "When I survey the wondrous cross" (B111, L482, M435); CM "God moves in a mysterious way" (B439, L483, M215); SM "I love thy kingdom, Lord" (B240, L368, M294); SMD "Crown him with many crowns" (B52, L170, M455); CMD "America, the Beautiful" (B508, M543), and LMD "Sweet hour of prayer" (B401, M275).

reverse of *iambic*), with first an accent and then a weaker pulse. This meter is more exciting and direct than the more stately and reserved *iambic*. Hymn meter indications do not specify the kind of poetic feet into which a given hymn is arranged. So two hymns can be in identical hymn meter (for example, 7.6.7.6.D., meaning stanzas of eight lines which alternate in number of syllables between seven and six) and yet one hymn could be in *iambic* and the other in *trochaic* accentual pattern. Compare the first two lines of the following two hymns, both of which are in this 7.6.7.6.D. meter:

Come, ye **faith**-ful, **raise** the **strain**	7
Of tri-**um**-phant **glad**-ness:	6 (Trochaic)
(L132, M448)	
Lead **on,** O **King** E-**ter**-nal,	7
The **day** of **march** has **come;**	6 (Iambic)
(B420, L495, M478)	

It is clear that one and the same 7.6.7.6.D tune could not possibly be used for both these hymns. To illustrate this, one might try to sing LANCASHIRE to "Come, ye faithful, raise the strain"!

In matching hymns to tunes, great caution must therefore be taken that even when in the same hymn meter, the musical and the textual *accents* agree. A brief perusal of a metrical index of tunes will reveal the many other patterns[6] into which hymns fall. It is a fascinating study!

Content and Expression

In addition to outward structure and form, a hymn may be considered a poem by its inner content and expression. The great poet Milton said that poetry in content should be *simple, sensuous,* and *passionate.* The hymn as a poem must possess something of all these qualities.

Ideally, a hymn is set out in clear, unambiguous language. Although it deals with profound thoughts, a hymn states them so simply and directly that "he who runs may read" and understand. Simplicity, which is the servant of clarity, is the first characteristic of hymnic expression.

But the hymn as poetry is also *sensuous.* It draws its themes from the commonplace materials of life. It conjures up familiar images which come from what ordinary folk see, feel, touch, and eat in everyday experience.

And a hymn by its very nature as poetry is *passionate.* It appeals to the heart as well as to the mind. A hymn stirs the emotions and lifts the soul,

---

[6]For a treatment of other meters, see Austin C. Lovelace, *The Anatomy of Hymnody* (Nashville: Abingdon Press, 1965), chap. 4 and 5. ·

comforting, challenging, making joyful or sorrowful, exalting sentiment, and quickening genuine feeling.

Often the finest hymnists are not known as outstanding poets. Conversely great poets are not particularly known for their hymn writing. It was the poet Alfred, Lord Tennyson who said: "A good hymn is the most difficult thing in the world to write."[7] He lived out that statement by giving the world only one genuine hymn and that one not written until his eighty-first year.

But a few outstanding literary persons have produced hymns that would qualify as fine poetry. Look, for example, at this stanza by Oliver W. Holmes:

> Lord of all being, throned afar,
>   Thy glory flames from sun and star;
> Center and soul of every sphere,
>   Yet to each loving heart how near! (M64).

This is a hymn of sincere praise and petition that also possesses the qualities of simplicity, sensuousness, and impassioned feeling.

Another example of vivid simplicity, contemporary imagery, and powerful feeling is this by Gilbert K. Chesterton:

> O God of earth and altar,
>   Bow down and hear our cry;
> Our earthly rulers falter,
>   Our people drift and die;
> The walls of gold entomb us,
>   The swords of scorn divide,
> Take not thy thunder from us,
>   But take away our pride (M484, L428).

Poetic Devices

Hymns also make discreet use of those rhetorical devices and figures of speech that are part and parcel of classical poetry. For example, many hymns use the device of allegory—the description of a subject under the guise of another subject of aptly suggestive resemblance. Sometimes a vignette of history may be made to carry religious significance for the singer-poet. This is seen in "Guide me, O thou great Jehovah" (B202, L343, M271), wherein the pilgrimage of the Israelites becomes a picture of the singer's life and hope beyond death with its references to manna (bread of heaven; 1:5), the pillar of fire (2:3), and crossing over Jordan (the river of death; 3:1) onto "Canaan's side" (heaven—the promised land; 3:4).

---

[7]Hallam, Lord Tennyson, *Tennyson: A Memoir* 11, 401.

pg 274 ΛΗ

Alliteration—the repetition of the same first sound in consecutive words—is used with care in hymn writing. Note, for instance, the use of the "s" sound in this line from Whittier's "Dear Lord and Father of mankind" (B270, L506, M235): "Take from our souls the strain and stress," and the "sh" and "l" sounds in this line from a contemporary hymn: "Shaping lives for sharing love."[8]

A much less used device sometimes found in hymns is that of anadiplosis (an-a-di-plo´sis)—using words or ideas ending one stanza as the start of the next. A fine example is found in Charles Wesley's "O for a thousand tongues to sing" (B69, L559, M1):

End of stanza 1:   The triumphs of his *grace*.
Start of stanza 2:   My *gracious* Master and my God,
End of stanza 2:   The honors of thy *name*.
Start of stanza 3:   Jesus, the *name* that calms my fears,

It is not by accident that many of these devices are to be found in the hymns of Charles Wesley. He benefited from a thorough training in classical poetry. In his hymns we also find the use of anaphora (a-naf´o-ra)—the repetition of the same word at the beginning of successive lines for rhetorical purposes. This is seen with the word *born* in both his "Hark! the herald angels sing" (stanza 3, B83, L60, M387), and "Come, thou long-expected Jesus" (stanza 2, B79, L30, M360).

Another literary artifice skillfully used by Wesley was the chiasmus (ki-a´zmus, from the Greek letter chi, X—the crossing of lines or clauses). A prime example of this is from "Jesus, lover of my soul" (A = The holy Savior, B = The sinful singer):

Just and holy is thy name,	A
I am all unrighteousness;	B
False and full of sin I am,	B
Thou art full of truth and grace.	A
(B172, M125)	

Here are two persons in bold contrast—the holy Savior and the sinful singer. Wesley the author starts with the Savior (A), then moves to two lines on the unrighteousness of the singer (BB), and then finally refers to the Savior again (A). This device can be an apt vehicle for setting forth the paradoxes of the Christian faith.

Paradox—a statement that is seemingly contradictory but nevertheless true—appropriately may be found at times in hymnic expression for it can dramatically set forth the paradoxical truths of Christian doctrine.

[8]From "To God we lift our voices"—an unpublished hymn by M. M. Pace.

Perhaps the best hymn to illustrate the use of *paradox* is George Matheson's "Make me a captive, Lord":

> Make me a captive, Lord,
>   And then I shall be free;
> Force me to render up my sword
>   And I shall conqueror be (M184). *pg 84 NH*

Closely akin to paradox is *antithesis* (an-ti´the-sis)—sharply contrasted ideas set in juxtaposition. This device is employed in hymns formulated according to what is often called the Hebrew pattern, involving the threefold: thesis, antithesis, synthesis.[9]

pg 104 NH

Hyperbole (hy-per´bo-lee)—a figure making use of exaggeration—is frequent in poetry and is often to be found effectively used in hymns. For example: "O for a thousand tongues to sing" (B69, L559, M1),

> In the cross of Christ I glory,
> Tow'ring o'er the wrecks of time (B70, L104, M416).

Personification—the representation of a thing or abstraction as a person or by a physical form—is often used in hymns for imaginative effect: "Rise, my soul, and stretch thy wings" (M474); "My faith looks up to thee" (B382, L479, M143); "Leaning on the everlasting arms" (B254).

pg 297 NH

Metaphor—the figure of speech using a word or phrase denoting one kind of idea or object in the place of another to suggest likeness or analogy between them—is sometimes found in hymnic lines:

> Prayer is the soul's sincere desire,
>   Unuttered or expressed.
> The motion of a hidden fire
>   That trembles in the breast (B400, M252).

> My heart an altar, and thy love the flame.
>   (B132, L486, M138, "Spirit of God, descend upon my heart")

Simile (sim-i-lee)—comparing unlike objects in one aspect—is used in hymnic poetry:

> Like a river glorious
> Is God's perfect peace (B208).

> It floateth like a banner
> Before God's host unfurled;
>   (B140, M372, "O Word of God Incarnate")

---

[9]See chap. 4, The Hymn and Theology.

Ambrose of Milan

Tautology—the repetition of the same thought in a slightly different way—is not infrequent in hymns:

> Jesus, thou art all compassion,
> > Pure, unbounded love thou art;
> > > (B58, L315, M283, "Love divine, all loves excelling")

This kind of literary device develops naturally from the synonymous parallelism of the Hebrew psalms and is therefore to be expected frequently in metrical psalm versions:

> The depths of earth are in his hand,
> Her secret wealth at his command;
> > (Psalm 95, Tate and Brady, B21, "O come, loud anthems let us sing")

> O magnify the Lord with me,
> > With me exalt his name;
> > > (Psalm 34, Tate and Brady, M56, "Through all the changing scenes of life")

Apostrophe—addressing inanimate objects or concepts—lends itself to effective devotional use in hymns: "Love divine, all loves excelling" (B58, L315, M283); "O perfect Love, all human thought transcending" (B395, L287, M333).

Climax—the arrangement of ideas in ascending order of intensity—lends progress and heightened emotion to meaningful hymn singing: "Ours the cross, the grave, the skies" (B114, M439, "Christ, the Lord is risen today"); "Demands my soul, my life, my all" (B111, L482, M435, "When I survey the wondrous cross"); "Our Maker, Defender, Redeemer, and Friend" (B30, L548, M473, "O worship the King").

All of these and other poetic artifices[10] are not really noticed by the ordinary worshiper. They become apparent when one seeks the secret of the expressive power of good hymns. Their presence is evidence of the true literary quality of many of our finest songs of devotion and praise.

Literary Patterns

In addition to the use of figures of speech, hymns are like fine pieces of crafted verse in the organized plan and symmetry of their thought structure.

---

[10]See Lovelace, *op. cit.*, chap. 4. Many other poetic devices frequently found in hymns are identified in this work, including *epanadiplosis* (repetition of a word at the beginning and end of a phrase), *epizeuxis* (immediate repetition of a word or phrase), and *synecdoche* (a part used rather than the whole).

Itemization

For example, many hymns make use of *itemization* to furnish thematic unity and progression. Note the plan of these hymns:

1. Holy Spirit, *Light* divine, Shine upon this heart of mine . . .
2. Holy Spirit, *Pow'r* divine, Cleanse this guilty heart of mine . . .
3. Holy Spirit, *Joy* divine, Cheer this saddened heart of mine . . . (B135).

1. O *Love* that wilt not let me go . . .
2. O *Light* that followest all my way . . .
3. O *Joy* that seekest me through pain . . .
4. O *Cross* that liftest up my head . . . (B368, L324, M234).

1. Open my *eyes* that I may *see* . . .
2. Open my *ears* that I may *hear* . . .
3. Open my *mouth* and let me *bear* . . . (B358, M267).

Dialogue

Other hymns are structured according to a question-answer or *dialogue* pattern. Consider carefully the conversational style of these hymns:

"Art thou weary , art thou languid" (M99)
"Watchman, tell us of the night" (M358)
"Ask ye what great thing I know" (B60, M124)
"Am I a soldier of the cross" (B388, M239)
"Christian, dost thou see them" (M238)

Litany

A particularly effective and useful literary pattern is that of the *litany*. This is most often found in hymns of petition and praise which are completed in thought by the same refrain or response:

"Jesus, with thy church abide" (each stanza ending with the petition):
    We beseech thee, hear us (B241, M311).

"For the beauty of the earth" (each stanza climaxing with the ascription of praise):
    Christ our God, to thee we raise
    This our hymn of grateful praise (B54, L561, M35).

Call and Response

A pattern developing out of the folk song tradition in non-literate societies is that of *call and response*. This is frequently seen in spirituals or songs based upon their model:

Lord, I want to be a Christian in my heart, (*call*)
   In my heart, (*response*; B322, M286)

When the storms of life are raging, (*call*)
   Stand by me (*response*; M244)

O when I get to heaven going to sing and shout, (*call*)
   I'm going to lay down my heavy load (*response*; B506)[11]

Sometimes this response is referred to as the "tag line," particularly in gospel songs:

O for a thousand tongues to sing,
   Blessed be the name of the Lord!
The glories of my God and King,
   Blessed be the name of the Lord! (B50).

There are various other ways in which songs and hymns make use of repetition to supply interest and cohesion.

The Hymn—a Distinctive Literary Form

Tennyson's statement referred to earlier concerning the difficulty of writing a good hymn highlights the nature of the hymn as one of the most rigorously limited of all types of literature. Its first limitation is that it must resemble lyric poetry. It must sing! Since it must also express religious truth, its strictures are even greater. But when it must be a medium of concerted action and feeling, simple enough to be used congregationally, its constraints are compounded and multiplied. So the construction of a good hymn is essentially an art of limitations. Yet such limitations can enhance rather than detract from greatness.[12]

In the final analysis, the hymn represents a unique form of literary art. It may not be as good as superior poetry, but it can have an excellence all its own. Poets, with few exceptions, speak first for themselves and only secondarily for or to others. By contrast the hymn writer has to produce something with others in mind, with the hope that others will take it as their own and sing it with meaning and conviction. The hymnist, moreover, is not only speaking to others but on behalf of others to God.

So the hymn, like a good piece of journalism, presents its theme clearly and memorably within a limited space. Like poetry, it has a touch of heightened imagination, but it must give expression to religious truth that is universal.

It has been suggested that the hymn may be conceived as having the same

[11]See chap. 9, Cultural Perspectives.
[12]V. M. Caird, "The Hymn as a Literary Form" in *Bulletin of the Hymn Society of Great Britain and Ireland* 38 (January, 1947), pp. 1-9.

relation to poetry as journalism has to "literature" in general.[13] Certainly it is a type of poetry existing of and by itself, possessing qualities that are distinctly its own. Those qualities are so distinctive that hymns may not fit the categories of either poetry or prose. Hymns in the final analysis are *sui generis*—the products of an art having its own qualities and requirements. They are poems, but they do not have to be great poems to achieve status as great hymns.

The purely literary appreciation of hymns as poetry has a legitimate function to perform in worship and devotion. Though hymns do not have to exhibit all the characteristics considered here to qualify as poems, when they do they have both religious and aesthetic value. The values need not strive the one against the other, for the informed critical faculty is not the opponent but rather the friend of true religion. The capacity to discern and appreciate the best in poetic expression is one that can and should be cultivated by anyone seeking in hymns and their singing to glorify God, the author of all art and beauty.

Evaluative Questions for Thought and Discussion

1. What percentage of the hymns chosen for the singing of your congregation would be judged as lyrical poems of quality?

2. Thinking of specific hymns such as "Love divine, all loves excelling" (B58, L315, M283) or "When I survey the wondrous cross" (B111, L482, M435), is there a relationship between literary character and spiritual effectiveness?

3. For the average person, is poetic beauty a hindrance or a help to spiritual edification?

4. What outstanding poets in British and/or American literature are represented by hymns in your hymnal?[14]

5. Which of these literary devices or patterns are to be found in the following hymns: Apostrophe, Alliteration, Anaphora, Hyperbole, Climax, Paradox, Hebrew pattern, Itemization?

   a. "O for a thousand tongues to sing" (B69, L559, M1)
   b. "Make me a captive, Lord" (M184)
   c. "Go to dark Gethsemane" (B112, L109, M434)
   d. "O God, our help in ages past" (B223, L320, M28)
   e. "How sweet the name of Jesus sounds" (B464, L345, M81)
   f. "O Love that wilt not let me go" (B368, L324, M234)

---

[13]Michael Hewlett, "Thoughts About Words" in *Bulletin of the Hymn Society of Great Britain and Ireland*, 115 (Spring, 1969), p. 11.
[14]Consult the hymnal's index of Authors, Composers, and Sources.

2

The Hymn and Music

To become a congregational song, a hymn text must be set to music. The musical setting of the hymn—even though it is usually harmonized for part-singing or accompaniment—is known as a tune, a hymn tune. A hymn text and its tune are so closely associated with each other that they have been likened to a marriage. The compatibility necessary for a good marriage is also necessary for a good match of hymn text and tune.

A hymn tune can be conveniently studied as melody, harmony, rhythm and meter, texture and form.[1]

Melody

The melody is usually found in the highest of the four voice parts used in most current hymnals. In addition to the highest (soprano) voice part, the vocal lines of the other voices—alto, tenor, and bass—may also be perceived as melodies, though they are subordinate to and generally lack the same melodic interest of the soprano.

Since the musical sounds that make up a melody consist of *pitch* and *duration*, melody really cannot be separated from rhythm. To distinguish between these two qualities of melody, pitch may be thought of as "high-low" and duration as "long-short." These two qualities may be referred to respectively as motion and rhythm and each melody may be illustrated as a motion skeleton and rhythm skeleton,[2] as in the following example from the hymn tune ANTIOCH (B88, L39, M392, "Joy to the world! the Lord is come"):

---

[1] A basic knowledge of the rudiments of music is necessary for a clear understanding of much of the material treated in this chapter. It is recommended that readers who encounter terms that may be unfamiliar utilize a good dictionary of musical terms, such as the *Harvard Dictionary of Music*, ed. Willi Apel, 2nd ed. rev. (Cambridge, Mass.: Belknap Press of Harvard University Press, 1969).

[2] "Melody," *Harvard Dictionary of Music*, 2nd ed.

The pitches of a melody are selected from a *scale*. Most hymn tunes in current use (including ANTIOCH) use a *major scale*. A relatively small percentage of tunes in hymnals of today use a *minor scale*. Two hymn tunes in minor are KIRKEN (B235, L365, "Built on the Rock, the church doth stand"; M355, "Lord Christ, when first thou cam'st to men") and EBENEZER (B385, M242, "Once to every man and nation"; L233, "Thy strong word did cleave the darkness"). A few hymn tune melodies are *modal*, being based on the medieval church modes. Examples of modal hymn melodies include KING'S WESTON (B363, L179, M76, "At the name of Jesus"), which is in the Dorian mode, and the plainsong-based melody, VENI EMMANUEL (B78, L34, M354, "O come, O come, Emmanuel") which is in the Aeolian mode.

Some hymn tunes—whether they are major, minor or modal—use less than the full seven notes of these scales. Of particular interest is the five-note or *pentatonic* scale, a scale often found in folk music and music of Africa and the Orient. One familiar form of the pentatonic scale omits the fourth and seventh degrees:

Folk melodies in the hymnal using pentatonic scales include the popular American folk hymn "Amazing Grace" (B165, L448, M92) and the Negro spiritual, "Lord, I want to be a Christian" (B322, M286). Two Oriental pentatonic hymn tunes are the Chinese SHENG EN (B250, M317, "The bread of life for all men broken") and the Indian ASSAM (B191, "I have decided to follow Jesus"). Although the melodies of pentatonic hymn tunes use only five notes, the harmonies generally make use of the full diatonic scale.

Most hymn melodies are *diatonic*, using the normal whole and half steps of their scales. The most common chromatic alteration in hymn tunes is the raised fourth modulating to the dominant in major keys, as found in ST. MAGNUS (B125, L173, M458, "The head that once was crowned").

In keeping with the need to be within the capabilities of an ordinary congregation, hymn tunes generally are limited in range. The melodies of most hymns fall within an octave or an octave plus an additional scale step. The general area where most pitches fall—the *tessitura*—is moderate in hymn tunes. Hymn tunes with high and low tessituras respectively are LASST UNS ERFREUEN (B9, L527, M60, "All creatures of our God and King") and ARNSBERG (B16, M788, "God himself is with us"; or WUNDERBARER KÖNIG, L249, "God himself is present").

In keeping with an increased emphasis on unison singing to accommodate the average singer in the congregation, hymn tunes have been appearing in lower keys in recent decades. The general range of hymn melodies is from c¹ (middle c) up to e♭, occasionally extended from b♭ (below middle c) to f.

Melodies of hymns move by step or skip, by scalar or triadic movement. The first phrase of ANTIOCH (B88, L39, M392, "Joy to the world") is a descending scalar progression encompassing a full octave of the major scale. OLD 100TH (B6, L564, M809, "Praise God from whom all blessings flow") begins with a scalewise progression descending from the tonic to the dominant. NICAEA (B1, L165, M26, "Holy, holy, holy") begins with an ascending triadic movement spelling out the tonic triad. Generally hymn tunes, as most melodies, combine scalar and triadic movement, both ascending and descending, to achieve a balance of melodic movement.

The melodies of hymns may develop with sequential repetition, as in the following third brace of ST. GEORGE'S WINDSOR (B233, L407, M522, "Come ye (you) thankful people, come"):

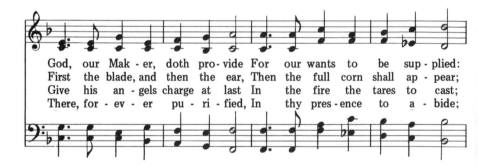

Note that these two melodic phrases are identical; the second one simply begins a fourth higher.

The melodic construction of DENNIS (B256, L370, M306) is also sequential:

1. Blest be the tie that binds Our hearts in Chris - tian love;
2. Be - fore our Fa - ther's throne We pour our ar - dent pray'rs;
3. We share our mu - tual woes, Our mu - tual bur - dens bear;
4. When we a - sun - der part, It gives us in - ward pain;

The fel - low - ship of kin-dred minds Is like to that a - bove.
Our fears, our hopes, our aims are one, Our comforts and our cares.
And of - ten for each oth - er flows The sym-pa - thiz-ing tear.
But we shall still be joined in heart, And hope to meet a - gain. A-MEN.

The second phrase of DENNIS is almost identical to the first, beginning a third lower. Although the third and fourth phrases are different, they nevertheless make frequent use of the third, an important melodic interval derived from the earlier phrases.

Many more of these interesting relationships can be discovered from the study of melodic construction in hymn tunes. Another aspect of melody—phrase repetitions—will be dealt with later under the discussion of form in hymn tunes.

Harmony

Hymn tunes are generally set in the harmonic style of the so-called "common practice period" in wide use from the time of Bach through the era of the Romantic composers. Relatively few hymn tunes have distinctive twentieth-century harmonies and these are used sparingly. The conservative style of hymn tune harmonies can be attributed to at least two factors. First, as congregational music to be sung largely by untrained singers, the emphasis of hymn tunes has been upon singable melodies unencumbered by elaborate harmonies. Second, this congregational music as "people's music" has, for practical reasons, embodied harmonic sounds with which untrained singers could readily identify and accept as a vehicle for their expression of faith in song.

Most hymn tunes in current hymnals are harmonized in a simple, straightforward style that has relatively few of the numerous passing tones, suspensions, and other nonharmonic tones associated with the Bach chorale harmonizations, as in the first score of the chorale LOBE DEN HERREN (B10, L543, M55):

LOBE DEN HERREN uses a large variety of chords; its harmonic rhythm is fast, for the chords change every beat until the final chord of the cadence. A simpler harmonization is that of the early American tune CORONATION (B40, L328, M71):

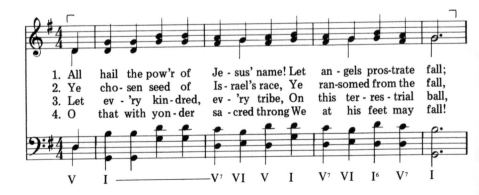

This first score of CORONATION uses only the tonic (I), dominant (V), dominant seventh (V⁷), submediant (VI), and the tonic second-inversion (I⁶) chords. Furthermore, the harmonic rhythm of this excerpt is somewhat slower, for the first full measure of harmony consists solely of the tonic (I) chord. Among the simplest harmonizations of hymns in American use are those of Lowell Mason and several of his contemporaries. This simplicity is also illustrated in the latter nineteenth-century gospel hymns, such as PROMISES (B335, M221):

1. Stand-ing on the prom-is-es of Christ my King, Thro' e - ter - nal a - ges
2. Stand-ing on the prom-is-es that can - not fail, When the howl-ing storms of
3. Stand-ing on the prom-is-es of Christ the Lord, Bound to him e - ter - nal -
4. Stand-ing on the prom-is-es I can - not fall, Lis - t'ning ev - 'ry mo-ment

The harmonies of these four measures consist basically of the tonic (I) and subdominant (IV), chords. The harmonic rhythm is quite slow, for the same harmonies are retained for one or two entire measures. In PROMISES, the harmonies are utterly subordinate to the driving march-like rhythms.

Most harmonizations of hymn tunes consist of the normal chords of the given keys, as illustrated by the following two scores of BEECHER (B58, M283, "Love divine, all loves excelling"):

Fix in us thy hum - ble dwell-ing; All thy faith - ful mer - cies crown.
Let us all in thee in - her - it, Let us find the prom - ised rest;
Sud -den - ly re - turn, and nev - er, Nev - er more thy tem - ples leave.
Let us see thy great sal - va - tion Per - fect - ly re - stored in thee:

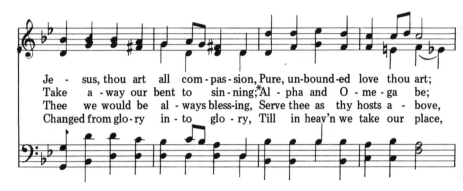

Je - sus, thou art all com - pas - sion, Pure, un-bound-ed love thou art;
Take a - way our bent to sin - ning; Al - pha and O - me - ga be;
Thee we would be al - ways bless-ing, Serve thee as thy hosts a - bove,
Changed from glo - ry in - to glo - ry, Till in heav'n we take our place,

The main key of the first score given is B♭, but the first two measures of the
second score of this excerpt are in its relative minor (G minor), the F♯
functioning as its leading tone. The latter two measures of this excerpt are
again the tonic key of B♭, the E♮ alteration resulting from a dominant chord.

The final cadences of nearly all hymn tunes (excluding appended plagal
"amen" cadences) involve a progression to the tonic from either the dominant
or dominant seventh chord. Internal cadences of hymn tunes are more varied,
including such progressions as V or V[7] to I, I to V, V[7] of V to V, VII[6] of V to V,
and I to IV.

Rhythm and Meter

Rhythm has already been mentioned in its relationship to melody as its time
quality and as it designates the rate of chord structure change (harmonic
rhythm). The rhythm of nearly all hymn tunes falls into the regular patterns of
accented and unaccented beats governed by musical meter.[3] Hymn tunes with
two-beat measures having an accent on the first beat utilize such meters as 2/2,
ARNSBERG (B16, M788, "God himself is with us"); or WUNDERBARER KÖNIG,
L249, "God himself is present"); 2/4, ANTIOCH (B88, L39, M392, "Joy to the
world"); and 6/8 (in fast tempo), WORDS OF LIFE (B142, M109, "Wonderful
words of life"). The three-beat pattern (-uu) in hymn tunes is found in such
meters as 3/2, ARLINGTON (B388, M239, "Am I a soldier of the cross") and
3/4, ST. CATHERINE (B143, L500, M151, "Faith of our fathers"). The six-
beat pattern, with its main accent on beat one and a secondary accent on beat
four, is utilized in such meters as 6/8 (in slow tempo), STILLE NACHT (B89,
L65, M393, "Silent night, holy night") and 6/4, MARTYN (B172, M126,
"Jesus, lover of my soul"). The more extended compound meters—9/8 and
12/8—are found mainly in the music of gospel hymns, such as "Blessed

---

[3]Plainsong and Anglican chant are two bodies of congregational music that are comparatively
nonmetrical.

assurance" (B334, M224) in 9/8 and "I will sing of my Redeemer" (B465), with its stanzas in 9/8 and refrain in 12/8.

The rhythms of hymn tunes are basically simple and straightforward in keeping with their role as music for the congregation. Part of this rhythmic simplicity is found in repetition. The four phrases of OLD 100TH (B6, L564, M809), for example, have the same rhythmic pattern. Other hymn tunes whose melodies repeat basically the same rhythmic pattern are ST. DENIO (B32, L526, M27, "Immortal, invisible, God only wise"), ST. THEODULPH (B39, L108, M424, "All glory, laud, and honor"), TOPLADY (B163, L327, M120, "Rock of Ages, cleft for me"), and WEBB (B391, L389, M248, "Stand up, stand up for Jesus").

Within each meter there are frequently recurring rhythmic patterns. For example, in 4/4 there is often the use of shorter note values followed by a longer note at the cadences of the first and/or second phrases, as illustrated by LEONI (B25, "The God of Abraham praise," or YIGDAL, L544; M30, "Praise to the living God"), HYMN TO JOY (B31, L551, M38, "Joyful, joyful we adore thee"), and PROMISES (B335, M221, "Standing on the promises").

Poetic meter* is a factor in determining the rhythmic patterns of hymns. Hymn texts in the iambic pattern use tunes that begin on an unaccented upbeat, such as EIN' FESTE BURG (B37, L228, L229, M20, "A mighty fortress") and AZMON (B69, L559, M1, "O for a thousand tongues to sing"). Conversely, hymns with trochaic texts use tunes that begin on an accented downbeat, such as MENDELSSOHN (B83, L60, M388, "Hark! the herald angels sing") and HYFRYDOL (B11, M42, "Praise the Lord, ye (o) heavens adore him").

Texture

The texture of most hymn tunes is *homophonic* or *chordal*, with the lower voice parts moving more or less in the same rhythm as the soprano melody. In the case of hymn tunes designed to be sung in unison, however, the texture is generally more *contrapuntal*, with a greater rhythmic independence of the accompanying voices. Examples of contrapuntal hymn tunes are Ralph Vaughan Williams' harmonizations of LASST UNS ERFREUEN (B9, L527, M60, "All creatures of our God and King") and SINE NOMINE (B144, L174, M536, "For all the saints"). Some popular tunes designed to be sung in harmony utilize counterpoint in the form of independent voice parts, such as the tenor and bass repetitions of "crown him" in DIADEM (B41, M72, "All hail the power of Jesus' name") and the alto-tenor-bass repetitions against the longer melody notes of PROMISES (B335, M221, "Standing on the promises").

---

*Poetic meter is discussed in more detail in chap. 1, The Hymn and Literature.

Form

By definition, the hymn is normally *strophic* in form, having the same music for each stanza. The number of phrases of the hymn tune correspond to its text, ranging generally from as few as four (B6, L564, M809, OLD 100TH) to as many as eight (B155, L554, TERRA PATRIS; or M45, TERRA BEATA), sometimes with a refrain of four or more additional phrases. Within its overall strophic form, examination of the phrases encountered in hymn tunes shows an interesting variety of patterns.

A pattern especially found in shorter hymn tunes is that of four different phrases (designated as ABCD), which can be also referred to as "through-composed." Short tunes with the ABCD pattern include OLD 100TH (B6, L564, M809), ST. ANNE (B223, L320, M28, "O God, our help in ages past"), ST. PETER (B464, L345, "How sweet the name of Jesus sounds"; M192, "In Christ there is no east or west"), and MARYTON (B369, M170, "O Master, let me walk with thee"; L492, "O Master, let me walk with you"). Longer tunes also following this through-composed structure include KREMSER (B229, M59, "We gather together"; B15, "We praise thee, O God, our Redeemer"; L241, "We praise you, O God, our redeemer"), EVENTIDE (B217, L272, M289, "Abide with me"), and SLANE (B212, M256, "Be thou my vision"; L469, "Lord of all hopefulness").

Other patterns of phrase relationships in hymn tunes consist of one or more repetitions. One of the simplest of these phrase-repetition structures, involving only two different phrase pairs, may be diagrammed as AB AB CD AB or more succinctly as AABA; this pattern is found in such hymns as FOREST GREEN (B154, M37, "I sing the almighty power of God"), NETTLETON (B13, L499, M93, "Come, thou Fount of every blessing"), and FOOTSTEPS (B325, "Sweetly Lord, have we heard thee calling").

Another pattern involves a repeated phrase or pair of phrases and then contrasting phrases (AAB); it is known in German music as *bar form*. Many chorales are in bar form, including EIN' FESTE BURG (B37, L228, L229, M20) and LOBE DEN HERREN (B10, L543, M55). The number of phrases in the "B" portion of bar form varies. When diagrammed in more detail, the bar form of EIN' FESTE BURG is AB AB CDEFB and that of LOBE DEN HERREN is A A BCD.

Some hymn tunes have repetitions of internal phrases such as the ABCDDEF pattern of ITALIAN HYMN (B2, L522, M3, "Come, thou Almighty King") and the ABABCCAB pattern of MADRID (B61; SPANISH HYMN M77, "Come, Christians, join to sing"). Phrases in hymn tunes are sometimes repeated with a variation in ending to effect a final cadence, as in the $AB^1 AB^2$ pattern of HAMBURG (B111, M435, "When I survey the wondrous cross") and the AB¹ AB² CD* pattern of Rescue (B283, M175, "Rescue the perishing").

A study of hymn tune phrases will reveal a number of additional patterns. An understanding of phrase relationships within hymn tunes, including not only repeated phrases but also the technique of sequential development treated earlier in this chapter, is important for an understanding of how hymn melodies are constructed.

Types of Hymn Tunes

The hymnal contains a wide variety of hymn tunes representing a number of different musical traditions. Not every hymn tune will fit into one of the categories described here, but these types represent most of the music used for present-day congregational singing in America.

Plainsong

Stemming from the Middle Ages, plainsong is also known as Gregorian chant (After Gregory I, who was Pope from 590 to 604). Gregorian chant is modal, based on the medieval church modes. It also has flexible rhythm which is articulated by means other than regular accentuation. Gregorian chant's modality and rhythmic flexibility are traits which account for its distinctive sound. Although traditionally sung without harmony and accompaniment, plainsong is also sung congregationally in unison with a harmonized accompaniment. Well-known examples of plainsong hymn tunes are Divinum mysterium (B62, L42, M357, "Of the Father's love begotten") and Veni Emmanuel (B78, L34, M354, "O come, O come Emmanuel").

One type of plainsong, called the psalm tone, is used for chanting the prose psalms from the Bible in worship, as in the following setting of Venite, exultemus (M663)[4]:

1. O come, let us sing unto the   Lord;
     let us heartily rejoice in the strength of   our salvation.
2. Let us come before his presence with thanks   giving,
     and show ourselves   glad in him with psalms . . . .

The most important feature of this type of chant, as distinguished from the

---

*The final cadential measure of B also appears in D.

[4]Instructions for chanting are given in *The Methodist Hymnal* (1966), at number 662. Another setting of Psalm 95 (in a modern translation) is at L4.

ordinary hymn tune, is that its rhythm seeks to emulate that of natural speech.

Another type of chant seeking to utilize the accentuations of natural speech is Anglican chant, which is written in four voice parts. Anglican chant, which may be derived from plainsong, consists of two or four short phrases of simple harmonic progressions as in Richard Farrant's BONUM EST CONFITERI (M667):

1. It is a good thing to give   thanks unto the Lord,
    and to sing praises unto thy name,   O Most Highest;
2. To tell of thy lovingkindness   early in the morning,
    and of thy   truth in the night season; . . .

Lutheran Chorale

From the impetus of the Protestant Reformation has developed, in addition to Anglican chant, a large body of German and Scandinavian hymn tunes known as chorales. The chorales reflect a variety of musical styles ranging from medieval plainsong and the song of the sixteenth-century Meistersinger to the baroque continuo accompanied *Lied*. Because of his masterful chorale harmonizations, many persons associate the chorale chiefly with J. S. Bach.

The phrase structure of the chorales in current use often adheres to the previously mentioned German bar form (AAB). In accord with the poetic structure of German chorale texts, few chorale tunes are in common, long, or short meter, utilizing rather a wide variety of other hymn meters. There are two main styles of rhythmic movement in the chorale. One consists of the sturdy rhythms using regular patterns of mostly quarter notes along with a few longer note values, especially for phrase endings. This style is sometimes called the "isometric" ("same meter") chorale, a style common in the eighteenth century and now associated with the Bach chorale harmonizations. Most of the older chorales found in American hymnals are isometric. The other style consists of the more irregular and often syncopated rhythms, such as those often found in the Reformation Era Chorales, as illustrated by the original rhythm (E25, L228) of Luther's EIN' FESTE BURG[5]:

---

[5]For the well-known isometric version, see B37, L229, M20.

Chorales are harmonized either in the Bach style (as in the PASSION CHORALE: B105, M418)[6] using a number of nonharmonic tones, or in a simpler style which uses nonharmonic tones sparingly and then mostly at cadences (as in LOBE DEN HERREN: B10, L543, M55).[7]

Calvinian Psalm Tune

From the influence of the Reformation theologian John Calvin of Geneva, arose the practice of singing the Psalms in meter to simpler tunes than the chorales. These psalm tunes may be divided into two categories: (1) those of the French language *Genevan Psalter*, characterized by a wide variety of hymn meters; (2) those of the English and Scottish psalters, largely falling into the patterns of common, long, and short meter. The French psalm tunes, like the Reformation Era chorales, are more often characterized by irregular rhythms and/or syncopations, as in RENDEZ A DIEU (M323):

[6]The original and isometric settings of the PASSION CHORALE at L116 and L117 are harmonized more simply than in Bach's style.

[7]For a detailed treatment of the musical style of the chorale, see Johannes Riedel, *The Lutheran Chorale—Its Basic Traditions* (Minneapolis: Augsburg Press, 1967).

Practically all the English and Scottish psalm tunes in current American hymnals are not only isometric; they also fall into 4/4 meter as illustated by WINCHESTER OLD (B96, M394, "While shepherds watched their flocks"; L264, "When all your mercies, O my God") and DUNDEE (B439, M215, "God moves in a mysterious way"; L464, 'You are the way; through you alone").

Both of these major groupings of psalm tunes are in accord with the Calvinian principle of simplicity in church song. They follow the practice of setting texts syllabically, with seldom more than one note per syllable of the words. Furthermore, most of these tunes (except a few longer Genevan melodies like RENDEZ A DIEU, M323) consist of four short unrepeated (ABCD) phrases, as in OLD 100TH (B6, L564, M809). The psalm tunes as used today are harmonized in a simple style, rarely using the nonharmonic tones characteristic of the Bach chorales.

Victorian Part-Song Tune

In Victorian England, a body of hymn tunes appeared which reflected the rich and often chromatic harmonies of the contemporary secular part-song. In addition to their harmonic emphasis, these Victorian hymn tunes are often characterized by repeated note melodies, as in ST. AGNES (B73, M82, "Jesus, the very thought of thee"; L316, "Jesus, the very thought of you"); stagnant bass lines, as in LANCASHIRE (B420, L495, M478: "Lead on, O King Eternal"); and mild rhythms, as also illustrated by ST. AGNES. Other familiar Victorian part-song hymn tunes illustrating one or more of these features are ST. GERTRUDE (B393, L509, M305, "Onward, Christian Soldiers"), AURELIA (B236, L369, M297, "The church's one foundation"), and LAUDES DOMINI (B44, L546, M91, "When morning gilds the skies").

Folk Tune

Although melodies of folk origin (existing first in oral tradition) have been used with hymns for centuries, in the present century folk melodies have achieved a prominent place in most American hymnals. An examination of the index of sources for most of our hymnals will reveal folk melodies from a number of countries. The majority of these tunes are from Britain and America. They fall largely into five categories: (1) the carol, (2) the English folk tune, (3) the Welsh folk tune, (4) the American folk hymn tune, and (5) the American spiritual.

(1) *Carol.* The carol, a form of a hymn whose words and music are joyful and festive, has been defined as a "traditional song for the celebration of Christmas" and "occasionally . . . other songs of joyful character."[8] The

[8]"Carol" *Harvard Dictionary of Music*, 2nd ed. rev., 1969. 136.

carol has been redefined in the light of twentieth-century use "as a quasi-religious song of folk-like spirit with reference to the joyful observance of something new in the life of Christ."[9] Carols in their medieval origin were associated with dance; some carols still in use are characterized by dance-like rhythm meters, such as IN DULCI JUBILO (B90, L55, M391, "Good Christian men, rejoice"), THE FIRST NOWELL, (B91, L56, M383), and GREENSLEEVES (L40, "What child is this"). If "folk-like spirit" is accepted as a main determinant of which hymns and tunes are carols, then Lowell Mason's arrangement from Handel's *Messiah*, ANTIOCH (B88, M392, "Joy to the world") and STILLE NACHT (B89, M393, "Silent night") might well be regarded as carols. On the other hand, more stately texts and tunes such as ADESTE FIDELES (B81, L45, M386, "O come, all ye faithful") and MENDELSSOHN (B83, L60, M388, "Hark! the herald angels sing"), would seem to fit more appropriately the category of Christmas hymns.

(2) *English Folk Tune.* English folk tunes other than carols were brought into English hymnals in the first decade of this century. In contrast to the harmonic interest of the Victorian hymn tunes, these melodies adapted from secular folk songs and harmonized are noted for their melodic interest. The English folk tunes often fall into four lines of paired phrases having one or more lines repeated, as in FOREST GREEN (B154, M37, "I sing the almighty power of God") and KINGSFOLD (B99, "O sing a song of Bethlehem"; L391, "And have the bright immensities").

(3) *Welsh Tunes.* Welsh folk or folklike tunes also frequently consist of a pattern of four lines with one or more of them repeated, as found in ST. DENIO (B32, L526, M27, "Immortal, invisible, God only wise"), LLANFYLLIN (B221, M231, "Sometimes a light surprises"), and LLANGLOFFAN (M260, "O gracious Father of mankind"; L430, "Where restless crowds are thronging"). The sturdy rhythms of these Welsh tunes are in striking contrast to those of the lilting dancelike carols.

(4) *American Tunes.* The American folk hymn tunes consist largely of folk melodies derived from secular folksong and set to sacred texts by rural singing schoolteachers and published in early nineteenth-century shape-note tunebooks. As first published, American folk hymns were set in three or four voice parts in open score with the melody in the tenor. They were harmonized in a style using "forbidden" harmonies and progressions. For example, AMAZING GRACE (B165, M92; or NEW BRITAIN, L448), as it appeared in William Walker's *Southern Harmony* (1835), included chords without thirds (first chord), and parallel fifths (bracket 1, treble and tenor) and octaves (bracket 2, treble and bass).

---

[9]"Carol" *A Dictionary of Protestant Church Music*, 1975. 74. A book-length treatment of this subject is Erik Routley's *The English Carol* (London: Herbert Jenkins, 1958).

NEW BRITAIN. C. M.

Baptist Harmony, p. 123.

1 Amazing grace! (how sweet the sound) That saved a wretch like me! I once was lost, but now am found, Was blind, but now I see

2 'Twas grace that taught my heart to fear, And grace my fears relieved: How precious did that grace appear, The hour I first believed!

3 Through many dangers, toils, and snares, I have already come; 'Tis grace has brought me safe thus far, And grace will lead me home.

4 The Lord has promised good to me, His word my hope secures; He will my shield and portion be, As long as life endures.

5 Yes, when this flesh and heart shall fail, And mortal life shall cease, I shall possess, within the veil, A life of joy and peace.

6 The earth shall soon dissolve like snow, The sun forbear to shine; But God, who call'd me here below, Will be for ever mine.

As they appear in present hymnals, however, American folk hymns are made more acceptable to people conditioned to more orthodox harmonies, as in E. O. Excell's well-known 1900 reharmonization of AMAZING GRACE (B165):

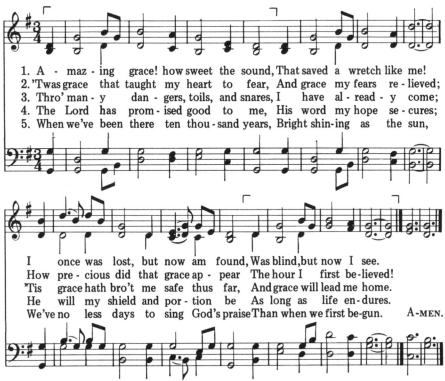

1. A - maz - ing grace! how sweet the sound, That saved a wretch like me!
2. 'Twas grace that taught my heart to fear, And grace my fears re - lieved;
3. Thro' man - y dan - gers, toils, and snares, I have al - read - y come;
4. The Lord has prom - ised good to me, His word my hope se - cures;
5. When we've been there ten thou - sand years, Bright shin-ing as the sun,

I once was lost, but now am found, Was blind, but now I see.
How pre - cious did that grace ap - pear The hour I first be - lieved!
'Tis grace hath bro't me safe thus far, And grace will lead me home.
He will my shield and por - tion be As long as life en - dures.
We've no less days to sing God's praise Than when we first be-gun. A-MEN.

Although most harmonizations of American folk hymns in present hymnals are out of character with their original style, some reharmonizations are attempts to retain some authenticity by the use of parallel fifths and some chords without thirds, as in Carlton R. Young's setting of KOHOUTEK (B93, "There's a song in the air"), MORNING SONG (B413, "Awake, awake to love and work"), FOUNDATION (M48, "How firm a foundation"), and WONDROUS LOVE (M432, "What wondrous love is this"). AMAZING GRACE also illustrates another important trait of American folk hymn tunes: the use of "gapped scales" employing less than the normal seven diatonic notes for their melodies. (They are generally harmonized using all seven notes.) The five-note pentatonic scale is used for AMAZING GRACE and other folk hymns.[10]

---

[10]See *American Traditions*, chap. 8, for discussion of additional folk hymns and spirituals.

American folk hymns make extensive use of repeated phrases, the most common pattern being AABA, found in NETTLETON (B13, L499, M93, "Come, thou Fount of every blessing"), and CLEANSING FOUNTAIN (B107, M421, "There is a fountain filled with blood"). This repetition pattern is slightly varied in FOUNDATION (B383, L507, M48), whose form is $A^1A^2BA^2$ and AMAZING GRACE, whose phrases consist of an $A^1A^2BA^1$.

Spirituals. The spiritual is a simplified type of American folk hymn characterized by text repetitions of phrases and usually a chorus. Although the Negro spiritual is better known, spirituals have been a part of the hymn repertory of both whites and blacks since at least the early nineteenth century.

The spiritual, although in a similar musical style to the folk hymn, is often characterized by livelier rhythm, sometimes involving syncopation, as in JACOB'S LADDER (B147, M287), BREAK BREAD (B252, L212, M330) and SOMEBODY'S KNOCKING (B480). The Afro-American spiritual was originally improvised, a practice facilitated by the use of a slow tempo and long-note values. Some of these longer notes which originally provided opportunity for improvisation are found in such spirituals as WERE YOU THERE (B108, L92, M436), BALM IN GILEAD (B205, M212), and BREAK BREAD (B252, L212, M330). Spirituals associated with whites stemmed from the frontier revivals of the early nineteenth century and were published with music in shape-note tune-books along with other folk hymns. White spirituals, although not generally characterized by syncopation, do exhibit driving, marchlike rhythms as in WARRENTON (B12, "Come, thou Fount of every blessing"), SHOUT ON (B436, "I know that my Redeemer lives"), and PROMISED LAND (B490, M291, "On Jordan's stormy banks I stand").

Gospel Hymn Tune

The gospel hymn developed in latter nineteenth-century America and reflects much of the simple musical style of contemporary popular song. Gospel hymns use simple major-key melodies and corresponding simple harmonies consisting largely of the tonic, subdominant and dominant chords in slow harmonic rhythm. They generally make fuller use of chromatic melodies than do most other bodies of hymn tunes. Although gospel hymns are frequently in simple meters such as 4/4 and 3/4, they make a greater use of compound meters than any other body of hymn tunes. Gospel hymns may use straightforward rhythms but dotted rhythms are more characteristic, such as the dotted eights and sixteenth rhythms of OLD RUGGED CROSS (B430, M228) and the dotted quarter and repeated eighths of CONVERSE (B403, L439, M261, "What a friend we have in Jesus"). Some gospel hymns also make use of syncopated rhythms, as in LIVING (B348, "Living for Jesus") and McDANIEL (B487, "Since Jesus came into my heart"). Gospel hymns are mainly homophonic but variety of texture is sometimes found in the use of "echo" voices, as in the alto, tenor, and bass parts of Old Rugged Cross (B430, M228).

Innovative Hymn Tunes

Some hymn tunes of the present century fall into one of the categories already described; other hymn tunes of more recent times are innovative and do not fit a simple characterization. The following descriptive list of innovative hymn tunes will show how some composers have sought to bring about new interest in this simple form.

Sine Nomine (B144, L174, M536, "For all the saints"), a "Baroque Trio" (bass, middle voice(s), and melody. The longer L174 has three more stanzas in harmony). Two devices found in this hymn tune common to a number of other innovative hymn tunes are its "walking" bass line and its downbeat in the accompaniment before the voices enter.

Purpose (B509, "God is working his purpose out") is a unison tune with a free accompaniment. The melody is given out a measure later in canon at a lower octave by a "walking" bass.

Little Flock (B225, L476, "Have no fear, little flock") is a unison tune in which the rhythm is derived from the natural speech rhythm of the hymn's biblical text; the remaining stanzas are written to fit the same text-derived rhythm.[11] The rhythm includes much syncopation and many of the harmonies are nontraditional, spiced with minor seconds and major sevenths.

Robin (B153, "My God is there, controlling") is a unison tune with its melody developed sequentially but with its accompaniment consisting solely of parallel fifth chords.

Santa Barbara (L563, "For the fruit of all creation") is quite venturesome harmonically. The first score, for example, begins with a first-inversion tonic chord in the key of C major and then moves through C minor to D major.[12]

Matching Tune and Text

For a happy marriage of hymn text and tune, they must be compatible in meter, accent, mood and association. If a hymn text consists of four lines of eight syllables each (long meter), its tune must also have four phrases with notes to fit eight syllables per phrase. Closely associated with meter is a consideration of accent. Although Antioch (B88, M392) and "Amazing

---

[11]See Heinz Werner Zimmerman, "Word and Tone in Modern Hymnody," *The Hymn* 24, 2 (April 1973), 44-55.

[12]For descriptions of this and other innovative hymn tunes, see Marilyn Stulken-Ekwo, "Contemporary Hymn Tunes: A Look at Some New Tunes in the Lutheran Book of Worship," *Journal of Church Music* 20, 2 (February 1978), 7-11.

Grace" (B165, M92) are both in common meter, the trochaic (long-short) accents of Antioch which are suitable for "Joy to the world" do not fit "Amazing Grace," for its initial unaccented syllable would be accented if sung to Antioch.[13]

Hymn tunes themselves cannot communicate nonmusical ideas, but they can express general moods, such as majesty, joy, solemnity, reflection or meditation, and marchlike enthusiasm. Although "All hail the power of Jesus' Name" and the tune Amazing Grace are both in common meter, the majestic character of this hymn text simply does not fit the more subdued mood of the tune Amazing Grace.

Finally, a hymn tune must not be tied too strongly to previous associations to be compatible with a particular text. So strongly identified are such tunes as Nicaea (B1, L165, M26, "Holy, holy, holy, Lord God Almighty") and Ein' feste Burg (B37, L228, L229, M20, "A mighty fortress") with their texts that it would be difficult for them to function as tunes for other words without reminding us of their more familiar associations. Tunes with secular associations for a particular congregation usually cannot be used with hymns without difficulties. Stephen Foster's tune to "Beautiful Dreamer" can be sung to "Blessed assurance" but the widespread knowledge of this tune by Americans as a love song renders it unsuitable for use as a hymn tune.

QUESTIONS FOR THOUGHT AND DISCUSSION

1. What are the forms (ABCD, ABB, etc.) of the following hymn tunes: Beecher (B3, M283), Old 134th (B26, M16), Hymn to Joy (B31, L551, M38), St. Theodulph (B39, L108, M424), Savannah (B227, M309), and Ebenezer (B385, L233, M242)?

2. How well do the following hymn texts and hymn tunes fit each other in regard to hymn meter, accent, mood, and association?

"Holy, holy, holy, Lord God Almighty"   and Nicaea
"Just as I am, without one plea"   and Woodworth
"O for a thousand tongues to sing"   and Hamburg
"Amazing grace"   and Arlington
"All hail the power of Jesus' Name"   and St. Agnes
"Jesus shall reign"   and Maryton

3. The following questions are applicable in considering hymn tunes for congregational singing. Apply them to several familiar hymn tunes in your hymnal.

A. How singable is the hymn tune for congregational use? (Consider the range, tessitura, and difficulty.)

B. How suitable is the style of the hymn tune for its intended use? (How familiar? For which group? For what occasion?)

C. Is there another readily available hymn tune that fits the hymn text better than the one given? (Consult the metrical index.)

[13]Note similar considerations above in chap. 1, The Hymn and Literature.

3
The Hymn and Scripture

Scripture is the basic raw material from which hymns are produced. A hymn cannot be useful unless and until it relates closely to the revealed truth about God and his mighty acts as written in the Scriptures. Therefore the effectiveness of any hymn is measurable in large part by the extent to which it functions as a vehicle for scriptural truth.

From one standpoint the entire history of the hymn could be delineated according to its varying relationship to the Scriptures.[1] Generally speaking, the line of evolution in that story, if it were retold, is from the actual singing of *parts of the Bible* (the psalms, for example) through the strict *paraphrasing of extended passages* and the dutiful use of *biblical allusion, language* and *figures* of speech to the *free expression* of *scriptural thought* and *teaching* in contemporary terms.

Variations in Hymn—Scripture Relationship

The familiar Shepherd Psalm (23) can illustrate the evolutionary process of moving from scriptural psalm to original hymn. First, there is the Psalm 23 itself in the original Hebrew or in a vernacular prose version such as those found in the responsive reading section of most hymnals (B575, L p.225, M560). In this form the psalm may be intoned or chanted to a form of plainsong[2] or to Anglican chant.[3]

Then there are the literal metrical versions of this psalm which are little more than rearrangements of the biblical words into patterns of meter and rhyme that accommodate simple measured tunes. Possibly the most famous version (among the hundreds that exist) is from the *Scottish Psalter* of 1650: "The Lord's my Shepherd, I'll not want" (B341, L451, M68).

James Montgomery's version of Psalm 23 is a slightly freer and more poetic paraphrase which appeared in his *Songs of Zion, Being Imitations of Psalms* (1822):

> The Lord is my Shepherd, no want shall I know,
>   I feed in green pastures, safe-folded I rest;

---

[1]This has been done by Louis F. Benson. See *The Hymnody of the Christian Church* (New York: George H. Doran, 1927. Reprint; Richmond: John Knox Press, 1956), "The Relation of the Hymn to Holy Scripture," pp. 57-95.
[2]See the *Lutheran Book of Worship*, pp. 290-91.
[3]See the *Bonum est* (Psalm 92) example in chap. 2, The Hymn and Music.

He leadeth my soul where the still waters flow,
Restores me when wandering, redeems when oppressed.[4]

A further step away from the original biblical text is seen in the New Testament allusions incorporated in the free paraphrase which Henry W. Baker included in the appendix to his 1868 edition of *Hymns Ancient and Modern*. "The King of love my Shepherd is" (B215, L456, M67). In the third stanza Baker actually breaks away from the psalm, personalizing it further by incorporating a related idea from the parable of the good shepherd recorded in Luke 15:3-7:

Perverse and foolish oft I strayed,
    But yet in love he sought me,
And on his shoulder gently laid,
    And home rejoicing, brought me.

Then in stanza four the hymnist adds to the comforting rod and staff of the shepherd the symbol of the cross for guidance through the shadow of death:

In death's dark vale I fear no ill.
    With thee, dear Lord, beside me,
Thy rod and staff my comfort still;
    Thy cross before to guide me.

Finally, there are hymns on the shepherd theme that are original compositions. For example, "Savior, like a shepherd lead us" (B213, L481, M121) starts with an allusion that may be from Psalm 23 but could just as easily have been inspired by the "I am the good shepherd" passage in John 10. Essentially, however, this is an original work, bearing only the suggestion of a relation to a particular Scripture passage and carrying the unmistakable impress of its author, Dorothy A. Thrupp.[5]

In these five examples related to Psalm 23, one can trace the progression from the precisely biblical to the clearly invented and original. And these representative examples epitomize the entire history of the Christian hymn in its relation to Scripture.

Examples of Hymns Based on Scripture

Though the book of Psalms is the natural and most used source of their inspiration, hymnists have turned to other portions of the Old Testament as well as the New Testament as bases for their hymns. For example, passages

[4]This four-stanza paraphrase may be found in many nineteenth and twenteth-century hymnals. See, for example, *Baptist Hymnal* (Nashville: Convention Press, 1956), 57.

[5]Another example: Joseph H. Gilmore's "He leadeth me" (B218, L501, M217) was inspired by thoughts from a prayer meeting devotional talk on Psalm 23.

from the Old Testament prophets have had unusual appeal, the prophet Isaiah being a particularly fertile source for hymnic ideas.

The anonymous author of "How firm a foundation" (B383, L507, M48) quotes almost literally verses from Isaiah in stanzas 2, 3, and 4:

Scripture	*Hymn*
Fear thou not; for I am	Fear not, I am with thee;
with thee; be not dis-	O be not dismayed,
mayed; for I am thy God:	For I am thy God.
I will strengthen thee;	and will still give thee aid;
yea, I will help thee; yea,	I'll strengthen thee, help thee,
I will uphold thee with the	and cause thee to stand,
right hand of righteousness.	Upheld by my righteous,
	omnipotent hand.
(Isa. 41:10).	
When thou passest through	When through the deep waters
the waters, I will be with	I call thee to go,
thee; and through the rivers,	The rivers of woe
they shall not overflow thee:	shall not thee overflow;
	For I will be with thee
	thy troubles to bless,
	And sanctify to thee
	they deepest distress.
When thou walkest through	When through fiery trials
the fire, thou shalt not be	thy pathway shall lie,
burned; neither shall the	My grace, all sufficient,
flame kindle upon thee.	shall be thy supply;
	The flame shall not hurt thee;
(Isa. 43:2).	I only design
	Thy dross to consume,
	and thy gold to refine.

The seventeenth-century German hymn "Comfort, comfort ye (now) my people" (B77, L29) is based on Isaiah 40:1-8—a passage made familiar by its use by Handel for the opening tenor recitative in *Messiah*. And Isaiah 33:20-21 is alluded to in the first two stanzas of John Newton's "Glorious things of thee are spoken" (M293; L358 "Glories of your name are spoken").

Partially because it includes the famous thrice-holy hymn of the cherubim as well as the prophet's poignant response of commitment "Here am I; send me," there are numerous hymns which refer to parts of the account of the call of Isaiah in the temple (Isa. 6:1-8). These include:

"Day is dying in the west" (M503)
"God himself is with us" (present) (B16, M788, L249)
"Hark, the voice of Jesus calling" (L381)
"Holy, holy, holy" (B1, M26, L165)
"Holy God, we praise thy (your) name" (M8, L535)
"Isaiah in a vision did of old" (L528)
"Let the whole creation cry" (L242)
"O day of rest and gladness" (M488, L251)
"Take my life, lead me, Lord" (B366)
"The voice of God is calling" (M200)

William Williams's "Guide me, O thou great Jehovah" (B202, M271, L343—"Guide me ever, great Redeemer") is an example of a hymn based predominantly on the Old Testament. Its general setting is the pilgrimage of the children of Israel from Egypt to Canaan. Its verses constitute a veritable scriptural mosaic, drawing upon other ideas as well from both Old Testament and New Testament:

Guide me, O thou great Jehovah, (Deut. 8:14-20; Ps. 78:52)
    Pilgrim through this barren land; (Heb. 11:13; Ex. 17:1)
I am weak, but thou are mighty; (Ps. 6:2; Isa. 1:24; Ps. 24:8)
    Hold me with thy powerful hand; (Ps. 139:10; Deut. 9:29)
Bread of heaven,   (Ex. 16:4, 12, 18)
    Feed me till I want no more. (John 6:48-51)

Open now the crystal fountain, (Ex. 20:11; Ps. 78:15-16)
    Whence the healing stream doth flow; (2 Cor. 10:4; Rev. 22:1-2)
Let the fire and cloudy pillar   (Ex. 13:21)
    Lead me all my journey through; (Deut. 8:2; Ps. 5:8)
Strong deliverer,   (Ps. 18:2; 70:5)
    Be thou still my strength and shield. (Ps. 28:7; 144:2)

When I tread the verge of Jordan (Josh. 3:8, 17)
    Bid my anxious fears subside; (1 Chron. 28:20; Isa. 35:4)
Death of death and hell's destruction, (2 Tim. 1:10; Heb. 2:14)
    Land me safe on Canaan's side;   (Num. 32:32)
Songs of praises,   (Ps. 27:6)
    I will ever give to thee. (Ps. 34:1; 146:2)

A prime example of literal paraphrase of a New Testament narrative is Nahum Tate's "While shepherds watched their flocks:" (B97, M394), a metrical version of the nativity story recorded in Luke 2:8-14. Other writers often start their hymns with a description of an event in the gospels, recalling some specific action of Jesus' ministry in order to remind the hymns' users of contemporary situations in which Christ's ministry may continue. Such is the case with Henry Twells's "At even, ere the sun was set" (M501) and Edward H. Plumptre's "Your hand, O Lord, in days of old" (L431), both based on the account of Jesus' healing the sick recorded in Mark 1:32-33. Both hymns go beyond description and recall to a prayer for Christ's healing presence amid the needy circumstances of today's world.

A few passages from the letters of the apostle Paul have been choice themes for hymnic treatment. One of these is: "But far be it from me to glory, save in the cross of our Lord Jesus Christ through which the world hath been crucified unto me, and I unto the world" (Gal. 6:14), reference to which is to be found in all the following hymns:

"Ask ye what great thing I know" (B60, M124)
"Beneath the cross of Jesus" (B360, L107, M417)
"In the cross of Christ I glory" (B70, L104, M416)
"The head that once was crowned with thorns" (B125, L173, M458)
"When I survey the wondrous cross" (B111, L482, M435)

Hymn writers have also been inspired by the great "self-emptying" passage in Philippians 2:5-11. "At the name of Jesus" (B363, L179, M76) is a nineteenth-century expression of its essential truths by the British woman, Caroline M. Noel. The American clergyman F. Bland Tucker has given it a twentieth-century setting in his "All praise to thee, for thou, O king divine" (B43, M74).

The doxological hymns in the book of Revelation have also been inspirational for hymn writing. For example, "Worthy is the Lamb that was slain to receive power, and riches, and wisdom, and strength, and honour, and glory, and blessing" (Rev. 5:12) is echoed in the following hymns:

"Blessing and honor" (L525)
"Come, let us join our cheerful songs" (B126, L254)
"Glory be to God the Father" (L167)
"O God of God, O Light of light" (L536)
"Ye (You) servants of God" (B292, L252, M409)

Biblical Images and Expressions

Hymnists through the years have made use of biblical images to impress upon the singing congregation, and evoke from it the truths of the faith. Many of these biblical images both illuminate and adorn the truths being expressed. Some of these images, though quite natural for the culture of biblical times, or even for the cultures of the hymnists using them in the eighteenth and nineteenth centuries, may need to be reexamined today because of the continuing cultural revolution of our time.

Shepherd

For example, the image of shepherd used in all the hymns discussed above may not have meaning for young persons who have lived all their lives in urban settings, where shepherds and sheep are rarely encountered except on the television screen. If one idea in the concept "Shepherd" is that of a reliable leader guiding one through hard and unfamiliar places when the going gets rough and confusing, then "The Lord is my guide" might be a more apt image for some urban folk.

Moreover, even when the word shepherd is a familiar concept, it connotes differing ideas to many people. "Shepherd" can either be the strong hero who relentlessly seeks out the lost and wounded lambs and defends them from the wolves or he can be the tender ethereal creature who gently carries the lambs "in his bosom." It was characteristic of the nineteenth century that it should ignore the idea of the "tough shepherd" and focus on that of the "tender shepherd." While the latter figure may be permissible in children's hymns, the idea of the tough shepherd would seem to come nearer the truth as portrayed in Scripture. The contrast is clear when comparing Henry M. Dexter's translation of the Clement of Alexandria hymn "Shepherd of eager youth" (M86—literal translation: "Bridle of colts untamed!")[6] with Mary L. Duncan's:

> Jesus, tender Shepherd, hear me.
> Bless Thy little lamb tonight;
> Through the darkness be Thou near me,
> Watch my sleep till morning light.[7]

Rock of Ages

> Trust in the Lord for ever,
> for the Lord God
> is an everlasting rock (Isa. 26:4, RSV).

The King James Version of this verse has in the marginal reading the phrase "Rock of Ages"—a familiar image in hymnody. But the phrase can be thought of in two ways: in the Old Testament, Elijah hid himself in a cave of the rock to get out of a storm (1 Kings 19). In the New Testament, Christ tells the story of the house built on the rock which stands when the storms come, in contrast to the house built on the sand which falls (Matt. 7:24-27).

---

[6]Kendrick Grobel's more recent translation, "O Guide to every child" (M84) is much closer to the thought of the original.

[7]This famous children's hymn is to be found in many hymnals of the late nineteenth and early twentieth centuries. See *The Hymnal* (Philadelphia: Presbyterian Board of Christian Education, 1933), 449.

Francis of Assisi

Which image expresses the greater truth? If the rock conjures up the image today of a sort of "bomb shelter" to which one can run and symbolically hide from life's dangers and demands, it could encourage a rather spineless religion. But if "Rock of Ages" calls to mind the firm foundation of faith on which one stands to face life's temptations and threats, then it can foster a strong and adventurous faith.

The "Rock of Ages" idea as "foundation" is found in John Newton's "Glorious things of thee are spoken" (M293, L358 "Glories of your name are spoken"); in F. S. Grundtvig's "Built on the Rock the church doth stand" (tr. Carl Doving, B235, L365—"Built on a rock the Church shall stand"); and the anonymous "How firm a foundation" (B383, M48, L507). The "Rock of Ages" as "protection and escape" seems to be the idea of Edward Hopper's "Jesus Savior, pilot me" (M247); Augustus Toplady's "Rock of Ages, cleft for me" (B163, L327, M120); and William O. Cushing's "O safe to the Rock that is higher than I" with its chorus:

> Hiding in thee, hiding in Thee
>   Thou blest "Rock of Ages"
> I'm hiding in Thee.[8]

Numerous other biblical expressions can be meaningless or misunderstood by many hymn singers. Given a proper explanation, hymns using these images can leap to new life and significance.

Ancient of Days

The expression "Ancient of days" (referring to God) found in several familiar hymns is often regarded as poetic nonsense since few worshipers know its scriptural base. The term is found in only one passage of the Bible: Daniel 7:9, 13, 22. In apocalyptic imagery the writer employs it to signify the eternal God, "one advanced in days," seated majestically on a throne of judgement.

Hymnists seeking to express the worship and adoration due God alone have incorporated the phrase "Ancient of days" with its majestic associations into these songs of objective praise. Note the first stanzas of each of these hymns:

"Ancient of Days, who sittest throned in glory" (M459)
"Immortal, invisible, God only wise" (B32, L526, M27)
"Come, Thou Almighty king" (B2, L522, M3)
"O worship the King" (B30, L548, M473)

Lord (of) Sabaoth

The word *Sabaoth* is Hebrew for "hosts" or "armies" and is used throughout the Old Testament to designate God's almighty power. It is

---

[8]Found in many earlier hymnals. See *Baptist Hymnal* (Nashville: Convention Press, 1956), 271.

retained untranslated in the older versions of the New Testament verses: Romans 9:29 and James 5:4, which refer to "the Lord of Sabaoth." The phrase entered into hymnic expression early on and nowhere more memorably than in the fourth-century *Te Deum laudamus* with its quotation of the seraphic song from Isaiah 6:

> "Holy, holy, holy, Lord God of Sabaoth;
>> heaven and earth are full of the majesty of thy glory" (M665, L3)

In Frederick H. Hedge's translation of Luther's Ein'feste Burg occurs the most familiar use of the phrase:

> "Lord Sabaoth, his name" (B37, M20)[9]

It is also found in several other modern hymns.[10] Because of similarities in their appearance and spelling, many worshipers have mistaken "Sabaoth" for "sabbath," thereby missing altogether the true significance of the term.

Alpha and Omega

Better known than the meaning of "Sabaoth" is the fact that "Alpha and Omega" indicate the first and last letters of the Greek alphabet and are used by the writer of the book of Revelation (1:8, 11; 21:6; 22:13) as a title for Christ, who is the first and the last, the beginning and ending of all things.

The phrase is found in stanza one of Prudentius' hymn of praise, as translated by John Mason Neale, "Of the Father's love begotten" (B62, L42, M357). Charles Wesley also used the words in "Love divine, all loves excelling": (B58, L315, M283). In characteristic fashion he links the "Alpha and Omega" reference from Revelation with a similar idea in Hebrews 12:2 with its prayer that Jesus will indeed be "the author and finisher of our faith."

Biblical Names and Places

Throughout hymnic history writers have made reference to biblical names and places. For people unfamiliar with the Bible these often need to be explained. An alphabetical listing of some of the names most commonly found would include:

Babel (Gen. 11:9)	Jesse (1 Sam. 16:1-22)
Bethlehem (Matt. 2:1-8)	Jordan (Josh. 1:2)
Calvary (Luke 23:33)	Lebanon (Ps. 29:5)
Canaan (Num. 33:50-53)	Macedonian (call, Acts 16:9)
Ebenezer (1 Sam. 7:12)	Martha (Luke 10:41)
Eden (Gen. 2:8)	Mary (Matt. 2:11)
Edom (Gen. 32:3; 36:21)	Messiah (John 4:25)

[9]The *Lutheran Book of Worship* (228, 229) provides a new translation, which changes the phrase to "Lord of hosts is he."

[10]See, for example "Praise the Lord, the King of glory" by Delma B. Reno, *Baptist Hymnal* (46): "Lord of Sabaoth his name."

Emmanuel (Immanuel, Matt. 1:23)	Moses (Ex. 2:10)
Galilee (Matt. 3:13)	Mt. Pisgah (Deut. 34:1)
Gethsemane (Matt. 26:36)	Nazareth (Luke 2:51)
Gilead (Jer. 8:22)	Pharisee (Luke 18:10)
Golgotha (Matt. 27:33)	Sharon (Song of Sol. 2:1)
Israel (Deut. 6:4)	Siloam (John 9:7-11)
Jacob (Gen. 25:26)	Stephen (Acts 6:5)
Joseph (Gen. 30:24)	Zion (Sion, Ps. 48:11)
Jerusalem (Luke 2:22)	

The terms that refer in narrative fashion to persons and places, such as Mary, Joseph, Jesus, Bethlehem, Nazareth, Gethsemane, and Golgotha are not as difficult for those with some knowledge of the gospel story. But some names carry symbolic meanings which may need explaining. These most often relate to the Old Testament.

For example, *Eden* may refer poetically to the garden where the first man and woman dwelt and thus be associated with the creation, as in the following hymns:

Show your face in brightness; shine in every land
As in Eden's garden when the world began.
(L153 "Welcome, happy morning").

Mine is the sunlight!
  Mine is the morning
Born of the one light
  Eden saw play.
(B151 "Morning has broken").

But the references to Eden include also the bliss of the garden before the fall and are associated with the glories of heaven, especially in gospel songs. For instance, here is Fanny Crosby:

Oh, the dear ones in glory, how they beckon me to come,
  And our parting at the river I recall;
To the sweet vales of Eden they will sing my welcome home,
  But I long to meet my Saviour first of all.
("My Saviour first of all").[11]

On the other hand, Eden is employed in a much more familiar song to symbolize neither creation nor heaven, but simply the opposite of gloom or trouble:

---

[11] *Baptist Hymnal* (1956), 472.

Sometimes 'mid scenes of deepest gloom,
Sometimes where Eden's bowers bloom.
(B218, L501, M217, "He leadeth me").

Similarly the use of *Jordan* and *Canaan* in hymnic expression often bears no literal reference to a particular river or to the land promised to the Israelites in Old Testament times. These two proper names are often found together, particularly in eighteenth-century hymns:

> When I tread the verge of Jordan,
>   Bid my anxious fears subside;
> Death of death and hell's destruction,
> [Bear me through the swelling current,]
>   Land me safe on Canaan's side.
>   (M271, B202, "Guide me, O thou great Jehovah")
>   (L343, "Guide me ever, great Redeemer").

> On Jordan's stormy banks I stand
>   And cast a wishful eye
> To Canaan's fair and happy land,
>   Where my possessions lie.
>   (B490, M291, "On Jordan's stormy banks").

The symbolism is that of passing over Jordan, the river of death, into the happy promised land of Canaan—the joys of heaven.[12]

   Zion (Sion) is one of the most common proper names found in hymnody. It is used to convey more than one idea. In the following instances, it transfers the earthly Mount Zion (Jerusalem, to which the Jews climbed for worship at the Temple) into a heavenly idea;

> The hill of Zion yields
>   A thousand sacred sweets,
> Before we reach the heavenly fields
>   Or walk the golden streets.
>   (B505, "We're marching to Zion").

> The ladder is long, it is strong and well-made
> Has stood hundreds of years and is not yet decayed;
> Many millions have climbed it and reached Sion's hill,
> And thousands by faith are climbing it still.
>   (B421, "As Jacob with travel").

[12]Many spirituals also make use of this imagery. For example, "Deep river" (black) and "Poor wayfaring stranger" (white).

Other hymns using Zion in reference to heaven include "Children of the
heavenly King" (M300), "Jerusalem the golden" (L347, M303), "Alleluia!
sing to Jesus" (L158), and "Oh, what their joy" (L337).

But in other hymns Zion refers to the church—the people of God on earth:

> Sure as thy [your] truth shall last,
>   To Zion shall be giv'n
> The brightest glories earth can yield
> And brighter bliss of heaven.
>   ("I love thy [your] kingdom, Lord," B240, L368, M294)

> Christ is made the sure foundation
>   Christ the head and cornerstone,
> Chosen of the Lord and precious,
>   Binding all the church in one;
> Holy Zion's help forever,
>   And her confidence alone.
>   ("Christ is made the sure foundation," L367, M298)

Other hymns using this word picture are "Glorious things of thee are spoken"
(M293), "Glories of your name are spoken" (L358), "O Zion, haste" (B295,
M299), "Praise God. Praise him" (L529), and "Zion stands with hills
surrounded."[13]

Guides to Biblical Sources of Hymns

Alongside the information for authors or sources many hymnals now also
indicate the scriptural references for terms such as those discussed above.
Some hymnals even place an appropriate verse of Scripture above each hymn
printed.[14]

For teachers, pastors, ministers of music and other church leaders, a
convenient index now found in most hymnals is one variously called Index of
Scripture References of the Hymns (M847), Index of Scriptural Bases of the
Hymns (B, p. 544).[15] These indices furnish a ready tool for correlating
appropriate hymns with public Bible readings and/or sermon texts. Insofar as
possible, such correlation should be sought in order that a service of worship
or instruction may form one artistic and logical whole. It will also help

---

[13]*Lutheran Hymnal* (1941), 474; *Baptist Hymnal* (1956), 378.

[14]See, for example *Worship Hymnal* (Fresno: General Conference of the Mennonite Brethren
Churches, 1971) and *Hymns for the Living Church* (Carol Stream: Hope Publishing Co., 1974).

[15]The *Lutheran Book of Worship* has a scriptural index in its Minister's Desk Edition (pp. 468-
69).

worshipers and learners become more keenly aware of the scriptural foundations of many of the finest hymns.[16]

For churches adhering closely to the Christian year, their lectionaries can be correlated with appropriate hymns through the use of suggested listings such as "Hymns for the Church Year" found in the *Lutheran Book of Worship* (pp. 929-31).

Using various helps that are available,[17] one can assure a meaningful hymn-Scripture correlation. For example:

The Ascension of Our Lord

(Observed the seventh week of Easter)

Epistle: Acts 1:1-11—Our Lord takes leave of his disciples with the promise of his everlasting presence till he come.

Gospel: Mark 16:14-20—The exalted Lord shows himself to be the one to whom all power in heaven and earth is given.

Hymns: "Look, ye saints (oh, look)! the sight is glorious" (B121, L156, M453)

"The head that once was crowned with thorns" (B125, L173, M458)

"Crown him with many crowns" (B52, L170, M455)

"A hymn of glory let us sing" (L157)

"Hail, thou once despised Jesus" (M454)

Most worthy hymns are biblical in the sense that they are either based directly upon, or express truths consonant with, Scripture. Therefore, drawing attention to their scriptural connections will not only enhance their meaningful use in worship and evangelism but also lead in an appealing way to a more interested consideration and study of the Bible. Many churchgoers today would not have any notion of the meaning of "Ebenezer" or "Mt. Pisgah" (to mention only two Old Testament place names) if they had not encountered them in "Come, thou fount of every blessing" (B12, 13, L499, M93) and "Sweet hour of prayer" (B401, M275). Careful attention to scriptural allusions in hymnody can lead to a renewed interest in Bible study!

Questions and Projects for Thought, Discussion, and Action

1. Compare and contrast the influence of the Psalms on hymn composition in each of the last three centuries: eighteenth, nineteenth, twentieth.

---

[16]A further resource for leaders, going much beyond the sometimes meager indication of biblical bases in some hymnals is Donald A. Spencer, *Hymn and Scripture Selection Guide* (Valley Forge: Judson Press, 1977).

[17]See especially the references to Gehrke and Boushong in the Bibliography.

2. What is the meaning of the biblical images like "milk and honey," "throne of David," "Paschal Lamb," "Jesse's stem," "Edom," and "Star of the East" found in the following hymns?

"Jerusalem the golden"

"Lord, enthroned in heavenly splendor"

"Brightest and best of the stars of the morning"

3. Use a hymnal concordance (see Bibliography) to locate hymns mentioning these biblical names: Emmanuel (Immanuel), Gilead, Sharon, Stephen, Bethel, Israel.

4. Look up the meaning of the following biblical words which are no longer in today's common language but are still found in hymns: Manna, psaltery, seraph, timbrel. Find hymns where these words occur.

5. Using a source such as McDormand and Crossman's *Judson Concordance to Hymns* or a tool such as Spencer's *Hymn and Scripture Selection Guide*, find hymns for worship and/or evangelism appropriate for use with the following passages of Scripture:

Isaiah 40:1-11

Psalm 91

Matthew 5:1-12 (The Beatitudes)

Colossians 3:15-17

6. How would you try to convince a pastor, minister of education, or Sunday School teacher that a thorough study of Christian hymnody could enhance Bible study?

7. For Sunday School lessons on the following Bible selections, choose appropriately related hymns:

Genesis 1

Psalm 103

John 20:19-29

Philippians 2:5-11

4
The Hymn and Theology

The Hymn—a Bearer of "Grass-roots" Theology

Someone has said that hymns are the poor person's poetry and the ordinary person's theology. Being the most popular kind of verse in living use, hymns do indeed express what common folk have believed through the ages and what can be affirmed today as true and reliable.

The recitation of creeds and confessions of faith makes up an important part of the public worship of many Christians; but in those worshiping groups where this is not the normal practice, the hymn stands as an alternate means of objectifying belief corporately. Replete with the lyric expression of universal doctrine which has been distilled from the church's twenty centuries of experience, the hymnal is truly a book of "grass-roots theology." For the person in the pew, a hymn like "O God, our help in ages past" (B223, L320, M28) sets forth in strong, vivid, and adequate language the eternity and omnipotence of the God being worshiped. A song like "The Solid Rock" (B337, M222, L293) voices his simple confession of faith in Jesus Christ as all-sufficient Redeemer. The hymnbook is not a formal volume of systematized dogma. However, by its general arrangement as well as the nature of its content, it is clearly theological.

The hymnal is also a ready means of presenting and teaching Christian doctrine, even though as an instructional tool it is often overlooked. The basic beliefs of most Christians have been formulated more by the hymns they sing than by the preaching they hear or the Bible study they pursue. Certainly one's disposition toward, or away from right belief is subtly but indelibly influenced by the hymns one repeatedly sings. And when talking about the faith, average churchgoers can quote more stanzas of hymns than they can verses of Scripture. This fact, far from lessening the importance of preaching and Bible teaching, is simply a testimony to the importance of the hymnal as a practical textbook in doctrine. Moreover, it focuses attention on the critical requirement that the content of the hymns taught to young and old, insofar as possible, accurately reflect theological and biblical truth.

Besides nurturing the faith, hymns figure prominently in spreading it. Christians from the first century on have proclaimed their beliefs in song, thereby helping spread the tenets of the faith. Many of the early Christian hymns were forged in theological controversy and consequently are creedal in nature.[1] Furthermore, every great religious awakening of the past has gone

---

[1]See the sections on Greek and Latin hymnody in chap. 5, Early Church and Pre-Reformation Traditions.

forward on wings of song.[2] And to the degree that hymns have been clearly theological, they have become the folk songs of the church militant. The evangelizing power of Christian song cannot be denied.

Because hymns were born out of the conscious human need of their authors to express their faith and devotion, they also minister to the spiritual needs of those who know and sing them. Thus the hymnal is a theological guidebook for meeting the challenges of daily living and the spiritual problems encountered in ordinary human relationships.

When Charles Wesley sought longingly for a thousand tongues to sing the praises of the One whose name calms fears and bids sorrows cease, ("Oh for a thousand tongues to sing" B69, L559, M1), he wrote from his own experience of the reassuring and comforting love of God revealed in Christ. And when Christians today sing the exuberant affirmations of this great hymn (written on the anniversary of Wesley's conversion experience), they too may be calmed and strengthened in their lives.

When John G. Whittier penned "Dear Lord and Father of Mankind" (B270, L506, M235), he was stating his quiet Quaker confidence in the eternal goodness of God and his sense of the wholeness of life given to those who are faithful in God's service. Amid the pressures of today's world, the confident singing of this hymn can undergird faith and purpose for one's own Christian walk. Since there exists a great reservoir of helpful spiritual truth within the covers of a good hymnal, it can function as a reliable handbook for believers, sustaining them in the daily round.

The hymn may thus be considered a ready tool for the major functions of today's church in *worship,* in *education,* in *evangelism,* and in *ministry.* In *worship* it can serve as a corporate affirmation of a congregation's faith. In *education,* it can make the doctrines of the faith memorable for Christian growth. In *evangelism* it can dramatize the truths of the gospel for mission appeal. In daily *ministry* its assuring lines can be constantly at hand to help in spiritual emergencies involving human need of every kind. The hymn can effectively function in all these areas owing to its nature as an expression of Christian theology couched in appealing lyric and mediated through personal experience.

The Hymn in Theological Controversy

The great hymns of the early centuries of the Christian church, such as the expanded *Gloria in excelsis Deo* and the *Te Deum laudamus,* were actually sung creeds. Moreover, the content of such hymns as Clement of Alexandria's "Shepherd of eager youth" and Prudentius's "Of the Father's love begotten" are best understood and appreciated when it is recognized that they

[2]For examples, see Chap. 10, The Hymn in Proclamation.

originated in the midst of theological struggle between those considered to be of the Orthodox faith and those of the Gnostic and Arian persuasions.[3]

We also know that it was after the great Christological controversies of the early centuries that the Trinitarian doxology became an integral part of medieval hymnody as well as of psalmody. Not only was the "Lesser Doxology" *(Gloria Patri)* appended to the chanting of every psalm in the divine offices; in the nineteenth century, praise to the Trinity became part and parcel of practically every hymn translated by the Oxford Reformers.[4] Look, for example, at the following hymns, the last stanzas of which include Trinitarian doxologies:

Prudentius, "Of the Father's love begotten" (B62; L42; M357)

Gregory, "Father, we praise thee" (M504)

Anonymous (seventh century), "Christ is made the sure foundation" (M298)

Rabanus Maurus, "Come, Holy Ghost, our souls inspire" (M467)

Peter Abelard, "O what their joy and their glory must be" (L337)

Bernard of Cluny, "Jerusalem, the golden" (M303)

Francis of Assisi, "All creatures of our God and King" (B9; M60)

These hymns also demonstrate that though often "born of controversy, the hymns that survive are those which express the universal faith of Christendom."[5] "Hymns which are exaggerated or one-sided in their doctrinal emphasis do not come into general use, and sooner or later are discarded."[6] If not discarded altogether, those parts unsuitable for universal use are generally omitted. Therefore most of the polemic elements in hymns have been largely excised for those who use them today.

For example, Samuel J. Stone's "The Church's one foundation" (B236; L369; M297) was in 1866 a rigid assertion of High Church dogma in disdainful opposition to those who were embracing the liberating accents of science and the higher criticism. However certain "mudslinging" allusions in the hymn have more recently been omitted, such as:

Though there be those that hate her [the Church]
    And false sons in her pale,
Against or foe or traitor
    She ever shall prevail.[7]

[3]See Chap. 5, The Early Church and Pre-Reformation Traditions.

[4]The members of the Oxford Movement even appended doxologies to existing hymns in their eagerness to imitate the medieval hymn. See Erik Routley, *Church Music and the Christian Faith* (Carol Stream, Il.: Agape, 1978), p. 98.

[5]Kenneth L. Parry, *Christian Hymns* (London: SCM Press, Ltd., 1956), p. 8.

[6]Robert Guy McCutchan, *Hymns in the Lives of Men* (New York, Abingdon-Cokesbury Press, 1945), p. 178, quoted from Howard Chandler Robbins, *Ecumenical Trends in Hymnody*, pamphlet issued by the Federal Council of Churches.

[7]Albert E. Bailey, *The Gospel in Hymns* (New York: Charles Scribner's Sons, 1950), p. 377.

Consequently the parts of the hymn now remaining in use constitute a sound lyrical exposition of what most Christians believe about the church.

Another issue causing more recent debate concerns the use of sexist language in hymns. Some theologians and worship leaders feel the pains of separation in the Christian community resulting from the use of noninclusive language in many (even classic) hymns. If such hymns are to continue to be effective in public worship, in their opinion, their sexist imagery must be avoided. In general, their concern is to eliminate exclusively male images of God, exclusively female images of the church and nature and the use of "generic" man (i.e., mankind, etc.).

An example of the kinds of emendation advocated is seen in the following excerpts from Henry van Dyke's "Joyful, joyful we adore thee" (B31, L551, M38):

Original	*Emendation*
Thou our Father, Christ our brother—	We on earth are all thy children;
All who live in love are thine;	All who live in love are thine;
Father-love is reigning o'er us	All creation sings before us,
Brother-love binds man to man.	Raise we now the glad refrain.[8]

Theological understandings that are quite meaningful in one generation may be rejected in later generations. Christian theologians are constantly struggling for better insight into the truth of God, and this struggle is often reflected in the emendation or abridgement of hymns.

For example, Reginald Heber's richly poetic "From Greenland's icy mountains" accurately stated the ardent convictions of nineteenth-century Englishmen in the days when the Christian missionary thrust was conceived as parallel to and intermingled with the spreading of the British Empire. But now the spiritually patronizing attitude implied by the questions in stanza 3:

> Can we, whose souls are lighted
> With wisdom from on high,
> Can we to men benighted
> The lamp of life deny?

has caused this hymn to fall into disuse. The few hymnals that still include it, usually omit the following stanza because of the words "heathen" and "vile" (in reference to those who are the objects of Christian missions).

---

[8]These and other changes in hymn texts seeking to affirm the femaleness and maleness of God and humanity may be found in *Because We Are One People: Songs for Worship* (Chicago: Ecumenical Women's Centers, 1975).

> What though the spicy breezes
> Blow soft o'er Ceylon's isle,
> Though every prospect pleases,
> And only man is vile;
> In vain with lavish kindness
> The gifts of God are strown;
> The heathen in his blindness
> Bows down to wood and stone.

Hymns thus expressing outmoded attitudes concerning the nature and mission of the church are being replaced. Newer hymns such as: Henry H. Tweedy's uplifting "Eternal God, whose power upholds" (M476) and Georgia Harkness' exuberant "Tell it out with gladness' (B275) are inspired, however, by the same basic Christian belief, which is that God's good news should be shared the world over with all persons in order that their lives may be transformed into the abundant life Christ died to give them.

John Wesley had a keen sense of importance of the hymn for encapsulating Christian dogma. He spoke of his collection of hymns as "a little body of experimental and practical divinity."[9] Furthermore, he was quite impatient with those who tried to mend his brother Charles' hymns to make what they thought to be better theological sense out of them. Yet John himself engaged in a considerable bit of emendation in order to satisfy his own theological and poetic requirements.

For instance, Charles Wesley's great hymn on the indwelling spirit of love, "Love Divine, all loves excelling" (B58; L315; M283) in its second stanza originally read: "Take away our *power* of sinning," concerning which the question was asked: "Is not this expression too strong?" "Can God take away our power of sinning without taking away our power of free obedience?" This extreme view of Christian perfection[10], though a cherished ideal of Charles Wesley, was so objectionable to John that he completely omitted this stanza in later editions. In American editions the stanza is retained but with "power of" changed to "bent to." Other wordings that have been changed are (in stanza 2) "second rest" becoming "promised rest"[11] and (in stanza 4) "sinless" becoming "spotless."

This doctrine of sinless perfection was a cause of much controversy in eighteenth-century England. One of its stoutest and most vituperative opponents was Augustus M. Toplady, the author of "Rock of Ages, cleft for

---

[9]John Wesley, preface to *A Collection of Hymns for the Use of the People Called Methodists* (London, 1780) quoted in the preface to *The Methodist Hymnbook with Tunes* (London: Methodist Conference Office, 1933), p. v.

[10]Also evident in stanza 4: "Finish then thy new creation; Pure and spotless let us be;"

[11]However, *The Methodist Hymnal* (1966), returns to "second rest" (M283).

me" (B163; L327; M120). Yet today Toplady's "Rock of Ages" and Wesley's "Jesus, lover of my soul" (B172; M125, 126), in spite of the strong theological differences between their authors, stand side by side as two of the most loved hymns in the English language. The fact that they do is dramatic proof of the truth stated above: though born of controversy, the great hymns express the one universal Christian faith. And they provide a powerful prod for Christians, regardless of denominational label, to continue the struggle toward the ultimate goal of unity expressed by Jesus in his high-priestly prayer: "That they may be one, even as we are one" (John 17:22).

The Hymnal's Table of Contents—a Theological Indicator

A look at the table of contents of a good hymnal quickly reveals the range and depth of its presentation of Christian doctrine. The manner and order of presentation may differ from hymnal to hymnal and yet most of the cardinal points of doctrine will find a place in a book claiming acceptance and respect by large bodies of believers. For example, a more liturgically-oriented hymnal may arrange many of its hymns according to the seasons of the Christian year while a book reflecting the beliefs and practices of worshiping groups inclined toward the free church tradition might list many of the same hymns under a heading such as "Jesus Christ" and the various events in his life and ministry.

By a similar token, hymns concerning the third person of the Trinity may be arranged systematically under "The Christian Year—Pentecost Season" in one hymnal and in another under "God—the Holy Spirit."[12] Hymns concerned primarily with the subject of outreach may appear in one hymnal under the heading of "The Church—Evangelism and Missions," while in another hymnal many of the same hymns will be found under the heading of "The Christian Year—Epiphany Season." Thus even the categorization of the hymns by subject headings will reveal the theological stance of a given hymnal's editors, publishers, and users.

Furthermore the number and variety of hymns under particular headings can be a clue to the theological bent of their compilers. For example, hymns and gospel songs having to do with confession, repentance, and salvation in one hymnal may number several times those on the same subjects in another hymnal. The latter hymnal however, may have a much richer and larger quantity of hymns on social concern and the relevancy of the gospel to the problems of today's world.

Hymn Patterns

Christian ministers, whether musicians or nonmusicians, have the

---

[12]However, in some hymnals both categories may be found. For example, *The Book of Hymns* (Methodist) has hymns about the Holy Spirit in sections headed "The Holy Spirit" (M131-8) and "Pentecost Season" (M459-67), as well.

opportunity, as well as the obligation, of knowing their hymnbook theologically; and they would do well to apply certain expository techniques to the task of revealing the theological implications of its individual hymns.

Objective-Subjective

One way this may be done is to think theologically about the patterns of thought in specific hymns. One basic approach is to regard hymns in terms of their objectivity and/or subjectivity. In its address, a hymn can be either objective (God or a person or a thing being the main object of attention and concern) or it can be subjective (the focus of attention being on the poet or singer, that is, the one who originally created the hymn or the one who re-creates the hymn when singing it).

For example, a quick analysis of a hymnal's table of contents will show how the hymns under the heading "God" are either addressed to him[13] or they are exhorting others or even one's own soul to make him the object of worship and thanksgiving. Sometimes there may be emphasis on only one aspect of the Godhead, as, for instance, on Christ[14] or the Holy Spirit.[15]

God is the chief object of prayer and praise in hymnic expression. Inanimate objects such as sunlight ("Heavenly sunlight") or a cross ("The old rugged cross") may certainly be referred to in worshipful song, but when they become the principal objectives of attention, they tend to be exalted to a status equal to or above God. In singing such songs one can unthinkingly give voice to a theological position that is in reality foreign to one's actual beliefs.

Predominant subjectivity is to be found in many a popular hymn. A healthy subjectivism is necessary to a wholehearted involvement of one's total person in dialogue with God. But subjectivity must be disciplined lest it lead to unwholesome self-centeredness. Consequently, songs weighted heavily toward subjectivity, like "O that will be glory" (B497) and "Pass me not, O gentle Savior" (B176, M145) would best be balanced with hymns of the God-centered type, such as "All praise to Thee" (B43, M74) and "All hail the power of Jesus' name" (B40, 41, 42; L328, 329; M71, 72, 73).

Better hymns and gospel songs combine the objective with the subjective by changing the object of address between or within successive stanzas. For example, Isaac Watts' hymn on the atonement, "Alas, and did my Savior bleed" (B113, L98, M415) is written with Christ, the Savior as the supreme object of attention, yet Christ is referred to in the third person. With stanza 4

---

[13]For example, in BH75, look at hymns numbers 1-15, in which those hymns not directly addressed to God (Numbers 8,9,10,11,14) bring him to mind as the sole object of praise. On the other hand, an analysis of the first fifteen God-centered hymns in M reveals only four (Numbers 3,6,8,12) addressed directly to God.

[14]See hymns B38-129, L22-159, and M71-130.

[15]See hymns B130-37, L486-513, 160-164, 376-403, and M131-38 and 461, 462, 467.

(beginning "Thus might I hide my blushing face") the hymn takes a more subjective turn; and in stanza 5, Christ is addressed directly, with the climaxing words of commitment:

> Here, Lord, I give myself away,
>   'Tis all that I can do.

Similarly in Cecil Frances Alexander's "Jesus calls us o'er the tumult" (B367, L494, M107) Jesus is spoken of in the third person, the singer addressing his fellow worshipers. But the final stanza becomes an intimate prayer to Jesus: ". . . by thy mercies (in your mercy) Savior, may we (make us) hear thy (your) call." A similar kind of shift to and from direct address to God can be observed in gospel hymns such as "He leadeth me! O blessed thought" (B218, L501, M217) and "Jesus, keep me near the cross" (B351, M433).

Paradox and Contrast

Some hymns make creative use of paradox and contrast in their thought content. This might well be expected when the many paradoxes implicit in the Christian faith are recalled. The burden of the teaching of Jesus was that whosoever would save his life shall lose it, and whoever would lose his life for Christ's sake would find it (Matt. 16:25). Furthermore, whoever would be chief must be servant of all (Matt. 20:27).

George Matheson's hymn "Make me a captive, Lord" (M184) is a masterful example of the symbolic use of such paradoxical thought. Note, for instance, stanza 1

> Make me a *captive,* Lord,
>   And then I shall be *free;*
> Force me to *render up* my sword,
>   And I shall *conqueror* be.
> I *sink* in life's alarms
>   When by myself I *stand;*
> *Imprison* me within thine arms,
>   And *strong* shall be my hand.

Charles Wesley's "Thou hidden source of calm repose" (M89) is another hymn rich in paradox, especially in its final two stanzas:

> Jesus, my all-in-all thou art:
>   My *rest* in *toil,* my *ease* in *pain,*
> The *healing* of my *broken heart,*
>   In *war* my *peace,* in *loss* my *gain,*
> My *smile* beneath the tyrant's *frown:*
> In *shame* my *glory* and my *crown.*

In *want* my plentiful *supply,*
In *weakness* my almighty *power,*
In *bonds* my perfect *liberty,*
My *light* in Satan's *darkest hour,*
In *grief* my *joy* unspeakable,
My *life* in *death,* my *heaven* in *hell.*

The "I know not" hymns also express some of the great contrasts implicit in the faith. Using the theme of 2 Timothy 1:12, Daniel Whittle movingly contrasts the "I know not's" of the poet or singer with the Pauline assurance: "I know whom I have believed" (B344).

The hymn of Harry Webb Farrington, "I know not how that Bethlehem's babe" (M123) also effectively illustrates this pattern of contrast, as does John Greenleaf Whittier's "I know not what the future hath" (B492, M290).

The Hebrew Pattern

A frequently overlooked thought design in many hymns is known as the Hebrew pattern because of its prevalent use by the Hebrew poets in the Psalms.[16] It consists of the conventional threefold plan: *thesis, antithesis,* and *synthesis.* The *thesis* contemplates God in all his perfection as holy, eternal, omnipotent, and loving. The *antithesis* presents the contrasting human situation with its sinfulness, ephemerality, weakness, and rebellion against God. Then in the *synthesis* man's sinfulness is caught up in God's holiness, his mortality into divine immortality, his weakness into God's power, and his rebellion into joyful reconciliation with the All-Merciful.

This pattern is most clearly discernible in the hymns of Isaac Watts, possibly because Watts followed closely the psalmodic model even when he was not paraphrasing a psalm. "O God our help in ages past" (B223, L320, M28), based on Psalm 90, can be thus analyzed:

Thesis	Stanza 1—	"O God, our help . . ."
	2 —	"Under the shadow . . ."
	3 —	"Before the hills . . ."
	4 —	"A thousand ages . . ."
Antithesis	5 —	"Time like an . . ."
	6 —	"The busy tribes of flesh and blood, With all their cares and fears, Are carried downward by the flood, And lost in following years."[17]

---

[16]See Carl F. Price, "Hymn Patterns," Hymn Society of America reprint from *Religion in Life,* Summer, 1947.

[17]If we had more of Watts' original paraphrase in our hymnals, the antithesis would include the stanza quoted.

Synthesis   7— "O God our help . . ."

Watts's great hymn on the Holy Spirit, "Come, Holy Spirit, heavenly Dove" (B134, M134) also follows the Hebrew model:

Thesis   Stanza 1— "Come, Holy Spirit . . ."
Antithesis   2— "Look how we grovel . . ."
                       3— "In vain we tune . . ."
                       4— "And shall we then . . ."
Synthesis   5— "Come, Holy Spirit . . ."

Since we are concerned here with a thought pattern (content) rather than a literary pattern (structure), we can not expect to find the design coinciding in every case with stanzaic construction. So John Bowring's hymn "God is love, his mercy brightens" (B36, M63) has the Hebrew thought pattern but it is not so neatly arranged according to stanzas:

Thesis   Stanza 1— "God is love . . ."
Antithesis   2— "Chance and change . . ."
 and Thesis
                       3— "E'en the hour . . ."
Synthesis   4— "He with earthly . . ."

An example of this pattern in a more recent hymn may be seen in Frank Mason North's "Where cross the crowded ways of life" (B311, L429, M204):

Thesis   Stanza 1— "Where cross the crowded . . ."
Antithesis con-   2— "In haunts of wretchedness . . ."
 trasting with thesis
                       3— "From tender childhood's . . ."
                       4— "The cup of water . . ."
Synthesis   5— "O Master, from . . ."
                       6— "Till sons of men . . ."

Other hymns too are cast in this mold.[18] Their theological teachings become apparent far more quickly and easily once the pattern is discerned.

Theological Interpretations

In addition to the analysis of patterns, theological meanings in hymns can also be highlighted through an exegesis of their content on a stanza-by-stanza basis. This can be done by verbal exposition either in a broad summary statement or by a detailed analysis. Some clergymen and other church workers have prepared short devotional commentaries on specific hymns; others have developed entire sermons using one or more hymns as sermon texts. A list of

---

[18]See, for example, "Praise, my soul, the King of heaven" (B8, L549, M66), "Savior, breathe an evening blessing" (M496), "O for a closer walk with God" (M268), and "O Thou, in whose presence" (B372, M129). To one intent on making a theological analysis, the Hebrew thought pattern will reveal itself in many other hymns.

Martin Luther

sources containing hymn interpretations may be found in the Bibliography of this volume.

Doctrinal content can also be brought into focus by paraphrasing a hymn's poetry in succinct prose. For example, John Greenleaf Whittier's hymn "Immortal love, forever full" (B329, M158) could be paraphrased in the following manner:

Immortal Love, forever full,
    Forever flowing fee,
Forever shared, forever whole,
    A never-ebbing sea!
	The eternal love of God,
	though constantly offered,
	is inexhaustible.

We may not climb the heav'nly steeps,
    To bring the Lord Christ down;
In vain we search the lowest deeps,
    For him no depths can drown.
	Christ's presence is not
	only to be found in the
	highest reaches of the
	stratosphere but also in the
	deepest ocean valleys.

But warm, sweet, tender, even yet
    A present help is he;
And faith has still its Olivet,
    And love its Galilee.
	Yet his loving spirit is
	always with those who
	follow his example in
	faith and love.

The healing of his seamless dress
    Is by our beds of pain;
We touch him in life's throng and press,
    And we are whole again.
	His healing presence can
	touch our busy, harried
	lives and restore whole-
	ness.

Through him the first fond prayers are said,
    Our lips of childhood frame;
The last low whispers of our dead
    Are burdened with his name.
	From earliest childhood
	until the hour of death,
	we pray in his loving name.

O Lord and Master of us all:
    Whate'er our name or sign,
We own thy sway, we hear thy call,
    We test our lives by thine.
	Regardless of our label, we
	all claim you, Lord, as
	the supreme master and
	model of our lives.

So in summary, Whittier's theology in this hymn postulates the boundless love of God which is freely given to those who acknowledge Christ as sovereign Lord in their present circumstance and need. Such basic doctrine becomes recognizable and clear when one engages in an exercise of simple paraphrase similar to that above.

Conclusion

It was the early nineteenth-century German poet Goethe who once said that noble architecture is frozen music. A twentieth-century hymnologist has rightly asked in response: "May we not say that a noble hymn is frozen theology that melts in the fervour of devotional song?"[19] Indeed we may. Yet regardless of how rich and correct a hymn's theological content may be, the hymn itself becomes a genuine expression of Christian belief only when the singer utters it from his heart.

Here is the crux of the matter of the hymn as theology. No matter how precise and correct the theological teaching of a hymn may be, its doctrine remains frozen in moribund wording and lifeless musical notation until its meaning is devoutly embraced by the one who sings it. George Herbert in his poem "A True Hymn" has put it aptly:

> The fineness which a hymn or psalm affords
> Is when the soul unto the lines accords.[20]

Questions for Discussion/Projects for Action

1. In what ways have specific hymns influenced your own beliefs?

2. Compare the table of contents of your hymnal with the contents of a hymnal of another church or denomination to determine their main theological emphases.

3. Some people have objected to the theology in the following songs:

"Pass me not, O gentle Savior" (B176, M145)

"I come to the garden alone" (B428)

"O that will be glory" (B497)

Can you find reasons for such objections? Do you agree or disagree with these objections?

4. Do you know of other hymns whose theology is questionable?

5. From your hymnal choose ten hymns that are totally objective in address and direction. Then choose ten more that are subjective. Make a list of your twenty-five favorite hymns and analyze them for subjectivity/objectivity.

6. Can you find and block out on paper the Hebrew pattern in these hymns?

"A mighty fortress is our God" (B37, L228, 229, M20)

"Praise, my soul, the king of heaven" (B8, L549, M66)

7. Choose one of the following three hymns:

"Look, ye saints (oh, look), the sight is glorious" (B121, L156, M453)

"Lord, speak to me, (us), that I (we) may speak" (B276, L403, M195)

"Abide with me, fast falls the eventide" (B217, L272, M289)

and write out in simple prose the thought contained in each of its stanzas. Then summarize the hymn's theological teaching in one or two sentences.

8. What are some ways by which you might lead others to consider more carefully the theology of the hymns they like to sing?

---

[19]Frank B. Merryweather, *The Evolution of the Hymn* (London: William Clowes and Sons, Ld., 1966), p. 17.

[20]Herbert, "A True Hymn" in *The Temple: Sacred Poems and Private Ejaculations* (9th ed.) (London: J. M. for Philemon Stephens, 1667), pp. 162-63.

5

Early Church and Pre-Reformation Traditions

When considering the worship song of the first-century Christians, one is inevitably drawn to a study of the Old Testament Psalter, which constituted the first Christian book of praise. Since the first Christians were mostly Jews, the well-known psalms were their only means of praise at the very beginning. Although the young Christian community was soon to add new songs resulting from its newfound hope and joy in Christ, even these new songs were to be based on psalmodic models.

Old Testament Backgrounds

The so-called "Nativity Canticles" in the Gospel of Luke are very much like the Psalms in both form and content. And it is significant that at the conclusion of the Last Supper Jesus and his disciples sang a hymn which was very likely a portion of the traditional psalms used for Passover—The Great Hallel (Ps. 113-118).[1]

The Psalms are the base upon which all subsequent church song has been built. Whether intended for corporate or private worship, they voice those universal sentiments that have constituted the themes of musical devotion throughout the centuries. Since in varied forms and styles they appear and reappear throughout the history of congregational song,[2] their supreme importance for worship prior to the formation of the Christian Church needs only to be recognized here.

New Testament Song

Nativity Canticles

Having come into a new and unprecedented knowledge of a loving fellowship through faith in the risen Christ, the first Christians felt the need to give fresh expression to their feelings in new songs of Christian experience. This is evidenced in the exuberant lyrics connected with the nativity of our Lord: the song of Mary (Luke 1:46-55), the song of Zacharias (vv. 68-79), the song of the angels (2:14), and the song of Simeon (vv. 29-32).

In later times these songs came to be known by their first words (incipits) in the Latin: the *Magnificat* (usually sung at Vespers or Evensong in liturgical

---

[1]There are other references to singing in the New Testament but it cannot be asserted with certainty that the songs used were drawn from the canonical Psalter. See *The Interpreter's Dictionary of the Bible* (1962 edition, S. V. "Hymns" by M. H. Shepherd).

[2]See elsewhere in this chapter, for example, Part III of the famous *Te Deum laudamus.*

churches) (M670, L6); the *Benedictus* (sung at morning hours) (M666, L2); the *Gloria in excelsis* (known as the "Greater Doxology" and expanded from the angelic message into a much longer song of prayer and praise)[3]; and the *Nunc Dimittis* (sung at Compline or Evensong or Communion) (M673, L159). The central note struck by these first truly Christian songs is one of exuberant joy occasioned by the fulfillment of ancient prophecy in the miraculous coming of Jesus Christ.

Pauline Hymn Fragments

In various other places in the New Testament, particularly in the letters of the apostle Paul, hymnlike fragments, possibly quoted from early worship usages in the churches, can be found. For example, there appear to be snatches from doctrinal hymns, which sound very much like the material from which the early creeds came:

> He appeared in human form,
> was shown to be right by the Spirit,
> and was seen by angels.
> He was preached among the nations,
> was believed in throughout the world,
> and was taken up to heaven. (1 Tim. 3:16b TEV).

Here is a fragment from a baptismal hymn:
> Wake up, sleeper,
> and rise from death,
> and Christ will shine upon you. (Eph. 5:14, TEV).

And there is a reference to the spontaneous use of hymns and prayers in the Jerusalem church. A marvelous incident recorded in Acts 4:24-31 affords just one glimpse of how the first Christians broke into singing compositions which were part of a great reservoir of poetry and prose regularly used in their common worship. Even in unlikely circumstances, as when Paul and Silas were beaten and locked in stocks at Philippi (Acts 16:25), they gave voice to well-known songs in praise to God.

The use of Christian song as an instrument of instruction is evident in parallel exhortations from Paul's writings: "Speak to one another in the words of psalms, hymns, and sacred songs; sing hymns and psalms to the Lord, with praise in your hearts." (Eph. 5:19, TEV). "Christ's message, in all its richness must live in your hearts. Teach and instruct one another with all wisdom. Sing psalms, hymns, and sacred songs; sing to God, with thanksgiving in your heart." (Col. 3:16, TEV).

[3]See the text at M618, L, pp. 58, 79, 100 and the discussion below.

Doxological Hymns

Certain doxological (praise) hymns in the book of Revelation, describing a visionary heavenly worship, provided another rich store of praise literature for the New Testament Christians. Among the many examples[4] is "The song of Moses, the servant of God, and the song of the Lamb":

> Lord, God Almighty,
> how great and wonderful are your deeds!
> King of all nations,
> how right and true are your ways!
> Who will not stand in awe of you, Lord?
> Who will refuse to declare your greatness?
> You alone are holy.
> All the nations will come
> and worship you,
> because your just actions are seen by all. (Rev. 15:3-4, TEV).

That the early churches actually engaged in singing praise is clear from the record of Pliny the Younger, governor of Bithynia, who in A.D. 112 reported to the Emperor Trajan that the Christians in his province held their worship assemblies on Sunday mornings before dawn and sang antiphonal hymns of praise to Christ as God.[5]

Greek Hymnody

Greek was the language of culture in the Eastern Mediterranean areas where Christianity got its start. Consequently the Hebrew Scriptures, originally translated into Greek (the *Septuagint*) in the third and second centuries B.C. to meet the needs of Jews in Egypt, were also appropriated by the first Greek Christians. Since the New Testament was originally written in Greek, it was natural that all the worship materials used by the early churches existed in this language as well.

Not until the nineteenth century was any of the hymnody of these Greek-speaking churchmen of the early Christian centuries translated into English. This finally happened as a result of the work of the Oxford Movement—a powerful force within nineteenth-century Anglicanism to revitalize the church by reasserting its ancient spirit and reclaiming its original power. This movement prompted a reexamination of the church's oldest documents and a reemphasis on its ritual and literature of worship.

---

[4]See Revelation 1:4-8; 5:9-10; 11:17-18; 19:1-3 among others.
[5]See Henry Bettenson, *Documents of the Christian Church* (London: Oxford University Press, 1946), pp. 3-7.

Early Prose Hymns

Our Greek hymnic legacy stems from three distinct types, insofar as form is concerned. The earliest hymns were proselike, coming from New Testament times and the era immediately thereafter. They are comparatively few in number. In addition to the biblical hymns mentioned above, two hymns from early centuries have continued to maintain an important place in the worship of the Greek church and through translation in other churches to this day.

One is the famous "Lamplighting Hymn" (third century A.D.) sung at the approach of night both in the family circle of Christian homes and at the gathering of the church for corporate devotion. Addressed to the heavenly Father and using the metaphor of "gladdening light," this hymn is one of pure praise. In the translation of John Keble it is known as "Hail! Gladdening Light, of His pure glory poured" and in Robert Bridges' more recent translation as "O gladsome light, O grace of God the Father's face" (L279, "Oh, gladsome light of the Father immortal").

The other hymn is a morning song—an expanded Greek form of the message of the angels at Christ's birth upon which the fully developed *Gloria in excelsis Deo* of the Western church was based. This expanded "greater doxology" is chanted as a canticle in liturgical churches with the familiar first line, "Glory be to God on high" (M618, L, pp. 58-59 "Glory to God in the highest").

Classical Meters

The second type of Greek hymn was written in classical meter. One of the very earliest of these is "Shepherd of Eager Youth" by Clement of Alexandria (c. 160—c.215). Clement was an outstanding Christian Gnostic scholar and head of the catechetical school at Alexandria. The original poem on which this hymn is based was appended to his guidebook in Christian manners and morals, variously called *The Pedagogue, The Tutor,* or *The Instructor (Paidagogos).* Not a hymn for children, it was written for the guidance and inspiration of Christian converts who were to be nurtured under the rule of the Word of Christ *(Logos).* "Shepherd of eager youth" (M86) is a nineteenth-century paraphrase by the American Congregational minister, Henry M. Dexter. A more recent unrhymed paraphrase by the late New Testament scholar, Kendrick Grobel is "O Guide to every child of thine" (M84).

Synesius of Cyrene (c. 375-c. 430), a philosopher-statesman as well as bishop in North Africa, wrote ten hymns setting forth the great themes of Christian doctrine in terms of Neoplatonic philosophy. The hymn "Lord Jesus, think on me" (M284, L309) is a translation of the final hymn of the group. It is a prayer to Jesus for forgiveness and inner purity (st. 1), for inward peace and rest (st. 2), for spiritual health and life (st. 3), for a guiding controlling hand (st. 4), for a sense of God's nearness amid life's tempests (st. 5), and for a future life of peace and joy (st. 6). These are universal needs.

Some of these early Greek hymns were originally in the form of prayers. Most notable are the eucharistic prayers in the *Didache (Teaching of the Twelve Apostles),* a second-century manual of church order. From these prayers for the church the contemporary American clergyman, F. Bland Tucker has paraphrased the hymn "Father, we thank thee who has planted" (M307, E1).

The original of "Let all mortal flesh keep silence" (M324, L198) is a prayer associated by tradition with the liturgy of St. James (the half-brother of our Lord) at the Jerusalem church. It was originally intended for use at the Communion but can also be used, as a call to worship or even as a Christmas or general hymn. Its plainsong-like tune, PICARDY, comes from seventeenth-century France.

Prose Canons

The third and most important type of Greek hymn came into existence after the decline of the classical meters. Though in prose format, these hymns have rhythmical affinities with Hebrew poetry. They are still included in the Service Books of the Greek Orthodox Church. They reached their culmination with the great canons of the eighth and ninth centuries. It is to this type of source that John Mason Neale (1818-1866) dedicated his unusual gifts to produce treasured English translations.

Andrew of Crete.—The earliest writer in this category who still claims attention today is Andrew of Crete (Andrew of Jerusalem 660-732). He was actually born in Damascus, but embraced the monastic life while under the influence of the Patriarch of Jerusalem (hence his second name above). However, after living both at the monastery of Mar Saba in the Judean desert and at Constantinople for a time, he was appointed Bishop of Crete (hence the name by which he is usually known).

Since no earlier examples have been found as yet, Andrew is considered the originator of that characteristic Greek worship form known as the canon *(kanon).* The most exalted form of Greek hymnody, the canon is an extended poem, consisting of eight (sometimes nine) odes, each of which in turn is made up of several stanzas. These odes were usually based on scriptural songs (canticles) such as the song of Moses (Exodus 15) and the nativity canticles of the Gospel of Luke. They are sung to this day in the Greek liturgy at the office of Lauds (early morning).

Andrew's most celebrated work was the "Great Canon," consisting of some 250 penitential stanzas, chanted during Lent prior to Holy Week. The rhythm of these exceedingly long and tiresome works is made up more of accents than of rhyme and thus would be somewhat comparable to modern free verse. Neale was the first to make translations of selections from these immense works for use in English worship. Without benefit of guidance as to form (neither from the original Greek nor from the example of any other translators), he made hymns which often bear more the stamp of his own genius than of their originals.

Such is the case with the hymn "Christian, dost thou see them?" (M238). Though it breathes the spirit of the monastic life, this hymn can also speak significantly to life today. When sung with a tune that powerfully expresses the dramatic contrast between the subtle manifestations of evil and the clarion call to fight against them with spiritual weapons,[6] this hymn can itself be used as a weapon in the struggle against present-day temptation. Note the climactic change of style in the final stanza, in which the insistent questioning of the Christian gives way to the Master's approbation and commendation.

The cloister of Mar Saba between Jerusalem and the Dead Sea was an important center for hymn writing in the eighth century. In addition to Andrew of Crete, who possibly found the inspiration there for his "Christian, dost thou see them?"; it was for many years also the home of John of Damascus.

John of Damascus.—At Mar Saba John of Damascus (d. c. 780) was educated under the tutelage of a learned Sicilian monk named Cosmas (the Elder). After a political career as chief councillor to the caliph of Damascus, the leading civil ruler of the Muhammadan faith, John and his foster brother Cosmas (the Younger) gave up their earthly possessions and retired to the monastery.

There John devoted himself to a life of writing, compiling huge works in the realms of science, philosophy, and theology. His main contribution was, however, to Greek hymnody and music. Indeed, what Gregory the Great (540-604) achieved in the collection and codification of Christian chant in the West, John achieved in the East, thereby giving a great impetus to music and hymnody in the Greek church. John's fame as a hymn writer rests mainly on his composition of both words and music for the canon, a form which he perfected.[7] The subject matter of his six canons was the Incarnation, expanded to include the entire Christ-event: birth, earthly ministry, death, resurrection, and ascension.

The most famous of these canons is the one for Easter, variously known as the "Golden Canon," "King of Canons," and "Queen of Canons" and

---

[6]ST. ANDREW OF CRETE by J. B. Dykes *(The Methodist Hymnal* [1935], 275), and WALDA (M238), by Lloyd A. Pfautsch.
[7]See above in connection with Andrew of Crete.

generally recognized as the grandest piece of Greek sacred poetry in existence. It is from the first ode of this canon that "The day of resurrection" (M437, L141) was freely translated by Neale. This is a glorious hymn of victory, making allegorical use of the Jewish Passover theme to apply to the triumph of Christ in the resurrection (st. 1). It also recalls the risen Christ's appearance to the three Marys (Matt. 28:9), on whom his "All hail" fell in a heavenly call to worship (st. 2); and it is climaxed by the joyous invitation for all things in heaven and on earth to join in the Easter praise (sts. 3 and 4).

Another fine Easter hymn, also by John, is "Come, Ye (You) faithful, raise the strain" (M446, M448, L132), translated by Neale from the first ode of the Canon for St. Thomas Sunday. In the Greek church this is the traditional name for the first Sunday after Easter. Based on the song of Moses (Ex. 15), this hymn employs the imagery of Israel's crossing the Red Sea, applying it to Christ's deliverance from the waters of death to the joys of the resurrected life. The final stanza is a Trinitarian doxology written and added by Neale.

Anatolius.—In the ninth century, Constantinople, the great center of culture, politics, and learning, became also the focal point of hymn writing in the Greek church. Here in a secluded monastery known as the Studium of St. John a group of holy men gave themselves to constant prayer and study. Under the inspiring example of their abbot, Theodore of the Studium (c. 759-c. 826), many of the monks also were devoted to hymn writing.

Anatolius (c. 810) was most likely a pupil of Theodore. Over a hundred short hymns are ascribed to him, including the original of "The day is past and over" (M491). This appealing prayer, intended for use upon retiring, has been freely translated by Neale. In its altered form it has found a place in evening worship and in Christian homes as a lullaby for children at bed time.

Traits of Greek Hymnody

The majority of Greek hymns in current use are characterized by objectivity (e.g., "Glory be to God on high") with little allowance for human emotions. This is true in part because they sprang up at the time the great doctrines concerning the mystery of the Trinity and the incarnation were being hammered out in the church creeds. Moreover, they were for the most part conceived liturgically, i.e., with the intention of glorifying the great scriptural lessons which were part and parcel of the daily and weekly orders of public worship. Consequently little opportunity is given for personal response to these doctrinal statements and scriptural expositions. The mind of the Greek hymn writer gloried in revealed truth, losing itself in sustained praise and ecstatic contemplation.

Dr. John Mason Neale and the other translators have left their unmistakable imprint on these hymns, carefully excising references which ascribe great honor and power to the virgin Mary; and often the hymns conclude with Trinitarian formulas, in keeping with nineteenth-century Anglican High Church worship practices. In contrast to this prevailing objectivity, there are a few compositions from among the shorter hymns (e.g., Synesius' "Lord Jesus, think on me") that reflect a tender introspection; in their affecting simplicity, these continue to appeal. The words of a British scholar aptly describe our hymnic legacy from Greek Christians, "the fountain of Christian hymnody is pure at its source."[8]

Latin Hymnody: Fourth and Fifth Centuries A.D.

Christian song in the Latin West developed at a time parallel with the later stages of Greek hymnic activity. Hymnody was slower in winning its way in the west because nonscriptural hymns were often forbidden (as an intended safeguard against heresy). In fact, the introduction of hymn singing in the Western church came by way of theological controversy.

In the fourth and fifth centuries the church was torn by doctrinal factions. Arius (c. 250-336), an influential leader at Alexandria, had led the battle against orthodoxy over the issue of the nature of Jesus Christ. To him, Jesus was a derived creature of God and therefore not fully divine. Though Arius was banished by his superiors, his teachings continued to be spread by means of appealing hymns, often sung in nightly processionals. As a counterforce, Bishop John Chrysostom, with the blessing of the Emperor, organized rival processions of orthodox hymn singers. Although confusion and even bloodshed sometimes resulted, the Christian custom of singing at evening was thereby greatly strengthened.

Hilary of Poitiers

It was this custom of nightly polemical singing that greatly impressed the eloquent and energetic Hilary of Poitiers (c. 310-366), who fought so strenuously against the Arian heresy in the West that he came to be called "The Hammer of the Arians." Hilary set hymns in the rhythm of the marching songs of the Roman soldiers in order to promote his theological convictions. Though none of his hymns survive, he is nevertheless important historically as the pioneer of hymn singing in the West. In this way he exerted a powerful influence on the true popularizer of Western hymnody, Ambrose of Milan (c. 340-397).

Ambrose

Ambrose led the battle against the Arians in Milan. When beseiged in his

---

[8]Frederick John Gillman, *The Evolution of the English Hymn* (London, George Allen and Unwin, Ltd., 1927), p. 51.

basilica by the heretical soldiers of the Arian Emperor Valentinian and his mother Justina, he composed for his followers simple, singable hymns to relieve their weariness during the long night watches. Ambrose's hymns were shorter and more disciplined than those of his predecessor, Hilary. Also adopting the meter of the marching rhythm of the soldiers, he standardized the form known in modern English hymnody as "Long Meter"—four lines of iambic tetrameter.[9]

Of the almost one hundred hymns attributed to Ambrose, only four can be proved to be his. But his pioneering work was so significant for metrical hymnody in the West that the term "Ambrosian" is applied to all hymns in the meter that he established, even though they may have been composed by some of his numerous imitators and disciples. Many of these hymns (especially those which came into being after the Arian struggle had calmed down and the church was again more serene), represent the earliest "office" hymns for use in the prescribed hours of prayer in the monasteries. These hymns are rugged in their simplicity and entirely objective and noncontroversial in content.

Two which were immensely popular and continue to be useful are:

"O splendor of God's glory bright" (M29) or
"O Splendor of the Father's light" (L271)
"O Trinity, O blessed Light" (L275)

The first two titles are translations of Ambrose's great morning hymn, *Splendor Paternae Gloriae.* Addressed to the Trinity (but especially to Christ as the Light of the world), it asks for divine guidance throughout the day. The second hymn is a translation of *O lux Beata Trinitas,* an evening hymn in praise of the triune God. In both these hymns the imagery of light is prominent. Light is a symbol found throughout the Scriptures as well as in earlier hymnody before Ambrose. An example is the famous Lamplighting Hymn of the early church. Intended for congregational singing in the monastic communities, these songs set the standard for a great body of systematic hymnody that was to develop throughout the Middle Ages.

TE DEUM LAUDAMUS

Contemporary with Ambrose was Niceta (c. 335—c. 414), missionary bishop of Remesiana in Dacia (Serbia), who also utilized hymns to wage battles for the orthodox faith. He is the probable author of at least part of the *Te Deum laudamus.* the most famous extrabiblical hymn of the Western church. This extended composition has enjoyed universal prestige and use for fifteen centuries, not so much for its intrinsic poetic qualities but because of its clear testimony to the Christian faith.

In the English version which was included in the 1549 and 1552 *Book of*

---

[9]For explanation of meter, see Chap. 1 The Hymn and Literature.

Common Prayer (M665, L139, E18), it falls into three parts:

Part I— *a paean of praise to God the Father* making liberal use of Hebrew heaven imagery by which all the powers of the celestial realm chant continually the "thrice holy" of Isaiah (6:3) joined by earthly apostles, prophets, and martyrs.

Part II—*a confession of faith in Christ,* the eternal Son, his miraculous birth, his triumph over death, his present reign in heaven, and his second coming to judge the world. This part concludes with a prayer that the redeemed may share in his everlasting glory.

Although these first two parts may be found in an early Greek version, the hymn was not used in the worship of the Eastern church. Therefore most scholars agree that it existed originally in the Latin of Niceta, though he borrowed extensively from the preexisting Apostles' Creed, the *Gloria in excelsis* and the *Sanctus.*

Part III—*a series of phrases culled largely from the Psalms* and added later. These psalm verses consist of petitions for God's blessing and guidance and affirmations of trust in his mercy, thus rounding out a comprehensive statement of worship and belief.

So here the essentials of the Christian faith are set forth in great majesty and beauty. The hymn expresses in the language of adoration the broad outlines of New Testament doctrine. Though usually given musical settings that are too elaborate for congregational singing,[10] the *Te Deum laudamus* remains as popular today as it was during more ancient times, being used throughout the Christian world on days of special thanksgiving and commemoration.

Two other outstanding men laboring near the outposts of Christian civilization in the late fourth and early fifth centuries made memorable hymnic contributions. Aurelius Clemens Prudentius (348-413) was a Spaniard who gave up a career in law to devote his life to Christian study and writing. The other, Patrick (c. 372-466), apostle and patron saint of Ireland, is remembered for a hymn known as "St. Patrick's Breastplate."

Prudentius

Prudentius has been variously designated in Christian literature as "the Horace and Virgil of the Christians," "the Christian Pindar," "the first really Christian poet," and "the Latin Watts." All these appellations are attempts by historians to honor him as the first poet of the West to bring scholarship and religion together, enlivening classic prosody with the vigor of a living

---

[10]Many world-famous composers, including Palestrina, Cherubini, Graun, Purcell, Handel, Tallis, Berlioz, Verdi, Vaughan Williams, and Walton have created music for the *Te Deum.* Other church composers have treated it in choral "Service" settings for Morning Prayer in the Lutheran, Episcopal, and Anglican churches. In some hymnals it is set out to be sung by the congregation in Anglican chant (see M665) or in some form of plainsong (see L, pp. 139-41, E18).

faith. Centos of the original poems of Prudentius were used throughout the Middle Ages. The most popular one to survive is "Of the Father's love begotten," in John Mason Neale's translation (B62, L42, M357).

Written in the early fifth century, this hymn is another intended to promote the orthodox doctrine of the nature of Christ (in opposition to Arian teachings). Based on Revelation 1:8, it affirms Christ to be "Alpha"—the source of all things—and "Omega"—the end of all things—and therefore coeternal with God the Father. Although the hymn is particularly appropriate for Christmas worship, its praise of the Trinity makes it suitable also for general use. The plainsong tune, DIVINUM MYSTERIUM, following the custom of performance often used, can be sung antiphonally between two bodies of singers who then come together on the refrain in the last line of every stanza: "Evermore and evermore."

St. Patrick

Legend assigns St. Patrick the authorship of the famous *Lorica* or "Breastplate Hymn." It came into being originally as an incantation but survives today in the translation of Cecil F. Alexander as a lengthy credal hymn, "I bind unto myself today" (L188, E23). It is considered somewhat rough in its grammar and loose in its poetic construction; yet it possesses the devotional fire of a courageous heart.

The characteristics of these early Latin hymns may be summarized. In the Latin original of these hymns, written while Roman law and order prevailed and when the church was growing rapidly, the verse structure remained classical, with no rhyme or accent. However, they utilized the "Ambrosian" metrical form of iambic tetrameter. In content they were primarily credal, forwarding the orthodox doctrines in the struggle against heresy.

The Dark Ages

The five centuries following the collapse of the Roman empire (A.D. 476) are often referred to as "the Dark Ages." However, during these centuries intellectual and cultural work of the highest order was accomplished, especially by the scholars and missionaries of the Benedictine order. This period forms a prelude, as it were, to medieval history and can be considered dark only by comparison to what followed. In this 500-year era (A.D. 500-1000) the foundations of medieval civilization were laid for every area of human endeavor. It is not surprising, then, that several important hymnists pursued their creative work during this relatively obscure time.

Gregory

Among these was Gregory I, the Pope called the Great (590-604) because of the extent of his accomplishments in the realms of administration, missions, theological writing, and preaching. He is remembered primarily for his contributions in the fields of liturgy and music, which he collected and codified for the Western church. The few hymns attributed to Gregory cannot be proved to be actually his. The most popular of those connected with his name, "Father, we praise you" (L267), has been assigned by the most recent scholarship to have been written in the tenth century. A simple morning hymn of objective praise, it is set in the unusual sapphic meter[11] in contrast to the more popular Ambrosian meter. The tune traditionally assigned to it, CHRISTE SANCTORUM, is a French "church melody" from the seventeenth century.

Fortunatus

The last of the classic writers and the first of the barbarian Christian poets was Venantius Honorius Clementianus Fortunatus (c. 530-609), born and educated in northern Italy. After traveling extensively in troubadour fashion as poet and secretary to the Frankish King Sigbert, he left court and settled at Poitiers, where, toward the end of his life, he became bishop. It was at Poitiers, for the reception into the convent of St. Croix of a relic of the true cross, that Fortunatus wrote his greatest hymn, *Vexilla regis proderunt.* In the translation of John Mason Neale, it begins "The royal banners forward go" (L124). It is sung at Evensong on Passion Sunday and daily until Wednesday in Holy Week. VEXILLA REGIS is the traditional plainsong melody for the text (L125).

For use at Easter is his great *Salve, festa dies,* known to us in John Ellerton's paraphrase, "Welcome, happy morning" (M452, L153).[12] This hymn gives universal expression to the Christian joy resulting from the Easter proclamation of Christ's triumph in the resurrection.[13]

One of the most venerable hymns from this period is *Urbs beata Jerusalem,* the second part of which (beginning *Angularis fundamentum*) is translated "Christ is made the sure foundation" (L367, M298). This seventh-century anonymous lyric is based upon 1 Peter 2:5, Ephesians 2:20, and Revelation 21:2. It has found wide use for the dedication of church buildings.

Theodulph of Orleans

Two other poets of the Dark Ages (ninth century), who kept the light of the Christian faith burning through their hymnic endeavors were Theodulph of

[11]Sapphic meter refers to the verse form used by the Greek lyric poetess, Sappho (600 BC), a line of which falls in the rare pattern for hymnody: 11. 11. 11. 5.

[12]See also L142 for an equally dramatic paraphrase of this same hymn.

[13]Another Fortunatus hymn extensively used at passiontide in his *Pange lingua gloriosi proelium certaminis* in Neale's translation "Sing, my tongue" (L118) and often considered to be his finest.

Orleans (c. 760-821) and Rabanus Maurus (776-856). Theodulph was born a barbarian but became a great Christian pastor and poet. So great was his poetic genius that he was called to the court of Carolus Magnus (Charlemagne), king of the Franks, to establish schools for the instruction of monks and other churchmen. He is remembered for his one hymn *Gloria, laus et honor,* familiar today in Neale's translation, "All glory, laud, and honor" (B39, M424, L108).

"All glory, laud, and honor" was composed about 820 while Theodulph was imprisoned in Angers by order of King Louis I. Based on the Gospel account of the triumphal entry in Jerusalem (Mark 11:1-10 and John 12:12-19), it is one of the best Palm Sunday processional hymns, picturing the only occasion when public homage was paid to Jesus.

Veni, Creator Spiritus

Although the authorship of *Veni, Creator Spiritus* has been variously attributed to Charlemagne, Ambrose, and Gregory the Great, it may be the work of Rabanus Maurus, bishop of Fulda and archbishop of Mainz (d. 856). This great prayer for the coming of the Holy Spirit exists in several English translations, attesting to its prominent use in connection with ordinations of priests, consecrations of bishops, the laying of foundation stones, and the consecration of churches. It was the only metrical hymn admitted to the English *Book of Common Prayer* (1549) at the time of the English Reformation. "Creator Spirit, by whose aid" (L164) is the paraphrase by John Dryden (1631-1700), the chief literary figure of the Restoration Era. "Come, Holy Ghost, our souls inspire" (M467, L472) is the earlier, more literal translation of John Cosin (1594-1672), bishop of Durham. Consecrated by the worship of centuries, this hymn continues to find use at all occasions when the gifts of the Holy Spirit are celebrated.

The Middle Ages

"The Middle Ages" is the convenient designation for that period extending from the end of the Dark Ages to those times when the spirit of the Renaissance became victorious in political, social, and artistic life. For the student of Christian hymnody it has special interest as the age which approached most nearly the realization of Western Christendom as a cultural unity. This was made possible by the complete and absolute supremacy of the papacy in all temporal matters as well as by the missionary and conserving zeal of the special orders of monks—the Benedictine, Cluniac, and Cistercian, and the new mendicant orders—the Franciscan and Dominican. From within the ranks of these orders came the hymnists of the day.

Little hymnody has survived from the eleventh century. But from the twelfth century, with the perfection of new forms of Latin verse using rhyme and accent, and inspired by the quiet contemplation of the cloistered life, some of the finest songs ministering to all that was true and holy in people's lives were produced. The seclusion of the monastic life exercised a special influence on the subject matter of these hymns. No longer confined to the worship of God—the Father, Son, and Holy Spirit, many were written in honor of the virgin Mary, the apostles, and other saints. Moreover, these songs were often refined into mystical meditations on the joys of heaven, the vanity of life, and the sufferings of Christ. From the twelfth century have come the hymns of three outstanding men of the medieval scholarly world—Abelard, Bernard of Clairvaux, and Bernard of Cluny.

Abelard

Peter Abelard (1079-1142), brilliant theologian, philosopher, and teacher, wrote an entire hymnal for use in the convent of the Paraclete (near Nogent-sur-Seine in France) which was under the charge of his beloved Heloise. From this Latin hymnal Neale has given us the English "O what their joy and their glory" (L337), a hymn celebrating the joy and peace of heaven. It is traditionally sung to O QUANTA QUALIA, another French "church melody" from a Paris antiphoner of 1681.

The contemporary American clergyman, F. Bland Tucker has translated from this Abelard hymn cycle a hymn for use on Good Friday, "Alone thou goest forth, O Lord" (M427).

Jesu, Dulcis Memoria

Many hymns have been ascribed to the greatest of medieval saints, Bernard of Clairvaux (1091-1153), just as the Psalms have been popularly attributed to David and the Proverbs to Solomon. Though he may not be the author of *Jesu, dulcis memoria* ("the sweetest and most evangelical . . . hymn of the Middle Ages"),[14] the hymn profoundly bears the stamp of his mind, and it may be taken as representative of his spirit.

Bernard was the most influential monk of his day, brilliantly debating with philosophers and theologians, passionately preaching to great throngs, and skillfully arbitrating among statesmen and popes. He was the founder and abbot of the model monastery at Clairvaux and the preacher of the Second Crusade.

Known in Italian as the "Jubilus rithmicus de amore Jesu," *Jesu dulcis memoria* was inspired by passages from the Song of Solomon. It repeats the name of Jesus in a manner that must have been enchanting to singers and

---

[14]The latest findings from an eleventh-century manuscript assigns this hymn to a Benedictine abbess. See Erik Routley, *Hymns and Human Life* (London: John Murray, 1952), pp. 204-205.

hearers alike. It has supplied to English and American hymnbooks several translations of sterling worth. Indeed few Latin hymns have been translated so often by so many different poets. Various centos from this hymn are the basis for the following two familiar translations:

"Jesus, thou joy of loving hearts" (B72, M329, L356)

"Jesus, the very thought of thee (you)" (B73, M82, L316)

The first is by the American Congregationalist poet and preacher, Ray Palmer, who is best known for his "My faith looks up to thee" (B382, M143). The second translation is the work of the British Roman Catholic scholar, Edward Caswall, to whom we are also indebted for other fine translations from both Latin and German sources.[15]

Bernard of Cluny

The other great Bernard (twelfth century, of the Cluny monastery) is known to posterity only as the poet of *De contemptu mundi,* a bitter satire that laments the moral corruption of his time. In contrast to the evil and darkness of that age, the hymn depicts the golden glories of the celestial city. From the long poem of 3,000 lines Neale translated 218, which have been arranged at various times into several different hymns. Of these, only "Jerusalem the golden" (L347, M303) has survived. Its durability could be due as much to its fine tune, EWING (named for the nineteenth-century Englishman who wrote it), as to its lofty recital of the joys of heaven.

Sequence-hymns

A most significant hymnic development of the Middle Ages was the invention of tropes and sequences. Tropes were both musical and textual interpolations to the prescribed liturgy of the medieval church; their purpose was to amplify, augment, or elucidate the Mass. The particular type of trope associated with the Alleluia chant of the Mass came to be known as a sequence. For aesthetically expressive reasons, lengthy melismas were developed upon the final syllable of the Alleluia. Then, as an aid to the musical memory of those singing them, special hymnlike texts were set to these extended vocalized passages. Yet another step came in the proliferation of thousands of these texts as independent entities to be sung for the various seasons and festivals of the Christian year.

In the Counter Reformation, the Council of Trent (1545-1563) decided to eliminate all but four of these many sequences: the *Victimae paschali* for Easter,[16] the *Veni, Sancte Spiritus* ("the Golden Sequence") for Pentecost

---

[15]See, for example, "Earth has many a noble city" (M405, L81) and "When morning gilds the skies" (B44, M91).

[16]See Chap. 6, Reformation Traditions, under the hymns of Martin Luther.

(from which we have "Come, Holy Ghost, God and Lord"—L163); the *Lauda Sion* by Thomas Aquinas (1227-1274) for the Feast of Corpus Christi; and the *Dies irae* by Thomas of Celano (13th century) for the Requiem Mass.

In 1727 there was added a fifth sequence, the *Stabat mater dolorosa,* attributed to Jacapone da Todi (1230-1306), for use on Good Friday. From this the hymn "At the cross, her station keeping" (L110) was translated. This hymn survives from a great body of medieval literature gathered about the cult of the virgin Mary. Its roots are probably traceable to the fourteenth-century *laudi spirituali* (praise songs) which glorify the sufferings of Mary and of Christ and which were sung by wandering bands of "flagellants." These heretical groups traveled about on their macabre processions scourging themselves for the sins of the world and pathologically brooding on sorrow.

Francis of Assisi

Two of these creators of sequences were part of the circle of St. Francis of Assisi (1182-1226), the most remarkable personality of the early thirteenth century. Jacapone da Todi was a lay brother in the mendicant order which (having been founded by him) bears Francis' name. Known as "God's Troubadour," Francis combined Provencal song style with the Italian vernacular to bring into being the *laudi,* from which Jacapone's *Stabat mater* is a surviving example. Thomas of Celano, author of the *Dies irae,* was also a Franciscan so intimately associated with the saint that he wrote Francis' biography.

Francis' famous "Canticle to the Sun" is said to be the first genuine religious lyric in the Italian language. It comes to us in the translation of the British clergyman, William H. Draper, as "All creatures of our God and King" (B9, L527, M60). It reflects Francis' childlike identification with all creation in the joyous praise of the Eternal. The exciting traditional tune, Lasst uns erfreuen can appropriately be sung antiphonally.

Thomas Aquinas

The most learned representative of the Dominican order in the thirteenth century was Thomas Aquinas (c. 1227-1274), the master schoolman who carried the medieval scholastic method, founded by Abelard, to consummation in his monumental *Summa Theologica.* Aside from the sequence hymn *Lauda sion,* Thomas was the author of several other hymns which were primarily expositions of the mysteries of the Eucharist and therefore suitable for Communion in liturgical churches. Of these communion hymns the best known is *Adoro te devote,* translated by J. R. Woodford as "Thee, we adore, O hidden Savior" (L199).

1980 Charles Massey, Jr.

John Calvin

Carols

The humanizing influence of Francis of Assisi helped produce a great flowering of religious song in the thirteenth and especially in the fourteenth century. These are generally known today as carols. Representative of this free, folksy kind of devotional expression are three carols found in most hymnals.

In dulci jubilo, in Neale's translation "Good Christian (friends) men, rejoice" (B90, L55, M391), is a macaronic carol[17] from fourteenth century Germany. Songs like these combining the Latin of the church with the vernacular of the people were common in Germany towards the close of the Middle Ages. The happy and joyous vein of the text is suitably matched with its swinging melody IN DULCI JUBILO, thus making it one of the most popular of all Christmas songs.

Surrexit Christus hodie, in the anonymous translation "Jesus Christ is risen today" (B115, L151, M443), is an Easter carol which appeared originally in German and Bohemian manuscripts of the fourteenth century. Its great popularity today is partly due to the LLANFAIR tune from Wales which gives jubilant expression to the Alleluia refrains.

O filii et filiae is probably the work of a French Franciscan, Jean Tisserand (d. 1494). As translated by Neale, it is a lovely narrative carol of Easter, "O sons and daughters, let us sing" (L139, M451). The tune O FILII ET FILIAE is a lilting folk melody of the same century. The gradual unfolding of the Easter story stanza by stanza, together with its repetitive Alleluia, make it particularly useful for teaching to children. It demonstrates the close connection that may have once existed between the trope and the carol, for *O filii et filiae* was originally a trope on the *Benedicamus Domino* chant used at the close of the prayers and praises of the offices.

Later Contributions

Latin hymnody declined from the late fourteenth century onward, thus paralleling the decline in the dominant position of the church itself. However, the following six hymns are representative of those excellent ones that have survived this era of decadence: "O come, O come, Emmanuel" (B78, L34, M354), an anonymous hymn first appearing in print in 1710 but doubtless existing in oral tradition from much earlier times as a hymn in preparation for the celebration of Christmas; "The strife is o'er" (L135, M447), an anonymous seventeenth-century hymn translated by Neale, intended for Easter worship; "Jerusalem, my happy home" (B488, L331), an anonymous sixteenth-century English hymn on heaven, based upon translations from a

---

[17]Using a mixture of two or more languages.

fifteenth century source and appealingly set to an American folk tune, LAND OF REST; "My (O) God, I love thee" (B57, L491), Edward Caswall's translation of a seventeenth-century Latin poem based on a Spanish sonnet which examines one's motives for loving God, often attributed to Francis Xavier (1506-1552), the Jesuit missionary and preacher; "On Jordan's banks the Baptist's cry" (L36), an Advent hymn by the distinguished French ecclesiastic and educator, Charles Coffin (1676-1749), who wrote over a hundred such hymns for *The Paris Breviary* (1736); and "O come, all ye faithful" (B81, L45, M386), Frederick Oakeley's translation of *Adeste fidelis laeti triumphantes,* written by the English layman, John Francis Wade (c. 1710-1786), who also wrote its tune. So popular has Wade's Latin hymn been that it exists in over a hundred English translations. The tune, ADESTE FIDELES exhibits the fuging characteristics of many tunes of its day.

The Latin Legacy

Hymns from the Latin, because they were produced over such a lengthy period of church history, are widely varied in their characteristics. Because many were born in theological controversy, they are credal in content and purpose, giving militant expression to what was considered the orthodox faith of their time. Because many were generated from within the monastic life, they are otherworldly and reflective in nature, giving tender expression to personal devotion, especially to the crucified Jesus. Because many were written for use in the canonical hours, they are liturgical in their intent. Because several are the product of the common folk, they are carol-like in nature, giving vent to simple religious joys. Because most were the result of an irrespressible universal urge to glorify the eternal God, they possess a dominant element of praise and thanksgiving.

Our hymnic legacy from the Latin is broad and rich though much of it, unfortunately, is neglected and forgotten. To appropriate it for today is the responsibility and privilege of today's worshiping Christians.

6

Reformation Traditions

The Chorale—Reformation to 1618

The German and Scandinavian chorales received their impetus from the thought and work of the German reformer Martin Luther (1483-1546). Luther was not only a theologian but also a musician, and he believed music to be of utmost importance in worship. As a part of Luther's emphasis on the priesthood of all believers, he advocated full involvement of the people and restored congregational singing to its rightful place as part of their worship. In 1524, seven years after Luther's ninety-five Theses were first posted, there appeared the first Lutheran hymn collection, the *"Achtliederbuch"* (*"Book of Eight Songs,"* eight hymns and four melodies), which included four hymn texts by Luther.

Of the thirty-seven hymns attributed to Luther, four which appear in many current hymnals are:

"A mighty fortress is our God"—based on Psalm 46 (B37, E25, L228, 229, M20)

"Out of the depths I cry to thee"—based on Psalm 130 (L295, M526)

"From heaven above to earth I come"—a Christmas hymn (L51)

"Christ Jesus lay in death's strong bands"—an Easter hymn based on earlier hymns, including the Latin Easter sequence, *Victimae paschali* (L134, M438)

Although Luther led the revolt against the abuses of the Roman Catholic Church, he continued to make use of its texts and tunes: "He modified Roman Catholic tunes and texts to fit his new theology. As a result, people recognized familiar hymns and chants and felt at home in the new church. He used music which was already familiar to the majority of the people in Germany."[1]

Luther may well have composed the melodies to "A mighty fortress" and to some of his other texts, but this is uncertain. Most surely he used melodies which reflected the German Meistersinger tradition, including EIN' FESTE BURG.[2]

Luther's "A mighty fortress" (B37, E25, L228, 229, M20), which became the "Battle hymn of the Reformation," mirrors his strong personality. This chorale depicts Luther's struggle with Satan (st. 1), including his belief in the

[1] Johannes Riedel, *The Lutheran Chorale, Its Basic Traditions* (Minneapolis: Augsburg Publishing House, 1967), p. 38.

[2] This melody has been compared to Hans Sachs' famous "Silberweise" (Silver Tone). See ibid., p. 39, and *Troubadours, Trouveres, Minne- and Meistersinger* ed. F. Gennrich, v. 2 of *Anthology of Music,* ed. K. G. Fellerer (Cologne, Germany: Arno Volk Verlag, 1960), pp. 64-65.

presence and power of devils (st. 3), and the triumph of Christ and God's kingdom over the forces of evil (st. 4).

In addition to those by Luther, another sixteenth-century chorale in current use is Nikolaus Hermann's (c. 1485-1561) Christmas text and tune "Let all together praise our God" (LOBT GOTT, IHR CHRISTEN, L47, M389; NICOLAUS to a different text in B431). At the close of the century, in 1599, appeared the "King and Queen of Chorales," Lutheran pastor Philipp Nicolai's (1556-1608) texts and tunes: "Wake, awake, for night is flying" (WACHET AUF, L31, M366) and "O Morning Star, how fair and bright" (WIE SCHÖN LEUCHTET DER MORGENSTERN, L76, M399). These two bar form (AAB) chorale melodies reflect the Meistersinger tradition, and the texts of both are rich in biblical imagery.

In the first two decades of the seventeenth century there were composed three German chorale melodies which still maintain a place in most hymnals of today. Hans Leo Hassler's PASSION CHORALE (1601), the tune originally set to a love song, became the setting of Paul Gerhardt's "O sacred Head, now wounded" (based on a Medieval Latin poem, B105, L116, 117, M418). Melchior Vulpius' GELOBT SEI GOTT (1609) is associated in English with the twentieth-century Easter hymn "Good Christian men, rejoice and sing" (B123, M449, "Good Christian friends, rejoice and sing," L144). A third familliar chorale melody from this era is Melchior Teschner's ST. THEODULPH (1615) named after Theodulph of Orleans, author of the Latin Palm Sunday hymn "All glory, laud and honor" (B39, m424, VALET WILL ICH DIR GEBEN, (L108), a text still associated with this tune.

The Protestant Reformation was not confined to Germany. The Lutheran movement spread especially to Scandinavia, where the countries of Denmark, Norway, Sweden, and Finland eventually established Lutheranism as their state church. The early Scandinavian Lutheran contributions found in most current hymnals stem from *Piae Cantiones (Sacred Songs)*,[3] a compilation of Theodoric Petri of Nyland (the largely Swedish-speaking province of southern Finland now referred to as Uusimaa), published in 1582. From this collection of old Scandinavian hymns and carols came four melodies now in American use: DIVINUM MYSTERIUM ("Of the Father's love begotten," B62, M357), PERSONET HODIE ("On this day earth shall ring," E17), PUER NOBIS ("On Jordan's banks the Baptist's cry," L36; "O God, thou giver of all good," M515) and TEMPUS ADEST FLORIDUM (Gentle Mary laid her child, M395).

Seventeenth Century: The Thirty Years' War and a Renewal of the Hymn

An estimated 20,000 hymns had been written in Germany by the end of the sixteenth century, and by 1618 (the beginning of the Thirty Years' War) this

---

[3]*Piae Cantiones* is described in Erik Routley's *The Music of Christian Hymnody* (London: Independent Press, 1951), pp. 21-23.

total had risen to perhaps 25,000. Nevertheless, German hymn writing had become stagnant. Ironically, the tragic political-religious conflict known as the Thirty Years' War (1618-48) exerted a profound positive influence on German hymnody. As described by Moore, "It was in this period of desolation and darkness of the night that there came about a real revival in the writing of hymns."[4]

Among the writers to participate in this renewal was the Lutheran pastor Johann Heerman (1585-1647), author of the hymn *Herzliebster Jesu, was hast du verbrochen?* (1630), which has been translated and supplemented by Robert Bridges as "Ah, holy Jesus, how hast thou offended" (L123, M412). The tune HERZLIEBSTER JESU is Johann Crüger's reworking of the *Genevan Psalter* setting of Psalm 23.

The best known hymn to appear during the Thirty Years' War is "Now thank we all our God." (NUN DANKET ALLE GOTT, B234, L533, 534, M49), written around 1636 by the Lutheran pastor Martin Rinkart and later set to music by Crüger. This hymn of thankgiving, originally intended as a table blessing, is based on the Apocryphal book of Ecclesiasticus 50:22-24 and includes only a brief allusion at the close of stanza 2 to the suffering experienced during this disastrous political conflict:

> And keep us in his grace,
> And guide us when perplexed,
> And free us from all ills
> In this world and the next.

These lines are followed by the triumphant praise of Rinkart's closing stanza, his paraphrase of the *Gloria Patri* (B4-5; M792-4). "Now thank we all our God," known as the *Te Deum* of Germany, has become not only the German national hymn of praise and thanksgiving, but also a popular expression of gratitude among English-speaking peoples.

The tragic Thirty Years' War is more fully reflected in a hymn of 1644 by the German nobleman, Matthäus von Löwenstern (1594-1648), translated and paraphrased by Philip Pusey as "Lord of our life and God of our salvation" (B145, L366). Bailey has revealed how Pusey's version of 1834 also reflects the situation in England at the time of Oxford Movement.[5] This version nevertheless retains the atmosphere of the original (as well as its use of the classical Sapphic meter—11. 11. 11. 5). Germans sing this hymn to a seventeenth century tune; but in English, "Lord of our life" is commonly sung

[4]Sydney H. Moore, *Sursum Corda, Being Studies of Some German Hymn Writers* (London: Independent Press, Ltd., 1956), p. 21. For a detailed discussion of this conflict, see "Thirty-Years' War" in *Encyclopedia Britannica.* 15th ed. Vol. 18, pp. 333-44.

[5]Albert Edward Bailey, *The Gospel in Hymns* (New York: Charles Scribner's Sons, 1950), p. 324.

to ISTE CONFESSOR (ROUEN), a French Roman Catholic tune published in 1746. How ironic that one of the finest Protestant hymns of this bloody war should today be sung today to a Roman Catholic tune!

The Sapphic meter of Löwenstern's hymn is one sign of the early seventeenth century literary flowering which involved literary efforts toward refining the German language and its poetry and bringing about a more refined hymnody. The effort of the Thirty Years' War was to make this hymnody more personal and subjective. Hymns from this time include those written for family devotions; these typically emphasize trust in God and a yearning for eternal life. Among the hymns written for the church year, those dealing with Christ's passion gained a prominent place in this period.[6]

The introspective qualities of the seventeenth-century German hymn are most fully exemplified in the work of the Lutheran minister Paul Gerhardt (1607-76), regarded, next to Luther, as the greatest German hymnist. Gerhardt is the most beloved and the most frequently represented writer in German hymnals today.[7] Four of his hymns often found in American hymnals are:

"All my heart this night rejoices"—a Christmas hymn originally containing fifteen stanzas ("Once again my heart rejoices," L46, M379).

"O sacred Head, now wounded"—Gerhardt's translation of part of a medieval poem on the suffering of Christ on the cross (B105, L116, 117, M418).

"Give to the winds your fears"—a personal hymn of trust in God (B224, M51).

"Jesus, thy boundless love to me"—a personal hymn giving the believer's response to the love of Jesus (B326, L336, M259).

Particularly illustrative of the subjective character of Gerhardt's hymns is "Jesus, thy boundless love to me" (1653) (translated in 1739 by John Wesley), in which the personal pronouns "I," "me" and "my" abound.

Hymn tunes of the seventeenth century, in contrast to the earlier Meistersinger practice, were generally no longer composed by the author of the hymn text, but rather by specialist musicians. Congregational singing was further popularized in this time by the adoption of the *Kantional* style, in which the melody appeared in the highest voice and the lower parts were harmonized in note-against-note treatment.[8] In addition, the Italian *basso*

---

[6]"The Period of the 30 Years' War" in *Evangelisches Kirchengesangbuch*. Edition for the Lutheran church in Bavaria. (Munich: Evang. Presserverband für Bayern e. V., 1957), p. 742. (This article in German appears with biographies of hymnists in the current German Lutheran hymnal.)

[7]Forty of Gerhardt's hymns are found in the above mentioned German Lutheran hymnal (1957 Bavarian edition). Further references to this hymnal indicate this Bavarian edition.

[8]Riedel, *The Lutheran Chorale*, p. 56.

continuo style exerted harmonic influence upon the chorale melodies in that they were most often fitted for accompaniement by a keyboard instrument such as the organ.[9]

Gerhardt's friend and colleague at St. Nicholas Church in Berlin and also his musical counterpart in the development of the chorale was the organist-composer Johann Crüger (1598-1662), whose chorale tune collection of 1644, *Praxis pietatis melica* ("Practice of Piety in Song"), was, in its numerous editions, the most important Lutheran hymnal of its century. Crüger tunes found in American hymnals today are:

HERZLIEBSTER JESU—"Ah, holy Jesus" (L123, M412)
JESU MEINE FREUDE—"Jesus, priceless treasure" (L457, M220)
NUN DANKET—"Now thank we all our God" (B234, L533, 534, M49)
GRÄFENBERG—to texts of English origin—(B357, M134; NUN DANKET ALL L254)
SCHMÜCKE DICH—"Deck thyself, my soul, with gladness" (M318, "Soul, adorn yourself with gladness, L224)

Crüger's tunes are conceived harmonically, as in the tonal and modal expressions of HERZLIEBSTER JESU. His melodies also reflect influences of the *Genevan Psalter* tunes, such as the repeated opening notes (typical of the psalm tunes) in his HERZLIEBSTER JESU and NUN DANKET.[10] Crüger's successor as organist of St. Nicholas Church in Berlin was Johann George Ebeling (1637-76), also a friend of Gerhardt and composer of chorale settings, including DIE GÜLDNE SONNE, the tune to Gerhardt's "Evening and morning" (L465).[11]

The increasingly personal and intimate character of German hymns of the mid-seventeenth century is exemplified by those of Johann Franck (1618-77), lawyer and friend of Crüger. His hymns include "Deck thyself with joy and gladness" (M318), "Soul, adorn yourself with gladness," (L224), and "Jesus, priceless treasure" (L457, 458, M220). Another personal hymn (both text and tune) written in 1641 by Georg Neumark (1621-81), a young student who later became court poet at Weimar, is "If you will only let God guide you" (B203; L453, "If you but trust in God to guide you"; M210, "If thou but suffer God to guide you"). In contrast to the hymns of Franck and Neumark there is the later hymn of 1671, "Comfort, comfort ye my people" (B77, L29, "Comfort, comfort now my people"), a paraphrase of Isaiah 40:1-8 written by the

---

[9]"The Period of the 30 Years' War."
[10]For a detailed discussion of Crüger's style, see Riedel, *The Lutheran Chorale*, pp. 64-69.
[11]Eight of Ebeling's melodies are in the current German Lutheran hymnal.
[12]Olearius' *Geistliche Singe-Kunst (Sacred Song-Art*, Leipzig, 1671), one of the most important Lutheran hymnals of the seventeenth century, included 302 of his hymns in its first edition. Five of his hymns remain in the current German Lutheran hymnal.

hymnal compiler[12] Johannes Olearius (1611-84). This text is traditionally sung to PSALM 42 (or FREU DICH SEHR) from the *Genevan Psalter*.

Late Seventeenth and Eighteenth Century Pietism

The Lutheran movement known as Pietism began with Jacob Spener at Frankfurt in 1670. Pietism was a reaction to the ever increasing formality and rigidity within the established church. It sought to give new life to the church and to underline the importance of a personal Christian experience. Pietistic hymns emphasized the tension between the transcendence of God and the personal relationship in repentance, conversion, and assurance of salvation. The personal emphasis of pietism was foreshadowed in earlier chorale texts, such as those of Gerhardt, Franck, and Neumark. Note the personal Pietistic emphasis in one of the earliest of this movement's hymns, "Sing praise to God who reigns above" (L542, B22, M4) by Spener's lawyer and friend, Johann Jakob Schütz (1640-90):

> Sing praise to God who reigns above,
>   The God of all creation,
> The God of power, the God of love,
>   The God of our salvation;
> With healing balm my soul he fills,
> And ev'ry faithless murmur stills:
>   To God all praise and glory.[13]

Another Pietist, of the Reformed (Calvinistic) Church in Germany, was Joachim Neander (1650-80). Though he lived only to the age of thirty, he bequeathed to us one of the most popular chorales, "Praise to the Lord, the Almighty" (B10, M55), which is both a hymn of adoration and a hymn of personal testimony. Also a gifted musician, Neander composed the tunes ARNSBERG ("God himself is with us," B16, M788; or WUNDERBARER KÖNIG, "God himself is present," L249) and UNSER HERRSCHER ("Open now thy gates of beauty," L250; "See the morning sun ascending," M7).

The leading hymnist of the Pietist movement, Johann A. Freylinghausen (1670-1739), was son-in-law and successor to the great Pietist leader at the Halle university and orphanage, August H. Franke. Freylinghausen's *Gesangbuch (Hymnal,* first part, 1704; second part, 1714) appeared in numerous editions and supplied hundreds of hymns and tunes for the Pietist movement. It included the tune GOTT SEI DANK ("Spread, O spread the mighty word," B284; "Spread, Oh, spread, almighty Word," L379).[14]

---

[13]A different translation of the hymn is found at L542.
[14]A dozen tunes from Freylinghausen's *Gesangbuch* appear in the current German Lutheran hymnal. For a description of this musical style, see "The Freylinghausen Tradition" in Riedel, *The Lutheran Chorale,* pp. 70 ff.

The most mystical of the Pietists whose hymns survive was Gerhard Tersteegen (1697-1769), a Reformed minister who later became an independent religious teacher and leader. In addition to "God himself is with us" (B16, M788; "God himself is present," L249), Tersteegen's mysticism is expressed in the fourth stanza of "Thou hidden Love of God, whose height" (M531), as translated by his contemporary John Wesley:

> Each moment draw from earth away
> My heart that lowly waits thy call;
> Speak to my inmost soul and say,
> "I am thy Love, thy God, thy all!"
> To feel thy power, to hear thy voice,
> To taste thy love, be all my choice.

The Moravians

The Moravians (also known as Hussites, Bohemian Brethren and the *Unitas Fratrum*—Unity of Brethren) were the much persecuted followers of John Hus of Bohemia (in present-day Czechoslovakia), who was martyred in 1415. These followers of Hus gave new emphasis to congregational singing. Their hymns were first published in a Czech hymnal in 1501, more than two decades before the first Lutheran hymnal. The earliest Moravian hymnic contribution to be found in American hymnals of today is MIT FREUDEN ZART ("Sing praise to God who reigns above"; B22, M4; "With high delight let us unite," L140).

After three centuries of persecution, a turning point came for the Moravians in 1722, when they were given refuge on the estate of the German nobleman, Count Zinzendorf (1700-60). Under his leadership at Herrnhut (the Lord's Shelter), the Moravians were mobilized into a great missionary force. Zinzendorf was a prolific hymn writer, and hymn singing played an important part in Moravian life. "No visitor to Herrnhut but was struck by the amazing "hymn-meetings," *Singstunden,* which he [Zinzendorf] conducted there. He seems to have felt a continual necessity to create. He would give forth one line, which the congregation would then sing; by that time the second line would be ready, perfect in rhythm, rhyme and sense. Many of his hymns indeed, improvised in this fashion, have been lost, since no one, in the earlier years at any rate, was deputed to copy them down.[15]

Because of their improvisatory nature, some of Zinzendorf's best hymns should be credited to Christian Gregor (1723-1801), the Moravian organist, hymnist and leader. From his critical and careful revision we have such hymns as "Christian hearts in love united" (B253) and "Jesus, still lead on" (B500,

[15]Moore, *Sursum Corda,* p. 84.

L341).[16] Two other Zinzendorf hymns found in American hymnals are in John Wesley's translations, "O thou to whose all-searching sight" (B470, M213) and "Jesus, thy blood and righteousness" (M127; L302, "Jesus, your blood and righteousness"). These hymns express the Pietist-Moravian emphasis on personal Christian experience.

Johann Andreas Rothe (1688-1758), although a Lutheran, almost became a pastor to the Moravians of Herrnhut. He contributed the hymn "Now I have found the ground wherein" (translated by John Wesley), which is viewed by Moore as "perhaps the greatest hymn of Herrnhut."[17] The strength and fervor of these Herrnhut Moravians is evident in this hymn (especially stanza 3):

> Though waves and storms go o'er my head,
>   Though strength and health and friends be gone,
> Though joys be withered all and dead,
>   Though every comfort be withdrawn,
> On this my steadfast soul relies
> Father, Thy mercy never dies.

Another Herrnhut hymn is one by Henriette Marie Luise von Hayn (1724-82); it describes the Christian's relationship with Jesus as being like that of a sheep with his shepherd:

> Jesus makes my heart rejoice,
> I'm his sheep, and know his voice;
> He's a Shepherd, kind and gracious,
> And his pastures are delicious;
> Constant love to me he shows,
> Yea, my very name he knows. (B386)

Other Eighteenth Century Developments

In addition to later Pietist hymnists and the Moravians, there were other writers of the Eighteenth century whose chorale texts are found in current American hymnals. Three representative hymnists are Erdmann Neumeister (1671-1756), Benjamin Schmolk (1672-1737), and Matthias Claudius (1740-1815).

[16]Although Gregor, who compiled the first Moravian European tunebook in 1778, has no hymns generally included in American hymnals, he is represented by one hymn text and one hymn tune in the current German Lutheran hymnal and by 15 hymns, 7 tunes, and numerous harmonizations in *Hymnal of the Moravian Church* (Bethlehem, Pa. and Winston Salem, N.C.: The Moravian Church in America, 1969). See John H. Giesler, "Bicentennial of Gregor's Hymnal 1778, *The Hymn* 29, 4 (October 1978), 211-13.

[17]Moore, *Sursum Corda*, p. 87. This hymn is given in William J. Reynolds, *A Joyful Sound*. 2nd ed. of *A Survey of Christian Hymnody*, rev. Milburn Price (New York: Holt, Rinehart, and Winston, 1978), no. 66.

Neumeister, a Hamburg Lutheran pastor and conservative who opposed the Pietists and Moravians, is even better known as a writer of many cantata texts for the Christian year which were set to music by J. S. Bach and others. Although a half dozen of Neumeister's hymns are found in current German hymnals, only one has achieved wide use in English, "Sinners Jesus will receive" (B167, "Jesus sinners will receive," L291). This hymn has the distinction of being known in English as a gospel hymn, its musical setting being in popular American style. (At L291, however, it is set to the chorale melody, MEINEN JESUM LASS ICH NICHT.) James McGranahan used four of its six lines in each stanza and the final couplet of the sixth stanza as the following refrain:

Sing it o'er and o'er again;
Christ receiveth sinful men;
Make the message clear and plain:
Christ receiveth sinful men.

The leading hymnist of the non-Pietist Lutherans in the first half of the eighteenth century was Benjamin Schmolk (1672-1777), a pastor in Silesia (between present-day Czeckoslovakia and Poland) who served under difficult circumstances in a predominantly Roman Catholic region. The hardships of his ministry rendered him bedridden and blind years before his death. Of his almost 1,200 hymns, eleven appear in the German Lutheran hymnal and three are often found in American hymnals: "My Jesus, as thou wilt" (M167), which apparently reflects Schmolk's sufferings; "Open now thy gates of beauty" (L250, M13), a personal hymn for the beginning of worship; and "Dearest Jesus, we are here" (L187), a baptismal hymn.

Matthias Claudius, the son of a Lutheran pastor, was one of the few German lay writers of hymns. Although he was a freethinker in early adulthood, he was brought to a deepened faith through a serious illness. His one hymn in American hymnals is "We plow the fields and scatter" (L362, M513); it is a harvest hymn, which was an especially appropriate expression for Claudius, a one-time agricultural commissioner. The tune WIR PFLÜGEN is by Claudius' contemporary Johann A. P. Schulz (1747-1800), a well-known composer of German art songs. Claudius was an opponent of the Enlightenment (German: *Aufklärung*), which sought to reconstruct hymnody in rationalistic terms and provide hymns with a new vocabulary to accord with the spirit of the age. For example, conversion became self-improvement; sanctification, betterment; God, the Supreme Being; and piety, virtue.[18] Hymns by Luther and Gerhardt were either remodeled or replaced by the rationalists.

---

[18]Moore, p. 103.

By the close of the second decade of the nineteenth century the winds of the Enlightenment had run their course, and the movement to restore the older hymnody was well on its way. One influence of the rationalistic mind set remains in the chorale melodies of many current American hymnals. This is the tenet that every measure should have an equal number of beats and that rhythms should be basically equal resulted in the development of the isometric ("same meter") chorale. Most of the older chorales (for example, Luther's EIN' FESTE BURG)[19] in American hymnals are cast in this isometric form.

By the time of Freylinghausen's famous Pietist hymnal in the early eighteenth century, the newly composed chorales clearly reflected the style of baroque solo song; they were mostly arias for single voice with *basso continuo* (frequently harpsichord and cello) accompaniment. These chorale arias were published with only the melody and figured bass parts written out. The keyboard instrumentalist would fill in the missing parts by improvising.[20] Although chorale arias were adapted in simpler arrangements for use in congregational singing, hymns for the soloist took precedence over hymns for the congregation. These solo chorales reflected the aesthetic principles of the late baroque, having melodies so constructed as to allow the singer and accompanist ample opportunity for embellishment.

Many of the later chorale melodies were built on the intervals of the triad (such as WIR PFLÜGEN, L362, M513 and UNSER HERRSCHER, L250, M13) and some of them used dance rhythms (such as NEUMARK, B203, L453, M210; and ARNSBERG, B16, M788; or WUNDERBARER KÖNIG, L249). These are only two of many stylistic traits which show the influence of general musical developments upon the chorale.[21]

The composer most commonly associated with the chorale is Johann Sebastian Bach. Bach's genius lay not in composing new tunes, but rather in harmonizing and embellishing the rich body of church song that already existed. He made extensive use of the chorale in his cantatas and passions, harmonizing most of the melodies in four parts for singing by trained choirs. Some of his ingenious harmonizations are found in hymnals today, either intact or simplified for congregational use. Bach's best known chorale harmonizations are for the PASSION CHORALE ("O sacred Head, now wounded," B105, M418), harmonizations he used both in his *Christmas Oratorio* and *St. Matthew Passion*. Other Bach chorale harmonizations in current American hymns include:

DARMSTADT ("Christ is the world's true light," B274)

[19]See chap. 2, The Hymn and Music.
[20]An illustration of the practice of ornamenting a chorale aria is found in Riedel, pp. 73 ff.
[21]See "The Freylinghausen Tradition (*ca.* 1644-1756)" in Riedel, pp. 70-89.

Du Friedensfürst, Herr Jesu Christ ("The day is past and over," M491)

Eisenach ("Captain of Israel's host," M46; O Thou who camest from above," M172)

Ermuntre dich (Break forth, O beauteous heavenly light," M373)

Ich halte treulich still "Jesus, my strength, my hope," M253)

Jesu, Joy of Man's Desiring ("Come with us, O blessed Jesus," L219)

Salzburg ("Let the whole creation cry," L242)

Wie schön leuchtet der Morgenstern ("O Morning Star, how fair and bright," M399)

Alongside the Protestant development of the chorale came the growth of hymn singing among Roman Catholics in German-speaking countries. Several Catholic hymn tunes now appear in American Protestant hymnals, including Lasst uns erfreuen ("All creatures of our God and King," B9, L527, M60), published in 1623 at Cologne; and Grosser Gott ("Holy God, we praise your name," L535; Holy God, we praise thy name, M8), published at Vienna about 1774.

Nineteenth Century

The nineteenth century was primarily a time of rediscovery for the German Protestant Church. Its heritage of song had been both ignored and weakened by the Rationalists. During this century original versions of the old chorales were restored to German Lutheran hymnals and scholars produced monumental scholarly studies concerned with the history of the chorale form.[22]

Although the nineteenth century focus was on the past heritage, some new German hymns were written. Karl Johann Philipp Spitta (1801-59), pastor from Hanover, was the leading Lutheran hymnist of his century, He was a hymnal compiler and author of "We are the Lord's" (L399). Another nineteenth-century German hymn now in American hymnals is "Spread, O spread the mighty word" (B284; "Spread, oh, spread, almighty Word," L379), a missionary hymn by Jonathan Friedrich Bahnmaier (1774-1841), outstanding Lutheran preacher and university professor at Tübingen.

The largest number of nineteenth-century German musical contributions to the development of the chorale are those of Felix Mendelssohn (1809-47). His large choral works contain harmonizations for the chorales Nun danket ("Now thank we all our God," M49) and Munich ("O word of God incarnate, B140, M372; "My Jesus, as thou wilt," M167; "O Thou who art

[22]Two monumental works treating the melodies of German church song are Johannes Zahn's *Die Melodien der deutsche Kirchenlieder* (6 vols., 1889-93). which includes some 8,806 melodies to German Evangelical hymns, and Wilhelm Bäumker's *Das katholische deutsche Kirchenlied* (4 vols, 1883-1911), a basic study of German Roman Catholic Church song from 1470 to 1800 containing 451 melodies.

the Shepherd," M201; "I lay my sins on Jesus," L305; "O Jesus, I have promised, " L503). His most famous tune (not intended as a hymn tune), is MENDELSSOHN ("Hark! the herald angels sing," B83, L60, M388). Although represented in American hymnals, Mendelssohn and other great composers (such as Mozart, Haydn, and Beethoven) have not found general acceptance in German hymnals.

From Lutheran churches of Scandinavia have come several nineteenth-century contributions. "Built on the Rock the church doth stand" (KIRKEN, B235; "Lord Christ when first Thou cam'st to man," E88, M355; "Built on a rock the Church shall stand," L365) was written by Nikolaus Frederik Severin Grundtvig (1783-1872). He and Sören Kierkegaard were the most influential religious personalities of nineteenth-century Denmark. The tune to Grundtvig's hymn was composed by Ludvig Matthias Lindeman (1812-87), an outstanding Norwegian organist of his time and the compiler of a Norwegian Lutheran hymnal.[23]

The largest number of Scandinavian hymns in American hymnals came from Sweden.[24] This nation's greatest hymnist was Johan Olof Wallin (1779-1839), whose hymnal of 1819 served the Church of Sweden without revision for over a century. Wallin, who became Archbishop of Sweden in 1837, still occupies the leading place in Swedish hymnals. His best known hymn in English translation is the Christmas text, "All hail to you, O blessed morn" (WIE SCHÖN LEUCHTET, L73).Other hymns of Wallin are "We worship you, O God of might" (VI LOVA DIG, O STORE GUD, L432) and "Christians, while on earth abiding" (WERDE MUNTER, L440).

Another Scandinavian hymnist was the Swede, Caroline Vilhelmina Sandell Berg (1832-1903), whose hymns reflect the spiritual awakening which swept Northern Europe in the latter part of the nineteenth century. Two of her hymns found in American hymnals are "Children of the heavenly Father" (to a Swedish melody of unknown origin: TRYGGARE KAN INGEN VARA, B207; L474) and "Day by day and with each passing monent" (BLOTT EN DAG, B222). The latter hymn is set to a tune by Oscar Ahnfelt (1813-82), a popular singer associated with Sweden's greatest lay preacher and religious leader, Carl Olof Rosenius. The most popular Scandanavian hymn in America is "How great Thou art" (O STORE GUD, B35, L532, M17), written in 1886 by the

[23]Additional contributions of these Danes are found in the *Lutheran Book of Worship* (1978). Hymns of Grundtvig are: "The bells of Christmas" (L62), "Bright and glorious is the sky" (L75), "O day full of grace" (L161), "Cradling children in his arm" (L193), "God's Word is our great heritage" (L239), "Spirit of God, sent from heaven abroad" (L285), and "Peace, to soothe our bitter woes" (L338). Hymn tunes of Lindeman are: FRED TIL BOD (Hallelujah! Jesus lives, L147; Peace to soothe our bitter woes, L338), DU SOM GAAR UD (Spirit of God, sent from heaven abroad, L285), NAAR MIT ÖIE (Come to Calvary's holy mountain, L301), GUD SKAL ALTING MAGE ("Jesus, priceless treasure," L458), and HER VIL TIES (Savior, like a shepherd lead us, L481).

[24]Information on many Swedish hymns now in English translation and a summary of Swedish hymnody are found in J. Irving Erickson, *Twice-Born Hymns* (Chicago: Covenant Press, 1976).

Swedish preacher, religious editor and parliament member, Carl Boberg (1850-1940). Set to a Swedish melody of unknown origin, this hymn was made popular in America through the Billy Graham meetings, beginning in 1955. The most popular nineteenth-century German text in America is the Austrian "Silent night, holy night" (STILLE NACHT, B89, L65, M393). It was written in the village of Oberndorf on Christmas in 1818 by the Catholic priest Joseph Mohr (1792-1849) and set to music by his church's acting organist, Franz Gruber (1787-1863). This Christmas hymn, first sung by two voices to guitar accompaniment because the church organ was out of order, has achieved international popularity.

Twentieth Century

Although the practice of hymn writing is very much alive in twentieth-century Germany, few of these contemporary hymns have been translated and published in American hymnals. The multilingual hymnal, *Cantate Domino* (3rd ed., 1974),[25] contains a representative number of recent German hymns in English translation. The two hymnists with the largest number of contributions to *Cantate Domino* are Dieter Trautwein (5 texts and 1 tune) and Rolf Schweizer (1 text and 4 tunes). Trautwein (b. 1928), a Lutheran minister at Frankfurt (Main), has written such provocative hymns as "God will, when he comes to earth" (CD60, *Kommt Gott als Mensch in Dorf und Stadt,* 1964; tr. by Fred Kaan, 1972). It depicts his view of how God would react upon returning in human form. Trautwein is also the author of "We're not just anyone; we're not just nobodies" (CD73, *Wir sind nicht irgendwer und nicht nur ungefähr,* 1965; tr. by F. Pratt Green, 1972), an innovative hymn based on 1 Peter 1:4-19, in which the refrain is sung and the stanzas are spoken above a background of improvised music. Schweizer (b. 1936), a church music director in Pforzheim, has composed pop-style hymn tunes with syncopations and off-beat entrances. These characteristics are evident in his 1963 setting of Paul Stein's "Sing to the Lord a new song" (CD47, *Singet dem Herrn ein neues Lied,* 1963, tr. by F. Pratt Green, 1972).[26]

In addition to recent hymnists represented in *Cantate Domino,* two Germans who have contributed to current American hymnals are Otmar Schulz and Heinz Werner Zimmerman. Schulz (b. 1938), a Baptist minister in Hamburg who is represented by one hymn in *Cantate Domino* (CD142), wrote text and tune for "Lord, you bid us ever" (B378, DU HERR, HEISST UNS HOFFEN, 1967: tr. by Harry Eskew, 1974). Zimmerman (b. 1930), a well-known Lutheran church music composer, has composed CARPENTER 1970 "Praise the Lord," B14), LITTLE FLOCK 1971 ("Have no fear, little flock,"

[25]See Chap. 9, Cultural Perspectives.
[26]Another Schweizer tune is his setting of Psalm 92, "How good to give thanks" (CD16, E6).

B225, L476), and Hymnus ("God is our defense and strength," E3).[27] The German theologian Dietrich Bonhoeffer (1906-1945) wrote "Men go to God" (Tr. by Geoffrey W. Young, Hinunter ist der Sonne, E90) and the German composer Hugo Distler (1908-1942) composed the tune Trumpets (adapted by Jan Bender for Martin Franzmann's "Weary of all trumpeting," E113).

The leading recent Scandinavian hymn writer whose hymns are available in English[28] is Anders Frostenson (b. 1906), a minister of the Church of Sweden who is represented by six hymns in *Cantate Domino*. Frostenson's hymns are remarkable for their fresh expression of biblical events, as in " 'It's Jesus we want,' requested the Greeks" (CD33, *Vi ville dig se, så grekerna bad,* 1971; tr. by Fred Kaan, 1972) and "They saw you as the local builder's son" (CD81, E105, *De såg ej dig blott timmermannens,* 1962; tr. by Fred Kaan, 1973). Also noteworthy are Frostenson's contemporary portrayals of faith and love in "Faith, while trees are still in blossom" (CD44, E74, *Ton sig sträcker efter frukten,* 1960; tr. by Fred Kaan, 1972) and "The love of God is broad like beach and meadow" (CD49, E104, *Guds kärlek är som stranden och som gräset,* 1968; tr. by Fred Kaan, 1972).

The centuries-old chorale tradition given its principal impetus by Martin Luther thus remains alive in Germany and in Scandinavia. As this tradition's twentieth-century contributions become increasingly available in English, some of them will likely find a place in the repertory of America's congregations as well.

The Metrical Psalm

French and Continental

Just as Luther gave the chorale its impetus, his contemporary—the French-Swiss Reformation theologian John Calvin (1509-64)—was the guiding hand behind the metrical psalm. A more radical reformer than Luther, Calvin rejected the musical heritage of the Roman Catholic Church, including organs, choirs and man-made hymns. He advocated singing only Scripture in worship, primarily the Psalms versified like hymns so that each could be sung to a particular tune. Furthermore, in Calvin's view the metrical psalms were to be sung only in unison and without instrumental accompaniment. The result of this philosophy of church song was the production of a series of gradually enlarged psalters in French, beginning with Calvin's Strassburg *Psalter* of 1539 and continuing with other psalters published in Geneva. The process culminated with the *Genevan Psalter* of 1562, which included all 150 psalms

[27]See chap. 2, The Hymn and Music.
[28]*Songs and Hymns from Sweden* ed. by Anders Frostenson and tr. by Fred Kaan (London: Stainer & Bell, Ltd., 1976). See the review of this collection in *The Hymn* 29, 1 (January 1978), 47-48.

plus the Ten Commandments and the *Nunc dimittis.* The complete *Genevan Psalter* contained 125 tunes in 110 different metrical forms.

Calvin, unlike Luther, was neither composer nor poet, but he was fortunate to have the assistance of others who did have these talents. Calvin's *Psalter* was versified in the French language by Clement Marot (*ca.* 1497-1544), who was succeeded several years after his death by Theodore de Beze (1519-1608). The chief musical contributor to the *Genevan Psalter* was Louis Bourgeois (*ca.* 1510—*ca.* 1561), who came from Paris to be director of music at St. Peter's Cathedral at Geneva, where Calvin preached for a number of years. In keeping with a common practice of the time, Bourgeois used many first phrases of secular chansons in his *Psalter* melodies. It is uncertain just how many of the Genevan Psalter tunes were actually composed by Bourgeois and how many were derived from other sources. Bourgeois's great influence upon this work has been attested by Pratt: "To him is plainly due the individual style that sets the French Psalter apart from all others of its age."[29] Among the *Genevan Psalter* tunes in present-day American hymnals are:

COMMANDMENTS ("Father, we thank thee who has planted," M307)—attributed to Bourgeois but with a first line from a secular chanson.

DONNE SECOURS ("Hope of the world," L493)—a Dorian melody attributed to Bourgeois and set to Marot's version of Psalm 12.

O SEIGNEUR ("When morning guilds the skies," L545)—

OLD 100TH ("All people that on earth do dwell," B17, E21, M21; "Praise God from whom all blessings flow," B6, 7, M809)—Originally to Psalm 134; attributed to Bourgeois but with a first line from a secular chanson.

OLD 107TH ("The Lord will come and not be slow," L318, M468)—original 7, 6, 7, 6, 6, 7, 6, 7 meter changed to C.M.D. in British-American use.

OLD 124 TH ("Your kingdom come, O Father, hear our prayer," L376; or GENEVA 124, "Turn back, O man, forswear thy foolish ways," M475).

OLD 134TH (or ST. MICHAEL, "Stand up and bless the Lord," B26, M16)—originally to Psalm 101 and in the metrical pattern 11, 11, 10, 4, this tune has been considerably altered in English use.

RENDEZ À DIEU ("Bread of the world in mercy broken," M323)—attributed to Bourgeois.

PSALM 42 (Comfort, comfort ye (now) my people, B77; or FREU DICH SEHR, L29; "Praise and thanks and adoration," L470)—this melody,

---

[29]Waldo Selden Pratt, *The Music of the French Psalter of 1562* (New York: Columbia University Press, 1939. Reprinted. New York: AMS Press, 1966), p. 62. This study, the most comprehensive treatment of the *Genevan Psalter* in English, contains all 125 tunes of the 1562 edition in modern notation.

eventually taken over into German use, was later used by Bach in seven of his cantatas.

The melodies of the *Genevan Psalter* gained extensive use in the sixteenth and seventeenth centuries, being spread not only in French-speaking areas but also through numerous translations in Germany, Holland, England, and Scotland, and from these lands to the American colonies. So great was the acceptance of these French Psalter tunes in Holland that their circulation there, even in our own century, is probably wider than that within their original French Protestant domain.[30]

Early English

Just as the first psalm versions of Marot had been written while he served in the court of Francis I of France, the beginnings of the first significant English psalter also took place amid royalty. Before 1549 Thomas Sternhold (1500-1549), a servant in the courts of Henry VIII and Edward VI, published nineteen psalm versions (which he sang to ballad tunes for his own private devotions) and dedicated them to young King Edward. A second edition containing thirty-seven psalms appeared in 1549 after Sternhold's death. In 1551 his friend John Hopkins (d. 1570), a clergyman and schoolteacher from Suffolk, added seven new versions to the previous thirty-seven. By the time this English *Psalter* was completed in 1562 (the same year of completion as the *Genevan Psalter*) Hopkins had contributed more than sixty psalm versions, thus giving it its popular designation—*The Sternhold and Hopkins Psalter*.

Before the completion of the English *Psalter,* however, political-religious developments in England caused English-language psalters to be published and used also on other than English soil. After the death of Edward VI in 1553, Roman Catholic Queen Mary (known as "Bloody Mary") succeeded to the throne. Under Mary's reign many Protestants fled from persecution to the Continent, and especially to Geneva. Editions of the *Anglo-Genevan Psalter* appeared in 1556, 1558, and 1561, the first being the initial English-language Psalter to include tunes. (Each of its fifty-one psalms had its proper tune, including some tunes reflecting Genevan influences.) The most lasting contribution from the *Anglo-Genevan Psalter* was made by William Kethe (d. c. 1593), among whose twenty-five versions in the 1561 edition was his rendition of Psalm 100, "All people that on earth do dwell" (B17, L245, M21). It was set to the tune previously used with Psalm 134 in the *Genevan Psalter,* known to English-Speaking churches as OLD 100TH.

The complete English *Psalter* of 1562, which included many versions from the *Anglo-Genevan Psalter,* was actually the work of at least twelve persons, but chiefly Sternhold and Hopkins. This *Sternhold and Hopkins Psalter,* later

[30]Ibid., p. 69.

known as the *Old Version* (to distinguish it from the 1696 *New Version* of Tate and Brady), was the official psalter of the Anglican Church until the second decade of the nineteenth century. Its metrical versions have almost completely passed out of common use today.

The greater influence of *Sternhold and Hopkins* upon current hymnody is musical rather than textual. Several of its tunes remain in common use. This complete psalter (the official title is *The Whole Book of Psalms, collected into English metre*), was published in melody-only edition (most melodies in double common meter) in 1562 in London by John Day and in a harmonized version in part-books (the melody in the tenor) in 1563. From Day's edition of 1562 the first four lines of the C.M.D. tune for Psalm 132 have become the presently used tune ST. FLAVIAN (M313, "Be known to us in breaking bread"). Other musical editions of *Sternhold and Hopkins* which have bequeathed tunes to present-day hymnals are:

1. William Damon's *Psalms* (1579), containing the S.M. tune to Psalm 14, later named by Ravenscroft SOUTHWELL (Lord Jesus, think on me," L309, M284).

2. William Damon's *Booke of Musicke* (1591, his *Psalms* revised by Este) containing the C.M. tune WINDSOR ("There is a green hill far away," L114; M428, "Behold the Savior of mankind").

3. Thomas Este's *Psalmes* (1592), containing the C.M. tune to Psalm 84, WINCHESTER OLD ("Awake my soul, awake my tongue," B96; "While shepherds watched their flocks by night," B97, M394).

4. Thomas Ravenscroft's *Psalmes* (1621), which included the common meter tunes BRISTOL (*The Hymnal 1940*, 7, "Hark! the glad sound! the Savior comes") and DURHAM (*The Hymnal 1940*, 297, "When all thy mercies, O my God").

In addition to these musical editions of *Sternhold and Hopkins,* one other early English psalter remains important for its music: Archbishop (of Canterbury) Matthew Parker's *Psalter* of about 1567 contained nine tunes of the pioneer Anglican composer Thomas Tallis (c. 1505-1585), including

> TALLIS'S CANON ("O Teacher, Master of the skill," B443; "All praise to thee, my God, this night," L278; "Awake, my soul, and with the sun," M180)
>
> TALLIS'S ORDINAL ("I waited for the Lord my God," B402; "According to thy gracious word," M316)
>
> THIRD MODE MELODY ("I heard the voice of Jesus say," L497)

Scottish

From about 1550 the English psalter begun by Sternhold was used in Scotland. A few years later the Scots, along with the English who fled from persecution to Geneva, used the *Anglo-Genevan Psalter*. Their great reformer, John Knox was pastor to the Genevan congregation of refugees for two years. After Knox's return to his homeland in 1559 the Scots began to revise the *Anglo-Genevan Psalter,* a process which resulted in their own *Psalter* in 1564 as a part of *The Book of Common Order.* Only about a third of this book's metrical psalms were of Scottish authorship. The *Scottish Psalter* contained 105 tunes (melodies only) and is regarded as musically superior to the *Sternhold and Hopkins Psalter* because of its greater use of French psalm tunes.

Two early editions of the *Scottish Psalter* are of particular musical interest. The edition of 1615 added to the "proper tunes" (tunes to be sung to only one metrical psalm) twelve "common tunes" (tunes which could be used with a number of psalms cast in the same meter). Two of this psalter's "Common tunes" in use today (both also in common meter) are:

> DUNDEE ("God moves in a mysterious way," B439, M215; "You are the way; through you alone," L464; "My God, how wonderful thou art," L524)—first called "French Tune." It was introduced to England by Ravenscroft in 1621 under the name "Dundy Tune."
>
> DUNFERMLINE ("Unto the hills I lift mine eyes," M57). This tune and DUNDEE also have several melodic motives in common.

The 1635 edition of the *Scottish Psalter,* edited by the skilled musician Edward Miller, had thirty-one common tunes harmonized (their melodies being in the tenor), including:

> CAITHNESS ("O Lord, throughout these forty days," L99; "How are thy servants blest, O Lord," M52)
>
> LONDON NEW ("God moves in a mysterious way," *The Hymnal 1940,* 310)—originally named NEWTON.This melody with its frequent leaps is in marked contrast to the more usual step-wise psalm tunes of its time.

LONDON NEW was introduced into English use by John Playford in his *Psalms & Hymns in Solemn Musick* (1671) and *The Whole Book of Psalms* (1677), the latter psalter being in circulation in England for a hundred years. Through Playford's as well as other English psalters, several Scottish psalm tunes gained a place in the repertory of English psalmody.

Although editions of the *Scottish Psalter* after 1564 had included music, the new *Scottish Psalter* adopted in 1650 contained no music. The 1650 *Scottish Psalter* has bequeathed several metrical psalms to American use, including:

> "The Lord's my Shepherd, I'll not want"—Psalm 23 (B341, L451, M68)
> "I waited for the Lord my God"—Psalm 40:1-5 (B402)
> "How lovely is thy dwelling place"—Psalm 84 (M295)

Although hymnals appeared in Scotland by the late 19th century,[31] the *Scottish Psalter* continued to be used well into the present century, its latest edition appearing in 1929.[32] The 1929 *Scottish Psalter* was used along with the 1927 edition of the Church of Scotland's *Church Hymnary* until 1973, when the third edition of the *Church Hymnary* was published. In the third edition of the *Church Hymnary,* metrical psalms and other scriptural paraphrases lost their time-honored special place and were mingled with the hymns. The small Free Kirk of Scotland, however, still sings only the psalms. When one enters a Free Kirk, he is handed a Bible with the metrical psalms bound in the book.[33]

Later English Psalmody

Although the *Sternhold and Hopkins Psalter* remained England's most widely used collection until its demise in the mid-nineteenth century, its leading rival made its initial appearance in 1696. This was entitled *A New Version of the Psalms of David, fitted to the tunes used in Churches.* The *New Version* was authored by two Irishmen, Nahum Tate (1652-1715), who had been made poet laureate by William III, and Nicholas Brady (1659-1726), a royal chaplain at that time. The *New Version* was dedicated to the King, who with his council designated it as "allowed and permitted to be used in all Churches, Chappels, and Congregations, as shall think fit to receive the same."

In contrast to the strict metrical renderings of the *Old Version* of Sternhold and Hopkins, the *New Version* made a freer and more polished literary paraphrase of the psalms, arousing such objections as the following: "David speaks so plain," said one old man, "that we cannot mistake his meaning, but as for Mr. Tate and Brady, they have taken away my Lord, and I know not where they have laid him."[34] The *New Version* never achieved the acceptance of the entire Anglican Church; it was used primarily by those who were most ready to sing hymns along with the psalms, particularly the churches of London.[35] Indeed, the polished metrical psalms of Tate and Brady seemed much more like hymns than those of the older psalters. Psalms from the *New Version* in American use include:

"As pants the hart for cooling streams"—Psalm 42 (L452, M255)
"O come, loud anthems let us sing"—Psalm 95 (B21)

[31]These are listed in Millar Patrick, *Four Centuries of Scottish Psalmody* (London: Oxford University Press, 1949), p. 219. This book is the definitive work on Scottish psalmody.
[32]*The Scottish Psalter* (London: Oxford University Press, 1929).
[33]We are indebted to Erik Routley for information on recent Scottish psalmody.
[34]Quoted in Millar, Patrick, *The Story of the Church's Song.* Revision of original 1927 ed. for American use by James R. Sydnor. (Richmond: John Knox Press, 1962), p. 98.
[35]Louis F. Benson, *The English Hymn.* Reprint of the original 1915 ed. (Richmond: John Knox Press, 1962), p. 50.

"O Lord, our fathers oft have told"—Psalm 44 (M54)

"Through all the changing scenes of life"—Psalm 34 (M56)

No music was included in the 1696 edition of the *New Version* but a *Supplement* in 1708 provided tunes, including several attributed to William Croft (1678-1727):

> St. Anne (to Watts's version of Psalm 90, "O God, our help in ages past," B223, L320, M28)
>
> Hanover ("Ye servants of God, your master proclaim," B292, M409; "O worship the King," L548)
>
> St. Matthew ("Come, let us rise with Christ our Head," M457)

This *Supplement* also included a familiar scriptural paraphrase of the announcement of the birth of Christ from Luke 2, "While shepherds watched their flocks by night" (B97, M394). Thus while the *New Version* did not achieve as widespread an acceptance as the *Old Version,* the *New Version* did gain a lasting place for some of its psalm versions (as well as its Christmas Gospel paraphrase) in current hymnals.

American

The old World metrical psalmody was brought across the Atlantic by a number of groups who settled in colonial America, notably the Pilgrims and the Puritans. The Pilgrims settled at Plymouth, Massachusetts, in 1620, bringing with them the *Ainsworth Psalter* (1612),[36] which they used until the close of the century. Nearly a decade later the Puritans established the Massachusetts Bay Colony (1628), bringing with them the *Sternhold and Hopkins Psalter* (1562). In other American colonies settled by French and Dutch Protestants, psalters from their respective homelands were used.

In 1640 at Cambridge, Massachusetts the Puritans published the *Bay Psalm Book* (for its actual title, see the title page.), the first book of any kind to be printed in British North America. The Puritan ministers sought to provide in the *Bay Psalm Book* a rendering of the psalms that was smoother and closer to the original Hebrew than those of *Sternhold and Hopkins.* The early editions of the *Bay Psalm Book* contained no music but referred the users to the *Ravenscroft Psalter* for tunes. Beginning with the ninth edition of 1698, music was provided, drawing from psalm tunes well known in England.[37] Although

---

[36]This was a psalter compiled by Henry Ainsworth, an English separatist minister and Hebrew scholar then in Amsterdam. Its 39 tunes drew from both English and Genevan sources. A detailed study of this psalter is Waldo S. Pratt, *The Music of the Pilgrims* (Boston: Oliver Ditson Co., 1921. Reprinted. New York: AMS Press, 1966).

[37]The tunes and musical instructions in this edition were taken from Playford's *Brief Introduction to the Skill of Musick* (London, 8th ed., 1679).

no psalm versions from the *Bay Psalm Book* remain in use in today's congregational repertory, this psalter was widely used for over a century in New England, England, and Scotland.[38]

THE

VVHOLE
BOOKE OF PSALMES
Faithfully
TRANSLATED *into* ENGLISH
Metre.

Whereunto is prefixed a difcourfe declaring not only the lawfullnes, but alfo the neceffity of the heavenly Ordinance of finging Scripture Pfalmes in the Churches of God.

Coll. III.
Let the word of God dwell plenteoufly in you, in all wifdome, teaching and exhorting one another in Pfalmes, Himnes, and fpirituall Songs, finging to the Lord with grace in your hearts.

Iames V.
If any be afflicted, let him pray, and if any be merry let him fing pfalmes.

Imprinted
1640

[38]Two significant studies of the *Bay Psalm Book* are Zoltan Haraszti, *The Enigma of the Bay Psalm Book,* published with a facsimile of the first edition of this psalter (Chicago: University of Chicago Press, 1956) and Irving Lowens, "The Bay Psalm Book in 17th-Century New England," in *Music and Musicians in Early America* (New York: W. W. Norton, 1964).

Eighteenth-Century Psalmody

In the eighteenth century the *Bay Psalm Book* was gradually replaced by other psalters. Watts's *The Psalms of David Imitated* was first reprinted in America by Benjamin Franklin's press at Philadelphia in 1729. The revival fervor of the Great Awakening shortly thereafter influenced many congregations to adopt Watts's *Psalms* and *Hymns.* A number of Watts's metrical psalms were also found in John Wesley's "Charlestown Collection" of 1737.[39] While some denominations changed with little difficulty from the older psalters to updated versions or to hymns, others (notably the Presbyterians) experienced major controversies.[40]

Nineteenth-Century Psalmody

After Americans gained political independence, various psalter editions sought, by removing references to Britain, to accommodate Watts's *Psalms* to America: Barlow (1785), Dwight (1801), and Worcester (1815). The second of these, edited by Timothy Dwight (1752-1817), a chaplain under George Washington and later president of Yale, included the editor's version of Psalm 137, "I love thy kingdom, Lord" (B240, M294; "I love your kingdom, Lord," L368) the earliest American congregational song remaining in common use. In the eighteenth and early nineteenth centuries most American denominations changed from singing only metrical psalms to singing freer psalm versions as well as the hymns of Isaac Watts and other English authors.

In the latter nineteenth century a second psalm paraphrase appeared which has gained a place in the broad stream of American hymnody. "O my soul, bless God the Father" (B34, M65), a version of Psalm 103, was first published in 1871 in the United Presbyterian *Book of Psalms.*

Twentieth-Century Psalmody

Although metrical psalmody in America was superceded by hymnody in most of its churches by the early nineteenth century, several denominations of the Calvinist tradition continue to the present day to use metrical psalters. An Associate Reformed Presbyterian Church's psalter is entitled *Bible Songs* (Due West, S. C.: Executive Board, Associate Reformed Presbyterian Church, 1930, 7th ed., 1975). Although restricted to the metrical psalms, the music of *Bible Songs* is largely American, making use of many gospel-hymn settings. Along with the psalter most A.R.P. congregations use hymnals as well. Another American denomination using a metrical psalter is the Reformed Presbyterian Church of North America. Their psalter is *The Book of Psalms*

---

[39]See chap. 7, British Traditions.
[40]See Benson, *The English Hymn,* pp. 161-218 for a detailed treatment of "The Era of Watts in America."

for Singing (Pittsburgh: Board of Education and Publication, Reformed Presbyterian Church of North America, 1973; 2nd ed. 1975). This psalter, although incorporating American musical settings, makes fuller use of the European heritage than does the *Bible Songs* volume. For example, it includes such familiar psalm tunes as DUNDEE, CRIMOND, ST. ANNE, and TALLIS'S ORDINAL.

7

British Traditions

The Gathering Streams

In the sixteenth century the English reformers of the church chose to follow John Calvin of Geneva rather than Martin Luther of Wittenberg. This had decisive consequences for the history of the Christian church in England and greatly affected the type of church song which developed there. Since the Lutheran chorale was rejected by the British reformers,[1] the development of true hymnody (in contradistinction to metrical psalmody) was long delayed. Therefore the story of worship song from the Reformation until the eighteenth century in the British Isles is largely the story of the metrical psalm.

George Wither

Yet even while psalmody continued to be dominant in the established church and among the Nonconformists alike, there were rumblings of discontent with it; and several early attempts were made to widen the sphere of church song. Most notable was the publication by George Wither (1588-1667) of *Hymns and Songs of the Church* (1623), a book which has been described as the very earliest attempt at an English hymnal. In addition to the conventional paraphrases of Scripture, it contained some true hymns for festivals and special occasions. It initially won a royal patent; but because such a concession was jealously opposed by the Company of Stationers, the patent had to be withdrawn. Wither's bold experiment eventually came to naught. But the book appears to have been popular with the young people for a time, and its attraction was doubtless enhanced by the inclusion of sixteen tunes by the most eminent composer of the day, Orlando Gibbons (1583-1625). None of Wither's delightful lyrics have survived in our hymnals, but the Gibbons tunes remain as a notable legacy.[2]

George Herbert

The century that produced Wither also marked the emergence of a

[1]There was a brief period in the days of Henry VIII (1491-1547) that Lutheranism seemed likely to have some influence in English religious reform. Miles Coverdale's *Goostly Psalmes and Spirituall Songes* (c. 1537-43) represented an attempt to import Lutheran hymnody into England but this book was soon suppressed (burned). After some hesitation, Archbishop Cranmer (1489-1556) came down on the side of Calvin, thus turning church song in the direction of metrical psalmody.

[2]These tunes are still named according to the numbering given them in Wither's hymnbook. See, for example, SONG 1 (L206); SONG 13 (B241, M311, but altered and named CANTERBURY); SONG 34 (L505); SONG 46 (M229); SONG 67 (L438).

remarkable group of men known as the metaphysical poets. In this fellowship were John Donne (1573-1631), dean of St. Paul's in London, Richard Crashaw (d. 1649), Nicholas Ferrar (1592-1637), and George Herbert (1593-1633). Most of these were members of a distinguished circle of friends that gathered about Izaak Walton (1593-1683), author of *The Compleat Angler* (1683), one of the monuments of English literature. All of them wrote devotional poetry intended mainly for private reading and contemplation; but verses from many of their poems were later extracted for hymnic use.

In the realm of hymns the best known of these poets is George Herbert, the masterful orator of the University of Cambridge and self-effacing rector of the village church at Bemerton. Herbert's hymns for congregational use have all been taken from a little book entitled *The Temple*. This is a posthumous collection (1633) of 169 of some of the quaintest and most profound poems in the English language, written by a man who is generally considered to have been one of the saintliest characters in all the history of literature.

Throughout the next two centuries Herbert's hymns were included in numerous hymn collections. Today he is mainly remembered for one— the one he entitled "Antiphon" in *The Temple*. It has found universal use. Known by its first line "Let all the world in every corner sing" (B24, M10), it is appropriately set to Robert G. McCutchan's vibrant tune, ALL THE WORLD, though it is one of several tunes written for this text.

John Milton

Herbert's younger contemporary, John Milton (1608-74), represents a different development in the early history of the English hymn. While Herbert and his group produced religious verse that subsequently was edited for congregational singing, Milton's "hymns" are actually free paraphrases of portions of the psalms. The relaxing of adherence to the exact content and language of the Psalms by gifted men like Milton was a necessary step toward the eventual breaking altogether of metrical psalmody's stranglehold on church song. Two excellent hymns based on Psalms that Milton has contributed to our modern collections are: "The Lord will come and not be slow" (B128, M468, L318), based on portions of Psalms 85, 82, and 86, and "Let us with a gladsome mind" (B27, M61), based on Psalm 136.

Richard Baxter

Richard Baxter (1615-91), who has been called the greatest of the Protestant schoolmen, was also one of the pioneers of hymn making and hymn singing in this early period. At a time when most of his fellow Puritan clergymen were disapproving of music in church, he was its champion. At a time when most of his contemporaries were paraphrasing the Psalms, he boldly wrote original lyrics. The one hymn by which he is still remembered is "Lord, it belongs not to my care" (M218). It is a poignant expression of Christian trust resulting from great bereavement. A masterpiece of simplicity voicing a richness of thought with rare economy of expression, it truly reflects the spirit of this devout pastor and peerless preacher. In form it anticipates the pure congregational hymn soon to come from the pioneering pen of Isaac Watts. Though generally unrecognized, Baxter is nevertheless a real herald of the modern English hymn.

Samuel Crossman

Another seventeenth-century churchman who wrote of the intimacies of the faith was Samuel Crossman (1624-83), dean of Bristol Cathedral. He identified himself with the Puritan cause for a time and was expelled from the Anglican ministry, but later conformed and became one of the king's chaplains. He is remembered today for one poignant hymn on the Passion of our Lord, "My song is love unknown" (B486, L94). The naive directness and charm of this hymn strikes an old-world note that undoubtedly contributes to the high regard in which it is still held today.

John Bunyan

John Bunyan (1628-88), the great allegorist who spent much of his adult life in jail as punishment for preaching in a Baptist church, is now represented in most hymnals by his "He who would valiant be" (B384; M155). Beginning originally "Who would true valour see," this hymn was written as the epilogue to a chapter in Part II of *Pilgrim's Progress* (1684). It follows the conversation between Great Heart and Valiant for Truth and is a summary of all that Bunyan was attempting to say in his great story. Most likely Bunyan would have been pleased for this poem to be sung, since he cast it in metrical form and was known to have encouraged the singing of hymns in congregational worship. Today the hymn sounds a needed note of urgency and bold venture which is admirably captured also in the bracing vigour and direct rhythms of Winfred Douglas's tune, ST. DUNSTAN'S.

Thomas Ken

This period of the early struggles for true congregational hymnody is perhaps best represented by Thomas Ken (1637-1711). Ken occupied many positions during his somewhat checkered career—rector of Little Easton, curate of Brightstone on the Isle of Wight, chaplain to Princess Mary at the Hague, chaplain of the English Fleet at Tangiers, bishop of Bath and Wells; but his contributions to hymnody came in connection with his positions at

Winchester Cathedral. There he was chaplain to the bishop, a fellow at Winchester College, and a member of the cathedral staff. For the boys of Winchester College (where he himself had been a scholar), he prepared his *Manual of Prayers for the Use of the Scholars of Winchester College* (1674), to which his famous morning and evening hymns were later appended. Ken was well known in his lifetime for strength of conviction and fidelity to conscience—characteristics which ring out in his hymns: "Awake, my soul, and with the sun" (M180, L269), and "All praise to thee, my God, this night" (M493, L278).

Ken also wrote a midnight hymn, but it has not survived. For all three of these hymns Ken wrote his famous doxology beginning "Praise God, from whom all blessings flow" (B6,7; M809; L564). This doxology has undoubtedly been sung more than any other four lines in the English language.

Benjamin Keach

An adventurous pioneer in writing hymns with the express purpose of their being sung in public worship was Benjamin Keach (1640-1704). Keach was pastor of a Particular Baptist church in the vicinity of London. As early as 1673 he introduced to his congregation the singing of his own hymns at the observance of the Lord's Supper. In view of the fact that Baptists at this time were generally opposed to such practice, Keach's pioneering effort is all the more remarkable. He defended his church's singing of hymns in *The Breach Repaired in God's Worship, or Singing of Psalms, Hymns and Spiritual Songs proved to be a Holy Ordinance of Jesus Christ* (1691) and reinforced it with the publication of *Spiritual Melody,* a collection of three hundred hymns. Practically all of Keach's hymns were of poor quality. However, one Christmas hymn is available today—"Awake, my soul, awake my tongue" (B96)—a reminder of the significant role Keach once played in the history of congregational hymn singings.

An Anonymous Folk Ballad

Among other early writers of hymns was the anonymous author of "Jerusalem, my happy home" (B488, L331). This famous twenty-six-stanza hymn on the subject of eternal life was probably written in the early seventeenth century. It exists in manuscript in the British Museum, where it is headed "A Song Mad [*sic*] by F. B. P. to the tune Diana." Nothing is known of this tune nor of the author, but the hymn's fervid images of heaven constitute a delightful mixture of biblical and English garden allusions which Routley calls both its defense and its splendor.[3]

---

[3]Erik Routley, *Hymns in Human Life* (London: John Murray, 1952), p. 305.

Nahum Tate

The name of Nahum Tate (1652-1715) is to be associated principally with metrical psalmody;[4] but a supplement to the famous *New Version of the Psalms by Dr. Brady and Mr. Tate* (1700) included also some paraphrases of passages of Scripture other than the Psalms. Among these was "While shepherds watched their flocks by night" (B97, M394), Tate's paraphrase of Luke 2:8-14. This is the only "hymn" to survive from a man who in his day wrote considerably for the stage and who later became both poet laureate and royal historiographer. But he needs no greater monument than "While shepherds watched their flocks by night," one of the finest hymnic descriptions of the appearance of the angels to the shepherds at the birth of Jesus.

The Confluence of the Calvinist and Lutheran Streams

Isaac Watts

The stage was now set for the appearance of Isaac Watts (1674-1748), generally considered "the Father of the English Hymn." However, since there were men like Milton and Tate before him who struggled toward a lyrical freedom within the tradition of scriptural paraphrase; and since other writers like Herbert and Bunyan composed superb devotional verse which on occasion found use in public praise; and since other journeyman poets like Wither and Keach actually championed the singing of hymns in corporate worship, Watts cannot properly be thought of as the inventor of the English hymn.

Watts was a Congregational minister. He was the one who possessed both the vision and the ability to amalgamate the two main streams of church song—paraphrases of Scripture and devotional lyric poetry—and to produce from them the two types of true English hymn for which he is justly famous. These two types resulted from his twofold theory of congregational praise:

1. Truly authentic praise for Christian folk had to go beyond the mere words of Scripture to include original expressions of devotion and thanksgiving.

2. If the psalms were to be used in Christian worship, they must be renovated by Christianizing them.

Watts put the first part of his theory into effective practice by the publication of his *Horae Lyricae* (1705) and *Hymns and Spiritual Songs* (1707). From the latter book came his finest hymns, among which are some of the greatest in the English language:

"Alas! and did my Savior bleed" (B113, M415, L98)
"Am I a soldier of the cross" (B388, M239)
"Come, let us join our cheerful songs" (B126, L254)

[4]See Chap. 6, Reformation Traditions.

"Come, we that love the Lord" (B505 M5)
"Come, Holy Spirit, heavenly dove" (B134, M134)
"Give me the wings of faith" (B498, M533)
"I sing the almighty power of God (B154, M37)[6]
"When I survey the wondrous cross" (B111, M435, L482)
"I'm not ashamed to own my Lord" (B450)
"Nature with open volume stands" (L119)

With regard to the second of his principles, Watts brought the Psalter up to date and made its use meaningful for the Chrisitan worshipers of eighteenth-century England and America. Then he demonstrated how he could carry this idea of New Testament praise back into the Psalter itself when he published his *The Psalms of David Imitated in the Language of the New Testament* (1719). This contained such great paraphrases as:

Psalm 19—"The heavens declare thy glory, Lord" (M365)
Psalm 72—"Jesus shall reign" (B282, M472, L530)
Psalm 90—"O God, our help in ages past" (B223, M28, L320)
Psalm 95—"Come, sound his praise abroad" (M24)
Psalm 96—"Let all on earth their voices raise" (M39)
Psalm 98—"Joy to the world" (B88, M392, L39)
Psalm 100—"Before Jehovah's awful (awesome) throne" (M22, L531)[7]
Psalm 117—"From all that dwell below the skies" (M14, L550)
Psalm 118—"This is the day the Lord hath made" (B68, M789)
Psalm 146—"I'll praise my Maker while I've breath" (M9)[7]

With these Watts set the model for a permanent type of English hymn. Where others had tried and failed, he was able to create for the singing of such hymns a position which they have subsequently retained in public worship. All subsequent hymn writers, even when they surpass him, are indebted to him.

While it may be an oversimplication to say that before Watts English churches sang psalms and after him they sang hymns, it must be affirmed that until Watts the use of true hymns was the exception rather than the rule. "To Watts more than to any other man is due the triumph of the hymn in English worship.[8]

School of Watts

Furthermore, Watts gave a great impetus to hymn writing in England by teaching and by example. In his wake sprang up a veritable "school of Watts" which included such outstanding persons as:

Joseph Addison (1672-1719)

---

[6]This hymn appeared in *Divine and Moral Songs* (1715), designed for children.
[7]Altered by John Wesley.
[8]Bernard Manning, *The Hymns of Wesley and Watts* (London: The Epworth Press, 1942), p. 81.

"The spacious firmament on high" (M43),
"How are thy servants blest, O Lord" (M52)
"When all thy (your) mercies, O my God" (M70, L264),
Philip Doddridge[9] (1702-51)
   "How gentle God's commands" (M53),
   "Great God, we sing that mighty hand" (M509),
   "Awake, my soul, stretch every nerve" (M249),
   "O happy day, that fixed my choice" (B457, M128).
Joseph Hart (1712-68)
   "Come, ye sinners, poor and needy" (B196, M104).
Anne Steele[10] (1716-78)
   "Father of mercies, in thy word" (M367).

Traits of the Wattsian Hymn

These hymns bear the salient characteristics that left their mark on the form and content of the English hymn for many decades to come.

As to form, the Wattsian hymn is:

1. Simple: (a) in meter—only common, long, and short meter were used; (b) in vocabulary—predominantly Anglo-Saxon words, with preference given to monosyllables.

2. Striking in its opening line, tersely proclaiming the theme of the entire hymn like a headline.

3. Often using repetition and parallelism, following the structural principle of the Psalms.

4. Frequently only half-rhymed (lines 2 and 4) and with a liberal use of imperfect rhymes or mere assonances.

5. Sometimes found with a pairing of lines 2 and 3 in four-line stanzas.

6. Dramatic in its climax, usually expressed in a final stanza.

As to content, the Wattsian hymn is:

1. Comprehensive in scope and cosmic in background.[11]

2. Calvinistic in theology; emphasis on such doctrines as the glory and sovereignty of God, the depravity of human nature, the security of the elect, and the all-sufficient atonement of Jesus Christ on the cross for the sins of humankind.

[9]See Erik Routley, *Hymns and Human Life* (London, 1952), for a lucid portrayal of Doddridge as an early champion of the social application of the gospel in hymns (pp. 89-92).

[10]Miss Steele was the foremost of a group of Baptist hymnists, including Benjamin Beddome (1717-93), Samuel Stennett (1727-95) (B267, 490, M83, 291), Robert Robinson (1735-90) (B12, M93) and Samuel Medley (1738-99) (B436, M168, 445), who, because their hymns possess a quality unsurpassed before or since, constitute a "Golden Age of Baptist Hymnody."

[11]Watts was the "master of the enormous conception" (a Routley phrase) who in wondering awe sang of the omnipotence of God, the spaciousness of nature, the vastness of time, and the dreadfulness of eternity.

3. Christian in focus; Christ exalted and adored above all else as the very center of objective worship.

4. Liturgical in purpose; inspired by the setting of public worship and conceived for use in public praise.

5. Scriptural in flavor; faithfully paraphrasing the content of Scripture and masterfully incorporating biblical language, allusion, and thought.

With these characteristics the permanent type of English hymn became definitely set. Thus was brought into being a class of "religious song with his (Watts's) own ardent faith made devotional, which his manly and lucid mind made simple and strong, which his poetic feeling and craftmanship made rhythmical and often lyrical, and which his sympathy with people made hymnic."[12]

Isaac Watts is the one man who most changed the course of English speaking congregational praise. Though his own hymns made rather slow headway in many congregations in the latter part of the eighteenth century, they "rode to the dominating position they ultimately held on the wings of Revival."[13] And that revival came with the inspired and indefatigable work of the Wesleys. There was, however, an element of reciprocity here; for Watts's hymns were, in turn, a potent factor in promoting that Evangelical Revival.

The Wesleys

The first hymnbook to be published on North American soil was John Wesley's *Collection of Psalms and Hymns* (Savannah, Ga. but printed in Charlestown, S.C., 1737).[14] Of its seventy hymns, exactly one half were from Watts. But to the core of Watts's hymns of objective wonder and praise there was soon to be added the Wesleyan hymn of inner experience and evangelical concern. Theologically this represented a tempering of the Calvinistic stream of hymnody (psalmody) with the warmer current of Lutheran pietistic devotion.

Moravian Influences

This moderating stream was mediated through the Moravians, who exerted great influence on the Wesleys. During their voyage to Georgia (1736), John Wesley (1703-91) and his brother Charles (1707-88) were impressed with the

[12]Louis F. Benson, *The English Hymn* (London, 1915), p. 206. This book is still the classic on the subject.

[13]Arthur P. Davis, *Isaac Watts* (London: Independent Press, 1943), p. 207.

[14]This is available in facsimile reprint: *John Wesley's First Hymn-book: A Collection of Psalms and Hymns* (Charleston: The Dalcho Historical Society, 1964). This book has been described as "the first real Anglican hymnal" by Winfred Douglas. *Church Music in History and Practice,* Revised, with additional material by Leonard Ellinwood (New York: Charles Scribner's Sons, 1961), p. 195.

devout singing of the Moravians on board. John maintained contact with these Moravians while in Georgia, learning and translating several of their hymns. After the Wesleys returned to England, it was perhaps under Moravian influence that they underwent their "heartwarming" conversion experiences. Thereafter, they set out on a mission to evangelize England, Wales, and Ireland.

Wanting to learn more of Moravian life-style and worship, John Wesley soon journeyed to Herrnhut, the Moravian settlement on the border of Bohemia, where he spent several weeks in fellowship and prayer and where he again came under the spell of fervent Moravian hymn singing. As a result of these influences, John Wesley became an ardent lover of their hymnody though rejecting their pietistic excesses. He was the first important translator of Moravian hymns into English.

Contemporary hymnals are still in great debt to John Wesley for the following hymns from the German:

"Jesus, thy (your) blood and righteousness" (M127, L302)
"O thou to whose all-searching sight" (B470, M213)
"Give to the wind thy fears" (B224, M51)
"Jesus, thy boundless love to me" (B326, M259, L336)
"Thou hidden Love of God" (M531)

Charles Wesley

But John Wesley's main contribution to English hymnody was the collecting, editing, publishing, and promoting of his brother Charles's hymns. Charles was the hymn writer par excellence. Indeed, he is often acclaimed the greatest hymn writer of all time.

The picture of England during the opening decades of the eighteenth century was a sorry one—morals were decayed, education was practically nonexistent, sanitation was neglected, literature and the theater were debauched, intemperance was rampant, crime was widespread, politics were corrupt and the clergy were idle and uncaring. Into such a world came the Wesleys like a cleansing fire. The great organizer and promoter of the movement was John Wesley. But by all accounts much of the success of this remarkable religious awakening must be attributed to the singing of Charles Wesley's hymns.

These hymns resulted from a genuine conversion experience in Charles's life (actually coming prior to John's). Before this turning point he, like John, was an ordained Anglican clergyman and, together with John, a missionary for a brief period to the Georgia colony. He was also a gifted poet. But it was not until he was catapulted into a deeply personal relationship to Jesus Christ as Redeemer and Lord (Whitsunday, 1738) that there was released in him the gift of sacred song. Immediately he wrote his first hymn, "Where shall my wondering soul begin?" (M528).

Paul Gerhardt

"Thereafter hardly a day or an experience passed without its crystallization in verse. The result, 6500 hymns on hundreds of Scripture texts and on every conceivable phase of Christian experience and Methodist theology."[15]

Even to list the Wesleyan hymns that are in current use would require much too great a space. Methodist collections would be expected to contain the most Wesley hymns[16] but no hymnal could be considered complete without these:

"A charge to keep I have" (B407, M150)
"Come, thou long-expected Jesus" (B79, M360, L30)
"Christ the Lord is risen today" (B114, M439, L130)
"Christ whose glory fills the skies" (M401, L265)
"Forth in thy name" (M152, L505)
"Hark! the herald angels sing" (B83, M387, L60)
"Jesus, lover of my soul" (B172, M125)
"Lo, he comes with clouds descending" (M364, L27)
"Love divine, all loves excelling" (B58, M283, L315)
"O for a thousand tongues to sing" (B69, M1, L559)
"Praise the Lord who reigns above" (B23, M15)
"Rejoice, the Lord is king" (B120, M483, L171)

Wesleyan Hymn Traits

Taking a careful look at these hymns, one becomes aware of the following characteristics:

As to form, the Wesleyan hymn is:

1. Rich in the variety of poetic meters. Not content to remain with the old psalm meters, Wesley exhibited superb mastery of at least twenty meters.

2. So constructed that sound and sense coincide. Wesley rarely fails to make the ends of his lines correspond with natural pauses in thought, thus making them very suitable for singing.[17]

3. Bold and free in scriptural paraphrase. Rather than keeping strictly to a restatement of the original in a mechanical manner, Wesley also makes imaginative comment on his scriptural passages.

4. Skillful in the mixture of Anglo-Saxon and Latin vocabulary.

5. Masterful in the use of the conventional eighteenth-century literary devices—careful rhyme, repetition, chiasmus.[18]

[15]Edward Albert Bailey, *The Gospel in Hymns* (New York: Charles Scribner's Sons, 1950), p. 84.
[16]*The Methodist Hymnal* (M) contains over eighty hymns by the Wesleys.
[17]Manning, *The Hymns of Wesley and Watts,* p. 59.
[18]See chap. 1, The Hymn and Literature, for examples of Wesley's mastery as a poet. Two important sources for further study in this connection are Henry Bett, *The Hymns of Methodism in Their Literary Relations* (London: Epworth Press, 1945) and Bernard L. Manning, *The Hymns of Watts and Wesley* (London: Epworth Press, 1942).

As to content, the Wesleyan hymn is:

1. Replete with Christian dogma. Wesley, reflecting Moravian influence, is Arminian in his theology. His hymns taken together constitute a body of skillfully condensed doctrine, or, in the words of John Wesley, "a body of experimental and practical divinity."[19]

2. Full of scriptural allusion. Wesley's hymns are always disciplined by biblical truth, and many of them are finely wrought biblical mosaics.[20]

3. Expressive of passionate Christian experience. Every mood of the Christian soul is reflected with a fervour which is free of vulgarity and mawkish excess. The predominant note is one of joy and confidence.

4. Simple and smooth, speaking directly of important matters pertaining to God and the souls of men. With disarming simplicity and directness Wesley confronted plain men and women with the central concerns of the faith. The hymns were democratic in design and evangelistic in purpose.

5. Mystical, glowing with a luminous quality transfiguring history and experience.[21] This comes in the audacity of intimacy with which Wesley talks to God as friend, a quality that makes his hymns timeless and universal in their appeal.

Methodist Tunes

Because his restless genius expressed itself in meters never before utilized by hymnists, Charles Wesley posed a challenge to writers of hymn tunes. John Wesley, who believed, along with Martin Luther before him and General Booth after him, that the devil should never have all the good tunes, was constantly looking for music from every available source. Therefore by challenging and encouraging composers, amateur and professional alike, the Wesleyan Revival unleashed a flood of new hymn tunes, some of which have proved to be of permanent value.

Many of these "old Methodist tunes" were highly florid and repetitive (often to the point of irresponsibility); others, however, being intended for "all sorts and conditions of men," were simple and folklike in style.[22]

But whether they are of the sophisticated tradition of Purcell and Handel (Handel set three Wesley hymns) or of the popular tradition (sung by the folk in the fields and even in the jails!), many of the tunes are unforgettable. To whistle them is to bring to mind the memorable texts with which they are matched, and thereby one can be mysteriously confirmed again in the faith.

[19]From the famous Preface to *A Collection of Hymns for Use of the People Called Methodists* (London: 1780).
[20]See Bailey, *op. cit.,* pp. 95-97 where the scriptural tapestry of "Love divine, all loves excelling" is unraveled.
[21]Manning, *op. cit.,* pp. 29-30.

And this is precisely what the Wesleys hoped for.

"These hymns were composed in order that the men and women whom Hogarth depicted in his terrible pictures might sing their way not only into experience but also into knowledge; that the cultured might have their culture baptized and the ignorant might be led into truth by the gentle hand of melody and rhyme. This disciplined fervour was what made it possible for English hymnody to have a classical age before it fell into corruption and decay."[23]

It was this disciplined fervour that helped re-Christianize Britain, providing sufficient personal faith and moral backbone to save that land from the agonies that overtook France during the French Revolution.

To summarize, the Calvinist stream produced the liturgical hymn of Watts and the pietistic Lutheran stream nourished the evangelical hymn of the Wesleys. Together these two types of classic hymnody "reformed the Reformation."[24]

Full Course: The Evangelical Revival

So completely did the Wesleys dominate their age that most of their contemporaries and followers are dwarfed in comparison. However, the evangelical hymn stream, released initially by the work of the Wesleys, was fed also by certain tributaries which constituted major sources of revival inspiration.

George Whitefield and the Calvinistic Methodists

The first of these additional major sources of inspiration was the powerful preacher, George Whitefield (1714-70). Along with the Wesley brothers, Whitefield was the third most important herald of the revival movement. A member of the famous Oxford Holy Club (dubbed "Methodist" by its detractors), he was spiritually reborn, even before the Wesleys experienced conversion. It was also he who led the way into preaching in the open air after

---

[22]Among Wesleyan tunes are those:
1. of straightforward psalm type: DUKE STREET (B282, M14), ST. THOMAS (B240, M5);
2. of the flowing, suave type: RICHMOND (B460, M12), IRISH (B492, M56);
3. in architectonic structure: KENT (M350); DARWALL (B120, M483);
4. of florid nature: ST. MARTIN'S (M507); DIADEM (B41, M72);
5. in the folk style of the Moravians: SAVANNAH (M309), AMSTERDAM (B23, M15).

These last two tunes, together with some forty others, were published in 1742 in a small tunebook, *A Collection of Tunes Set to Music as they are commonly sung at the Foundery.* See a facsimile reprint of this "Foundery Collection," bound with a reprint of Wesley's *Collection of Psalms and Hymns* (Charles-town, 1737), with a preface by Rev. G. Osborn (London: T. Woolner, n.d.).

[23]Erik Routley, *Hymns and Human Life* (London: John Murray, 1952), pp. 71-72.

[24]Martha Winburn England and John Sparrow, *Hymns Unbidden* (New York Public Library, 1966), p. 40.

the established churches shut their doors to him. Whitefield's principal contributions to hymnody came after he broke with the Wesleys for theological reasons and became the leader of the Calvinistic Methodists, whose chief spheres of action were in the west of England and Wales.

Although not a hymn writer himself, Whitefield did edit an influential hymnbook. He also gave great impetus to the Welsh revival, which thrived on fervent hymn singing.

William Williams

The chief of all the Welsh revival hymnists was William Williams (1717-91), who produced 800 hymns in Welsh and over a hundred in English. His greatest hymn (still existing in both languages) is "Guide me, O thou great Jehovah" (B202, M271). It is a hymn supremely representative of Welsh religious verse of his time. Its spirit, character, nature imagery, and emotional style is very much like that of Hebrew poetry. Known as "the Welsh Watts" and "the sweet singer of Wales," Williams today is little sung except for this one masterpiece. The reasons lie not only in the thorny problems of translating from the Welsh language but also in the nature of Williams's religious idiom. This idiom, though popular in Calvinistic Wales, has proved to be difficult for use elsewhere.

The greatest legacy of the Welsh to hymnody is in the realm of tunes. The appealing folklike character of these melodies, supported by strong fundamental harmonies, give them an admirable congregational quality. They provide solid evidence of a deep-rooted and vigorous singing tradition. The twentieth century has discovered the enduring qualities of such tunes as: HYFRYDOL (B11, M132, L158), CWM RHONDDA (B202, M271, L343), ST. DENIO (B32, M27, L526), EBENEZER (B340, M242, L233), LLANFYLLIN (B221, M136). [25]

John Cennick

Among the more noteworthy of the lesser lights in Whitefield's circle was John Cennick (1718-55). He was typical of many in that age whose denominational loyalty swung indecisively from one religious group to another. He first followed the Wesleys, then Whitefield but ended as minister among the Moravians. He is the author of the so-called "Wesley Graces"—"Be present at our table, Lord" and "We thank Thee, Lord, for this our food" (M518); but he is best known for the hymn "Children of the heavenly King" (M300).

---

[25]Those tunes now used from Wales, however, are primarily products of the nineteenth century (CWM RHONDDA excepted). See chap. 9, Cultural Perspectives.

Thomas Olivers

Thomas Olivers (1725-99), a Welsh shoemaker who was converted as a result of Whitefield's preaching, first became one of Whitefield's itinerant preachers. But later he switched his allegiance to the Wesleys. In hymnody he is honored for his Christianization of the thirteen articles of the Jewish Yigdal (a sort of creedal doxology), which he heard chanted to its traditional melody one Friday evening in the Great Synagogue in London. "The God of Abraham praise" (B25, L544) is the opening line of Olivers' version. It continues to be used with great effect both in England and the United States.[26]

Lady Huntingdon

A second rallying source for the Evangelical Revival centered in the person and work of Selina (1707-91), Countess of Huntingdon, a brilliant noblewoman who used her wealth and influence to sponsor itinerant preachers and patronize hymnists and musicians. She edited hymnals and even wrote tunes for use in the chapels she erected.

Edward Perronet

One of Selina's protégés for a time was a man of French Huguenot ancestry, Edward Perronet (1726-92). Though brought up in the Church of England, he worked energetically with the Wesleys for about eight years. Being somewhat volatile and strong-willed, he later disagreed with them and served for a while as a Chaplain of Lady Huntingdon. Eventually he became an independent pastor in Canterbury.

Perronet's hymnic fame rests on his masterful "All hail the power of Jesus' name" (B40, M71, L328). Often considered the grandest of all church songs on the lordship of Jesus Christ, this popular hymn is sung to three well-known tunes, MILES LANE, its first tune by the young Canterbury organist William Shrubsole (1760-1806) (B42, M73, L329); CORONATION, the oldest American hymn tune in continuous use, by the Yankee tunesmith, Oliver Holden (1765-1844); and DIADEM, a florid "Methodist tune" by the nineteenth century lay musician, James Ellor (1819-99) (B41, M72). The hymn was considerably altered by the prominent Baptist preacher, historian, and editor, John Rippon (1751-1836),[27] who is credited with adding the lines which now almost always

---

[26]More recently a complete recasting of the Yigdal in a metrical version more faithful to the Hebrew has been done through the collaboration of three American clergymen, Rabbi Max Landsberg and Unitarian ministers Newton Mann and William C. Gannett of Rochester, N.Y. Known by its opening line "Praise to the Living God" (M30), the hymn is still sung to its traditional melody, LEONI. However, the Newton-Mann version is also found with Olivers' original opening line (B25). L544 retains the greater part of Olivers' work.

[27]Rippon figures prominently in British hymnic circles because of *A Selection of Hymns from the Best Authors* . . . (London, 1787) and its sequel, *A Selection of Psalm and Hymn Tunes from the Best Authors* (London, 1791), both of which were widely used in America as well as England.

constitute the final stanza:
>O that with yonder sacred throng
>We at his feet may fall!
>We'll join the everlasting song,
>And crown him Lord of all.

Thomas Haweis

A second follower of Lady Huntingdon was Thomas Haweis (1734-1820) who served as manager of her chapels, in addition to holding his posts in the established church. Haweis was an important promoter of hymn singing and the author of a collection of hymns. He was also the assistant for a time to Martin Madan, chaplain of Lock Hospital chapel, and one of the founders of the London Missionary Society. The most musical of Lady Huntingdon's chaplains and the composer of many tunes, Haweis today is remembered mainly for the suave "Methodist tune" RICHMOND (B460, M12).

Olney Hymns

A third source of the Evangelical Revival came from within the established church itself under the robust leadership of the Olney curate, John Newton (1725-1807). The story of Newton's early profligate life as a slave trader, his miraculous conversion, and his late flowering in the Anglican ministry is one of the great romances of Christian hymnic history.

Newton is remembered today for his hymns written for the epoch making little collection *Olney Hymns* (1779), in which he collaborated with his poet friend, William Cowper (1731-1800). *Olney Hymns* was compiled (according to the custom of local hymnals prevailing at that time) for the parish church of Olney, i.e., "for the use of plain people." It envisaged the needs of the village congregation as it gathered weekly in the "Great House" for prayer and praise.

Cowper, who excelled in lyrics of personal devotion, contributed sixty-seven hymns to the book before periodic lapses into depression and insanity prevented him from continuing. With characteristic industry, Newton wrote more than four times as many hymns (281) for the book. Like Watts, Newton was a Calvinist. He wrote his best hymns with a churchly intent. On the other hand, personal experience and evangelical concern are clearly expressed in many of his hymns which are still sung today.

Cowper's hymns are illustrative of the hesitating faith of the solitary Christian. Those in use today are:
>"Sometimes a light surprises" (B221, M231)
>"God moves in a mysterious way" (B439, M215, L483)
>"O for a closer walk with God" (M268)
>"There is a fountain filled with blood" (B107, M421)

Newton's hymns express a virile confidence in God and a passionate zeal for souls. They were written to be sung in corporate worship. Those hymns for which he is remembered include:

"How sweet the name of Jesus sounds" (B464, L345, M81)
"Glorious things of thee are spoken" (M293)
("Glories of your name are spoken"—L358)
"May the grace of Christ our Savior" (M334)
"Amazing grace, how sweet the sound" (B165, L448, M92)
"Safely through another week" (M489)
"Day of judgment! Day of wonders!" (B502)

Augustus Toplady

One hymnist influenced at many points by the evangelical revival but somewhat apart from them all was Augustus Toplady (1740-78). Brought up in the established church, he was converted to Methodism but later turned Calvinist and entered the Anglican ministry as one of the earliest members of the Evangelical Party (along with John Newton, Thomas Haweis, and others).

Toplady's vituperative theological battles with the Wesleys is one of the less-than-edifying episodes in British hymnic history;[28] but fortunately most of that controversy is now forgotten and the memorable residue is the world-famous hymn "Rock of Ages, cleft for me" (B163, M120, L327). In spite of some confusing images, this hymn continues to have great power; for it voices a universal human need—the need for confessing sin and receiving God's forgiveness.

John Fawcett

A Baptist contemporary of Toplady was John Fawcett (1740-1817), whose fidelity to his struggling church at Wainsgate in spite of opportunities to leave for more secure positions in London and Bristol is of special romantic interest. Greatly impressed by Whitefield's preaching, Fawcett was connected for a while with the Methodists. However, he was ordained into the Baptist ministry and thereafter spent his life as a clergyman and in educating others for the ministry. Fawcett is remembered for two hymns of parting: "Blest be the tie that binds" (B256, M306, L370) and "Lord, dismiss us with thy blessing" (M165, L259). Despite the fact that the latter hymn is more precisely a dismissal hymn, the former is just as frequently used at the end of worship. Together they bring lasting recognition to a dissenting minister who, during his lifetime, sought little of it.

---

[28]See chap. 4, The Hymn and Theology.

Anonymous Hymns

Several of the hymnic masterpieces of this revival period were produced anonymously. Among these, the following are classics:

"Come, thou Almighty King" (B2, M3, L522)

"Praise the Lord! ye (O) heavens adore him" (B11, M42, L540)

"How firm a foundation" (B383, M48, L507)

The tunes to which these three hymns are set furnish a cross section of the typical musical sources for hymnody during the eighteenth-century revival period. "Come thou almighty King" is now usually found with ITALIAN HYMN, by Felice de Giardini (1716-96), Italian singer and violinist. Befriended by Lady Huntingdon, Giardini wrote several tunes for the famous Lock Hospital Collection, compiled by Martin Madan (1726-90);[29] but only this tune from that collection has survived. HYFRYDOL, often found with "Praise the Lord, ye heavens adore him," is a Welsh tune composed about 1830 by Roland Hugh Pritchard (1811-87), a prominent Welsh amateur musician. Welsh tunes possess that singable quality which render them durable under hard use. FOUNDATION, sung to "How firm a foundation," is an anonymous American tune, representative of a rich shape-note tradition which matched folk melodies to scores of hymns from the Evangelical Revival.[30]

The Romantic Flood

It was Charles Wesley who paved the way for bringing the hymn into the domain of true poetry. Much of what he wrote was rhymed dogma for teaching converts. But often Wesley's muse took wings for he was blessed with the natural gifts of a poet as well as trained in the disciplines of eighteenth-century literary expression. Outside of Methodism, William Cowper was the poet of the Evangelical Revival. His sensitive gifts were brought to bear on the deep personal aspects of the Christian faith.

But the full acceptance of poetic emotion into hymnic expression had to await the flowing of that greater stream in English literature known as the Romantic Movement. It broke over England just before the turn into the nineteenth century with such inspired works as the *Lyrical Ballads* (1798) of William Wordsworth, *Childe Harold* (1812) of Lord Byron and similar masterpieces by the "Romantics"—Scott, Coleridge, Southey, Shelley, and Keats.

Reginald Heber

The three principal characteristics of the "romantic" hymn writers are lyric expression of emotion, imaginative description of natural beauty, and a

---

[29]Madan is probably the alterer of the hymn "Hail, thou once despised Jesus" (M454).
[30]Concerning American shape-note hymnody, see chap. 8, American Traditions.

careful regard for elegance of form. These became the marks of English hymnody through the work of two important men: Bishop Reginald Heber of the established church and James Montgomery, a layman connected with the Moravians and Methodists as well as the Anglicans.

Bishop Heber (1783-1826) led the way to the "literary" hymn by attempting to compile a national church hymnal which was to be made up of contributions from Southey, Scott, and the other romantic poets. His plan never matured. However, up until his untimely death in India, Heber had gathered over a hundred hymns, more than half being his own. These were published posthumously in 1827. The three distinguishing characteristics of this collection were: (1) its hymns were arranged in the order of the Christian year; (2) they were emotionally sensitive, albeit restrained in feeling; and (3) they brought English hymnody into the mainstream of the Romantic Movement in literature.

These three characteristics are marks of a significant stage in the evolution of the English hymn and are aptly demonstrated by Heber's own hymns. First, his "Brightest and best of the stars (sons) of the morning" (L84, M400) (for Epiphany), "The Son of God goes forth to war" (L183, M419) (for St. Stephen's Day, December 26), and "Bread of the world in mercy broken" (M320, 322, 323) (for communion) show his concern to make hymns fit the various emphases of the Prayer Book and the ecclesiastical year. Second, as evidence of his concern for sober restraint his "Holy, Holy, Holy" (B1, M26, L165) praises, not the intimate God of the mystics, nor the fearful God of the Calvinists, but the Lord "Perfect in power, in love and purity." Third, his "God that madest earth and heaven" (M497; "God, who made the earth and heaven," L281) and "From Greenland's icy mountains" (the first real missionary hymn after Watts's "Jesus shall reign") beautifully exhibit his romantic use of the imagery of nature as background for hymnic thought.

But the essence of Heber's work is pointed out by Erik Routley in the following quotation taken from the preface to Heber's first hymn collection (1811):

"No fulsome or indecorous language has been knowingly adopted; no erotic addresses to him whom no unclean lips can approach; no allegories, ill understood and worse applied.[31]

James Montgomery

James Montgomery (1771-1854), journalist of Scottish Moravian background, would not be considered a greater poet than many of his hymn-writing contemporaries. However, he seemed to have possessed the gift of writing religious verse which expresses the inner life in forms of beauty suitable

[31]Quoted in Erik Routley, *Hymns and Human Life* (London: John Murray, 1952), p. 131.

for the corporate worship of ordinary Christians. Consequently Montgomery's hymns continue to wear well. Their number and current usability demonstrate his claim to being "the greatest of Christian lay hymnwriters."[32] His hymns sung today include:

"Prayer is the soul's sincere desire" (B400, M252)
"Go to dark Gethsemane" (B112, M434, L109)
"Angels from the realms of glory" (B87, M382, L50)
"Stand up and bless the Lord" (B26, M16)
"Hail to the Lord's Anointed" (M359, L87)
"God is my strong salvation" (B343, M211)
"Be known to us in breaking bread" (M313)
"In the hour of trial" (M237, L106)

These hymns possess something of the enthusiasm and subjectivity of the Wesleys combined with the churchliness and objectivity of Watts. Not only have such qualities contributed to the continuous use of Montgomery's hymns, but one scholar thinks they entitle him to be called "the typical English hymn-writer"[33] of the nineteenth century.

These two creative hymnists, Heber and Montgomery, each representing two of its principal streams, moved nineteenth-century British hymnody on its triumphant way. Following Watts, Heber was a continuing fountainhead of the churchly stream in hymnody. On the other hand Montgomery followed Wesley, feeding the evangelical stream with his hymns of revival and personal devotion.

The Evangelical Stream

The pioneering work of Heber, though seminal for the onrush of liturgical hymnody soon to come within Anglicanism, was undertaken in the midst of an evangelical hymnody that was already at high tide. Appearing first among the independents, the evangelical hymn, emphasizing individual experience, became so popular that it forced its way gradually into established church use as well. In the early decades of the nineteenth century, therefore, there is no strong line of demarcation between Anglicans and Dissenters insofar as the hymns they produced are concerned.

It has already been noted that the Wesleys lived and died as ministers of the Church of England and that both Cowper and Toplady wrote their hymns of individual piety in connection with that church. It was not long before scores of clergymen (Anglican and Dissenting) and not a few lay persons were also writing hymns of personal devotion. Some of the Oxford Movement leaders produced a high churchly hymnody, and some went to the Roman Catholic

---

[32] *Ibid.*, p. 124.
[33] *Ibid.*, p. 125.

Church. Among these were some who gave expression to deeply felt personal emotions, making their hymns indistinguishable from those of the Evangelicals. From a long list of hymnists representing widely differing theological backgrounds these must be mentioned for their expressions of personal experience:

Clergy

William Hiley Bathurst (1796-1877)
   "O for a faith that will not shrink" (B390, M142)
John Ernest Bode (1816-74)
   "O Jesus, I have promised" (B365, M164, L503)
Horatius Bonar (1808-89)
   "I heard the voice of Jesus say" (M117, L497)
   "No, not despairingly" (B173)
   "I bless the Christ of God" (B286)
   "Fill thou my life, O Lord my God" (B460)
   "Here, O my Lord, I see thee" (M326, L211)
George Croly (1780-1860)
   "Spirit of God, descend upon my heart" (B132, M138, L486)
Frederick William Faber (1814-63)
   "There's a wideness in God's mercy" (B171, M69, L290)
   "My God, how wonderful thou art" (L524)
   "Faith of our fathers, living still" (B143, M151, L500)
Edwin Hatch (1835-89)
   "Breathe on me, Breath of God" (B317, M133, L488)
Thomas Kelly (1769-1854)
   "Look, ye saints (oh, look)! The sight is glorious" (B121, M453, L156)
   "The head that once was crowned with thorns" (B125, M458, L173)
Henry Francis Lyte (1793-1847)
   "Abide with me" (B217, M289, L272)
   "Praise, my soul, the King of heaven" (B8, M66, L549)
   "God of mercy, God of grace" (B297)
   "Jesus, I my cross have taken" (M251)
John Marriott (1780-1825)
   "Thou whose almighty word" (B303, M480)
George Matheson (1842-1906)
   "O love that wilt not let me go" (B368, M234, L324)
   "Make me a captive, Lord" (M184)
John Henry Newman (1801-90)
   "Lead, kindly light" (M272)

Lay Persons

Sarah Flower Adams (1805-48)
"Nearer, my God, to thee" (B333, M263)
Cecil Frances Alexander (1818-95)
"Jesus calls us o'er the tumult" (B367, M107, L494)
"All things bright and beautiful" (M34)
"There is a green hill far away" (M414, L114)
Anonymous
"Savior, like a shepherd lead us" (B213, M121, L481)
John Bowring (1792-1872)
"In the cross of Christ I glory" (B70, M416, L104)
"God is love, his mercy brightens" (B36, M63)
"Watchman, tell us of the night" (M358)
Elizabeth Cecilia Clephane (1830-69)
"Beneath the cross of Jesus" (B360, M417, L107)
James Edmeston (1791-1867)
"Savior, breathe an evening blessing" (M496)
Charlotte Elliott (1789-1871)
"Just as I am, without one plea" (B186, M119, L296)
Arabella Katherine Hankey (1834-1911)
"I love to tell the story" (B461, M149, L390)
Frances Ridley Havergal (1836-79)
"Take my life and let it (that I may) be consecrated'" (B373, M187, L406)
"Like a river glorious" (B208)
"Lord, speak to me (us) that I (we) may speak" (B276, M195, L403)
"I gave my life for thee" (B417)
"Truehearted, wholehearted" (M179)
Jane Eliza Leeson (1807-82)
"Savior, teach me day by day" (B291, M162)
Thomas Moore (1779-1852)
"Come, ye disconsolate" (B211, M103)
Anna Laetitia Waring (1803-1910)
"In heavenly love abiding" (B204)

The Churchly Stream

Up until the early years of the nineteenth century hymn singing was not an integral part of the official Service Orders for the worship of the Church of England. Archbishop Cranmer at the time of the English Reformation dispensed with hymns altogether.[34] His rubrics for the Book of Common

---

[34]The one exception was the *Veni, Creator Spiritus.*

Prayer, insofar as music was concerned, provided only for canticles, psalms, and anthems.

Actually, however, the singing of hymns was allowed in public worship as a result of the impact of the hymnic giants, Watts and Wesley. Through a liberal interpretation of psalmody, Watts's Christianized psalms were admitted. It was then only one mere step from the use of his free psalm paraphrases to his true hymns, especially since these latter verses were liberally laced with Scripture. Moreover, the Methodist hymnic cause functioned as a "fifth column," so to speak, from within the church itself. The Wesleys remained clergymen of the established church to the end of their lives, and their revival enthusiasm was shared by other ordained ministers of that church. These clergymen constituted a lively Evangelical wing, (including George Whitefield, Martin Madan, John Newton, Augustus Toplady, Roland Hill, and others), in which hymn singing was most welcome.

Even though hymns were officially proscribed in the public worship of the church, others factors encouraged their use. For instance paraliturgical services in which hymn singing was fostered sprang up within the established church. The *Olney Hymns* were intended by Newton and Cowper for prayer meetings during the week in the Olney manor house rather than for Morning and Evening Prayer on Sunday in the parish church. The chapels of charity hospitals were also centers of hymnic activity.[35] And the early Methodist meetings, regardless of where they were held, were always considered extraliturgical services of the church.

Many Anglicans, therefore, were gradually won over to this great interest in hymns. In the first decades of the nineteenth century numerous individuals made and published collections of hymns for use in the established churches.

The Oxford Movement

The invasion of the evangelical type of hymn into established usage caused considerable alarm among many leaders. Some sought to counteract the trend by seeking acceptable antidotes in a more liturgical type of hymn. Guided by the ideals of the Oxford Movement, hymnists soon began to write lyrics for the various emphases of the Christian year, as adjuncts to the Book of Common Prayer.

The Oxford Movement[36] was a High Church school of thought which sought to restore the church to the ancient glory of those times when it reigned

---

[35]The Lock Hospital and the Foundling Hospital were two of the most prominent charity institutions in whose chapels hymn-singing was not only allowed, but for which now-famous collections of hymns were published. See, for example, the source of "Praise the Lord! ye heavens adore him" (B11, M42).

[36]Erik Routley suggests the movement should be called the London Movement because it was there that much of the early action centered. See his *A Short History of English Church Music* (London: Mowbray's, 1977), p. 55.

supreme in all matters temporal and spiritual.

John Keble and John Henry Newman, two of the leaders of the movement, felt that the drastic severing with the past which the Reformation had appeared to effect, had cut the English Church off from many valuable aids to worship. They believed that the Anglican Church was not Protestant but rather a part of the Holy Catholic Church. Therefore, in an attempt to restore liturgical continuity with past centuries, they sought to recover some of the lost treasures of the Breviaries and Service Books of the ancient Greek and Latin churches. It was under the impetus of this Oxford Movement,[37] with its Romantic reverence for history, that Greek, Latin, and even German hymns in translation entered the mainstream of English hymnody.[38]

But the Oxford Reformers, inspired by Heber's work and led by Keble, also began to write original hymns. Soon a stream of liturgical hymnody was being produced by clergymen of the established church and by members of their families. The list of these High Churchly hymnists is long and impressive.

Clergy

Henry Alford (1810-71)
"Come, ye thankful people, come" (B233, M522) (harvest and thanksgiving)
"We walk by faith and not by sight" (B357) (Feast of St. Thomas)
"Ten thousand times ten thousand" (processional for saints' days)
Henry Williams Baker (1821-77)
"The king of love my Shepherd is" (B215, M67, L456)
"O God of love, O King of peace" (L414) (in times of trouble)
Sabine Baring-Gould (1834-1924)
"Onward Christian soldiers" (B393, M305, L509) (processional)
"Now the day is over" (M495, L280) (evening)
John Ellerton (1826-93)
"Savior, again to thy (your) dear name we raise" (B65, M236, L262) (choir festival)
"The day Thou gavest (you gave us), Lord, is (has) ended" (M500, L274) (evening)
"Behold us Lord, a little space" (M549) (mid-day service)
William Walsham How (1823-97)
"For all the Saints who from their labors rest" (B144, M536, L174) (All Saints' Day)
"O Word of God incarnate" (B140, M372, L231) (the Scriptures)

[37]Also called the Tractarian Movement since its promoters urged their views in a series of *Tracts for the Times,* the logic of which drove many into the Roman Catholic Church.
[38]See the sections above dealing with these traditions. John Wesley should be remembered for pioneering the translation of German hymns in the eighteenth century. However, the main flow of translation from this language did not come until the nineteenth century.

"We give thee but thine own" (M181, L410) (offertory)

"O Jesus, thou art standing" (M108)

John Keble (1792-1866)

"New every morning is the love" (M499) (morning)

"Sun of my soul, thou Savior dear" (M502) (evening)

"Blest are the pure in heart" (M276) (presentation of Christ in the Temple)

Henry Hart Milman (1791-1868)

"Ride on! ride on in majesty" (M425, L121) (Palm Sunday)

John Samuel Bewley Monsell (1811-75)

"God is love, by him upholden" (M62) (first Sunday after Trintiy)

"Fight the good fight" (B394, M240) (nineteenth Sunday after Trinity)

"Light of the world, we hail thee" (M398) (sixth Sunday after Epiphany)

"Sing to the Lord of harvest" (B232, L412) (harvest and thanksgiving)

Edward Hayes Plumptre (182-91)

"Rejoice, ye pure in heart" (B28, M233) (choir festival)

Thomas Benson Pollock (1836-96)

"Jesus, with thy Church abide" (B241, M311) (litany)

Godfrey Thring (1823-1903)

"Crown him with many crowns" (B52, M455, L170) (coronation)
(stanza beginning "Crown him the Lord of life, only")

Walter Chalmers Smith (1824-1908)

"Immortal, Invisible God only wise" (B32, M27, L526)

Samuel John Stone (1839-1900)

"The Church's one foundation" (B236, M297, L369) (the creed)

Christopher Wordsworth (1807-1885)

"O day of rest and gladness" (M488, L251) (Sunday)

"Lord of heaven and earth and sea" (M523) (Harvest and thanksgiving)

"Alleluia! Alleluia! hearts to heaven" (B117) (Easter)

Lay Persons

Matthew Bridges (1800-94)

"Crown him with many crowns" (B52, M455, L170) (coronation)

William Chatterton Dix (1837-98)

"As with gladness men of old" (M397, L82) (Epiphany)

Robert Grant (1779-1838)

"O worship the King" (B30, M473, L548) (divine service)

Dorothy Frances Gurney (1858-1932)

"O perfect love, all human thought transcending" (B395, M333, L287) (Wedding)

Folliett Sandford Pierpoint (1835-1917)

"For the beauty of the earth" (B54, M35, L561) (communion)
William Whiting (1825-78)
"Eternal Father, strong to save" (M538, L467) (mariners)

Hymns Ancient and Modern

Aside from the above individual hymnic achievements, possibly the greatest legacy from the Oxford Movement was the publication of *Hymns Ancient and Modern* (1859-60). In the four decades prior to this important event there was feverish activity in the production of individual hymnals for parochial use.[39] The sheer number of these collections prevented any one of them from being successful. Recognizing the lack of unanimity in the church's hymnic uses, certain leaders, the chief among them being Henry W. Baker, made a united effort to compile one book which would command general confidence. An appeal was made to the clergy and to their publishers to withdraw their individual collections and to support this new combined venture. The result was *Hymns Ancient and Modern* which experienced immediate and overwhelming success, becoming possibly the most popular English hymnal ever published.

This great collection, which has subsequently gone through many editions,[40] in its blending of the old and the new set a standard to which most later responsible hymnals have adhered. In *Hymns Ancient and Modern* a great many of the hymns listed above first appeared; in addition it contained the finest work of those leaders who were translators from the Latin, Greek, and German languages.[41]

The musical character of this pivotal collection also contributed to its popularity. Under the editorship of William H. Monk, many composers contributed. They created a type of hymn tune which, whatever may be its artistic merits, satisfied the musical longing of the churchgoers of the last four decades of the nineteenth century. Consequently, this book (including its later editions) is the original source for such well-known Victorian tunes as:

John Bacchus Dykes (1823-76)
NICAEA (B1, M26, L165),
MELITA (M538, L294)
DOMINUS REGIT ME (B215, M67)
VOX DILECTI (M117)

---

[39]See John Julian, *Dictionary of Hymnology* (London: John Murray, 1907), pp. 334-38 for the listings of over one hundred hymnals compiled in this period.

[40]The history of the editions of this influential book can be read in W. K. Lowther-Clarke, *A Hundred Years of Hymns Ancient and Modern* (London: Clowes, 1960).

[41]See above under Greek, Latin, and German hymnody concerning the contributions of such outstanding translators as Edward Caswall, John M. Neale, Jane Borthwick, Catherine Winkworth, and others.

William H. Monk (1823-89)
  EVENTIDE (B217, M289, L272)
  DIX (B54, M35, L82)
Henry W. Baker (1821-77)
  STEPHANOS (M99, L460)
Joseph Barnby (1838-96)
  LAUDES DOMINI (B44, M91, L546)
These Victorians influenced and were imitated by many other late nineteenth-century writers including:
  S. S. Wesley (1810-76)—AURELIA (B236, M297, L197)
  Henry Smart (1813-79—REGENT SQUARE (B87, M382, L50)
  John Goss (1800-80)—LAUDA ANIMA (B502, M18, L549)
  John Stainer (1840-1901)—ALL FOR JESUS (B485)
  Arthur Sullivan (1842-1900)—ST. EDMUND (B307, M188)
    ST. GERTRUDE (B393, M305, L509)
  Alexander Ewing (1830-95)—EWING (M303)
Hymns Ancient and Modern also established the practice of writing tunes for specific texts and publishing both texts and tunes together rather than in separate collections, which had been the earlier practice till that time. This new practice has resulted in many lasting text-tune marriages such as:
  LAUDES DOMINI for "When morning gilds the skies"
    (B44, L546, M91)
  MELITA for "Eternal Father, strong to save" (L467, M538)
  NICAEA for "Holy, Holy, Holy" (B1, M26, L165)
As its title indicates, *Hymns Ancient and Modern* also dipped back into the past to include the hymns of those associated with the "dissent" of the Nonconformists and the "enthusiasm" of the Methodists. It therefore brought together into one collection the two mainstreams of hymnody—the evangelical and the churchly—which had been running parallel in English religious life since the beginning of the century. With its initial publication in 1861, hymns reached the accepted and respected position which they still hold today. Later hymnals, even though admitting newer hymns, continued to reflect the character, aims, and ideals of *Hymns Ancient and Modern*. The contents of this hymnal therefore represent the mainstream of English hymnody throughout the remainder of the nineteenth century.

Carols

Another important development in the latter part of the nineteenth century was the revival of carols and their restoration to a place in the congregation's repertoire. As an important by-product of the Oxford Movement and as a

---

[42]For a collected edition of all of Barnby's tunes, see *Hymn-Tunes by Joseph Barnby* (London: Novello, 1897). Around 1900 Novello also published the collected tunes of Dykes, Stainer, and Sullivan.

result of the general thrust toward historical research fostered by the Romantic Movement, carols from both medieval written sources and oral traditions were revived, edited, and made more generally known.

John Mason Neale and Thomas Helmore (1811-90) were not only leaders in the revival of medieval hymnody and plainsong, but they were also pioneers in adapting carols from certain ancient sources, notably *Piae Cantiones*.[43] Other researchers, among them William Sandys, H.R. Bramley, John Stainer, and R. R. Chope, published legendary songs from the oral tradition of the West Country of England. The unearthing of these old carols also led to the composition of new ones. Carols (chiefly but not exclusively of the Christmas variety) thus began to be incorporated into the regular worship of the churches.[44]

Hymnology

The nineteenth century also marks the burgeoning of hymnological investigation on a broader scale. This was but a part of a broader scholarly enterprise associated with the dawning of the science of musicology. Again, aided and abetted by the Romantic passion for the past, the century produced several students of hymns who may be represented by four men whose work spans the century: James Montgomery (1771-1854), John Mason Neale (1818-66) Daniel Sedgwick (1814-79) and John Julian (1839-1913).

In a now famous essay prefixed to his *Christian Psalmist* (1825) Montgomery took stock of the Wattsian, the Wesleyan, and other Evangelical hymns of his day and made value judgments mainly of a literary nature. Being no mean hymn-poet himself and fired by the ideals of the Romantic Movement, he produced a perceptive critical review that ranks as the first English work in hymnology.

A generation later, championing not only a scholarly but a High Anglican theological standard, was John Mason Neale. Although known and honored first as a translator from the Greek and Latin as well as a writer of original hymns inspired by the ancient sources, Neale must also be reckoned a hymnologist. In an article entitled "English Hymnology: Its History and Prospects,"[45] he set forth, like Montgomery, his opinion concerning the merits of his predecessors in hymn-writing. Although somewhat captious in its criticisms of Watts, Wesley, and the Evangelicals (mostly on doctrinal grounds), this lengthy article remains an important one for English hymnology.

[43]Published originally in Finland, *Piae Cantiones* (1582) yielded its riches to Helmore and Neale when a rare copy was brought to England in 1853. See chap. 6, Reformation Traditions for a listing of the melodies from this source that are in current use.
[44]The fascinating story of the carol is told by Erik Routley in *The English Carol* (London: Berrie & Jenkins, 1958).
[45]Published in *The Christian Remembrancer, XVIII* (October 1849), 303ff.

Contemporary with (but quite at the opposite pole from) Neale was Sedgewick, a self-taught student and publisher of hymns who by dint of industry and perseverance became possibly the most prominent hymnologist of his time. He amassed an impressive library in the course of his work as a bookseller and became a valued consultant to the compilers of *Hymns Ancient and Modern* (1861), to Sir Roundell Palmer for his *Book of Praise* (1862), to Charles Haddon Spurgeon in *Our Own Hymnbook* (1866), and to Josiah Miller in his hymnological work, *Singers and Songs of the Church* (1869). Although he was limited in education and theological perspective, Sedgwick, through careful collection, comparison, and annotation of hymns and hymnological literature may well qualify as the real father of English hymnology.[46]

But the prince of all hymnologists came a generation later. Dr. John Julian, in compiling his monumental *Dictionary of Hymnology* (1891),[47] examined over 400,000 hymns. Enlisting the aid of over forty other historians and specialists, he accomplished a work which is still the definitive source book on the origins and history of Christian hymnody of all ages and nations although it is now in need of radical revision and updating.

Summary of Nineteenth Century

Taking into account all these major developments, nineteenth-century British hymnody can be characterized in the following ways:

I. Under the impact of Evangelical Revival, it was:

1. Intense in its expression of personal devotion

2. Enthusiastic in proclaiming the evangelical faith

3. Produced mainly by Nonconformists

4. Fostered with vigor by the evangelical wing of the established church

II. Under the impact of the Oxford Movement, British hymnody was:

1. Produced with a high churchly intent to adorn the festivals of the liturgical year and accompany the various emphases of the prayer book and catechism

2. Enriched by a recovery of the treasures in the liturgical books of the ancient Greek and Latin churches

3. Influential on the work of tune writers who composed music for specific hymn texts

4. Written by many who espoused the Roman Catholic faith

III. Under the impact of Romanticism, it was:

[46]Montgomery and Neale, though perceptive critics, did not give themselves, as did Sedgwick, to hymnology as a profession. See J. Vincent Higginson, "Daniel Sedgwick: Pioneer of English Hymnology" in *The Hymn* 4 (July 1953), 77-80.

[47]John Julian, *Dictionary of Hymnology* (London: John Murray, 1891). Revised edition with new supplement was published in 1907.

1. Written in colorful, elegant language, appealing vividly to the imagination
2. Concerned with natural beauty as a backdrop for hymnic truth
3. Receptive of the hymnic contributions of noted poets
4. Enriched by a reverence for the past, encouraging translations from ancient sources and the oral traditions (carols) as well as fostering scholarly research (hymnology)

Twentieth Century Currents

Toward the end of the nineteenth century, a rising stream of dissatisfaction with Victorian hymnody had gathered momentum. Although more recent views have encouraged a more favorable reappraisal of that period, there is ample evidence that Victorian congregational song was in need of rejuvenation.

1900-1955—Protest and Change

Insofar as music was concerned, a small start toward hymnic revival was made by a group of composers in the latter decades of the century. From Sir Hubert Parry (1848-1918), professor, author, organist, and composer came a few broadly sweeping hymn tunes like INTERCESSOR (L283) and RUSTINGTON (L408). Because Sir Charles V. Stanford (1852-1924), prominent conductor and composer, thought in expansive festival rather than congregational terms, his hymn contributions were minimal. He is remembered for ENGELBERT set now to a baptismal hymn by John B. Geyer (b. 1932) "We know that Christ is raised" (L189, E111). Like Stanford, Sir Basil Harwood (1859-1949), a cathedral and collegiate organist, wrote little for the churches; yet his THORNBURY (L77) has enjoyed some success. These tunes signaled a new trend during a period of general musical complacency. However, the 1904 edition of *Hymns Ancient and Modern,* incorporating these and other tunes in this newer musical vocabulary, failed to win popular acceptance.

At this juncture several energetic men began to challenge the conventionalities of prevailing hymn usage: Robert Bridges (1844-1930), poet laureate in succession to Alfred, Lord Tennyson; George R. Woodward (1848-1934), a learned Tractarian priest of Oxford; Percy Dearmer (1867-1936), an Anglican vicar who became professor of ecclesiastical art in King's College, London, and canon of Westminster; and Ralph Vaughan Williams (1872-1958), greatest British composer of his generation.

In 1899 Bridges prepared the *Yattendon Hymnal,*[48] which championed the restoration of old metrical psalm, chorale, and plainsong tunes. To supply suitable words for many of these, Bridges found he either had to retranslate or

[48] *Yattendon Hymnal* (Oxford: Clarendon Press, 1899).

create completely new texts. This resulted in an excellent group of hymns, including "Ah, holy Jesus" (L123, M412), "O splendor of God's glory bright" (M29) and "All my hope on God is founded" (E51). Woodward edited *Songs of Syon*[49] (1904, 1910), a much larger collection following much the same general plan of Bridges, i.e., reviving for British use the finest tunes from the Latin, Genevan, and German traditions and writing texts that could fit their unusual meters.[50]

Neither of these scholarly hymnals achieved wide use, but they paved the way for Percy Dearmer and his musical collaborator, Ralph Vaughan Williams in the publication of *The English Hymnal* (1906).[51] This hymnal was an important landmark for several reasons:[52]

1. It began with an often-quoted preface which declared the book to contain "the best hymns in the English language" and ventured the epic statement that "good taste is a moral rather than a musical issue."[53]

2. It contained, for the first time in an Anglican book, a group of hymns embracing liberal theology and the social gospel, including many that were American in origin, such as Whittier's "Immortal love, forever full" (B329, M157), Sears' "It came upon the midnight clear" (B86, L54, M390), Hosmer's " 'Thy kingdom come,' on bended knee,"[54] and Johnson's "City of God, how broad and far."[55]

3. It included newly written hymns such as Gilbert Chesterton's "O God of earth and altar" (L428, M484), Scott Holland's "Judge eternal, throned in splendor" (L418, M546), and Charles Kingsley's "From thee all skill and science flow" (M485).

4. Most memorably, it represented the first hymnic use of a large number of traditional English folk songs. Thanks to the sure editing of Vaughan Williams, many folk melodies were rescued from England's past: KINGSFOLD (B230, L391), KING'S LYNN (L178, M484), and FOREST GREEN (B309, M33). Moreover, his sure craftsmanship resulted in original tunes, including

---

[49] *Songs of Syon* (London: Schott and Co., 1904, 1910)

[50] Although he had as his musical editor Dr. Charles Wood (1866-1926), Cambridge music professor, Woodward harmonized many of the tunes himself. See, for example, PUER NOBIS NASCITUR (L36, M515). Insofar as texts are concerned he is best remembered for his earlier work with carols ("This joyful Eastertide," L149).

[51] *The English Hymnal* (London: Oxford University Press, 1904).

[52] For evaluations of *The English Hymnal* and its influence see these articles in *The Bulletin of the Hymn Society of Great Britain and Ireland* (Henceforth BHSGBI), Erik Routley, *"The English Hymnal* 1906-56," No. 75 (IV/2 Spring 1956), pp. 17-26; A. J. B. Hutchings, "The Literary Aspects of *The English Hymnal,"* No. 76 (IV/3 Summer, 1956), pp. 33-49; Cyril Taylor, *"The English Hymnal Service Book,"* No. 96 (V/8, Summer, 1962), pp. 111-18; Erik Routley, "Percy Dearmer, Hymnologist," No. 111 (VI/9, Winter, 1967), pp. 169-86.

[53] *The English Hymnal,* ix.

[54] *The Hymnal* of the Protestant Episcopal Church in the United States of America (New York: The Church Pension Fund, 1940), 391.

[55] Ibid., 386.

RANDOLPH (M540), DOWN AMPNEY (M466, L508) and SINE NOMINE (B144, L174, M74), the latter two being generally considered among the great tunes of the twentieth century.

The pioneering work of Dr. Vaughan Williams was followed by the work of a group of outstanding teachers of music, including Sir Walford Davies (1869-1941) and the Shaw brothers, Martin (1875-1958) and Geoffrey (1879-1943). Davies' style (more conventional than that of Vaughan Williams but less so than that of the Victorians) is epitomized in GOD BE IN MY HEAD (M813) and CHILDHOOD (M525). Martin Shaw, like Vaughan Williams, was versatile and uncompromising in his hymn-tune style. Along with the older composer he was musical editor of both *Songs of Praise* (1926, Enlarged ed., 1931),[56] the direct successor of *The English Hymnal,* and *The Oxford Book of Carols* (1928),[57] the carol equivalent of *The English Hymnal.*

These books contained further adaptations of early folk tunes, such as KING'S WESTON (B319, L179, M76), NOEL NOUVELET (L148, M441), and NOUS ALLONS (L541). Martin Shaw also wrote original tunes intended for unison singing in the chapel services of the public schools. His PURPOSE (B509), first appearing in *Songs of Praise* (1931) and subsequently in many public school hymnals, is a good example of his broad melodic style. His younger brother, Geoffrey Shaw, a public school musician, wrote tunes like LANGHAM (L413), a forcible melody rising to a climax on the refrain of Laurence Housman's "Father eternal, ruler of creation" (L413, M469), for which it was written.

Songs of Praise was no less fresh and zestful in its selection of texts. Percy Dearmer, its editor, continued the liberal theological policy he had established in *The English Hymnal.* In his choosing, editing, translating, and writing of hymns he boldly confronted the new mood of doubt and experimentation prevalent at that time. An example of his translation from the Latin is "Father, we praise thee (You) (L267, M504). "He who would valiant be" (B384, L498, M155), based on John Bunyan, is a good example of his adapting earlier English devotional poetry. "Book of books, our people's strength" (M370) reveals his talent as a hymnist in his own right.

Among other important hymnwriters of the early twentieth century George Wallace Briggs (1875-1959), Anglican clergyman and educator, is outstanding.[58] His "Christ is the world's true light" (B274, M408) and "Come, risen Lord" (L209, E69) are typical of his contributions to *Songs of Praise.* His "God hath spoken by his prophets" (L238, M460) was one of "Ten New

[56]*Songs of Praise* (London: Oxford University Press, 1926).

[57]*The Oxford Book of Carols* (London: Oxford University Press, 1928).

[58]For an appraisal of Briggs' contribution as hymn-poet, tune writer, and hymnologist see an obituary written by Erik Routley, *Bulletin of the Hymn Society of Great Britain and Ireland* (BHSGBI), No. 88 (IV/14, Winter 1960), pp. 245-49.

Hymns on the Bible" solicited by the Hymn Society of America and originally published in American hymnals. Cyril A. Alington (1872-1955), Anglican priest and Dean of Durham, also contributed to *Songs of Praise* "Good Christian men (friends), rejoice and sing" (B123, L144, M449).

Other writers of this period whose hymns have achieved wide use are John Oxenham, pseudonym for William A. Dunkerly (1852-1941), Congregationalist churchman and novelist, with his "In Christ there is no east or west" (B258, L359, M192, E86) and "Mid all the traffic of the ways" (M225); Clifford Bax (1886-1962), painter and man of letters, with his "Turn back, O man" (M475); Geoffrey A. Studdert-Kennedy (1883-1929), preacher and chaplain to the king, with his "Awake, awake to love and work" (B413, M190); and Jan Struther (pen name for Joyce Anstruther; 1901-1953), poetess and novelist, with her "When Stephen, full of power and grace" (B392) and "Lord of all hopefulness" (L469).

In the area of tunes, David Evans (1874-1948), Welsh Prebyterian editor of the revised *Church Hymnary* (1927),[59] brought enrichment through his harmonizations of the Celtic tunes, LLANFAIR (B115, M443), SLANE (B212), NYLAND (B204, M230, KUORTANE, L339), LLANGLOFFAN (L430), and LLANFYLLIN (B221). Eric H. Thiman (1900-1975), Congregationalist organist and professor, served in nonconformist circles the role that Martin Shaw had played in the established church. His smooth flexible style of tune writing is typified in SHERE (B286). Kenneth G. Finlay (b. 1882), Scottish shipbuilder and teacher, has composed pleasing folklike melodies such as AYRSHIRE (M157), GLENFINLAS (M791) and GARELOCHSIDE (L78). The latter two men were major contributors to *Congregational Praise* (1951),[60] which was the first collection from British nonconformity to rise above the conventionality characterizing most of the denominational hymnals in the first half of the twentieth century. *Congregational Praise* was published in the same year as *The BBC Hymn Book*[61] and one year after the release of the third complete revision of *Hymns Ancient and Modern*.[62] These collections, in their breadth of vision and balanced regard for all the main traditions, typify the state of British hymnody at mid-twentieth century.

Outstanding names connected with these hymnals include Dr. Walter K. Stanton (1891-1978), editor-in-chief of *The BBC Hymn Book* and composer of CANNOCK (L201); the Rev. Cyril V. Taylor (b. 1907), former warden of the Royal School of Church Music and composer of SHELDONIAN (L160) and

[59] *Church Hymnary Revised* (London: Oxford University Press, 1927).

[60] *Congregational Praise* (London: Independent Press, 1951).

[61] *The BBC Hymn Book* (London: Oxford University Press, 1951). An excellent critical review of this book is written by Leonard Blake, BHSGBI No. 58 (III/1, December, 1951), pp. 2-11.

[62] *Hymns Ancient and Modern Revised* (London: William Clowes & Sons, Ltd. 1950). See Erik Routley's appraisal of this book in BHSGBI No. 51 (II/10, April, 1950), pp. 145-59.

ABBOT'S LEIGH (his finest tune); and Sir Sydney H. Nicholson (1875-1947), the leading contributor of new tunes to *Hymns Ancient and Modern* (1950). That collection's content in both text and tune can be fairly represented by Nicholson's CRUCIFER, set to "Lift high the cross" by G. W. Kitchin (1827-1912) and M. R. Newbolt (1874-1956) (L377).

The British hymnic stream flowed deep and wide in the period 1900-1955. Periodically fed by fresh and sometimes turbulent springs (*English Hymnal*, 1906, *Songs of Praise*, 1926, and *Hymns Ancient and Modern Revised*, 1950), it ran in full force near mid-century. Aided by subtle cross currents springing from the ecumenical movement, the Anglican main course exerted a favorable pressure on nonconformist hymnody resulting in a general change of taste.

1955-1970—Innovation and Crisis

After 1955 British hymnody suddenly ran into troubled waters. They were stirred in part by the emergence of the twentieth-century Church Light Music Group. Founded by Geoffrey Beaumont (1905-71), who in 1956 published the *Twentieth-Century Folk Mass* (sometimes called the "Jazz Mass"), this group of lay musicians produced tunes in various secular styles in the hope of popularizing the singing of familiar hymns for the evangelizing of youth.[63] Causing a shock wave in some church music circles, Beaumont deliberately wrote in the "big tune" style of the Broadway musical and succeeded in having two of his best tunes published in a standard English hymnal—*The Baptist Hymn Book* (1962).[64] This hymnal is a comprehensive and eclectic collection after the manner of *Congregational Praise,* but its chief claim to distinction may be its inclusion of Beaumont's CHESTERTON to H. W. Baker's "Lord, thy word abideth" and his GRACIAS to "Now thank we all our God" (Rinkart-Winkworth).

Other tune writers of this movement have continued to compose music reminiscent of the popular stage songs of the 1920's and 1930's, but their creative output has not successfully included innovative texts commensurate with their unconventional tunes. Church leaders regard the style of this group as "old hat," patronizing, and too compromising to accomplish its goal of reaching the unchurched.

Another violent disturbance in the hymnic stream of the 1960's was caused by Sydney Carter (b. 1915), journalist and songwriter. Carter, a master in the use of modern satire, has written informal texts which are set to folk melodies

---

[63]The work of this group may be studied in three collections, all published in London by Josef Weinberger, Ltd.: *Eleven Hymn Tunes by the Rev. Geoffrey Beaumont* (1957), *Thirty 20th Century Hymn Tunes* (1960), and *More 20th Century Hymn Tunes* (1962).
[64]*The Baptist Hymn Book* (London: Psalms and Hymns Trust, 1962). See review by Caryl Micklem. BHSGBI No. 95 (V/7, Spring, 1962), pp. 118-20.

or to folklike melodies newly composed.[65] One of his most widely known songs, "The Lord of the dance" (set to the early American Shaker tune, SIMPLE GIFTS), is written in the style of a carol, reminiscent of the medieval carol, "Tomorrow shall be my dancing day."[66]

Carter is the patron saint of a modern school of conversational style hymnody which includes, among others, Malcolm Stewart (b. 1926). Stewart's songs, lacking Carter's irony and satire, are based mainly on narratives and incidents from the Bible sensitively arranged in an easy folk style.[67] The work of the "Light" music group and the "folk" hymnody of Carter and his followers represent deviations from the main stream of British hymnody. However, that current itself was soon to flow more deeply and widely again.

The coming tide was not yet evident in *The Anglican Hymnbook* (1965).[68] This hymnal represented a conservative reaction, ignoring much in the mainline contemporary styles and omitting altogether the new "pop" styles in favor of the older schools of the eighteenth-century Evangelicals and the nineteenth-century Victorians. Though not presenting any development textwise beyond *Hymns Ancient and Modern Revised,* this hymnal was slightly more adventurous in its tunes.

Textually, the diverging currents of "light" and "pop" hymns were reducing the mainstream of hymnody to a trickle. But it did not run completely dry. One of the most active of mainstream hymnists after 1950 was the Congregational minister, Albert F. Bayly (b. 1901), who wrote his first hymns at the close of World War II and subsequently has published over a hundred.[69] Bayly's work, while imaginatively relating the church's worship to the issues of contemporary life, is thoroughly theological and basically conservative in language. After years of local use, his hymns have achieved major representation in hymnals throughout the world.

Bayly's best-known hymn in the United States is "Lord, whose love in

---

[65]Carter's "Folk" hymns are to be found in standard hymnals published after 1970. Roman Catholics have been particularly hospitable to him; see *New Catholic Hymnal* (1971), 99 and *Praise the Lord!* (1972), 92. He is also well represented in the hymnal supplements.

[66]*Oxford Book of Carols* (London: Oxford University Press, 1928), p. 71. His most controversial song is "Friday Morning," the words of which are imaginatively put in the mouth of one of the thieves crucified with Jesus. See *Songs of Sydney Carter in the Present Tense 2* (London: Galliard, Ltd. and New York: Galaxy Music Corporation, 1969), pp. 6-7. The inclusion of this song in the *Book of Worship for United States Forces* (1974) caused a considerable furor. See *The Hymn* 27/4 (October 1976), pp. 134-35.

[67]See *Gospel Song Book* introduced by Sydney Carter (London: Geoffrey Chapman, 1970) also published as *Now Songs* (Nashville: Abingdon Press, n.d.).

[68]*Anglican Hymn Book* (London: Church Book Room Ltd., 1965). The title is somewhat misleading in that it represents only the evangelical side of the Anglican communion.

[69]Bayly has published four booklets of hymns: *Rejoice, O People* (1950), *Again I Say Rejoice* (1967), *Rejoice Always* (1971), and *Rejoice in God* (1977) available from the author at 3 Church Lane, Springfield, Chelmsford, Essex. CM1 55F, England.

(through) humble service'' (L423, M479).[70] Other hymns dealing with social and ecological concerns are "Lord, save your world" (L420), "Lord of all good, our gifts we bring" (L411) and "Praise and thanksgiving" (L409). Hymnal supplements recently released in England contain many of Bayly's hymns, testifying to their usefulness as contemporary utterances combined with a true classic poise.

Another promising post-1950 hymnist was Donald W. Hughes (1911-67), headmaster of a boy's school. His creative work was cut short by an untimely death. Like Bayly, he was a master of the art of combining the timeless with the timely. His craft is evident in "Beyond the mist and doubt" (E64). Another who claims attention in this period is Timothy Rees (1874-1939), who wrote "God of love and truth and beauty" (set to the modern tune CAROLYN by Herbert Murrill in E79).

Post-1970—Revival and Opportunity

"New English Renaissance"[71] is the term applied to a group of writers and composers whose work appeared in several new supplemental hymnals during the six-year period—1969-75. These hymnal supplements are vivid evidence of the rapidity of style change in recent British hymnody. They also indicate the concern on the part of publishers to keep parent books in use while exploring for new treasures during an era characterized by trial and experimentation. Each major denomination now has at least one hymnal supplement.[72]

Hymns and Songs is important as the earliest of these books to include a sizable selection of the hymns of Frederick Pratt Green (b. 1903). Pratt Green[73] is a Methodist clergyman and playwright who turned to hymn writing late in his career. With the exception of *English Praise*, all the supplements include some of his hymns, as do most of the standard hymnals produced after 1970. His dynamic hymn on the Trinity, "Rejoice with us in God the Trinity" (E101)

[70]The words were originally published in "Seven New Social Welfare Hymns," 1961 by the Hymn Society of America.

[71]See Erik Routley, "Hymn Writers of the New English Renaissance" in *The Hymn* 28, 1 (January, 1977), pp. 6-10.

[72]*100 Hymns for Today* (London: William Clowes and Sons, Ltd., 1969) is a supplement to *Hymns Ancient and Modern Revised. English Praise* (London: Oxford University Press, 1975) is a supplement to *The English Hymnal* (Revised edition in 1933).

Hymns and Songs (London: Methodist Publishing House, 1969) is a supplement to *The Methodist Hymn Book* (1933).

Praise for Today (London: Psalms and Hymns Trust, 1974) is a supplement to the *Baptist Hymn Book* (1962).

The United Reform Church is a merger of the Presbyterian and Congregationalists in England. Therefore *New Church Praise* (Edinburgh: The Saint Andrew Press, 1975) is a supplement both to *The Church Hymnary Revised* (1973) and *Congregational Praise* (1951).

[73]Though he has written many other hymns, *26 Hymns* (London: Epworth Press, 1971) is Pratt Green's first published collection. See Erik Routley's review in BHSGBI No. 123 (VII/9, Jan. 1972), pp. 180-85. See also *The Hymn*, July 1979, pp. 154-58.

and two hymns on Christ's life and work, "Christ is the world's light" (E66) and "Glorious the day" (E63) are among his finest expressions. In his direct and unaffected way he has also supplied excellent new hymns for:

Sunday—"The first day of the week" (L246)

Easter—"This joyful Eastertide" (B124)

Thanksgiving—"For the fruit of all creation" (L563)

Musicians—"When in our music God is glorified" (L555)[74]

Pratt Green also has the distinction of having written "A Hymn for the Nation" that was authorized for use in the churches at the 1977 observance of the jubilee of Queen Elizabeth II's accession to the British throne.[75]

Another important hymnist on the contemporary scene is Fred Kaan (b. 1929). Kaan is Dutch by birth but has spent a good part of his career as a United Reform minister in England and has written his hymns in English.[76] He is a world Christian, a caring citizen of the modern city, and a passionate advocate of social action. These ideas permeate his hymns.[77] Combining inspiration with audacity, he often reveals a deft use of metaphor and double meaning.

Often-published Kaan hymns include:

For worship—"Praise the Lord with joyful cry" (E100)

For Communion—"As we break the bread" (E60) and

"Now let us from this table rise" (E85)

On God's Word—"God who spoke in the beginning" (E80)

On love and service—"Lord, as we rise to leave this shell of worship"

(E87)

The major contributor of new texts to *New Church Praise*[78] is Brian Wren (b. 1936), another minister of the United Reform Church. He works with that church's Committee on World Development. Erik Routley describes Wren as

[74]Other hymns by Pratt Green may be found at B319, L360, L433, E75, and E57 (a translation from Dietrich Bonhoeffer). See also p. 260 below.

[75]See Erik Routley, "The Two Jubilee Hymns" in *The Hymn* 28, 3 (July, 1977), pp. 151-52.

[76]For ten years Kaan worked as an executive secretary at the World Alliance of Reformed Churches, with headquarters in the ecumenical center at Geneva, Switzerland. In 1978 he returned to England in an executive position with the United Reform Church.

[77]Most of Kaan's hymns are published in three volumes: *Pilgrim's Praise* (London: Galliard, 1972); *Break not the Circle* with tunes by Doreen Potter (Carol Stream, IL: Agape, 1975); and *Worship the Lord* with Canada's Walter Farquharson (Oakville, ONT.: Harmuse Publications, 1977). He is also an accomplished translator of hymns from the Swedish language. See *Songs and Hymns from Sweden* (London: Stainer and Bell, Ltd., 1976). For a personal account of his hymn writing see "Saturday Night and Sunday Morning," in *The Hymn* 27, 4 (October 1976), pp. 100-108. See also p. 263 below.

[78]See the reviews of this fine supplement by Norman P. Goldhawk in BHSGBI 134 (November 1975), 125-30 and by Carlton Young in *The Hymn* 28, (January 1977), 28-30.

Isaac Watts

being "as theological as Pratt Green, and often as abrasive as Kaan."[79] His command of an exhilarating but unaffected contemporary idiom is evident in hymns such as:

"Thank you, Lord, for water, soil and air" (on ecology, E78)

"Christ, upon the mountain peak" (on the transfiguration, E67)

"Christ is alive!" (the resurrection and reign of Christ, L363, E68)

"I come with joy to meet my Lord" (the Lord's Supper, E84)

The revival in writing hymn texts has been a powerful stimulus also for the composition of new tunes during the 1965-75 decade. Among those who have been most active in this field are John Wilson (b. 1905), who has written LAUDS[80] for Brian Wren's "There's a spirit in the air" and a fine tune (unfortunately unnamed) for Pratt Green's "Rejoice with us in God the Trinity";[81] John Gardner (b. 1917), ILFRACOMBE[82] for Pratt Green's "Glorious the day when Christ was born" (E63) and Erik Routley[83] (b. 1917), WOODBURY (E30), MAPLE GROVE (E38), MAIDEN WAY (E64) for Donald Hughes' "Beyond the mist and doubt," ALTHORP (E78) for Brian Wren's "Thank you, Lord, for water, soil and air," CORBRIDGE (E80) for Fred Kaan's "God, who spoke in the beginning," and WANSBECK (E87) for Kaan's "Lord, as we rise."

General characteristics to be found in the work of these tune writers are:

1. Well constructed tunes, for unison singing, basically diatonic, sometimes folklike, often spare and lean in style

2. Rhythm that is free, flexible, and written without meter signature

3. Harmony which is uncomplicated and strong, avoiding chromaticism, sometimes modal, often minor

Malcolm Williamson (b. 1931), the Master of the Queen's Music, stands apart from these composers as something of a contradiction. He is an accomplished composer who is at home in many varieties of musical style. Yet he deliberately writes hymn tunes in a simplistic "pop" idiom that comes close to that of the Twentieth-Century Church Light Music Group. Williamson is astute enough to put into his tunes enough musical wit—some unconventional and yet logical melodic interval, some fresh rhythmic turn, some change of meter or mode—to preserve them from banality or sentimentality. Unlike

---

[79]Erik Routley, "Hymn-Writers of the New English Renaissance" in *The Hymn* 28 (January 1977), 6-10. Wren has written two helpful articles giving encouragement to would-be hymnwriters: "Making Your Own Hymn" in BHSGBI 142 (May 1978), 21-24 and "Genesis of a Hymn" in BHSGBI 143 (September 1978), 39-45.

[80]*New Church Praise*, 98.

[81]F. Pratt Green, *26 Hymns*, 9.

[82]*New Church Praise*, 28.

[83]A collection of fifteen of Routley's tunes together with interesting notes on the circumstances of their creation, written by the composer, are published in *Eternal Light* (New York: Carl Fischer, 1971).

other composers, he has no particular interest in setting new texts. Rather he chooses those of the eighteenth-century evangelicals (Watts, Wesley, Kelly), nineteenth-century Victorians (Ellerton, Wordsworth, Keble), and others from the various strands of traditional hymnody.[84] Three tunes in his offhand style are OBEDIENCE (E31), LIFE OF CHRIST (E37), and MERCER STREET (E108).

Hymological Activity

The flood of activity in twentieth-century hymnody has been accompanied by a commensurate growth in the work of hymnologists. Nowhere is this more evident than in the scholarly service rendered by the compilers of the numerous hymnal companions which have appeared in recent years. Two important names connected with *Hymns Ancient and Modern* are W. H. Frere (1863-1938), who wrote an extended historical introduction for the "Historical Edition" of that collection in 1909; and Maurice Frost (1888-1961), who enlarged upon Frere's work to prepare the monumental *Historical Companion to Hymns Ancient and Modern* in 1962.[85] Frost was the most eminent of all twentieth-century British hymnologists. His massive *English and Scottish Psalm and Hymn Tunes, c. 1543-1677*[86] is an authoritative source.

In the field of Scottish hymnology the outstanding scholars were James Moffatt and Millar Patrick, with their *Handbook to the Church Hymnary Revised* (1927, enlarged 1935).[87] Dr. Millar Patrick was the founder and first editor of the *Bulletin of the Hymn Society of Great Britain and Ireland* and the author of both *The Story of the Church's Song* and *Four Centuries of Scottish Psalmody*.[88]

By far the most versatile of all twentieth-century British hymnologists has been Congregationalist clergyman, scholar, and musician, Erik Reginald Routley (b. 1917). Routley is a rare individual, equally competent in the theological and musical disciplines. For three decades he has exercised his scholarly gifts in the fields of Bible, hymnology, and worship.

A partial listing of his hymnological works includes:

I'll Praise My Maker (London: Independent Press, 1951), a study of the

---

[84]Many of Williamson's tunes may be studied in *12 New Hymn Tunes* (London: Josef Weinberger, Lts., 1962) and *16 Hymns and Processionals* (Carol Stream, IL: Agape, 1975).

[85]Maurice Frost, editor, *Historical Companion to Hymns Ancient and Modern* (London: William Clowes & Sons, Ltd., 1962)

[86]Maurice Frost, *English and Scottish Psalm and Hymn Tunes, c. 1543-1677* (London: Oxford University Press, 1953).

[87]James Moffatt and Millar Patrick, editors, *Handbook to the Church Hymnary with Supplement* (London: Oxford University Press, 1935).

[88]Millar Patrick, *The Story of the Church's Song* (Edinburgh: The Scottish Churches Joint Committee on Youth, 1927; Reprinted and revised, James R. Sydnor, editor, Richmond: John Knox Press, 1962). Millar Patrick, *Four Centuries of Scottish Psalmody* (New York: Oxford University Press, 1949).

hymns of certain authors who stand in or near the tradition of English Calvinism, 1799-1850.

Hymns and Human Life (London: John Murray, 1952), a serious yet entertaining account of the human background of Christian hymnody.

Hymns and the Faith (Greenwich, Conn.: Seabury Press, 1956), a devotional and theological study of forty-nine hymns considered to be among the most popular in English Protestantism.

The Music of Christian Hymnody (London: Independent Press, 1957), the only extensive survey of hymn tunes in English.

Hymns Today and Tomorrow (Nashville: Abingdon Press, 1964), a detailed investigation of the language, images, and literary style of hymns with the view to sharing constructive insights for the writing of new hymns.

Words, Music, and the Church (Nashville: Abingdon Press, 1968), a series of essays loosely gathered about the theme of worship as drama in a changing society and the relation of music (including hymns) in its ordering.

A Panorama of Christian Hymnody (Collegeville, Minnesota: The Liturgical Press, 1979).

An English-Speaking Hymnal Guide (Collegeville, Minnesota: The Liturgical Press, 1979).

From 1947 to 1974 Routley served as editor of the *Bulletin of the Hymn Society of Great Britain and Ireland,* often furnishing the greater part of each quarterly issue with his own scholarly articles and reviews of hymnals. He has served on the editorial board of several hymnals published during the past quarter century and is the author of numerous periodical articles and other works pertaining to all aspects of hymnody. Being also a creator as well as a student of hymns, Routley is representative of the whole of late twentieth-century hymnic activity.

Owing much to the imaginative work of such scholars in England, America, and elsewhere English hymnody is in a vigorous state of revival, its study a matter of lively interest, and its increasingly effective use a cause for excitement and gratitude. The future of the hymn is bright!

8

American Traditions

The European Heritage

Beginning in the seventeenth century, colonists from Europe started arriving in the New World, bringing with them, along with other traditions, their Old World heritage of song. Two main types of congregational song were transplanted by these "Euramericans":

1. Metrical psalmody,[1] from the English-, French-, and Dutch-speaking settlers, and
2. The chorale,[2] from the German and Scandinavian settlers.

The transplanting was so effective that both traditions were maintained almost exclusively for nearly 100 years until the American singing school movement developed in the eighteenth century.

The Singing School

The singing school arose as a reform movement in early eighteenth-century New England. Harvard-educated ministers sought to improve what they regarded as poor congregational singing[3] by teaching their people to read music instead of singing by ear. The Massachusetts pastor John Tufts compiled in 1721 the first singing school manual, *An Introduction to the Singing of Psalm Tunes* (11 eds. to 1744).[4] This modest volume was the first of hundreds produced for singing school or church use, each containing two basic ingredients: an introduction to the rudiments of music and an anthology of music (usually with sacred texts) for singing. By the latter eighteenth century the singing school textbooks had become standardized in an oblong shape and were known as *tune*books, for most of their tunes had only one stanza of text. In contrast to tunebooks, hymnals and psalters of this time generally had texts only. Singing school tunebooks contained tunes for metrical psalms and hymns in addition to more elaborate noncongregational music (this category

---

[1]See chap. 6, section on metrical psalmody.

[2]See chap. 6, section on the chorale.

[3]One Massachusetts minister (Thomas Walter) described congregational singing as "an horrid Medley of confused and disorderly Noises." Gilbert Chase has made a strong case for viewing this singing as a folk style. See Chase's *America's Music*. Rev. ed. (New York: McGraw-Hill, 1966), chap. 2.

[4]A facsimile reprint of the fifth edition contains an introduction by Irving Lowens (Philadelphia: Printed for *Musical Americana* by Albert Saifer, Publisher, 1954). Lowens treats the early history of Tuft's *Introduction* in his *Music and Musicians in Early America* (New York: The W. W. Norton Co., 1964), pp. 39-57.

consisting of fuging tunes[5] and anthems[6]). The singing school movement is important for American hymnody and American music history because it brought forth, in the latter eighteenth century, our first native composers of hymn tunes. (The period of development for indigenous hymn texts was not to come until several decades later, in the nineteenth century.)

The earliest American hymn tune in common use today is CORONATION ("All hail the power of Jesus' name," B40, L328, M71), composed in 1793 by Oliver Holden (1765-1844), a Massachusetts pastor, state legislator, music teacher, and tunebook compiler. Following the practice of the singing school tradition, the melody was originally in the tenor voice. Note also the repetition of the latter portion of this tune and the rests in the inner voice parts; these are features related to the fuging tune.

An example of a fuging tune now used in American hymnals is LENOX ("Blow ye the trumpet blow," M100; "Arise, my soul, arise," M122), composed by Lewis Edson (1748-1820) of Massachusetts, New York, and Connecticut, blacksmith and singing schoolteacher. LENOX (published in 1782 or 1783) begins with a homophonic section followed by an imitative section which is repeated, thus forming an ABB structure typical of the fuging tune.

LENOX appears in *The Methodist Hymnal* in a "defuged" version with the imitative entrances filled in to make it more easily singable by a twentieth-century congregation.

A third piece of music from the early American singing school still in use is the tune WINDHAM ("How beauteous were the marks divine," M80; "We sing the praise of him who died," L344), composed by Daniel Read (1757-1836) of Massachusetts and Connecticut. Read, an ivory comb manufacturer and book publisher, compiled several tunebooks and began the first American music magazine. WINDHAM was published in Read's *The American Singing Book* (New Haven, Conn., 1785).

All three of these early American tunes—CORONATION, LENOX, and WINDHAM—have remained in continual use through their publication in *The Sacred Harp*[8] and other Southern shape-note tunebooks. These tunes of the singing school thus represent the earliest of America's musical contributions to current hymnic practice.

---

[5]A good introduction to the fuging tune may be seen in Lowens, "The Origins of the American Fuging Tune" in *Music and Musicians in Early America*, pp. 237-48.

[6]The anthem in early America is treated in Elwyn Wienandt and Robert H. Young, "The Beginnings of the American Anthem" in *The Anthem in England and America* (New York: Free Press, 1970), pp. 169-205.

[7]See David W. McCormick, "Oliver Holden, 1764-1844," *The Hymn,* (July 1963), 69-77,79.

[8]The most recent edition of *The Sacred Harp,* compiled by B. F. White and E. J. King, is *The Original Sacred Harp* (Cullman, Alabama: Sacred Harp Publishing Co., 1971). Available from P.O. Box 185, Bremen, Georgia 30110.

CORONATION, from Holden's *Union Harmony, or Universal Collection of Sacred Music* (Boston, 1793). The text, credited to Medley, is by Perronet. (See Chap. 7, British Traditions.)

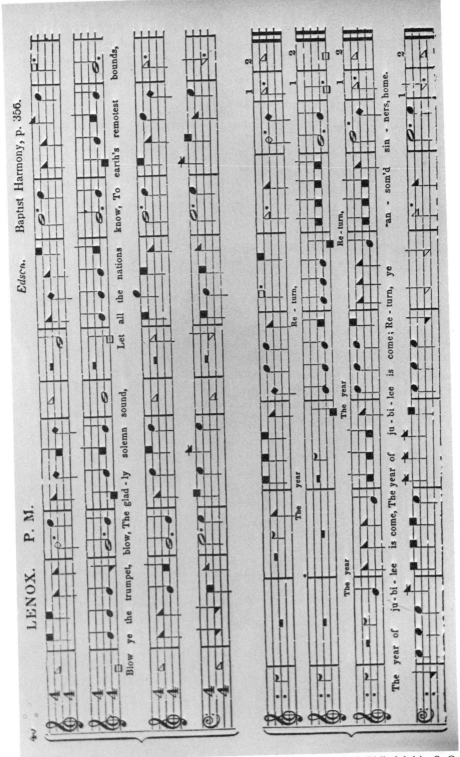

LENOX, from B. F. White and E. J. King, *The Sacred Harp*. 3rd ed. Philadelphia: S. C. Collings, 1860, p. 40.

WINDHAM, from Read's *The American Singing Book* (New Haven, Conn., 1785), p. 55. "158th Hymn 2nd Book" refers to the text source, Watts' *Hymns and Spiritual Songs* (London, 1707), a collection of his hymns divided into three "books" but actually in one volume.

Folk Hymnody

Introduction

Folk music is distinguished from cultivated music by the manner in which it is transmitted. Rather than conforming to one authentic version published in musical score, the folk song is transmitted by oral tradition, thus resulting in numerous variants. Since people hear and perform folk music from memory, a folk song may be sung in highly distinctive ways by different persons, especially if the singers come from contrasting cultures.

American folk hymnody has both an *unwritten* and a *written* history. The melodies of American folk hymns are mostly related to the secular folk-song tradition brought by early settlers, primarily those from Great Britain. Some folk hymns have been traced by scholars, especially George Pullen Jackson (1874-1953),[9] to specific secular folk-song melodies. Others are related to "families" of folk melodies or are in a musical style very similar to the Anglo-American folk-song idiom. The most common style trait of this tradition is the use of five-note (pentatonic) and other gapped scales. Another characteristic of these folk hymns is modal melody (e.g., Dorian, Mixolydian, etc.).

In its early history the folk hymn existed solely in oral tradition. The *written* or *printed* history of the American folk hymn began when singing schoolteachers either notated them from oral tradition (both words and music), took a printed hymn text (usually of English origin) and adapted a folksong melody to it, or composed a melody themselves in a style practically identical to that of other folk hymns. The earliest singing school tunebook to contain a significant number of folk hymns surviving to the present was John Wyeth's *Repository of Sacred Music, Part Second,* published at Harrisburg, Pennsylvania in 1813.[10]

Shape-Note Hymnody

The printed folk hymn and the singing school movement came together with the invention of shape notes, a device to simplify music reading first appearing in William Little's and William Smith's tunebook, *The Easy Instructor* (Albany, NY, 1802).[11] Little's and Smith's system (which corresponded to the Elizabethan sol-fa solmization brought by American colonists from England), used four shapes, three of which were repeated to form a diatonic scale:

---

[9]Beginning with his *White Spirituals in the Southern Uplands* (Chapel Hill: University of North Carolina Press, 1933; reprint, New York: Dover, 1964), Jackson's books are essential reading for a detailed knowledge of American folk hymnody. See his books listed in the bibliography of this text. See also *The Hymn,* Oct. 1979, pp. 240-42.

[10]See *Wyeth's Repository of Sacred Music, Part Second* with a New Introduction by Irving Lowens. Reprint of the 2nd ed. of 1820. (New York: Da Capo Press, 1964).

[11]For a detailed study of this tunebook, see Lowens, *Music and Musicians,* pp. 115-37.

fa   sol   la   fa   sol   la   mi   fa

Through shape-note tunebooks, folk hymns (along with New England psalm
tunes, fuging tunes, and anthems) were widely circulated in the pre-Civil War
period, especially in the rural South and Midwest.[12] Four leading shape-note
tune books of this period, each containing a number of folk hymns, are
Ananias Davisson's *Kentucky Harmony* (the first Southern shape-note
tunebook, Harrisonburg, Va., 1816),[13] Allen Carden's *Missouri Harmony* (St.
Louis, but printed in Cincinnati, 1820; later eds. to 1857), William Walker's
Southern Harmony (Spartanburg, S.C., but printed first in New Haven,
Conn. and later in Philadelphia, 1835; later eds. to 1854),[14] and B. F. White's
and E. J. King's *The Sacred Harp* (Hamilton, Ga., but printed in Phila-
delphia, 1844; later eds. to the present time).[15]

After about 1850 most shape-note tunebooks were printed in various seven-
shape systems corresponding to the do-re-mi solmization advocated by Lowell
Mason and other leading Northern musicians. They united in the 1870's to use
Jesse B. Aikin's seven-shape notation[16] first published at Philadelphia in 1846
in his *The Christian Minstrel:*

do   re   mi   fa   sol   la   ti   do

[12]These tunebooks are listed in Richard J. Stanislaw, *A Checklist of Four-Shape Shape-Note
Tunebooks* (New York: Institute for Studies in American Music, Brooklyn College, 1978).
[13]See *Kentucky Harmony*, Facsimile Edition with introduction by Irving Lowens. Reprint of 1st
ed. of 1816. (Minneapolis: Augsburg Publishing House, 1976).
[14]See *Southern Harmony*, Facsimile of 1854 ed. (Los Angeles: Pro Music Americana, 1966).
Available from Box 649, Murray, Ky 42071.
[15]See *The Sacred Harp*, Facsimile of the third ed., 1859, including as a historical introduction
The Story of the Sacred Harp by George Pullen Jackson, with a Postscript by William J.
Reynolds. (Nashville: Broadman Press, 1968). Descriptions of these four tunebooks and
biographical sketches of their compilers are found in Jackson, *White Spirituals.*
[16]A variety of seven-shape systems was developed because Aikin's shapes were thought to be
patented (hence the term "patent notes" was used to refer to shape notes). A comparison of
several of these seven-shape systems is given in Jackson, *White Spirituals,* p. 337.

Folk hymns from oral tradition thus became a part of the rural singing school through their publication in numerous shape-note tunebooks, some of which survive in present-day singings.[17]

An increasing number of early American folk hymns (texts and tunes or hymn tunes for more recent texts) have appeared in most American hymnals of recent decades. Eight of the most frequently found are:

KEDRON ("O thou to whose all-searching sight," B470; "God send us men whose aim 'twill be," M191) is an Aeolian, hexatonic melody, one of the earliest folk hymns to be printed, appearing in 1799 at Boston in Amos Pilsbury's *United States Harmony* to an earlier text.

MORNING SONG ("Awake, awake to love and work," B413, M190; "O holy city, seen of John," M481) is an Aeolian melody, slightly florid like KEDRON, which appeared in Wyeth's *Repository of Sacred Music, Part Second* (Harrisburg, Pa., 1813) to an earlier text with the tune name CONSOLATION.

NETTLETON ("Come, thou Fount of every blessing," B13, L499, M93) was also published in Wyeth's tunebook under the tune name HALLELUJAH and with this same text. Compare the original duple meter version and melodic differences with the present-day hymnal version of this tune.

AMAZING GRACE ("Amazing grace! how sweet the sound," B165, L448, M92) is a pentatonic melody, probably the most popular American folk hymn. It first appeared in print in the Shenandoah Valley of Virginia in James P. Carrell and David L. Clayton's *Virginia Harmony* (Winchester, Va., 1831, 2nd ed., 1836). Its tune name in this tunebook is HARMONY GROVE and its text is Watt's "There is a land of pure delight." This folk hymn is equally popular among black and white congregations and had the distinction of becoming an international hit in 1972 through the bagpipe recording of the Royal Scotch Dragoon Guards.

FOUNDATION ("How firm a foundation, ye saints of the Lord," B383, L507, M48) is a pentatonic melody originally entitled PROTECTION but associated with this same text. It was first printed in another Shenandoah Valley tunebook, Joseph Funk's *Genuine Church Music* (Winchester, Va., 1832, later eds. to the present day; now entitled *New Harmonia Sacra*).

HOLY MANNA ("Brethren, we have met to worship," B260; "Glorious is thy name, Most Holy," B419; "God, who stretched the spangled heavens,"

---

[17]A singing is an informal gathering organized for fellowship and singing. Many singings take place annually on weekends, beginning by mid-morning and followed by a noonday break for "dinner on the grounds" and a concluding afternoon session. Though nondenominational, singings mostly take place in church buildings. Singings are generally organized into conventions, often on the county and state level. *The Sacred Harp* is by far the most widely used of the shape-note tunebooks. A list of "Traditional Sacred Harp Singings: Dates and Locations" is given in Buell E. Cobb, Jr., *The Sacred Harp, A Tradition and Its Music* (Athens: University of Georgia Press, 1978), pp. 163-85.

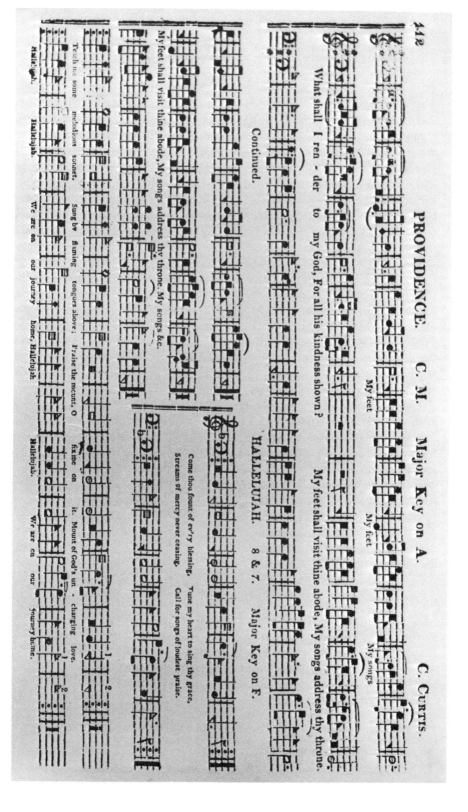

HALLELUJAH from Wyeth's *Repository . . . Part Second*, p. 112.

E81, L463) is a pentatonic melody credited to William Moore of Wilson County, Tennessee, in his *The Columbian Harmony* (Cincinnati: Printed for the compiler by Moran, Lodge, and Fisher, 1825). At the annual Southern Harmony Singing at Benton, Kentucky, it is a long-standing tradition to begin with the singing of HOLY MANNA. "Brethren, we have met to worship," the hymn traditionally associated with HOLY MANNA, appeared as early as 1819 in George Kolb's *Spiritual Songster Containing a Variety of Camp Meeting and Other Hymns* (Frederick-town, Md.), where it is attributed to George Atkins (identity unknown).

WONDROUS LOVE[18] ("What wondrous love is this, O my soul, O my soul," B106, E46, L385, M432) is a Dorian, pentatonic melody first printed in the 1843 edition of Walker's *Southern Harmony* (1st ed., 1835, later eds. to 1854), where it bears the name "Christopher" as composer. In his later *Christian Harmony* (Spartanburg, S.C., but printed at Philadelphia, 1867, 2nd ed. 1840), p. 359, Walker indicates this tune to be "Arranged by James Christopher, of Spartanburg, S.C. A very popular old Southern tune." The anonymous text of WONDROUS LOVE, probably by an American, appeared in print as early as 1811 at Lynchburg, Va., in the second edition of Stith Mead's *A General Selection of the Newest and Most Admired Hymns and Spiritual Songs Now in Use.*

WEDLOCK ("God is my strong salvation," B343, M211; "O Lord, send forth your Spirit," L392), like WONDROUS LOVE, is a Dorian, pentatonic melody. The similarities and variations of its four double phrases are interesting to compare. WEDLOCK, published by G. P. Jackson in his *Down East Spirituals and Others* (New York: J. J. Augustin, 1939), p. 76, was collected by Cecil Sharp and Maude Karpeles in the North Carolina Appalachians in 1918.[19] A variant of WEDLOCK, entitled EDMONDS, appears in the *Original Sacred Harp,* Denson Revision (Cullman, Ala.: Sacred Harp Publishing Co., 1971), p. 115.

Camp-Meeting Hymnody

In addition to its connection with the singing school, American folk hymnody was influenced by the growth of revivalism, particularly that of the frontier camp meeting. Beginning in Kentucky in 1800, the camp meeting revivals became a significant means of communicating the gospel in sparsely populated frontier areas. Hymns were an important means of expressing the emotional fervor of these revival meetings. The need for hymns simple and

[18]For a comparative study involving this tune, see Ellen Jane Porter, *Two Early American Tunes: Fraternal Twins?* Papers of the Hymn Society of America, XXX (1975).

[19]*English Folk Songs from the Southern Appalachians,* Vol. 2 (London: Oxford University Press, 1932), p. 272.

contagious enough to appeal to unlettered frontier folk brought into being a simplified folk hymn, a type then known as a spiritual song and now commonly referred to as a spiritual.

The basic technique of simplification in the spiritual is repetition, as in

> Give me that old time religion,
> Give me that old time religion,
> Give me that old time religion,
>   It's good enough for me.[20]

Another way to simplify a folk hymn was to add a chorus to a standard hymn such as the following, appended to Robinson's "Come, thou Fount of every blessing" (B12):

> I am bound for the kingdom,
> Will you go to glory with me?
> Hallelujah, praise the Lord.

A third way hymn texts were simplified in the camp-meeting tradition was to insert tag lines into a standard hymn text, such as "glory hallelujah" in Cennick's "Jesus, my all to heaven is gone," as given in the *Original Sacred Harp* (1971 ed., p. 324):

> Jesus, my all, to heav'n has gone,
>   Glory Hallelujah;
> He whom I fix my hopes upon!
>   Glory Hallelujah!
>
> *Chorus:*
> I want a seat in Paradise,
>   Glory Hallelujah!
> I love that union never dies [*sic*],
>   Glory! Hallelujah!

Numerous collections of camp meeting hymn texts appeared in the early decades of the nineteenth century. Later their tunes were published (but in harmonized form) in such tunebooks as *The Sacred Harp* (1844) and John G. McCurry's *The Social Harp* (Hart County, Ga., but printed at Philadelphia, Pa., 1855). This latter collection contained the largest single tunebook concentration of spirituals in this period.[21]

[20]Both white and black versions of this spiritual are given in George Pullen Jackson, *White and Negro Spirituals*. Reprint of 1st ed. of 1943 (New York: Da Capo Press, 1975), pp. 184-85.

[21]John Gordon McCurry, *The Social Harp* (Philadelphia: T. K. Collins, 1855; reprint ed. by Daniel W. Patterson and John F. Garst with an Introduction by Daniel W. Patterson. Athens: University of Georgia Press, 1973).

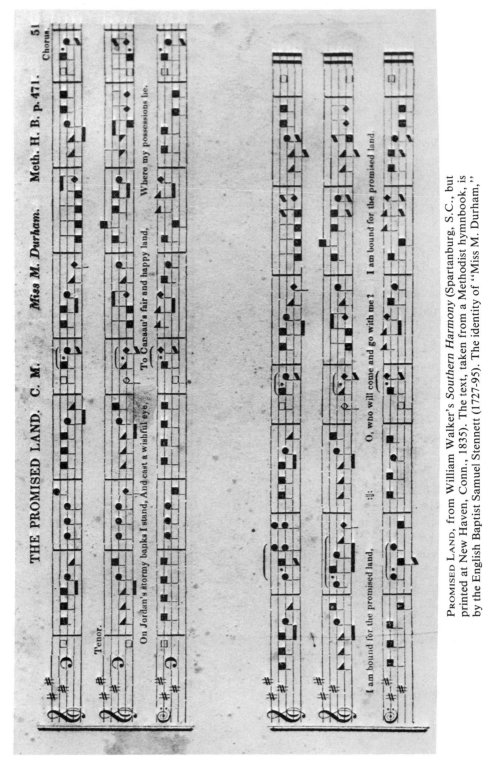

PROMISED LAND, from William Walker's *Southern Harmony* (Spartanburg, S.C., but printed at New Haven, Conn., 1835). The text, taken from a Methodist hymnbook, is by the English Baptist Samuel Stennett (1727-95). The identity of "Miss M. Durham," Walker's tune source, is unknown.

Two white spirituals to be found in present day hymnals are WARRENTON ("Come, thou Fount of every blessing"; refrain: "I am bound for the kingdom," B12) and PROMISED- LAND ("On Jordan's stormy banks I stand"; refrain: [B only] "I am bound for the promised land," B490, M291). Both of these tunes[22] have English hymn texts, with refrains added during their association with early nineteenth-century American revivalism. Although PROMISED LAND now appears in a major key, its early version in shape-note tunebooks is in minor, as in this appearance in Walker's *Southern Harmony* (1835).

Negro Spirituals— Although Negro slaves developed spirituals (then generally called plantation melodies)[23] in the pre-Civil War period, the first collection of Negro spirituals, *Slave Songs of the United States,* was not published until 1867.[24] Negro spirituals after the Civil War branched into two streams. One stream—the grassroots spiritual—continued among the common folk. The other stream—the concert arrangements of spirituals harmonized in "correct" European style—was spread through popular performances of groups such as the Fisk Jubilee Singers (Fisk University in Nashville), beginning in 1871.

While the grassroots spiritual continued to be sung by blacks in their traditional ways with less polished harmonies and free improvisations, the more acceptable concert versions became known to the public at large. Negro spirituals were not published to an appreciable extent in collections designed for congregational singing until the twentieth century; only in recent decades have they been included in most major American hymnals. As they appear in current hymnals, their harmonies are more akin to the concert versions than to folk practices.

The following Negro spirituals[25] are among the most often included in American hymnals today:

"Go, tell it on the mountain" (B82, L70, M404)
"Let us break bread together on our knees" (B252, L212, M330)
"Lord, I want to be a Christian" (B322, M286)

[22]In addition to these two, the well-known tune BATTLE HYMN (Mine eyes have seen the glory of the coming of the Lord, B510, M545) is regarded as a variant of a camp-meeting melody.

[23]For treatment of the musical traits of the spiritual see chap. 2, The Hymn and Music and chap. 9, Cultural Perspectives.

[24]William Francis Allen, Charles P. Ware, and Lucy McKim Garrison (eds.), *Slave Songs of the United States* (New York: A. Simpson and Co., 1867; reprint, New York: Peter Smith, 1951; Rev. ed., New York: Oak Publications, 1965).

[25]The earliest of these spirituals to be published in a hymn collection seems to be "Were you there," 1911, in *Songs of Evangelism* by Harvey R. Christie (Cincinnati: Standard Publishing Co.) and "We are climbing Jacob's ladder," 1905, in *Joy Bells of Canaan, Burning Bush Songs No. 2,* ed. by Arthur F. Ingler (Chicago: The Burning Bush). It is interesting that these earlier printings of Negro spirituals were in revivalistic songbooks and that only in recent decades has it become "respectable" to include these in denominational hymnals.

"There is a balm in Gilead" (B205, M212)
"We are climbing Jacob's ladder" (B147, M287)
"Were you there when they crucified my Lord" (B108, L92, M436)

Although white spirituals were published in shape-note tunebooks two decades before Negro spirituals began to appear in print, both bodies of congregational folk song existed side by side in the pre-Civil War period. It is clear that these bodies of song intermingled and influenced each other but the evidence is insufficient for either tradition to claim priority.[26] Regardless of their label, spirituals have become a deeply meaningful expression of a common faith for many American congregations.

Thus American folk hymnody developed in the nineteenth century with a variety of associations: Anglo-American secular folk song, the singing school with its shape notation, revivalism (including the frontier camp meetings), and the Afro-American tradition (later influenced by the European tradition). All of these associations continue to influence congregational song.

Nineteenth Century Northern Developments

Musical Reformers and Revivalists

While folk hymnody and the singing school flourished in the nineteenth-century South and the frontier areas of the Midwest, a second reform movement in American church music was taking place in the urban North. Led by Lowell Mason and others, this movement considered the music of the earlier American composers (e.g., Billings, Read, and Jeremiah Ingalls) generally inferior, preferring European music, which they regarded as "scientifically" conceived (or correct). These reformers based their hymn tunes on European models, or they used melodies arranged from famous composers for congregational singing. In the early nineteenth-century more sophisticated means of music education, including the introduction of music instruction in public schools, gradually replaced the singing school, at least in the larger cities.

The dominant figure in this reform movement and the leading composer of hymn tunes of his time was Lowell Mason (1792-1872), whose main activities centered in Boston and in New York City.[27] Mason is particularly renowned for having pioneered in introducing music instruction on a regular basis into the Boston public schools in 1827. He composed or arranged some 1,600 hymn tunes and compiled some eighty collections of music. Among the best known of his surviving hymn tunes are:

[26]The most extensive collection of sources documenting the early spiritual is Dena J. Epstein, *Sinful Tunes and Spirituals* (Urbana: University of Illinois Press, 1977).

[27]See J. Vincent Higginson, "Notes on Lowell Mason's Hymn Tunes," *The Hymn* 18 (April 1967), 37-42; and George Brandon, "Some Classic Tunes in Lowell Mason's Collections," *The Hymn* 18 (July 1967), 78-79.

ANTIOCH ("Joy to the world," B88, L39, M392), an arrangement (1839) of themes from Handel's *Messiah*

AZMON ("O for a thousand tongues to sing," B69, L559, M1; "Jesus, thine all-victorious love," M278; "I'm not ashamed to own my Lord," B450), an arrangement (1839) from the music of Carl G. Glaser

BETHANY (Nearer, my God, to thee," B333, M263), a tune composed for this text in 1856

HAMBURG ("When I survey the wondrous cross," B111, M435), arranged from a Gregorian chant in 1824

OLIVET ("My faith looks up to thee," B382, L479, M143), a tune composed for this text in 1832

Mason's leading contemporary in musical reform was Thomas Hastings (1784-1872),[28] who from 1832 onward was active in New York City. Hastings wrote some 600 hymn texts, 1,000 hymn tunes, and compiled more than fifty collections of music. Three of Hastings's hymn tunes which survive are:

ORTONVILLE ("Majestic sweetness sits enthroned," B267, M83), composed for this hymn in 1837

RETREAT ("From every stormy wind that blows," M232), composed for this hymn in 1842

TOPLADY ("Rock of ages cleft for me," B163, L327, M120), composed for this hymn in 1830.

While Mason and Hastings advocated hymn tunes in a devotional style characterized by simplicity and dignity, Congregationalist minister and journalist Joshua Leavitt (1794-1873) brought out (in his *The Christian Lyre,* New York, 1831) hymns set to certain secular melodies which Mason and Hastings regarded unfit for religious use. Leavitt's collection sought to supply hymns (including some songs with choruses) suitable for the new urban revivalism of evangelist Charles G. Finney (1792-1875).[29] Among the anonymous hymn tunes bequeathed to current hymnals by *The Christian Lyre* are:

ELLESDIE ("Jesus, I my cross have taken," M251)

HIDING PLACE ("O Jesus, king most wonderful," L537)

PLEADING SAVIOR ("Sing of Mary, pure and lowly," E61; Come, ye sinners, poor and needy," M104; "Lord, with glowing heart I'd praise thee," L243)

Although revivalistic in its orientation, *The Christian Lyre* also contains the first publication of Presbyterian minister James W. Alexander's translation of

[28]See Lee Hastings Bristol, Jr., "Thomas Hastings, 1784-1872," *The Hymn* 10 (October 1959), 105-10.
[29]See Paul Hammond, "The Hymnody of the Second Great Awakening," *The Hymn* 29 (January 1978), 19-28.

Gerhardt's "O sacred Head, now wounded" (B105, L116 and 117 [a composite tr.], M418).

Mason and Hastings, alarmed by the secular orientation of *The Christian Lyre,* sought to supply the revival movement with more dignified church music in their *Spiritual Songs for Social Worship* (Utica, N.Y., New York, and Philadelphia, 1833). This collection provided an introduction to the public for Ray Palmer's "My faith looks up to thee" (to Mason's OLIVET) and other widely used hymns of Hastings and others.

Mason's associate during his later Boston years was George J. Webb (1803-87), a native of England. While on a ship bound for America, Webb composed music for a secular text, " 'Tis dawn, the lark is singing.'' This tune later came to be used with hymns and is now known as WEBB (B391, L389, M248), the hymn tune for "Stand up, stand up for Jesus.''

Denominational Hymnody

In the nineteenth century most American denominations underwent a gradual transition from the use of metrical psalmody (or Watts's and other hymns of English origin) to the development of their own hymn writers. They also began to publish their own hymnals as well.[30] In this period a number of hymns emerged which are still found in American hymnals. Although some hymn texts of this period reflect the particular doctrines of individual denominations, those which have survived tend to embody beliefs held by most of America's Christians. These hymns, however, may best be treated according to their denominational origin.

Baptists. A Massachusetts Baptist minister, Samuel F. Smith (1808-95), produced one of America's enduring patriotic hymns, "My country 'tis of thee" (AMERICA, B511, L566, M547), written in 1831 and first sung by a choir of Boston Sunday School children directed by Lowell Mason. This hymn's New England origin is reflected in such phrases as:

> I love thy rocks and rills,
> Thy woods and templed hills.

Smith was also one of the editors of *The Psalmist* (Boston, 1843), the leading Baptist hymnal of the first half of the century. Three other Baptist ministers, each of whose hymns were written in the latter half of the century, are Joseph H. Gilmore (1834-1918), author of "He leadeth me, O blessed thought" (1862; B218, L501, M217); Sylvanus D. Phelps (1816-95), author of "Savior, thy dying love" (1864; B418, M177); and Adoniram J. Gordon (1836-95),

---

[30]The best survey of American denominational hymnals in the nineteenth century is found in Louis F. Benson, *The English Hymn* (New York: George H. Doran, 1915; reprint, Richmond: John Knox Press, 1962). See chapter 8 and portions of chapters 9 and 10.

composer of the hymn tune GORDON (1876; "My Jesus, I love thee," B76; "Lord Jesus, I love thee," M166). Each of these hymns reflects the strong Baptist emphasis on a personal relationship to the Savior.

Congregationalists. Congregationalists have contributed to current hymnals a number of hymns from the nineteenth century. Their greatest contributions in the pre-Civil War period came from Ray Palmer (1808-87), author of "My faith looks up to thee" (1830, OLIVET, B382, L479, M143) and translator of "Jesus, thou joy of loving hearts" (1858, QUEBEC, B72; ROCKINGHAM (MASON), M329; "O Jesus, joy of loving hearts," WALTON, L356). Other Congregationalist contributors, all writing in the latter half of the century, are: Daniel March (1816-1909), the minister who wrote "Hark, the voice of Jesus calling" (1868, pub. 1878, GALILEAN, L381); Samuel Wolcott (1813-86), a missionary to Syria and later a pastor in this country who wrote the missionary hymn, "Christ for the world we sing" (1869, ITALIAN HYMN, M292); John Zundel (1815-82), a native of Germany who gained fame as organist of Henry Ward Beecher's Plymouth Congregational Church, Brooklyn, composer of the hymn tune BEECHER (1870, "Love divine, all loves excelling, B58, M283); Washington Gladden (1836-1918), minister and early advocate of the social application of the gospel who wrote "O Master, let me walk with thee (you)" (1879, MARYTON, B369, L492, M170); and Ernest W. Shurtleff (1862-1917), minister who wrote "Lead on, O King Eternal" (1887, LANCASHIRE, B420, L495, M478).

Episcopalians. The earliest nineteenth-century Episcopalian hymn found in today's hymnals is " 'Take up thy cross,' the Savior said" (GERMANY, B370, M160; "Take up your cross," the Savior said," NUN LASST UNS DEN LEIB BEGRABEN, L398), written in 1833 by Connecticut minister Charles W. Everest (1814-77). A second Episcopal contribution is the hymn tune CAROL ("It came upon the midnight clear," B86, L54, M390), composed in 1850 by the music critic Richard S. Willis (1819-1900). The popular Christmas hymn "O little town of Bethlehem" (1868, ST. LOUIS, B85, L41, M381) was written for Sunday School children by the famed preacher Phillips Brooks (1835-93) following a visit to Bethlehem.[31] The organist of his Holy Trinity Church in Philadelphia, Lewis Redner (1830-1908), composed its tune, interestingly named ST. LOUIS. The missionary hymn "O Zion haste, thy mission high fulfilling" (TIDINGS, B295, L397, M299) was written in 1868 by the English-born Philadelphian Mary Ann Thompson (1834-1923). Another of this century's patriotic hymns, but one not restricted to a single nation, is "God of our fathers, whose almighty hand" (NATIONAL HYMN, B149, L567, M552), written in 1876 for America's centennial by Daniel C. Roberts (1841-1907).

[31]See J. Vincent Higginson, "Phillips Brooks and Sunday School Music," *The Hymn* 19, 2 (April 1968), 37-43.

The unusual hymn tune with fanfares was composed in 1892 for the centennial of the United States Constitution by the New York organist, George W. Warren (1828-1902).

Methodists. Only one Methodist American hymn writer of the nineteenth century (apart from gospel hymnists) is commonly represented in today's hymnals. The artist and editor Mary A. Lathbury (1841-1913)[32] wrote in 1877 for the summer assemblies at Lake Chautauqua, New York, the hymn "Break thou the bread of life" (B138,[33] M369). Miss Lathbury's beautiful evening hymn, "Day is dying in the west" (CHAUTAUQUA, st. 1 and 2, 1877; st. 3 and 4, 1890; M503) has declined in use because of the gradual passing of vesper services.

Mormons. The Mormons or Latter-Day Saints have contributed a well-known hymn which, in altered form, has found a place in at least one other denominational hymnal. "Come, come, ye saints" (ALL IS WELL,[34] B210) was written in 1846 by William Clayton (1814-79), a native of England and one of the pioneer Mormons who journeyed to Utah. This hymn has been altered in *Baptist Hymnal.*

Presbyterians. Three Presbyterians whose hymns are commonly found in current hymnals are Elizabeth P. Prentiss (1818-78),[35] George Duffield, Jr. (1818-88), and Edward Hopper (1816-88). Mrs. Prentiss, an invalid who authored the religious best seller *Stepping Heavenward* (1869), wrote "More love to thee, O Christ" (1856, B484, M185). Duffield, one of a family of Presbyterian ministers, wrote "Stand up, stand up for Jesus" (WEBB, B391, L389, M248) during the 1858 revival in Philadelphia. Hopper, pastor of the Presbyterian Church in Sag Harbor, Long Island, New York, wrote "Jesus, Savior, pilot me" (1871, PILOT, L334, M247).

Quakers. The one Quaker hymnist of the past century whose hymns still flourish is one of the giants of American poetry, John Greenleaf Whittier (1807-92).[36] Although he did not write hymns as such, hymns have been extracted from his poems. His surviving hymns include:

"All things are thine" (1872, HERR JESU CHRIST, DICH ZU, M347)
"Dear Lord and Father of mankind" (1872, REST, B270, L506, M235)
"I know not what the future hath" (1867, IRISH, B492; COOLING, M290)

---

[32]See Gladys E. Gray, "Mary Artemisia Lathbury," *The Hymn* 14 (April 1963), 37-46.

[33]The additional two stanzas given in this hymnal were written by Englishman William Groves and published in 1913.

[34]This hymn tune is found in *The Sacred Harp* (1844) and even earlier. See David W. Music, "A New Source for the Tune 'All Is Well' " *The Hymn* 29, 2 (April 1978), 76-82.

[35]Mrs. Prentiss and her minister husband were first Congregationalists and later became Presbyterians.

[36]See David H. Kidder, "John Greenleaf Whittier's Contribution to American Hymnody," *The Hymn* 8 (October 1957), 105-11.

"Immortal Love, forever full" (1866, SERENITY, B329; AYRSHIRE, M157)

"O brother man, fold to thy heart thy brother" (1848, pub. 1850, WELWYN, M199)

The last of these hymns reflects the social application of the gospel: feeding the widow and orphan (st. 2) and replacing earth's wars with peace (st. 4).

Unitarians. One hymn by an American Unitarian from the first half of the nineteenth century has found a firm place in current hymnals. "It came upon the midnight clear" (CAROL, B86, L54, M390) was written in 1849 by Edmund H. Sears (1810-76), a Massachusetts minister. With no mention of Jesus, this hymn focuses upon the portion of the angels' message dealing with peace and forecasts its eventual achievement on earth. The Unitarian hymnist of the last century with the largest number of hymns in use today is Samuel Longfellow (1819-92), brother of the poet Henry Wadsworth Longfellow. Samuel Longfellow wrote:

"God of the earth, the sky, the sea" (1864, GERMANY, M36)

"Holy Spirit, Truth divine" (1864, SONG 13 or CANTERBURY, L257, M135)

"Now on land and sea descending" (1859, VESPER HYMN, M505)

"O God, thou giver of all good" (1864, PUER NOBIS NASCITUR, M515)

"One holy church of God appears "(1864, ST. STEPHEN, M296)

Samuel Longfellow and his fellow hymnist Samuel Johnson (1822-82) edited the Unitarian hymnals of 1845 and 1864.[37] Unitarians have also contributed the patriotic hymn "Mine eyes have seen the glory of the coming of the Lord" (1861, BATTLE HYMN OF THE REPUBLIC, B510, M545) by Julia Ward Howe (1819-1910), an influential speaker and advocate of abolition and pacifism. A Unitarian hymn that anticipated the space age, "Eternal Ruler of the ceaseless round" (SONG 1, L373), was written in 1864 by John W. Chadwick (1840-1904) for his graduation from Harvard Divinity School.

Nondenominational. One nineteenth-century American poet, essayist, and critic who never affiliated with any church is James Russell Lowell (1819-91), author of "The Present Crisis" (1845), an antiwar poem from which we have the hymn "Once to every man and nation" (EBENEZER, B385, M242). Katherine Lee Bates (1859-1929), an English professor at Wellesley College and daughter of a Congregationalist minister, also did not affiliate with any denomination. She wrote "O beautiful, for spacious skies" (MATERNA, B508, M543). This patriotic hymn, written after the author visited the Rocky Mountains in 1893, is reflective of America's experience of geographical expansion to the West in that century. Mention should also be made of the

---

[37]Two of Johnson's hymns in *The Hymnal 1940* (Episcopal) are "Life of ages, richly poured" and "City of God, how broad and far."

Sing with Understanding

© 1980 Charles Massey, Jr.

John Wesley

anonymous American Christmas hymn for children, "Away in a manger, no crib for a bed" (MUELLER or AWAY IN A MANGER, B80, L67, M384). This hymn appeared in 1885 in Philadelphia. Its hymn tune was first published in 1887 by James R. Murray (1841-1905).

Most of America's major denominations during the nineteenth century made some contribution to current hymnody. However, two principal church groups, the Roman Catholics and Lutherans, had not yet developed a considerable original hymnody because of their strong ties to their European heritages. The Roman Catholics were singing very little in the vernacular, and the Lutherans were using either German chorales (increasingly in English translation) or the hymns of their English-speaking neighbors.

Although the hymnody of America's churches in the nineteenth century is characterized by much diversity, the hymns that have continued in current use reflect certain emphases:

1. Americans have been well supplied with national hymns, including "My country, 'tis of thee," "Mine eyes have seen the glory," "God of our fathers," and "O beautiful, for spacious skies," all perhaps an outgrowth of the sense of patriotism necessary to weld the United States into a cohesive nation.

2. America's involvement in the modern worldwide missionary movement is illustrated by such hymns as "Hark, the voice of Jesus calling," "Christ for the world we sing," and "O Zion, haste."

3. The few hymns written for seasons of the church year focus mostly on Christmas," e.g., "O little town of Bethlehem," "It came upon the midnight clear," and "Away in a manger."

4. There is an emphasis on hymns of devotion to Jesus, such as "More love to thee, O Christ" and "Savior, thy dying love"; and of a personal relationship to Christ, as in "He leadeth me" and "Jesus, Savior pilot me."

5. Much nineteenth-century American hymnody is concerned with the afterlife. This is especially true of folk and gospel hymnody. Among the hymns mentioned in this section, note the reference to heaven in the final stanzas of "He leadeth me," "More love to thee," "Away in a manger," and "Jesus, Savior pilot me." The emphasis on heaven gave hope to most Americans who worked long and hard but with little realization of riches in this life.

6. There are hymns reflecting a growing social concern, such as "O brother man," "It came upon the midnight clear," and "Once to every man and nation."

7. Finally, with the exception of women hymn writers, the hymn text writers from the nineteenth-century churchly stream of American congregational song were nearly all clergymen rather than laypersons.

Gospel Hymnody

Just as the rural camp meeting in the early decades of the nineteenth century produced its popular hymnody, the urban revivals in the latter decades of this century brought forth a body of popular church song—a type known as the gospel song or the gospel hymn. The use of these terms to refer to this body of revival hymnody can be traced to two popular collections, Philip P. Bliss's *Gospel Songs* (1874) and Bliss and Ira D. Sankey's *Gospel Hymns and Sacred Songs* (1875). Gospel hymn texts utilized the same devices of simplification found in the camp-meeting hymn. The musical style of the gospel hymn has been described in chapter 2, The Hymn and Music.

Sunday School Era

Although the term "gospel hymnody" emerged in the mid-1870's, this hymnody actually appeared more than a decade earlier, especially in collections designed for America's rapidly growing Sunday schools.

Some of the common features of the gospel hymn were anticipated in hymn tunes of Lowell Mason and Thomas Hastings. But Mason's student, William B. Bradbury (1816-68), a leading composer of Sunday School music, is the first composer in this idiom whose works survive to any extent in current American hymnals. The compiler and publisher of numerous collections with titles designed to appeal to Sunday School children (e.g., *Fresh Laurels,* New York, 1867; *Golden Chain,* New York, 1861), Bradbury composed the musical settings for:

"Jesus loves me" (1862, CHINA, B336),

"He leadeth me" (1864, B218, L501, M217),

"Sweet hour of prayer" (*ca.* 1861, B401, M275),

"Just as I am, without one plea" (1849, WORDSWORTH, B187, L296, M119), and

"My hope is built on nothing less" (1863, SOLID ROCK, B337, L293, M222).

Two successors to Bradbury in providing music for the Sunday School were Baptists Robert Lowry (1826-99)[38] and William H. Doane (1832-1915). Lowry, a pastor who succeeded Bradbury as editor of Sunday School songbooks for the New York firm of Biglow and Main, wrote both words and music. He wrote both text and tune of "Shall we gather at the river"[39] (1864, HANSON PLACE, B496) the tune NEED for "I need thee every hour" (1892, text by Baptist Annie S. Hawks, B379, M265), and the tune SOMETHING FOR JESUS

---

[38]See John F. Zellner, III, "Robert Lowry: Early American Hymn Writer," *The Hymn* 26 (October 1975), 117-24, and 27 (January 1976), 15-21.

[39]This hymn has been arranged for solo voice by Aaron Copland in his collection, *Old American Songs Newly Arranged* (New York: Boosey & Hawkes, 1950).

(1871) for "Savior thy dying love" (1864, text by Baptist Sylvanus D. Phelps, B418, M177). Doane, (president of a Cincinnati firm manufacturing woodworking machinery), found time to compose more than 2,200 hymn tunes and compile more than forty collections. He is particularly known for his musical settings of hymns by Fanny Crosby (1820-1915), such as:

"I am thine, O Lord," (1875, B352, M159),
"Jesus, keep me near the cross" (1869, B351, M433),
"Pass me not, O gentle Savior" (1868, B176, M145),
"Rescue the perishing" (1869, B283, M175), and
"To God be the glory" (1875, B33).

Doane also composed the tune to Elizabeth P. Prentiss' previously mentioned hymn, "More love to thee."

Fanny Crosby, the leading poet of the gospel hymn movement,[40] was a remarkable blind Methodist teacher from New York who wrote some 8,000 hymn texts (the exact number is uncertain). A recognized popular secular poet before she turned to writing hymns, she incorporated in her hymns such words of sentiment found in the popular song of her day as *gentle, precious,* and *tenderly.* In addition to her hymns set by Doane, other texts of Crosby still in use include:

"All the way my Savior leads me" (1875, tune by Lowry, B214, M205),
"Blessed assurance, Jesus is mine" (1873, tune by Methodist Phoebe P. Knapp, B334, M224), and
"Jesus is tenderly calling thee home" (1883, tune by George C. Stebbins, B188, M110).

One of the most popular gospel hymns of the Sunday School era is "What a friend we have in Jesus" (CONVERSE, B403, L439, M261), which was written in 1855 by Joseph M. Scriven (1820-86), a native of Ireland who from 1844 lived in Canada; it was later set to music in 1868 by the distinguished American composer, Charles C. Converse (1832-1918). Another was "I love to tell the story" (HANKEY, B461, L390, M149), written in 1866 by Londoner Katherine Hankey (1834-1911) and set to music in 1869 by William G. Fischer (1835-1912), a college music professor who from 1868 was associated with J. E. Gould (composer of PILOT) in a Philadelphia piano business.

Moody-Sankey Era

From the 1870's gospel hymnody came forth as a major force in urban revivalism especially through the meetings of evangelist Dwight L. Moody (1837-99) and his musical associate Ira D. Sankey (1840-1908). During the Moody-Sankey era, the hymns previously associated with the Sunday School

---

[40]An authoritative biography of Fanny Crosby is *Fanny Crosby* by Bernard Ruffin (Philadelphia: United Church Press, 1976).

came to be known as gospel hymns. In their mass meetings Sankey introduced many gospel hymns as he accompanied himself at his portable reed organ. Much of Moody and Sankey's work was related to the Young Men's Christian Association (founded in London, 1844; in Boston and Montreal, 1851), an organization which utilized the popular hymns of Bradbury, Lowry, Fischer, and others. Moody and Sankey first met at a YMCA convention at Indianapolis in 1870. Sankey was hired to direct music at Moody's church in Chicago. In 1872, when Moody was invited to hold evangelistic meetings in England, he at first sought the services of the more experienced musicians Philip Phillips (1834-95)[41] and Philip P. Bliss (1838-76); both declined. Moody then invited the less experienced Sankey, who during their British tour gained international fame. Such was the demand for the hymns used by Sankey that a series of popular gospel hymn collections emerged.

Although he was more important as a compiler and a popularizer of gospel hymnody than as a composer, Sankey composed three tunes in the hymnals of this study (SANKEY, B377, TRUSTING JESUS, B441, and SANKEY, M514; B377 and M514 are not the same). Sankey did much to spread gospel hymnody through the collection he began in London in 1873 entitled *Sacred Songs and Solos,* a small sixteen-page pamphlet that by 1903 became a mammoth volume of 1,200 selections. Its American counterpart, the "Gospel Hymns Series," began with Bliss and Sankey's *Gospel Hymns and Sacred Songs* (1875), followed by numbers *2* (Bliss's and Sankey), *3, 4, 5,* and *6* (Sankey, McGranahan, and Stebbins), and culminating in *Gospel Hymns Nos. 1-6 Complete* (1894).[42]

Sankey's co-compilers, all associated with Moody at various times, were more successful than he in writing gospel hymns. Bliss, a Pennsylvanian like Sankey, was an evangelistic singer who worked with Moody and with the evangelist Daniel W. Whittle (1840-1901). Bliss wrote words and music to such popular gospel hymns as "Wonderful words of life" (1874, first line: "Sing them over again to me," B142, M109); "Let the lower lights be burning" (1871, first line: "Brightly beams our Father's mercy," M148), and the music to "I gave my life for thee" (1873, KENOSIS: text by Frances R. Havergal, 1858, B417) and "It is well with my soul" (1876, VILLE DU HAVRE:[43] first line: When peace like a river attendeth my way," Horatio G. Spafford, 1873: B339; hymn without refrain, L346).

---

[41]Phillips's *Hallowed Songs* (Cincinnati, 1865) was at first used by Sankey in London before compiling his own collection. Phillips, known internationally for his services of song, did much to popularize gospel hymnody and prepare the way for Sankey.

[42]This collected edition has been reprinted with a new introduction by H. Wiley Hitchcock (New York: Da Capo Press, 1973).

[43]Although VILLE DU HAVRE has a refrain, its straightforward rhythm and harmonic variety are more typical of "churchly" hymnody than of gospel hymnody. Other Bliss tunes in this more churchly idiom are those to " 'Man of sorrows,' what a name" (1875, B56) and "More holiness give me" (1873, *Baptist Hymnal,* 1956, no. 338).

McGranahan (1840-1907), who after Bliss' death became Whittle's song leader, composed music for such gospel hymns by Whittle as "I know whom I have believed" (1883, EL NATHAN, first line: "I know not why God's wondrous grace," B344) and "There shall be showers of blessing" (1883, B273). McGranahan also composed the music to Bliss's "I will sing of my Redeemer" (1876, tune 1877, B465) and a German hymn of 1718 by Neumeister, "Sinners Jesus will receive" (1883, NEUMEISTER, B167).

George C. Stebbins (1846-1945), an evangelistic singer with Moody and others for some twenty-five years, composed the music to such popular gospel hymns as "Jesus is tenderly calling thee home" (1883, text by Crosby, B188, M110), "I've found a friend, O such a friend" (1878, text by James G. Small, 1863, B423, M163), and "Have thine own way, Lord" (1907, ADELAIDE, text by Adelaide A. Pollard, B349, M154).[44] Daniel B. Towner (1850-1919), the youngest of Moody's associates whose hymns survive, is especially important as an educator of evangelistic musicians, for he was head of the Music Department of Moody Bible Institute in Chicago from 1893 until his death. Of the more than 2,000 compositions credited to him, two which remain in use are the settings of "Trust and obey" (1887, first line: "When we walk with the Lord," text by John H. Sammis, B409, M223) and "Grace greater than our sin" (1910, MOODY, first line: "Marvelous grace of our loving Lord," text by Julia H. Johnson, B164).

Two gospel hymnists not associated with Moody whose surviving hymns were produced in the late nineteenth century are John R. Sweney (1837-99) and William J. Kirkpatrick (1838-1921), both Pennsylvanians. Sweney, a Presbyterian and a popular song leader for summer assemblies, composed more than 1,000 gospel hymns and compiled more than sixty collections. He wrote tunes for three gospel hymns in the 1880's which remain in use: "Tell me the story of Jesus" (1880, text by Crosby, B437), "More about Jesus would I know" (1887, text by Pennsylvania Presbyterian Eliza E. Hewitt, B327), and "There is sunshine in my soul today" (1887, SUNSHINE, text by Hewitt, B447).[45] Kirkpatrick, a Methodist active in Philadelphia, was associated with the publication of about 100 gospel hymn collections of various publishers. He wrote words and music for the invitation hymn, "Lord, I'm coming home" (1892, first line: "I've wandered far away from God," B174) and the music for "Jesus saves" (1882, first line: "We have heard the joyful sound," text *ca.* 1882 by Priscilla Owens, B277).

---

[44]Like Bliss, Stebbins also composed hymn tunes in other idioms. His tune EVENING PRAYER ("Savior, breathe an evening blessing," *Baptist Hymnal* 1956, no. 34), for example, is in a typical Victorian hymn tune style.

[45]It is of interest that both Sweney and Kirkpatrick were associated with Civil War military bands, a factor that may have influenced their gospel hymn melodies. Note, for example, the trumpet-call like melody to Kirkpatrick's setting of "Jesus saves" (B277).

The Early Twentieth Century

Following the era of Moody and Sankey, the pattern of each evangelist's having his own professional musicians became the norm. Among the musicians associated with evangelists, particularly important contributions to gospel hymnody were made by Charles M. Alexander (1867-1920) and Homer A. Rodeheaver (1880-1955).

Alexander, who was briefly associated with Moody in 1893, became famous through his meetings with evangelists Reuben A. Torry (1856-1928) and later J. Wilbur Chapman (1859-1918) in America, England, and Australia. Alexander, the opposite in personality from Sankey, eliminated all vestiges of dignity and formality in his revival services, leading the singing with wide sweeping motions of his hands and preferring improvised trills and cadenzas on the piano to simple organ accompaniment. In keeping with the lighthearted mood of his song services, Alexander popularized "The Glory Song" (1900, first line: "When all my labors and trials are o'er," text and tune by Charles H. Gabriel, B497), a gospel hymn that lent itself to interpretive effects. Although not a composer, Alexander compiled widely used collections of gospel hymns; and some of his copyrights are solos and congregational hymns still in use, the latter category including "One day when heaven was filled with his praises" (*ca.* 1909, CHAPMAN, by Charles H. Marsh, text by J. Wilbur Chapman, B127).

Rodeheaver became famous as the song leader for William (Billy) Sunday (1862-1935). His approach to music in evangelism (similar to Alexander's) was enhanced by his vocal and trombone solos. To those who criticized his use of a secular-sounding gospel hymn, Rodeheaver replied:

"It was never intended for a Sunday morning service, not for a devotional meeting—its purpose was to bridge the gap between the popular song of the day and the great hymns and gospel songs, and to give men a simple, easy lilting melody which they could learn the first time they heard it, and which they could whistle and sing wherever they might be."[46]

Rodeheaver established his own music publishing firm in 1910, later locating it at Winona Lake, Indiana (now a part of Word Music, Incorporated). Rodeheaver composed little but published many gospel hymns; two of his most popular copyrights were "In the Garden" (1912, first line: "I come to the garden alone," text and tune by C. Austin Miles, B428) and "The Old Rugged Cross" (1913, first line: "On a hill far away stood an old rugged cross," text and tune by George Bennard, B430, M228).

The music editor for Rodeheaver from 1912 until his death in 1932 was the prolific Charles H. Gabriel (b. 1856), who produced numerous gospel hymn

[46]Homer Rodeheaver, *Twenty Years with Billy Sunday* (Nashville: Cokesbury Press, 1936), p. 78.

collections. Like Bliss and Lowry before him, Gabriel wrote both words and music of gospel hymns. Hymns of Gabriel still in use include "Send the Light" (1890, McCABE, "There's a call comes ringing o'er the restless wave," B304), "I stand amazed in the presence" (1905, MY SAVIOR'S LOVE, B63), and the music to "Higher Ground" (text 1892, HIGHER GROUND "I'm pressing on the upward way," Johnson Oatman, Jr., B324) and "Since Jesus came into my heart" (1914, McDANIEL, "What a wonderful change in my life has been wrought," Rufus H. McDaniel, B487).

Shape-note Gospel Hymnody

Following the Civil War, the impact of urban influence from the North was increasingly felt upon the rural shape-note hymnody of the South. The seven-shape tunebooks included smaller portions of indigenous folk hymns, and larger portions of European music and music by such European-oriented composers as Mason, Hastings, and Bradbury, together with a Southern type of gospel hymn. One nineteenth-century Southern gospel hymn tune that has survived is the setting of "Footsteps of Jesus" (1871, text by Massachusetts schoolteacher Mary B. C. Slade, FOOTSTEPS, "Sweetly Lord, have we heard thee calling," B325) by the Virginian (and European-trained) Asa B. Everett (1828-75). This hymn tune, while embodying the slow harmonic rhythm and limited harmonic vocabulary of a gospel hymn, is a quasi-pentatonic[47] melody, a reflection of the earlier folk hymn tradition.

"Leaning on the everlasting arms" (1887, SHOWALTER, "What a fellowship, what a joy divine," Elisa A. Hoffman, B254) was set to music by Anthony J. Showalter (1858-1924), a Virginian who established in 1884 at Dalton, Georgia, the A. J. Showalter Music Company. The tune SHOWALTER has a hexatonic melody, omitting the fourth degree of the scale. "Victory in Jesus" (1939, HARTFORD, "I heard an old, old story," B475) was both written and composed by Eugene M. Bartlett (1885-1941), president of the Hartford (Arkansas) Music Company (1918-35), who was later associated with the leading shape-note publishing firms, the Stamps-Baxter Music Company,[48] Dallas, Texas, and the James D. Vaughan Music Company, Lawrenceburg, Tennessee.[49] Shape-note gospel hymns have found a firm place in the churches of several Southern denominations, including the Church of God, Cleveland, Tennessee.

In contrast to Northern gospel hymnody, the environment of Southern

[47]The seventh of the major scale is missing and the fourth occurs only once.
[48]Now under Northern ownership, this firm is known as Stamps-Baxter Music of the Zondervan Corporation. For a study of the texts and music of shape-note gospel hymnody based on Stamps-Baxter publications, see Shirley Beary, "Stylistic Traits of Southern Shape-Note Gospel Songs," *The Hymn* 30 (January 1979), 26-33,35.
[49]This firm, no longer owned by the Vaughan family, is now located at Cleveland, Tennessee.

shape-note gospel hymnody has been largely rural or small town. Its context has been the singing school and the singing convention rather than mass revivalism. More recently this tradition has been dominated by professional concert and recording artists in the gospel music field.[50] Although some congregational singing remains in current shape-note gospel singing, it has generally taken second place to professional performance.

Recent Gospel Hymnody

Mass urban revivalism declined after the early decades of this century; but gospel hymns have continued to be written, published, and widely sung. These hymns have gained a substantial place in the congregational singing of fundamentalist churches as well as in a number of America's evangelical denominations, such as Assemblies of God, Southern Baptists,[51] Churches of Christ, Churches of the Nazarene, Seventh-Day Adventists, Churches of God, and various Pentecostal bodies.

"Great is thy faithfulness" (FAITHFULNESS, B216), one of the few gospel hymns addressed to God rather than to one's fellowman, was written in 1923 by the Methodist minister Thomas O. Chisholm (1866-1960) and set to music by another Methodist minister and music editor who for many years was associated with the Moody Bible Institute, William M. Runyan (1870-1957). The words and music to "He Lives" (ACKLEY, "I serve a risen Savior," B438) were written in 1933 by the Presbyterian minister Alfred H. Ackley (1887-1960),[52] who was associated with the Rodeheaver Publishing Company as a compiler and editor. This exuberant gospel hymn incorporates an expanded harmonic vocabulary and vocal range. A third representative newer gospel hymn is "Surely Goodness and Mercy" (GOODNESS, "A pilgrim was I and a wand'ring," B228), whose text and tune were jointly written in 1958 by John W. Peterson (b. 1921) and Alfred B. Smith (b. 1916), both active gospel hymn composers and editors. This gospel hymn, an expression of the Christian pilgrimage based on Psalm 23, incorporates a florid style and an expanded form that includes a coda. Smith, the first song leader for Billy Graham, established in 1941 the music publishing firm of Singspiration, which he sold to the Zondervan Publishing House, Grand Rapids, Michigan, in 1962. A prolific hymn writer and composer, Peterson has published more than 1,000

---

[50]The primary organization that serves the interests of the gospel music industry is the Gospel Music Association, Nashville, Tennessee.

[51]The leading gospel hymn writer-composer among Southern Baptists was B. B. McKinney (1886-1952), who edited the popular *Broadman Hymnal* (Nashville: Broadman Press, 1940) and is represented by more than a dozen hymns in *Baptist Hymnal* (1975). See William J. Reynolds, *Companion to Baptist Hymnal* (Nashville: Broadman Press, 1976), pp. 376-77.

[52]His brother, Bentley D. Ackley (1872-1958), also a hymn writer, was pianist for many years in the Sunday-Rodeheaver meetings.

songs. Another recent gospel hymn, written in 1971, is "Because He Lives" (RESURRECTION, "God sent his Son, they called him Jesus," B448). An Indiana couple, Gloria (b. 1942) and William J. Gaither (b. 1936), wrote the text; and William J. Gaither composed the music. "Because He Lives," which shares a similar theme with Ackley's "He Lives," also has in common with this earlier gospel hymn an expanded range and harmonic vocabulary. The Gaithers are widely known in America as performers, recording artists, and publishers of gospel music.

Black Gospel Hymnody

Black gospel hymnody is based on elements of the spiritual and the blues as well as the white gospel hymn, but its style of performance is distinctively black. Important factors in its performance are its improvised melodies and rhythmic piano accompaniments, which since the 1940's have been combined with the Hammond electronic organ. In black holiness churches various percussion instruments are also used. Although black gospel hymnody is a twentieth-century development, its roots lie in a much older tradition of preaching, singing (including a continuing tradition of lining-out[53]), shouting, and clapping. Black gospel music is known to whites primarily through professional performers, such as Mahalia Jackson (1911-1972) and Andraé Crouch (b. 1942) and the Disciples.

The distinction between congregation and choir (or ensembles or soloists) is blurred in black worship; for the congregation often sings along with the choir and expresses its joy or affirmation in terms of hand-clapping, "hallelujahs," or "amens."

Two representative composers of black gospel hymnody are Charles A. Tindley (1851-1933) and Thomas A. Dorsey (b. 1899). Tindley, pastor of the Tindley Temple Methodist Church in Philadelphia from 1902 until his death, wrote both words and music to "We'll understand it better by and by" (1905, first line: "We are often tossed and driv'n on the restless sea of time"[54]; BY AND BY, altered version: "Trials dark on ev'ry hand, And we cannot understand," B499) and "Stand by me" (1905, first line: "When the storms of life are raging, Stand by me," M244[55]). Both of these hymns reflect the life of poverty and discrimination that many black Americans have experienced. Note, for example, the second stanza of "We'll understand it better by and by":

[53]Ben E. Bailey, "The Lined-Hymn Tradition in Black Mississippi Churches," *The Black Perspective in Music* (spring 1978), 3-17.
[54]*The New National Baptist Hymnal* (Hereafter: N) (Nashville: National Baptist Publishing Board, 1977), no. 325; *A.M.E. Hymnal* (Hereafter: A) (N. P.: A.M.E. Sunday School Union, 1954), no. 542.
[55]A287, N500.

We are often destitute of the things that life demands,
Want of food and want of shelter—thirsty hills and barren lands,
We are trusting in the Lord, and according to His Word,
We will understand it better by and by.

Dorsey, a native of Georgia who has lived in Chicago throughout his adult life, composed both blues and gospel in his early years, but since 1929 he has devoted himself exclusively to gospel music. Two of his best-known hymns for which he wrote both words and music are "Precious Lord, take my hand" (1932)[56] and "There'll be peace in the valley for me" (1939), first line: "I am tired and weary, but I must toil on").[57] These hymns, like those of Tindley, offer encouragement and hope to the discouraged and weary.

To understand the significance of black gospel hymnody and black church music in general, it is necessary to go beyond the pages of a hymnal to experience these hymns amid the enthusiastic mood of traditional black worship. Black church music, and black gospel hymnody in particular, cannot be adequately studied from a printed page; the musical score provides only a skeleton which when clothed through embellishments and other variations in performance, assumes a form that has an expressive character of its own.

Summary

Gospel hymnody, forged in the setting of the urban Sunday School and mass revivalism, exemplifies the same freedom of personal expression found in the earlier rural hymns and Negro spirituals. The more artistic gospel hymns have survived and can be found in many hymnals, especially those of churches involved in revivalism. Gospel hymnody has not been limited to America and Britain. Through the work of missionaries and evangelists this hymnody has been translated into many languages and has spread to every continent. It is of interest to note, for example, that some gospel hymns which are no longer in current use in this country still survive in Spanish and Portuguese hymnals used by Latin American Evangelicals. Gospel hymnody has not remained static in musical style or language; it has continued a process of development in its more than a century of existence. A gospel hymn of Sankey's day, for example, will be recognizably different from most gospel hymns of Peterson or Gaither. Furthermore, offshoots of gospel hymnody, such as shape-note gospel hymnody (based on folk hymnody) and black gospel hymnody (based on the spiritual), have also developed from the older traditions.

Hymnology in America

Many major American hymnals now have companions or handbooks which

[56]A333, N339.
[57]N446.

provide background information on each of their hymns and tunes and biographical sketches of their authors and composers. Behind these companion volumes lies a wealth of hymnological scholarship dating back to the nineteenth century.

Two American hymnologists who contributed to Julian's *A Dictionary of Hymnology* (1892) are Philip Schaff (1819-1893) and Louis F. Benson (1855-1930). Schaff, a Reformed Church minister born in Switzerland and with university training in Germany, came to Pennsylvania at the age of twenty-four to teach theology. His hymnological works include an important Julian *Dictionary* article on "German Hymnody."[58] Benson, a Presbyterian minister who is recognized as America's greatest hymnologist, was also a hymnal editor and hymn writer. Benson's *The English Hymn* (1915) continues to be the most definitive history of the hymn in English.[59]

Whereas Schaff and Benson were concerned mainly with the *texts* of hymns, two other American hymnologists dealt with the *music* of congregational song. Waldo Selden Pratt (1857-1939), a musicologist who taught church music and hymnology at Hartford Theological Seminary, wrote two works dealing with the music of metrical psalmody: *The Music of the Pilgrims* (1921) and *The Music of the French Psalter of 1562* (1939).[60] Robert Guy McCutchan (1877-1958) was a college music teacher and administrator who edited *The Methodist Hymnal* (1935) and authored its companion, *Our Hymnody* (1937), the first hymnal companion of significance to be published in America.[61]

Hymnology in America has advanced significantly through the work of the Hymn Society of America, an interdenominational organization founded in 1922. In addition to its activities encouraging the writing of new hymns and tunes and giving impetus to congregational singing in general, it has published a series of scholarly papers (from 1930 on) as well as numerous hymnological studies in its quarterly, *The Hymn* (from 1949 on).

The Dictionary of American Hymnology Project (DAH) is a mammoth endeavor of the Society to produce an American equivalent of Julian, *Dictionary of Hymnology.* The DAH, which grew out of efforts to update the American sections of Julian, was first under the editorship of Henry Wilder Foote[62] in the early 1950's and since 1955 has been edited by Leonard

[58]Richard G. Appel, "Philip Schaff, Pioneer American Hymnologist," *The Hymn* 14 (January 1963), 5-7.

[59]Morgan Phelps Noyes, *Louis F. Benson, Hymnologist,* Paper XIX of the Hymn Society of America, 1955.

[60]"Waldo Selden Pratt," *The Hymn* 6, 2 (April 1955), 38. See also Pratt's *The Significance of the Old French Psalter,* Paper IV of the Hymn Society of America, 1933.

[61]Helen Cowles McCutchan, *Born to Music,* Paper XXVIII of the Hymn Society of America, 1973.

[62]See Arthur Foote, 2nd, *Henry Wilder Foote, Hymnologist,* Paper XXVI of the Hymn Society of America, 1965.

Ellinwood.[63] As of early 1979, the DAH files contained approximately 900,000 hymn data cards resulting from the indexing of over 4,000 American and Canadian hymnals in addition to numerous biographical sketches and essays on American hymnody. The DAH is nearing completion and publication is expected in the 1980's.

Twentieth-Century Churchly Hymnody

Hymns in Ecumenical Use

Six American hymn texts and two American hymn tunes of this century have found a place in most major hymnals issued in this country in recent years.

Four of the six hymn texts were written before World War I. The earliest, a favorite hymn for children as well as adults, is "This is my Father's world" (TERRA PATRIS, B155, L554, M45; MERCER STREET, E108), written in 1901 by Presbyterian minister Maltbie D. Babcock (1858-1901) and set to music in 1915 by his friend Franklin L. Sheppard (1852-1930). In 1903 appeared "Where cross the crowded ways of life" (GERMANY or WALTON, B311, L429, M204), written by the Methodist minister Frank Mason North (1850-1935). North, who from 1892 to 1912 edited *The Christian City,* incorporated his concern for reaching the urban masses with the Christian message into this hymn, which has become the classic American hymn on the city. In 1907 "Joyful, joyful we adore thee" (HYMN TO JOY, B31, L551, M38) was written (to fit the famous melody from Beethoven's *Ninth Symphony*) by the Presbyterian minister and professor of English literature, Henry Van Dyke (1852-1933). Van Dyke's exuberant hymn together with Beethoven's joyful melody is a fine example of unity in text and tune. This joyous hymn is often used for processionals and is appropriate at weddings. The fourth pre-World War I hymn now in general use is "Rise up, O men of God" (ST. THOMAS, B268; FESTAL SONG, M174), written in 1911 by Presbyterian minister William P. Merrill (1867-1954). This hymn emphasizes brotherhood, a significant theme of twentieth-century hymnody. All three of these Presbyterian hymn writers of the early twentieth century served at one time as pastors of New York City's historic Brick Presbyterian Church: Van Dyke from 1883-99, Babcock from 1899-1901, and Merrill from 1911-38.[64]

In 1917 the hymn tune ST. DUNSTAN'S (B384, L498, M155) appeared. It was composed for Bunyan's "He (All) who would valiant be" by Episcopal Canon C. Winfred Douglas (1867-1944). Douglas was a leading influence in restoring plainsong to use in the Episcopal Church. He was editor of the Episcopal *New*

[63]Leonard Ellinwood, "The Dictionary of American Hymnology Project," *The Hymn* 19 (January 1968), 19-22.

[64]See Edith Holden and George Litch Knight, "Brick Church's Role in American Hymnody," *The Hymn* 3, 3 (July 1952), 73-78.

Hymnal (1918) and greatly influenced *The Hymnal 1940.*[65]
"God of grace and God of glory" (CWM RHONDDA, B265, L415, M470) was written for the dedication of the Riverside Church in New York City in 1930 by its prominent minister, Harry Emerson Fosdick (1878-1969). Fosdick, a Baptist, sought to make the Riverside Church an ecumenical congregation, serving the needs of all classes of people. This hymn, his prayer for wisdom and courage, has become a prayer of worshiping groups throughout America.[66]

The most recent American hymn to gain general use in major hymnals is "Hope of the world, thou Christ of great compassion" (O PERFECT LOVE, B364; DONNE SECOURS, L493: VICAR, M161). It was written in 1954 for the Second Assembly of the World Council of Churches at Evanston, Illinois, by the Methodist minister and theologian Georgia Harkness (1891-1974). This hymn, like Fosdick's earlier hymn, is a fervent prayer affirming Christ as "Hope of the world" and ending with a strong assertion of God's victory.[67] "Hope of the world" was the winning hymn of a competition sponsored in 1954 by the Hymn Society of America. This is one of a number of hymns resulting from the Hymn Society's "searches."

Hymns of Wide Acceptance

In addition to the above hymns and tunes of twentieth-century America, twelve other hymn texts and one additional hymn tune are frequently found in current hymnals.

Three of these hymns appeared before 1920. "We praise thee, O God, our Redeemer, Creator" (KREMSER, B15; "We praise you, O God, our redeemer, creator," L241) was written by Presbyterian[68] Julia Cady Cory (1882-1963) in 1902 before she was twenty years of age. William P. Merrill wrote "Not alone for mighty empire" (GENEVA, L437; HYFRYDOL, M548) in 1909. This text, appropriate for use at Thanksgiving or other national holidays, expresses the need for social justice.

> God of justice, save the people
> From the clash of race and creed;
> From the strife of class and faction,
> Make our nation free indeed.

[65]See Mrs. Winfred Douglas and Leonard Ellinwood, *To Praise God: the Life and Work of Canon Winfred Douglas.* Papers of the Hymn Society of America, XXIII, New York, 1958.
[66]See Linda Clark, "God of Grace and God of Glory: A Very Urgent Personal Prayer," *The Hymn* 29 (October 1978), 206-210,213.
[67]See Deborah C. Loftis, "The Hymns of Georgia Harkness," *The Hymn* 28 (October 1977), 186-91.
[68]She was also associated with New York City's Brick Presbyterian Church and wrote this hymn for the tune KREMSER at the request of this church's organist, J. Archer Gibson.

Keep its faith in simple justice
Strong as when its life began,
Till it find complete fruition
By the guiding of your hand.

Another hymn concerned with social justice is "O holy city seen of John" (MORNING SONG, M481), written in 1910 by Walter Russell Bowie (1882-1969), a distinguished Episcopal clergyman and seminary professor. In 1928 he wrote "Lord Christ when first thou cam'st to men" (you came to earth) (MIT FREUDEN ZART, L421; KIRKEN DEN ER ET GAMMELT HUS, M355), an Advent hymn with an emphasis on judgment written for inclusion in the English hymnal *Songs of Praise* (1931).

Two more of these hymns were written in the 1920's. Louis F. Benson (1855-1930) wrote in 1924 the communion hymn "For the bread which thou hast broken" (KINGDOM, M314; "For the bread which you have broken," OMNI DIE, L200). In 1925 Lutheran minister and hymnologist Ernest E. Ryden (b. 1886) wrote "How blessed is this place, O Lord" (SOLOTHURN, L186; KENT, M350), a hymn appropriate for church dedication.

The first of three hymns from this group written in the 1930's is "And have the bright immensities" (KINGSFOLD, L391; HALIFAX, M456), an unusual hymn on Christ's ascension and living presence written in 1931 by Episcopal minister and seminary professor Howard Chandler Robbins (1876-1952). A second hymn from the 1930's is "O Spirit of the living God" (LLANFYLLIN, B264, M136) (one of the relatively few hymns of this century on the Holy Spirit), written in 1935 by Congregationalist minister and hymnal compiler Henry H. Tweedy (1868-1953). The third hymn from this decade is "All praise to thee, for thou, O King divine" (SINE NOMINE, B43, M74), a paraphrase of Philippians 2:5-11 by Episcopal minister F. Bland Tucker (b. 1895).

Of the three remaining hymns, one was published in the 1950's and two in the 1960's. One hymn appeared as part of a Hymn Society of America publication, *Ten New Hymns on the Bible* (1952) a booklet for the celebration of the initial publication of the Revised Standard Version of the Bible. "O God of light, thy Word, a lamp unfailing" (WELWYN, M371; "O God of light, your Word, a lamp unfailing," ATKINSON, L237) was written by Sarah E. Taylor (1883-1954), a Rhode Island Primitive Methodist schoolteacher. In 1959 the hymn "Where charity and love prevail" (CHRISTIAN LOVE, B257; TWENTY-FOURTH, L126), a paraphrase of a ninth-century Latin hymn, was written by the Roman Catholic church musician and publisher, Omer Westendorf (b. 1916). Westendorf founded the World Library of Sacred Music in 1950 and compiled a widely used hymnal, *The People's Mass Book* (Cincinnati, 1964, later eds. 1966, 1970, 1976). The tune CHRISTIAN LOVE was written at the request of Westendorf by the Luxemburg organist, Dom Paul

Benoit (b. 1893) at Nancy, France). The hymn tune PERRY ("This is the Spirit's entry now," L195; "Beneath the forms of outward rite," E62, M321) was composed in 1962 for use in *The Methodist Hymnal* (1966) by the distinguished Episcopalian organist, teacher, and composer, Leo Sowerby (1895-1968). One twentieth-century trait of PERRY is its lack of a time signature and its varying number of beats per measure.

Summary

Twentieth-century American hymn *texts* in the churchly stream that have achieved broad acceptance are few; even fewer American hymn *tunes* of this tradition are widely used. In contrast to England, American hymnists of this century have not yet written a significant number of widely accepted hymns.

Several themes are recognizable in twentieth-century American hymns:

1. Brotherhood is a prominent emphasis, exemplified by "Joyful, joyful we adore thee" and "Rise up, O men of God."

2. No longer strictly rural in their context, hymns also recognize the needs of urban Americans. The classic American hymn on the city is "Where cross the crowded ways of life."[69]

3. There is an increasing emphasis on justice and social responsibility. These related themes are especially prominent in "God of grace and God of glory," "Not alone for mighty empire," and "O holy city seen of John."

4. America's experience in the tragic wars of this century is reflected in hymns emphasizing the tragedy of strife and the need for peace (e.g., "Hope of the world").[70]

5. Many recent hymns are occasional, having been written for specific events. "God of grace and God of glory" was written for the dedication of the Riverside Church in 1930. "Hope of the world" was written for the Second Assembly of the World Council of Churches in 1954. "O God of light, thy Word a lamp unfailing" was written for the initial publication of the Revised Standard Version of the Bible in 1952.

Most American denominations have issued hymnals in recent years, each compiled to fit the needs of its own constituency. Thus each hymnal is distinctive, mirroring a particular heritage which in turn reflects a history of theological beliefs and musical tastes. In some cases several denominations, especially those of similar background, have combined their efforts to produce a single hymnal. The *Lutheran Book of Worship* (1978), for example, was

---

[69]Other city-oriented American hymns include "Jesus, friend of throning pilgrims" (B100), "Stir thy church, O God our Father" (B269), "Where restless crowds are thronging" (L430), "O Jesus Christ, may grateful hymns be rising" (L427), and "The voice of God is calling" (M200). See chap. 13, The Hymn in Ministry.

[70]Other American hymns reflecting these themes include "Peace in our time, O Lord" (B310), "O God of every nation" (L416), and "O God, empower us" (L422).

Reginald Heber

compiled by several cooperating Lutheran bodies in this country. Some have also sought to encourage ecumenism in hymnody. The Consultation on Ecumenical Hymnody[71] has published lists of hymns and tunes recommended for ecumenical use. But in spite of ecumenical influences, each denomination's hymnal still tends to embody much of its own heritage. Practically all recent major American hymnals have incorporated a greater representation of early American folk hymnody (including Negro spirituals) than in the past. These recent hymnals are also admitting hymns from the Third World cultures of Africa and the Orient.[72] America's pluralistic society is reflected in the great variety of its religious denominations, and this pluralism is accurately pictured in the wide diversity of its hymnals and in its varied congregational singing practices.

Recent Canadian Hymnody

Hymn writing has flourished in Canada since the middle of this century. In *The Hymn Book* (1971), a joint project of the Anglican Church of Canada and the United Church of Canada,[73] there are no less than forty-five Canadian authors represented. Of these, twenty-four had not appeared in any previous hymnal.[74]

Among Canadian hymnists represented in American hymnals are Robert B. Y. Scott (b. 1899), Moir A. J. Waters (b. 1906), and Thomas B. McDormand (b. 1904). Scott, a United Church minister and former theological seminary professor now in Toronto, is best known for his hymn of judgment, "O day of God, draw nigh" (1939, ST. MICHAEL, M477). Waters, also of the United Church of Canada, wrote in 1968 a hymn on John the Baptist as the herald of Jesus, "Herald! sound the note of judgment" (NEW MALDEN, L556). McDormand, of Amherst, Nova Scotia, is perhaps the best-known Baptist hymnist in Canada. Two of his hymns for the observance of the Lord's Supper are "From every race, from every clime" (1970, DAUGAVA, B247) and "Where can we find thee, Lord, so near" (1974, FEDERAL STREET, B245).

A leading representative of a younger generation of Canadian hymn writers is Walter H. Farquharson (b. 1936), a United Church pastor and a high school English teacher at Saltcoats, Saskatchewan. "God who gives to life its

[71]See Ford Lewis Battles and Morgan Simmons, "The Consultation on Ecumenical Hymnody," *The Hymn* 28 (April 1977), 67-68,87; "Hymns and Tunes Recommended for Ecumenical Use," *The Hymn* 28 (October 1977), 192-209; and Robert J. Batastini, Donald P. Hustad, Austin C. Lovelace, and Cyril V. Taylor, "The CEH List: Four Diverse Appraisals." *The Hymn* 29 (April 1978), 83-90.

[72]See examples in chap. 9, Cultural Perspectives.

[73]The United Church of Canada is a union of Congregational, Methodist, Presbyterian, and United Brethren bodies.

[74]Stanley L. Osborne, "Recent Canadian Hymnody," *The Hymn* 29, 3 (July 1978), 135. This article is an excellent survey of recent Canadian hymn texts.

goodness" (1969, ABBOT'S LEIGH) is one of his four hymns in the 1971 Anglican-United *Hymn Book*. Stanley L. Osborne writes that this hymn "expresses a basic tenet of the Christian faith, namely, that man's chief end is 'to glorify God and enjoy him forever.' It celebrates God's limitless giving, his blessing of our work and leisure, and his mighty acts both in the physical and primal things of life.'"[75]

> God who gives to life its goodness,
>   God creator of all joy,
> God who gives to us our freedom,
>   God who blesses tool and toy;
> teach us now to laugh and praise you,
>   deep within your praises sing,
> till the whole creation dances
>   for the goodness of its King.
>
> God who fills the earth with beauty,
>   God who binds each friend to friend,
> God who names us co-creators,
>   God who wills that chaos end:
> grant us now creative spirits,
>   minds responsive to your mind,
> hearts and wills your rule extending,
>   all our acts by Love refined.[76]

Canada has thus experienced a flowering of hymn writing in recent decades similar to that of England. Perhaps in the coming decades a similar resurgence of hymn writing will take place also in the United States of America. Meanwhile an impressive body of recent Canadian hymnody awaits the consideration of hymnal committees south of its border.

---

[75]Stanley L. Osborne, *If Such Holy Song, The Story of the Hymns in The Hymn Book 1971* (Whitby, Ontario: The Institute of Church Music, 1976), no. 88.
[76]© 1970 Walter Henry Farquharson. Used by permission.*

9

Cultural Perspectives

Cultural Diversity of Congregational Song

The typical hymnal of our time is an anthology of poetry and music representing many diverse cultures. Culture, which may be described simply as the "man-made part of the environment,"[1] includes to some extent what we eat and drink, what we wear, what we read, and what we sing. A hymn is man-made and therefore is a work of culture reflecting a particular heritage.

The cultural diversity of current hymnals may be described in various ways. Hymns in most American hymnals primarily come from Great Britain and the United States, with a lesser proportion from Continental Europe and a much smaller number from other continents. Cultural diversity is also evident in the many languages in which hymns have been written. Beginning with the Greek and Latin tongues of Medieval Christianity, hymns have been written in each of the major modern languages of Europe (with an especially large number in German and English). With the spread of Christianity to Africa, Asia, Australia, and the Americas, hymns are found in the various native tongues of these continents. Today hymnals may be seen in every country where there are Christian churches. Although these hymnals typically contain a large number of hymns from Europe and/or North America (the traditional nineteenth and twentieth century missionary-sending areas), hymnals in Third World countries are evidencing the development of congregational song in the language and musical idiom of each indigenous culture.

The cultural diversity of congregational song exists not only in reference to different continents and nations but is also found within a single nation. In the United States, for example, there exists a large number of religious denominations, each with its own heritage of hymns. Although some denominations have similar enough heritages to enable them to use the same hymnal, most religious bodies have one or more hymnals, compiled specifically for their own use. Cultural diversity also exists in congregational song among regions of a nation. For example, the southern part of the United States in particular developed a large body of folk hymnody, including expressions of song from both white and black communities.

Diversity in congregational song also exists in congregations of the same community and denomination. Among denominations that have no official hymnal it is not uncommon for some of its churches in the same city to use

---

[1]Melville J. Herskovits, *Cultural Anthropology* (New York: Alfred A. Knopf, 1958), p. 305. Note that this definition of culture as used by anthropologists differs considerably from the elitest sense which signifies that some people have culture and others do not.

different hymnals. Even when congregations use the same hymnal, their preferences may vary, depending on their cultural backgrounds.

Cultural diversity in hymns and hymn singing may also be viewed on an individual level. Why do you prefer to sing hymns of a particular type? If you have a favorite hymn, why is it your favorite? The answers to these questions must involve an examination of one's own cultural background, including experiences with congregational song from the time of childhood to the adult years.

Since New Testament times Christianity has been a singing faith, a faith which broke out of the bonds of a narrow nationalism to spread to every continent. The message of Christianity is expressed in hymns which parallel to some extent the cultural diversity that exists among nations and continents, among language groups and races, among religious denominations, among regions, among local congregations, and among individuals.

Understanding Hymnic Diversity

To understand the diversity of congregational song from a cultural perspective, one views the hymn as a human expression of religious thought reflecting a particular culture or cultures in which it originated. Study of the origin of a hymn may help us to understand why the author wrote the hymn, why the composer wrote the hymn tune, and why each is written in a particular style.

Each hymn originates within a particular cultural setting, a human environment shaped by numerous factors, such as geography, race, language, economic status, religion, family life, and social customs. A cultural understanding of a hymn involves examination of its setting, including both the circumstances of its origin and of its continuing use.

In addition to a consideration of its human context, the hymn must be studied in regard to how it functions within its setting. Does the hymn function as an expression of formal worship within a liturgical service? Does the hymn function as a tool of evangelism within an informal revival service? Does the hymn function in a very personal way to comfort an individual or family in a time of sorrow? Questions such as these involve a study of the hymn beyond its existence as words and music printed in a hymnal. From this perspective one views the hymn as it again comes alive in human experience, functioning in a certain way in a particular cultural context.

Traditions Illustrating Cultural Diversity

The cultural diversity of congregational song can be illustrated by many Christian traditions. Several of these will be briefly described in this section, with a focus first on several traditions of the United States of America and then on one tradition each of Europe, Africa, and Asia.

Lining-out

This first example illustrates conflict between those who wanted to sing in an established tradition and those who wanted to replace it with another tradition of congregational music. Early eighteenth-century New England congregations were lining-out their psalms, following a practice brought over from England. It originated because the people either could not read or did not have hymnbooks.

In lining-out, the minister or deacon would read or sing the metrical psalm (or hymn) line by line before it was sung by the congregation. In time the psalm tunes used in early New England became considerably altered, so much that one of their ministers observed that in their congregations it was "hard to find two that sing exactly alike"; he further observed concerning their singing that "Your usual way of singing is handed down by tradition only, and whatsoever is only so conveyed down to us, it is a thousand to one if it be not miserably corrupted, in three or four-score years' time."[2] Several of these New England ministers had studied music at Harvard and become greatly concerned for the state of their congregational singing which one of them viewed as a "horrid Medley of confused and disorderly Noises."[3]

Singing schools to teach music reading eventually brought the practice of lining-out and its accompanying style of singing to an end in early New England. In spite of widespread ridicule, lining-out has survived even today in some Primitive Baptist and in certain black Baptist congregations.[4]

Although one may take the view that lining-out was simply an inferior type of congregational singing practiced only by the uneducated, Gilbert Chase has made a strong case for regarding it as an "Early New England Folk Style" with the same call-and-response pattern and traits of oral tradition found in the Negro spiritual and in certain other bodies of folk song.[5]

To come to an appreciation of what lining-out meant and still means to those who practice it, it is important for us to suspend temporarily our own cultural conditioning and to seek with imagination and empathy to adopt the perspective of those who carry on this tradition. When one adopts this

[2]Thomas Symmes, *The Reasonableness of Regular Singing, or Singing by Note* (Boston, 1720); Quoted in Gilbert Chase, *America's Music* 2nd ed. rev. (New York: McGraw Hill, 1966), pp. 28-29.

[3]Thomas Walter, *The Grounds and Rules of Musick Explained, or An Introduction to the Art of Singing by Note* (Boston: Printed by J. Franklin, 1721); quoted in Chase, p. 26.

[4]See Terry W. York, "Lining-Out in Congregational Singing," *The Hymn* 28, 3 (July, 1977), 110-117.

[5]Chase, p. 33. For an interesting and provocative description and interpretation of this early New England cultural conflict, see Chase's chapter, "New England Reformers," pp. 22-40. Lining-out has also survived in Gaelic congregational singing in certain isolated areas of Scotland. See the phonorecord, *Gaelic Psalms from Lewis*, recorded and documented by the School of Scottish Studies, University of Edinburgh. Tangent Records TNGM 120 (52 Shaftesbury Avenue, London WIV 7DE).

perspective—an attitude and an approach known as cultural relativism[6] and practiced by anthropologists—one can gain new insight into the meaning of congregational song to persons in cultures that are different from his own.

Old Order Amish

This Swiss-American denomination, stemming from the Anabaptist-Mennonite branch of the Reformation, has sought to maintain its cultural heritage through its religious faith, its strong family ties, its use of the Pennsylvania Dutch (German) dialect in their homes, and through its separation from the world by rejecting many elements of present-day culture. These conservative people are largely farmers or carpenters by trade. They are well-known for conflicts with governmental authorities over their objection to having their children attend school beyond the elementary grades, for they believe that modern high school education destroys their agricultural way of life.

The Old Order Amish do not build church buildings but meet in homes, where worship services are conducted in the standard German of their European forefathers.[7] Their singing is from the Anabaptist *Ausbund* (1564), a German-words-only hymnal whose content has been little changed since the sixteenth century.[8] The Amish do not use musical instruments in worship and have refused to notate their music. They have developed a style of embellished singing which may not be far from that associated with lining-out in early New England. Scholars who have transcribed the hymn singing of the Amish and eliminated notes considered to be embellishments have discovered both secular and sacred melodies from the sixteenth century,[9] preserved in oral tradition by the Amish and their forefathers for more than 400 years! Although their embellished singing of these old melodies may sound strange to an outsider, to

---

[6]See David Biley, "Culture: Cultural Relativism," in *International Encyclopedia of the Social Sciences*, edited by David L. Silles, Vol. 3 (New York: The Macmillan Co., and The Free Press, 1968), p. 543.

[7]For an interesting introduction to Amish culture, see John A. Hostetler, *Amish Life* (Scottdale, Pa.: Herald Press, 1952, 1959).

[8]A reprint of the first American printing of the *Ausbund* was made in 1975 by the Lancaster Press, Inc., Lancaster, Pennsylvania. Copies can be ordered from Gordonville Bookstore, Gordonville, PA 17529. See Martin E. Ressler, "Hymnbooks Used by the Old Order Amish," *The Hymn* 28 (January 1977), 11-16. One hymn from the *Ausbund* sung by the Old Order Amish as the second hymn in every morning service is the *Lob Lied* (Praise Song), *O Gott Vater, wir loben dich*, translated by Ernest A. Payne as "Our Father God, thy name we praise" (B206). See Martin E. Ressler, "A Song of Praise," *Pennsylvania Mennonite Heritage* 1 (October 1978), 10-13.

[9]Paul M. Yoder, "The Ausbund" in *Four Hundred Years with the Ausbund* (Scottdale, PA.: Herald Press, 1964), pp. 7-10. For an extensive study of Old Order Amish hymnody, see Rupert Karl Hohmann, "The Church Music of the Old Order Amish of the United States" (Ph.D. dissertation, Northwestern University, 1959).

the Old Order Amish these hymns have a deep significance which can be appreciated by one adopting a cultural perspective of hymnody.[10]

Shape-note

This tradition of hymnody, in general use in singing schools and churches of the South and Midwest in the mid-nineteenth century, takes its name from a system of notation in which the solmization syllables are represented by different shaped noteheads designed to simplify music reading. In spite of the rejection of shape notes by leading music educators and the devastation of Southern culture by the Civil War, this system has survived and today has two bodies of hymnody associated with it: (1) the older folk hymnody stemming from the pre-Civil War period, represented mainly in singings using the famous tunebooks, *Southern Harmony* (1835) and *The Sacred Harp* (1844); (2) the post-Civil War gospel hymn tradition combining traits of the Northern gospel hymn and the Southern folk hymn, represented in gospel singing using paperback songbooks. This shape-note gospel hymnody is still alive, but is confined chiefly to singing conventions in the South.[11]

The older folk hymn tradition of four-shape-note hymnody has become increasingly evident in major church hymnals in recent years. Included are such tunes as NETTLETON (B13, L499, M93, "Come, thou Fount of every blessing"), FOUNDATION (B383, L507, M48, "How firm a foundation"), and MORNING SONG (B413, M140, "Awake, awake to love and work"). The harmonies of these shape-note tunes have been generally changed in order to accommodate them to the styles of harmony common to hymns of today.[12] This change of harmonies illustrates how folk music undergoes a transformation when it passes from its home in one culture to find a new home in a different culture.[13]

Afro-American

As its name implies, Afro-American music is a syncretism, made up of both African and American elements. Afro-American music in turn owes much of its character to the European musical heritage. In the black churches of

[10]In addition to the Old Order Amish, other religious bodies in America who have maintained distinctive traditions of hymnody which have particular cultural interest include the Mennonites, the Moravians, the Seventh-Day Baptists of Ephrata, Pennsylvania, and the Shakers. See "Singing Dissenters," chap. 3 of Chase, *America's Music*, pp. 41-64.
[11]See Shirley Beary, "Stylistic Traits of Southern Shape-Note Gospel Songs," *The Hymn* 30, 1 (January 1979). See additional treatment of shape-note gospel hymnody in chap. 8, American Traditions.
[12]See the original and altered harmonizations of "Amazing Grace" in chap. 2, The Hymn and Music.
[13]For additional treatment of four-shape-note hymnody see chap. 8, American Traditions.

America, particularly those which hold closely to older traditions, congregational singing reflects this Afro-American heritage.

While this heritage of congregational song is too extensive a subject to be treated in depth, we can illustrate two important aspects of black African music that are prominent in black church music of today: melodic embellishment (or improvisation on a basic melody) and rhythmic prominence.[13] When a black congregation sings an old hymn such as "Amazing Grace," they will normally sing it in a much slower tempo than that common to most white churches, for the slow tempo allows the time needed for embellishments on the melody. Although this folk hymn is of white origin, its manner of performance in black worship is clearly Afro-American.[14] This freedom of embellishment is in keeping with the freedom of expression found in traditional black worship, ranging from singing and improvising accompaniment to spontaneous "amens," clapping, body movement, and shouting, as well as preaching which intensifies into a songlike speech. The rhythmic emphasis of the African heritage is evident in the drive and syncopation of many black spirituals, such as "Joshua fit the battle of Jericho," "Every time I feel the Spirit," and "Somebody's knocking at your door" (B480), and in the performance of the more recent gospel music.[15]

Black spirituals have appeared in increasing numbers in the hymnals of predominantly white denominations in recent years. The singing of these spirituals by white congregations can result in a meaningful worship experience, but their performance by whites will inevitably be adapted to fit a different culture. Herein lies a basic reason for the existence of separate black and white churches. There is a desire on the part of both races to maintain their worship through music in their own cultural contexts.[16]

Welsh

Perhaps no culture has given a greater place to hymn singing than that of the Welsh. The people of the little country of Wales, a beautiful land of mountains and valleys to the west of England, speak a Celtic language that was in use in Britain at the time of the ancient Romans. Although nearly all the

---

[13]For a fuller description of elements of this African heritage in relation to American music, see Chase, *America's Music*, chap. 4, "African Exiles," pp. 65-83; and Eileen Southern, chap. 1, "The African Heritage," in *The Music of Black Americans, A History* (New York: W.W. Norton, 1971), pp. 3-24.

[14]George Pullen Jackson, *White and Negro Spirituals*. Reprint of original 1944 ed. (New York: Da Capo Press, 1975), pp. 249ff.

[15]For a personal and perceptive view of black worship with an emphasis on music, see Charles G. Adams, "Some Aspects of Black Worship," *Andover Newton Quarterly* ii (January 1971): 124-138; *Music Ministry* 5 (September 1972), 2-9; *Journal of Church Music* 15 (February 1973), 2-9, 16.

[16]See additional treatment of the Negro spiritual in chap. 8, American Traditions.

Welsh now speak English rather than Welsh, there is presently an increased effort to preserve this country's language which is so closely bound up with its national heritage.

Wales holds a special interest to Americans, for large numbers of the Welsh have emigrated to the United States, and such states as Pennsylvania and Ohio have substantial Welsh-American populations.

Hymn singing in Wales, in contrast to that of the United States, is a much more conspicuous activity, for it is not limited to regular church services. Welsh hymn singing today finds its expression in the *Gymanfa Ganu* (pronounced *Ga mon' va Gon' ee*), meaning an "assembly or festival of sacred song."[17] David G. Jenkins has described the cultural setting in which this hymn-singing activity originated in the nineteenth century: "The beginnings of the Gymanfa Ganu were humble: it began in the little chapels and churches which dot the hills and valleys of Wales. After the religious service was over the congregation would remain for an hour of song. Unaccompanied by any instrument—for the Puritan spirit was never stronger in New England than in Old Wales—led by a leader who sounded the pitch, the congregation would be drilled for the forthcoming Gymanfa. For months a few selected hymns and an anthem or two would be rehearsed; then in a common meeting place congregations of one neighborhood or denomination would unitedly render the selections so prepared, under a conductor specially qualified and chosen."[18]

The present-day *Gymanfa Ganu* is similar to that described here, except that piano and organ accompaniment are generally used and its purpose is usually not to bring into use new material for congregational worship but rather the singing of a limited number of old favorites.

Part of the prominence of hymn singing in Welsh culture is due to its having been secularized. Welsh hymnody received its biggest thrust from the Calvinistic Methodist movement and other revivals of the eighteenth and nineteenth centuries which produced William Williams, author of "Guide me, O thou great Jehovah" (B202, M271, L343, "Guide me ever, great Redeemer"), this nation's greatest hymnist. The puritanical character of this movement almost brought about the death of the old secular folk songs. In the course of time this cultural vacuum came to be filled by hymns, causing them to serve in places where other cultures would use secular songs. As Robert R. Williams has observed of the Welsh, "Today wherever they congregate in small or large groups, on the football field or during the meetings of the

[17]Frank C. Issacs, "The Gymanfa Ganu in America," *The Hymn* 14, 2 (April 1963), 47.

[18]David G. Jenkins, "The Gymanfa Ganu" in *Favorite Welsh and English Hymns and Melodies* (Warren, Ohio: printed for the National Gymanfa Ganu Association of the United States and Canada by Printing Service, Inc., n.d.), p. 92. Quoted in Isaacs, "The Gymanfa Ganu," 47-78.

National Eisteddfod (singing competition), the hymns of the church are sung with fervor to popular tunes such as CWM RHONDDA, ABERYSTWYTH and CRUGYBAR."[19]

Although Welsh hymns and tunes have increasingly appeared in English language hymnals in the present century, certain distinctive traits have prevented their being used to a great extent outside of their own cultural setting. Welsh poetry has certain features that cannot be easily transferred to our language, such as their predilection for unusual meters, their preference for repetition of words, and the fact that many words in Welsh have an unaccented penultimate short syllable.[20] Furthermore, Welsh hymnody gives a central place to the atonement, often expressed in a way that is not in line with much present-day preaching and theological expression.[21]

Nevertheless, the Welsh have produced a few hymns and tunes that have transcended cultural barriers to achieve wide acceptance among English-speaking congregations in both Great Britain and America, such as "Guide me, O Thou great Jehovah" to CWM RHONDDA (B202, M271, L343, "Guide me ever, great Redeemer"), and the tunes LLANFYLLIN ("Sometimes a light surprises," B221, M231), EBENEZER ("Once to every man and nation," B385, M242, L233, "Thy strong word did cleave the darkness"), ABERYSTWYTH ("Jesus, lover of my soul," B172, M125, L91, "Savior, when in dust to you"), LLANFAIR ("Jesus Christ is risen today," B115, "Christ the Lord," L128, M443), and HYFRYDOL ("Praise the Lord! ye heavens adore him," B11, "Alleluia! Sing to Jesus," L158, M42).

Black African

Until relatively recent times, nearly all of the hymns sung by black African Christians were imported from Europe or America and translated into African languages. Although African Christians accepted these hymns as a part of the Christian faith, they do not express their faith in a way that is natural to them. As Weman has observed, in the African's church and school he "does his best to sing the stipulated tunes, but since these are—almost without exception—European, it is seldom that song succeeds in loosening his tongue. He is moving in an alien world, and if his heart fails to beat in time with the music, that is only to be expected."[22]

The music of black Africa contrasts with Euro-American music in numerous ways but especially in regard to its rhythmic freedom—a characteristic "which

[19]Robert R. Williams, "Some Aspects of Welsh Hymnody," *The Hymn* 4, 1 (January 1953), 6.
[20]Alan Luff, "Welsh Hymn Melodies: Their Present and Future Use in English Hymn Books," *Bulletin*, The Hymn Society of Great Britain and Ireland, 4 (Spring 1970), 76-77.
[21]Isaacs, "The Gymanfa Ganu," p. 50.
[22]Henry Weman, *African Music and the Church in Africa* (Uppsala, Sweden: Ab Lundequistska Bokhandeln, 1960), p. 9.

lies far above the conformity of the Westerner to fixed groupings according to simple rhythmic schemes."[23] Thus the rhythmic simplicity of imported Christian hymns lacks the rhythmic expressiveness which is inherent in African song. Furthermore, hymns which modulate are unsuitable for the African, for a basic rule of African melody is that "there is no key change in the course of the tune."[24] Thus the climactic modulation from F major to C major in the following score of NUN DANKET- ("Now thank we all our God"):

Who, from our moth-er's arms, Hath blessed us on our way

was observed by Weman in his visits to South Africa, Rhodesia, and Tanzania to be sung as follows:

This chorale melody is sung by the African in the way that fits his musical tradition but the climax, so expressive of joy and thanksgiving to Western ears, is taken away by this change.

These rhythmic and melodic contrasts between Euro-American and African music focus clearly on the problems found in the use of imported music by African Christians. So strong has the tradition of Western sacred music become among Christians of Africa that they often come to regard their own musical heritage as inferior.[25]

"Jesus, we want to meet" (E65, M487), one of the few African hymns which has appeared in any American and European hymnals, has several traits

[23]Ibid., p.62.
[24]Ibid., p. 46.
[25]A recent collection of African hymns in English translation compiled by Howard S. Olson is *Lead Us Lord* (Minneapolis: Augsburg Publishing House, 1977). See also *The Hymn*, July 1979, 159-66.

of African music: rhythmic freedom (note the frequent shifts in rhythmic patterns and accents), a pentatonic melody which remains in one key, and optional drumbeat patterns. In addition to the two optional drumbeat patterns given with this hymn in the hymnals, a third and fourth have been added to further exemplify the great rhythmic variety and expressiveness of African music.[26]

The text of "Jesus, we want to meet" has the element of repetition ("On this holy day"), another important feature of African song. This hymn also lends itself to the typical call and response pattern often found in African music:

Leader: "Jesus, we want to meet"
Congregation: "On this thy holy day."

Chinese

China, one of the world's oldest cultures, has a long and complex history, for organized civilizations have lived continuously on her mainland since at least 3000 B.C. As in black Africa, music in China has occupied a prominent place in everyday life and continues to do so. In China, "There is hardly any phase of the life of the people in which music does not function, whether it be social, recreational, business and professional, or religious."[27]

Chinese music is distinctively different from Western music. The following traits are characteristic of Chinese vocal music:

1. Duple time is usual, with little use of triple time.

2. Modal endings to phrases are frequent.

3. The pentatonic scale is common, but the seven-tone scale is also used. The most characteristic trait of Chinese melody is that it never proceeds upwards by a half step but it may proceed downward by a half step.

4. Chinese melodies often sound out of tune to Western ears because they do not use the tempered scale.

5. There is no concise combination of tones (harmony) in vocal music.

6. Melodies associated with poetry have been influenced by poetic structure and poetic form has been influenced by music.[28]

These traits of Chinese music seldom appeared in the hymns of Chinese Christians before the 1930's, for both Roman Catholic and Protestant

---

[26]These rhythms have been suggested by Dr. Mary Oyer of the Music Department, Goshen College, Goshen, Indiana, who is both a hymnologist and a specialist in African music. (The first two drumbeat patterns were dictated by the translator in 1962 to Austin C. Lovelace and Carlton R. Young.)

[27]Bliss Wiant, *The Music of China* (Hong Kong: Chung Chi Publications, 1965), p. 95.

[28]Summarized from ibid., pp. 3-4.

Jesus, We Want to Meet

1. Je - sus, we   want_ to meet   On   this_ thy   ho - ly day;
2. We kneel in   awe_ and fear   On   this_ thy   ho - ly day;
3. Thy bless - ing,   Lord,_ we seek   On   this_ thy   ho - ly day;
4. Our minds we   ded - i - cate   On   this_ thy   ho - ly day;

We   gath - er   round_ thy throne   On   this_ thy   ho - ly day.
Pray God to   teach_ us   here   On   this_ thy   ho - ly day;
Give joy of   thy vic -to - ry   On   this_ thy   ho - ly day.
Heart and soul   con - se - crate   On   this_ thy   ho - ly day.

Thou _ art _ our heav'n - ly Friend, Hear our prayers as they as - cend;
Save _ us _ and cleanse our hearts, Lead and guide our acts of praise,
Through grace a- lone are   we saved; In thy flock may we be found;
Ho-ly Spir - it, make us whole; Bless the ser - mon in this place;

Look in - to   our hearts and minds to - day, On   this _ thy ho-ly day.
And our faith from seed   to   flow-er raise, On   this _ thy ho-ly day.
Let the mind of Christ a - bide in   us On   this _ thy ho-ly day.
And _ as we go, _ lead us Lord; We shall be thine ev - er-more.

Optional drumbeat patterns:

Words and Music by A. T. Olajide Olude, *Nigeria.* Translated by Biodun Adebesin.
Versed by Austin C. Lovelace. Words © copyright 1964 by Abingdon Press. Used
by permission. Music used by permission of A. T. Olajide Olude.

missionary efforts had produced a church that was largely foreign in form and in control.[29]

In the early 1930's, six Chinese Protestant bodies united their efforts to produce the first hymnal to include a significant number of Chinese texts and tunes. This epoch-making hymnal, *Hymns of Universal Praise* (Shanghai, 1936), contains, alongside Western hymns, sixty-two original Chinese hymn texts. Seventy-two of its hymn tunes originated in China; these include fourteen of relatively ancient origin and fifty-seven new compositions, including twenty-three tunes "by foreign missionaries who, having lived in China for a considerable length of time, have learned to think in characteristically Chinese music idioms," and thirty-four tunes by Chinese.[30]

One Chinese hymn from *Hymns of Universal Praise* (HUP) which illustrates several traits of Chinese music is SHENG EN ("The bread of life, for all men broken," B250, M317). The melody of this Chinese hymn is pentatonic, omitting the notes *e* and *b♭*. SHENG EN is harmonized as an accommodation to Western practice; Chinese tradition would require that it be sung in unison.

The rhythm of this Chinese melody is atypical, for rather than falling strictly into groups of two, its rhythm consists of groups of two and three. In HUP the time signature of this hymn tune is 5/4. Here (from M317) no time signature is listed and bar lines occur only at the ends of phrases. SHENG EN's rhythm has been accommodated to Western tradition in another version in 3/4 time (B250).

In accordance with Chinese practice, this melody does not ascend by half step (nor does it in this case descend by a half step). Furthermore, SHENG EN's phrase endings are modal, the final notes being approached from above or below by a minor third. The melodic form also conforms to Chinese practice in that it is free, having no repeated phrases.

Other examples of Chinese-Christian hymns which have appeared in American hymnals include "My heart looks in faith" (SONG OF THE YANGTZE BOATMAN, B332), "Rise to greet the sun" (LE P'ING, M490), and "Ne'er forget God's daily care" (WIANT, M519).

Cantate Domino: Unity in Diversity

Through the foregoing examples of hymn-singing cultures we have seen

---

[29]In 1928 Latourette reported: "With occasional splendid exceptions, throughout China and among both Roman Catholics and Protestants, the Church was still dependent on the foreigner for ideas, leadership, and financial support. Little first-class Christian literature had yet appeared from Chinese pens. No outstanding apologia, no great work of devotion had yet been written by a Chinese." Kenneth Scott Latourette, *A History of Christian Missions in China* (New York: The Macmillan Co., 1929), p. 833.

[30]*Hymns of Universal Praise* (Shanghai, 1936), pp. 10-11.

1. The bread of life, for all men bro - ken! He drank the
2. With god - ly fear we seek thy pres - ence; Our hearts dis -
3. O Lord, we pray, come thou a - mong us, Light - en our

cup on Gol - goth - a. His grace we trust, and spread with rev - erence
tressed by peo - ple's grief. Thy ho - ly face is stained with bitter tears;
eyes, bright - ly ap - pear! Im - man - u - el, heaven's joy un - end - ing,

This ho - ly feast, and thus re - mem - ber.
Our hu - man pain still bearest thou with us.
Our life with thine for - ev - er blend - ing. A - men.

Words by Timothy Tingfang Lew, 1936; translated by Walter R. O. Taylor, 1943. Tune SHENG EN, Su Yin-Lan, arranged by Bliss Wiant, 1934.

something of the diversity of Christian hymnody. Although each hymnal reflects the cultural heritage(s) of its constituency, there has been in recent decades a growing trend in American collections to be inclusive of representative hymns from Third World countries.

By far the most internationally inclusive hymnal is *Cantate Domino* (CD), whose title is taken from the Latin of Psalm 96:1, *"Cantate Domino canticum novum"* ("Sing unto the Lord a new song"). This unique multilanguage hymnal, first published in 1924 by the World Student Christian Federation, was published in its fourth edition under sponsorship of the World Council of Churches in 1974.[31]

The purpose of CD has been described by Erik Routley, the spokesman for its editorial board: "At an early stage it was agreed that the purpose of the book was to serve the church at its 'growing points.' The Church is at present growing, we believe, through the meeting of cultures and races, as well as through experiments in text-writing, music and liturgy; an international hymn book with an experimental emphasis was clearly called for, and we have sought to include in the book material of many styles. Not only hymns of the familiar kind will be found here, but also antiphonal canticles and folk songs. We hope to make available not only the hymnody of the west to the east, and of the north to the south, as did the older missionary enterprises, but some of the new and vital hymnody of the southern hemisphere to the north, and of the east to the west."[32]

In accord with its purpose, CD contains a fascinating array of hymns representing many cultures. These hymns are given in their original languages in addition to English and in other languages which communicate their thoughts best, often including French and German. Furthermore, CD is an ecumenical hymnal, for its preparation involved active participation by Orthodox, Roman Catholic, and Protestant Christians.

The following citations from CD will give an idea of the varied multicultural scope of this unique hymnal. African hymns include the melody of a Malawi wedding song to Psalm 148, "O praise the King of Heaven" (18), and a Yoruba tune to the text "Blessed Word of God" (104). Contributions from the Americas include the Negro spiritual "He is King of Kings" (85), the Jamaican folk song melody to "Take the dark strength of our nights" (31) and the Argentine hymn "Christ is risen, Christ is living" (89). East Asian hymns include, in addition to Chinese hymns, a Thai traditional melody to Psalm 1, "Happy is he who walks in God's wise way" (7), an old Japanese melody with Japanese text, "In this world abound" (106), and a melody of Philippine origin to "Father in heaven" (121). Hymns in CD from other parts of Asia include an Indian text and tune, "God is love!" (70) and a Persian text and tune, "Spread the news!" (90).[33]

This collection of church songs from many cultures is thus a repository of words and music demonstrating the unity in diversity that characterizes Christianity at its best. Christians express their faith in song in ways that are

---

[31]*Cantate Domino*, New edition. Published on behalf of the World Council of Churches (Kassel, Germany: Bärenreiter-Verlag, 1974).

[32]Ibid., "Editor's Introduction" by Erik Routley, pp. xiii-xiv.

[33]See also the following nations or cultures represented by hymns in *Ecumenical Praise*: Chinese (53), Ghana (58, 77), Hungarian (66), Irish (23), and Shaker (45).

natural to them, whether they are from Europe, Asia, Africa, Australia, or the Americas. At the same time, however, they may sing one another's hymns in the realization that

In Christ there is no East or West,
In him no South or North,
But one great fellowship of love
Thro'out the whole wide earth.[34]

Questions for Thought and Discussion

1. What cultural conditions have exercised a strong influence on your views of hymns and hymn singing?

2. To what extent can one accept the validity of a hymn and/or hymn tune that evidently expresses the religious experience of another Christian but not one's own?

3. Can one accept someone of another cultural background and have genuine respect for his hymn preferences, though they are different?

4. To what extent in hymn singing is cultural unity feasible or desirable?

5. How many cultural traditions are represented in your congregation's hymn singing? How fully do these traditions represent the backgrounds of these people?

6. To what extent is your congregation able to worship through hymns set to music of unfamiliar cultural traditions? To what extent is this desirable?

---

[34]This hymn of Oxenham (B258, L359, M192) so expressive of Christian unity has been in CD since its first edition of 1924. ©Copyright in U.S.A. by Fleming H. Revell Co. Used by permission.*

10

The Hymn in Proclamation

Hymns function in the mission of the church in several ways. In *proclamation* the hymn functions as a vehicle for sharing the good news. In *worship* the hymn is an instrument of corporate devotion. In *education* the hymn is a means for Christian instruction. And in *ministry* the hymn functions as an inspiration for social service. Some hymns relate to several of these functions; other hymns focus primarily on one. Persons who bear leadership responsibility for congregational singing can profit greatly from an awareness of the potential use of hymns in fulfilling the church's mission and their specific application in accomplishing the tasks of proclamation, worship, education, and ministry.

The Meaning of Proclamation

A proclamation is a public declaration. In the context of the church, proclamation is the public declaration of the gospel of salvation in Jesus Christ and of its day-to-day application in people's lives. Proclamation of the gospel may take place within a worship service, in an evangelistic meeting, or in a conversational setting. The manner in which this proclamation occurs varies according to the particular heritage and theology of each congregation. Proclaiming the gospel at a church gathering may be done formally in a variety of ways: through the preaching of a sermon, the reading of Scripture, the recitation of a creed, or the singing of a hymn.

Three important terms describing aspects of proclamation are evangelism, witness, and missions. *Evangelism* (or evangelization), which comes from New Testament Greek words meaning to "bring good news," refers to the public preaching and dissemination of the gospel. Among the hymns which encourage evangelism are such hymns as "Tell it! tell it out with gladness" (Hymn To Joy, B275), "Christ is the King! O friends, rejoice" (Beverly, L386), "Lord of the harvest, hear" (St. Bride, M339), and "Tell the good news" (Rhea, B288).

Witness as an aspect of proclamation signifies the activity in which individual Christians share their experience of faith with others. Hymns of witness recount Christian experiences, giving personal testimony in hymnic form to the love of Christ, as in "I know that my Redeemer lives" (Duke Street, L352; Truro, M445), "I know whom I have believed" (El Nathan, B344), "My song is love unknown" (Robertson, B486; Rhosymedre, L94), and "I heard the voice of Jesus say" (Third Mode Melody, L497; Vox

DILECTI, M117). In addition to hymns of witness to others, there are hymns of prayer for the one who bears witness, such as "Lord, speak to me that I may speak" (CANONBURY, B276, L403, M195) and "O Master, let me walk with thee (you)" (3rd stanza, MARYTON, B369, L492, M170).

When evangelism is pursued across national and cultural lines, it is considered more particularly *missions* (from the Latin, meaning to "let go" or "send"). Hymns also express the concerns of missions: "We've a story to tell to the nations" (MESSAGE, B281, M410), "O Zion haste, thy mission high fulfilling" (TIDINGS, B295, M299, ANGELIC SONGS, L397), and "Thou (God), whose almighty word (Word)," (SERUG, B303; ITALIAN HYMN, L400, DORT, M480).

Biblical Basis

Music and the proclamation of the gospel have a considerable history of close association in the Scriptures. In the Old Testament the psalmist calls on worshipers to proclaim God's salvation with singing:

Sing a new song to the Lord!
Sing to the Lord, all the world!
Sing to the Lord, and praise him!
Proclaim every day the good news that he has saved us.
Proclaim his glory to the nations,
    his mighty acts to all peoples (Ps. 96:1-3, TEV).

"A new song" testifies to the mercy and compassion of God in Psalm 40:1-3, 9-10 (TEV):

I waited patiently for the Lord's help;
    then he listened to me and heard my cry.
He pulled me out of a dangerous pit,
    out of the deadly quicksand.
He set me safely on a rock
    and made me secure.
He taught me to sing a new song,
    a song of praise to our God.
Many who see this will take warning
    and will put their trust in the Lord.
In the assembly of your people, Lord,
    I told the good news that you save us.
You know that I will never stop telling it.
I have not kept the news of salvation to myself;
    I have always spoken of your faithfulness and help.
In the assembly of all your people I have not been silent
    about your loyalty and constant love.

In the New Testament the Gospel of Luke describes how the proclamation of the birth of Jesus was accompanied by song: "Suddenly a great army of heaven's angels appeared with the angel, singing praises to God:
'Glory to God in the highest heaven,
    and peace on earth to those with whom he is pleased!' "
(Luke 2:13-14 TEV).
Singing the good news is associated with one of the most dramatic conversions recorded in the New Testament. As the apostle Paul and his associate Silas sang during their imprisonment in a Philippian jail, an earthquake occurred; and the jailer and his household were converted (Acts 16:25-31). In Colossians 3:16 Paul exhorted the churches to make known the word of Christ through singing, and the Pauline hymn fragments in 1 Timothy 3:16*b* and Ephesians 5:14 also sound the note of proclamation.[1]

Historical Use

Through much of Christian history the hymn has been an effective vehicle for proclaiming the gospel. In the thirteenth century Francis of Assisi gave impetus to the creation of *laudi spirituali*, popular hymns in the language of the Italian people.[2] The Protestant Reformation gained momentum partly from Luther's chorales and Calvin's metrical psalms. These songs permeated the homes, schools, and churches of Germany, Switzerland, and other countries where they were used. The effectiveness of congregational song for communicating the good news has been underscored by other spiritual awakenings, such as the Wesleyan revival of eighteenth-century England, the frontier camp meeting revivals of early nineteenth-century America, and the British and American urban revivals which were led by Moody and Sankey during the last three decades of the nineteenth century.[3]

Using Hymns in Proclamation

For a hymn to proclaim the gospel in its New Testament sense, it must incorporate the good news of salvation in Jesus Christ. Hymns which proclaim this good news are not limited to any single century, culture, or style. For example, note the diversity of sources for the following stanzas which proclaim the good news:

From the Scottish-English Moravian James Montgomery's hymn of 1824, "Stand up and bless the Lord," stanza 4 (OLD 134TH, B26, M16):

[1]See "New Testament Song" in chap. 5, Early Church and Pre-Reformation Traditions.

[2]His own "All creatures of our God and King," although a poem of praise, contains a word of proclamation urging forgiveness toward others and the casting of one's cares on God (LASST UNS ERFREUEN, B9, st. 3; L527, M60, st. 5).

[3]Hymns written during these awakenings are treated in the historical chapters of this book.

Timothy Dwight

God is our strength and song,
  And his salvation ours;
Then be his love in Christ proclaimed
  With all our ransomed pow'rs.

From an anonymous Latin hymn of about the eighth century, stanzas 1 and 2 (Lobt Gott, ihr Christen, L300):

O Christ, our hope, our hearts' desire,
  Creation's mighty Lord,
Redeemer of the fallen world,
  By holy love outpoured:
How vast your mercy to accept
  The burden of our sin,
And bow your head in cruel death
  To make us clean within.

From the anonymous Negro spiritual, "New born again" (B474):

I found free grace and dying love, I'm new born again,
Been long time a-talking 'bout my trials here below.

Refrain:
Free grace, free grace, free grace, sinner,
Free grace, free grace, I'm new born again.
So glad, so glad, I'm new born again,
Been long time a-talking 'bout my trials here below.

And from Fanny Crosby's gospel hymn of 1882, "Redeemed, how I love to proclaim it" (B446):

Redeemed, how I love to proclaim it!
  Redeemed by the blood of the Lamb;
Redeemed through his infinite mercy,
  His child, and forever, I am.

Good News Hymns

The heading "Good News Hymns" is chosen here rather than "Gospel Hymns" to convey more clearly that many kinds of hymns proclaim the gospel. The kinds of hymns used to proclaim the gospel differ according to the liturgical heritage and cultural outlook of particular congregations and their leadership. Two contrasting approaches to proclaiming the gospel—each with its traditions of good news hymnody—are the Christian calendar and revivalism.

The Christian calendar is generally known by its major festivals of Christmas, Easter, and Pentecost, festivals which are widely observed. The calendar is biblically based, proclaiming in an annual cycle God's mighty acts in the birth, life, death, and resurrection of Jesus Christ, the coming of the Holy Spirit on Pentecost, and the nature of the triune God on Trinity Sunday.[4] The good news of salvation in Jesus Christ is found in hymns written for use in the various seasons of the Christian calendar. The following excerpts from hymns for Advent, Christmas, Holy Week, Easter, and Pentecost are representative of those used to proclaim the good news.

Advent

Come, thou long-expected Jesus,
   Born to set thy people free;
From our fears and sins release us;
   Let us find our rest in thee. . . .
Born thy people to deliver,
   Born a child, and yet a King,
Born to reign in us forever,
   Now thy gracious kingdom bring.
      (HYFRYDOL, B79, M360; JEFFERSON, L30)

Christmas

How silently, how silently
   The wondrous gift is giv'n!
So God imparts to human hearts
   The blessings of his heav'n.
No ear may hear his coming,
   But in this world of sin,
Where meek souls will receive him still
   The dear Christ enters in.
      (stanza 3, "O little town of Bethlehem, ST. LOUIS, B85, L41, M381)

Holy Week

There is a green hill far away,
   Outside a city wall,
Where the dear Lord was crucified,
   Who died to save us all
      (WINDSOR, L114, M414)

---

[4]Additional treatment of the Christian calendar is given in chap. 11, The Hymn in Worship.

Easter

The three sad days have quickly sped;
He rises glorious from the dead.
All glory to our risen head!
　Alleluia!
Lord, by the stripes which wounded you,
From death's sting free your servants too,
That we may live and sing to you.
　Alleluia!
　　　　　("The strife is o'er, the battle done," Victory, L135,
　　　　　　　stanzas 3, 5; M447, stanzas 3, 4)

Pentecost

Come, Holy Ghost, our souls inspire,
And lighten with celestial fire;
Thou the anointing Spirit art,
Who dost thy seven-fold gifts impart.
　　(Veni, Creator Spiritus, L472, M467)

The revivalism of the nineteenth century in particular played a significant role in the development of American Christianity and continues to function as a means of proclaiming the good news in a number of church bodies and nondenominational evangelistic organizations. In contrast to the annual cycle of the Christian calendar, revivalism focuses on shorter periods of intensive effort, such as a weekend, half a week, or a week or more of daily evangelistic meetings. Hymns associated with revivalism tend to be more person-centered than those of the Christian calendar, focusing to a greater extent on the experiences and emotions of the individual singers. The personal pronouns I, me, and my abound in the hymns of revivalism. Furthermore, most hymns of revivalism emphasize personal testimony, sometimes even to the extent of excluding an explicit statement of God's work in Jesus Christ. Much revivalistic hymnody emphasizes "what Jesus means to me" rather than what he has done for the salvation of the world.

On the other hand, revivalistic hymns in their simplistic language and musical style bring the message of the gospel to persons who find it difficult to relate to more sophisticated styles of hymnody. The following themes and the hymns that illustrate them are representative of revivalistic hymnody that has found a firm place not only in revival meetings but also in the weekly (especially Sunday evening) services of a significant number of America's churches.

The Love of Jesus

I stand amazed in the presence
Of Jesus the Nazarene,
And wonder how he could love me,
A sinner, condemned, unclean.

Refrain:
How marvelous! how wonderful!
And my song shall ever be;
How marvelous! how wonderful!
Is my Savior's love for me! (B63).

The Atonement

I will sing of my Redeemer
And his wondrous love to me;
On the cruel cross he suffered
From the curse to set me free.

Refrain:
Sing, oh, sing of my Redeemer,
With his blood he purchased me;
On the cross he sealed my pardon,
Paid the debt and made me free. (B465).

The Atonement and Resurrection

Tell of the cross where they nailed him,
Writhing in anguish and pain;
Tell of the grave where they laid him,
Tell how he liveth again.

Refrain:
Tell me the story of Jesus,
Write on my heart ev'ry word;
Tell me the story most precious,
Sweetest that ever was heard.
("Tell me the story of Jesus," st. 3, B437)

Testimony of Salvation

I've found a friend, O such a friend!
Christ[5] loved me ere I knew him;
He drew me with the cords of love,
And thus he bound me to him;
And round my heart still closely twine
Those ties which naught can sever,
For I am his and Christ is mine,
Forever and forever (B423, M163).

As we have already noted, the proclamation of the gospel is not limited to any single tradition of hymnody. Both the Christian calendar and revivalism have proved to be effective means of proclaiming the good news. Churches observing the Christian calendar make a greater use of hymnody designed to present the good news in the context of its seasonal emphases. Churches with a revivalistic heritage sing more hymns giving emphasis to personal testimony.

Balance is a key to evaluating proclamation hymnody. There is *objective* truth to be proclaimed: God's mighty acts which have bought salvation through the Jesus of history. There is also *subjective* experience: one's response to salvation history and how one feels about the experience of knowing God's love in Jesus Christ. Both objective and subjective expressions are valid when a balance is maintained between them. However, for use in congregational singing, subjective hymns present a particular difficulty. Since the subjective focuses on individual feelings, these feelings may not be valid for the entire congregation. The emotions and experiences that hymns express need to convey the sentiments of the congregation as a group of Christians.

Hymns of Call, Hymns of Response

When the gospel has been proclaimed (whether in the spoken word or in song), those who hear are called upon to respond. This response to the proclamation of the good news is often expressed in hymns. In many congregations individuals are invited to make public decisions to accept the gospel of Christ during the singing of a hymn following the sermon. Hymns calling for a response to the proclamation of the gospel often emphasize the *call* of Christ or urge persons to *come* to the Savior:

"Jesus *calls* us o'er the tumult" (GALILEE, B367, L494, M107)
"God *calling* yet! Shall I not hear?" (FEDERAL STREET, M105)
"Jesus is tenderly *calling*" (B188, M110)
"Softly and tenderly Jesus is *calling*" (THOMPSON, B190)

---

[5]In the interest of clarity, "Christ" has twice been substituted for the original "He" in this stanza at B423.

"Today your mercy *calls* us" (ANTHES, L304)
"*Come*, ev'ry soul by sin oppressed" (STOCKTON, B183, M101)
"*Come*, follow me, the Savior spake" (MACHS MIT MIR, GOTT, L455)
"*Come*, sinners to the gospel feast" (WINCHESTER NEW, M102)
"*Come*, ye disconsolate" (CONSOLATOR, B211, M103)
"*Come*, ye sinners, poor and needy" (BEACH SPRING, B196;
  ARISE, B197; PLEADING SAVIOR, M104)

In other congregations a hymn of individual commitment is sung, but without any similar public decision being called for. Hymns of response to the gospel may be prayers which involve acts of repentance, faith, dedication, and a sense of joy and peace. One of the most frequently sung hymns of response is "Just as I am, without one plea" (WOODWORTH, B187, L296, M119). This hymn expresses the confession of a person in spiritual need and how fears and conflicts are resolved in Christ, concluding with the response, "O Lamb of God, I come." A Christian hymn of the fifth century which is also a positive response to the gospel is "Lord Jesus, think on me" (SOUTHWELL, L309, M284):

Lord Jesus, think on me
  And purge away my sin;
From selfish passions set me free
  And make me pure within.

Although this chapter has focused on proclamation, it is important to recognize that proclamation is inseparable from worship in the mission of the church. As stated by Davies, "Personal commitment, worship, daily life, proclamation or witness are all parts of our response to Christ: to separate them is to distort."[6] Furthermore, many of the procedures for the use of evangelistic hymns are similar to those employed with hymns of worship. In the next chapter then, many of the practical points concerning hymns in worship are also valid for employing hymns in proclamation.

Questions for Thought and Discussion, Projects for Action

1. Using an order of worship in your church bulletin and/or book of worship for a recent Sunday, list those actions which involve proclamation of the gospel. List all the spoken and sung parts of the service which proclaim the message of God's love in Jesus Christ.

2. Evaluate your church's hymnal in terms of hymns encouraging witnessing, evangelism, and missions. Are the sections containing these hymns adequate in number or in encouragement to evangelism? Are there other hymns encouraging proclamation and missions that you would add?

[6] J. G. Davies, *Worship and Mission* (New York: Association Press, 1967), p. 71.

3. Cite some instances in which music has been associated with proclamation in the Scriptures and in Christian history.

4. Contrast and evaluate the Christian calendar and revivalism as approaches to proclaiming the good news and the traditions of hymnody associated with each.

5. Citing appropriate examples, describe how hymns can express an invitation to Christian discipleship and an individual's response to the proclamation of the good news.

6. Plan a hymn service that proclaims the good news, using hymns and Scripture passages taken from festivals and seasons of the Christian calendar.

7. Using revivalistic hymns, plan a hymn service designed to proclaim the good news and to show how hymnody has developed in association with great spiritual awakenings.

11
The Hymn in Worship

The setting most natural to the function of the hymn is the service of public worship. A hymn's worship function cannot be explained apart from some understanding of the nature of corporate devotion. Public worship is a multifaceted phenomenon, subject to consideration from many perspectives. One of the most fruitful is to think of it in terms of drama.

Worship as Drama

In a real sense, worship is dramatic action. The principal actors in the drama of corporate worship are the people of the congregation who are aided and equipped for their role by the leaders of worship—the prompters from the wings. The drama, often scripted, has a structure and sequence based upon the nature of God's dialogical encounter with his people. A general pattern of progress in the worshiping action emerges from that dialogue. The Bible is the record of that dramatic encounter. Though encapsulated within the time and space limits of formal worship with others each Lord's day, the drama actually continues in the daily life of the individual worshiper through the week.

The Danish religious thinker Sören Kierkegaard (1813-55) has suggested the above analogy.[1] Worship is indeed drama, a real-life drama because all of life is on the stage. The people of the congregation are the actors—the active participants in the work (the service) of worship. The principal audience then is God himself. He hears and accepts the prayers and praise offered by the congregation. He looks at the hearts and lives of the performers, discerning the motives of their worship and their service.

The pastor, the minister of music, the choir members, the organist, and/or other instrumentalists are the prompters. They are the enablers of worship, seeking to help and guide the congregation to do its work of worship well in the presence of God before whom they also stand as participants in the dramatic action.

Furthermore, the drama continues in daily life, where the liturgy—the service of the people of God—is carried out while the church is dispersed (Rom. 12:1). The word *liturgy* has differing connotations according to the church tradition of those using it. In essence, "liturgy" (as used above) simply

---

[1] Sören Kierkegaard, *Purity of Heart.* Tr. Douglas V. Steere (New York: Harper and Brothers, Torchbooks, 1956), 177-84.

means the service rendered by human beings to God.[2] It carries the meaning of worship as work, and it applies equally to the activity of the people of God whether they are assembled for worshipful acts or dispersed for their everyday work in the world. Its form is not necessarily fixed or ecclesiastically prescribed; but when its texts are written out as the agreed-upon order for doing things together, it may be considered the script for the drama of worship.[3]

A Dialogical Model—Isaiah's Vision in the Temple

Within the Scriptures may be found many worship experiences whose natural components can be analyzed and, by God's grace, relived in the experience of today's worshipers. The experience of the prophet Isaiah, when he received and responded to the call of the Lord in the temple, has often been cited as one model for the structuring of the drama of worship. The structure is that of dramatic dialogue in which God speaks first, revealing himself in mystery, majesty and power.

I. Initiating Grace (Is. 6:1-4)

God always takes the initiative in worship. The great and gracious God is the prime mover, requiring an adoring response on the part of his worshipers. The first movement of the worship dialog is therefore downward and inward from God to the worshiper. By God's own grace we see him revealed in transcendent power and holiness.

II. Confession of Sin (Is. 6:5)

Seeing God in all his majesty and goodness, Isaiah by painful contrast saw himself as sinful and in need of forgiveness. His feeling of contrition and repentance was both individual and social; so, as the dialogue continues, the upward and outward moving response is that of confession of sin and unworthiness.

III. Pardon and Renewal (Is. 6:6-7)

Again the dramatic flow reverses, with God responding by providing cleansing, forgiveness, and relief. Then he issues the call to service.

IV. Dedication of Life (Isa. 6:8).

After having experienced spiritual renewal and thus a new sensitivity to the voice of God, Isaiah finally responds with a commitment of his life to God's

---

[2]Liturgy is from the Greek, *leitourgia*, a compound word from *laos*—people and *ergon*—work. Therefore its basic meaning is "the work of the people." The New Testament uses it frequently (Acts 13:2, Heb. 8:6). See Paul W. Hoon, *The Integrity of Worship* (New York: Abingdon Press, 1971), pp. 30-33.

[3]Erik Routley treats the subject of worship as drama in *Music Leadership in the Church* (Nashville: Abingdon Press, 1967) 106-120; and *Words, Music, and the Church* (Nashville: Abingdon Press, 1968) 192-70.

purposes. True and complete worship ends with the offering of self as the climax of the dramatic action.

Since this structure is universal, deriving from the nature of God's dramatic dealings with his people, it can be discerned in the Christian liturgies that have developed through the ages as well as in great pieces of devotional literature. Although God's Spirit cannot be limited to liturgical formulae, a service of true worship is generally never haphazard or unstructured. In fact, spontaneity often comes because of, rather than in spite of, structure. To sum up, a service of worship is a two-way conversation between God and his people with a given pattern and sequence. The dramatic sequence outlined above is a channel through which the Spirit of God has acted throughout history. Thus, ideally, every service of worship reflects this structural unity, i.e., a general form and movement in which each part is logically related to the whole. Whether its tradition is "liturgical" or "free," a service of true worship represents a devotional whole.

The Function of Hymns in the Drama of Worship

With this concept of public worship as dramatic action, the place of the hymn becomes clear. Hymns are not only an important part of the sacred script of the worship drama, but at every point in the dramatic sequence, they can also be instruments of congregational action. Since the worship leaders are prompters of that action, they can utilize hymns as precision instruments selected accurately, intelligently, and sensitively to help the people say what they should or want to say at specific places in the dramatic sequence.

The people must be made aware of the place and purpose of their singing in worship. Hymns are never to be regarded as "musical breaks" for physical relaxation, nor to relieve boredom nor to cover up awkward pauses, nor to function as traveling music for the ministers as they move from one part of the sanctuary to another. Rather, to use another figure of speech, it is the offering of a sacrifice of praise requiring the commitment of mind, body, spirit, and will (Ps. 107:22).

In order to grasp this view of the hymn's function, the congregation may need patient instruction. The participation of congregational representatives in the planning and doing of the worship may be required. But the purpose of the planners of worship as they select hymns for the people to sing should be clearly understood by them. After all, the actors must not only know the meaning of every part of the play; they must also be enlisted in a teamwork of endeavor with the "playwrights," the prompters, and all the others who are committed to bringing off the performance.

Hymns and the Dialogical Pattern of Worship

As in Isaiah's vision, worship may begin with hymns depicting the holiness, power, and majesty of God. These enable the people to express their recognition of the divine object of their worship as well as their adoring response:

"Holy, Holy, Holy" (B1, L165, M26)
"Immortal, invisible, God only Wise" (B32, L526, M27)
"All hail the power of Jesus' name" (B40, L328, M71)
"Let us with a gladsome mind" (B27, L521, M61)

Then if hymns are used to give corporate response (i.e., recognizing human weakness and sin as well as asking for forgiveness), selections of penitence and confession might be:

"When I survey the wondrous cross" (B111, L482, M435)
"Beneath the cross of Jesus" (B360, L107, M417)
"I lay my sins on Jesus" (L305)
"Savior, like a shepherd, lead us" (B213, L481, M121)

The dramatic word of God in forgiveness and renewal comes most specifically in the actual words of Scripture. Yet the worship leader who knows the hymnbook's resources well, and who is concerned that hymns function as worship tools can find those which appropriately express God's forgiving and saving action:

"I heard the voice of Jesus say" (M117)
"How can a sinner know" (M114)
"Jesus, thy (your) blood and righteousness" (L302, M127)
"No, not despairingly" (B173)

Finally, hymns giving utterance to commitment and dedication of life at the climax of the drama will be imaginatively chosen:

"Take my life and let it be (that I may be) consecrated" (B373, L406, M187)
"O Master, let me walk with thee (you)" (B369, L492, M170)
"Send me, O Lord, send me" (B293)
"O Jesus, I have promised" (B365, L503, M164)

It is obvious from the content of the hymns here suggested that a dimension of experience beyond the vision of Isaiah is assumed in the context of Christian worship, namely the life, redeeming death, and resurrection of Jesus Christ. All Christian worship now is in and through Christ.

Hymns in the Larger Drama of the Christian Year

For historical and ecclesiastical reasons some Protestants have been denied the powerful dramatic aid that the observance of the church year (beyond that of Christmas and Easter) provides for Christian worship. In a manner more extended than any one single worship service, the Christian year is essentially the dramatic proclamation of the mighty acts of God in Christ and in his body, the church. The gradual return of many of the free churches to an acknowledgment of the seasons of preparation for the high festival days (Advent in preparation for Christmas, and Lent in preparation for Easter) is beginning to restore something of a sense of the drama of salvation to their corporate worship.

This renewal of church year observance can also enrich the knowledge and use of the great hymnic heritage bequeathed us from earlier centuries. Hymns, if known and carefully chosen, can help reinforce the theme of the season and underline the special teaching of a particular Lord's day or festival day, thus reenacting God's dramatic acts in the redemption of mankind.

For example, "Easter hymns" would not be indiscriminately used during Holy Week, nor would Christmas carols be used during Advent. Instead, hymns would be sensitively selected for the logical, sequential rehearsal of the events of the last days of Jesus' earthly life. For Palm Sunday hymns such as:

"Hosanna, loud hosanna" (M423)
"All glory, laud and honor" (B39, L108, M424)
"Ride on, ride on in majesty" (L121, M425)

would be sung to celebrate the triumphal entry into Jerusalem. For the observance of the Lord's Supper on Maundy Thursday, communion hymns would be sung:

"Here, O my Lord, I see thee face to face" (L211, M326, 327)
"In memory of the Savior's love" (B249, M319)
"Let us break bread together on our knees" (B252, L212, M330)

For Good Friday worship hymns like:

"Ah, Holy Jesus" (L123, M412)
"O, sacred Head now wounded" (B105, L117, M418)
"There is a green hill far away" (L114, M414)

would be used to recall the suffering of Christ on the cross. Not until Easter Sunday and during Eastertide would joyous hymns of the resurrection be selected:

"The day of resurrection" (L141, M437)
"Christ the Lord is risen today" (B114, L130, M439)
"Come, Ye (You) faithful, raise the strain" (L132, M446)

These are obvious examples of the choices that can also be made when considering worship planning for other seasons and days of the Christian year as well. For instance, there are hymns appropriate for Ascension, Pentecost, and Trinitytide.[4] Such of these hymns as may not be in a particular

---

[4]See "Hymns for the Church Year" in the *Lutheran Book of Worship*, pp. 929-31; and "Index of Hymns by Classification: The Christian Year" at M852.

congregation's hymnal could be printed in its worship folders and sung to familiar tunes. The precise use of hymns for observing the Christian Year is one way of making sure that all of God's mighty acts are declared in the dramatic course of worship during each twelve-month period.

The Nature of the Hymn—Congregational

It is sometimes forgotten that hymns are the offerings of the entire congregation, not merely those of the clergy and the choir. In the worship of most Christian groups (even those with a prescribed liturgy) hymns are preeminently that part of corporate worship in which the congregation has assumed the largest and most direct part. In the current stress on the role of the laity in the work of the church, the importance of the full participation of the congregation in hymn singing should therefore be accentuated.

Indeed, congregational singing is presupposed if the church as the body of Christ is in actuality engaged in the action of worship. "The hymn . . . *is* the church singing corporately in praise of God, and not just the worshipper 'taking part' in the service over against what the priest or preacher may do."[5]

Every person—young and old, homemaker, business executive, teacher, storekeeper—all—are included in the work of singing praise. As John Wesley exhorted in the third of his famous directions for singing: "Sing *all.* See that you join with the congregation as frequently as you can. Let not a slight degree of weakness or weariness hinder you. If it is a cross to you, take it up, and you will find it a blessing."[6]

In order for hymns to qualify for use by the entire congregation, they must of necessity be within the comprehension of most of the people. After all, hymns are designed for the use of "plain folk." The church is a voluntary body in which the "foolish" are of no less account than the "wise." In both thought and expression hymn texts must be easily grasped and free from elaborate or involved structure. Their basic message must be clear, direct, and understandable upon first encounter.

Models of such directness and clarity are Isaac Watts's "O God, our help in ages past," John Kebles's "Sun of my soul, thou Savior dear," and Georgia Harkness's "Hope of the World." In these hymns there are no words or images that even the simplest people would have to stop and think, "What do these words mean?" Hymns like these, when put to singable tunes, are best calculated to formulate a meaningful and useful script for the people as they enter together into the drama of worship.

[5]Cecil Northcott, *Hymns in Christian Worship* (Richmond: John Knox Press, 1964), p. 33.

[6]Wesley, John, Preface to *Sacred Melody*, 1761, quoted by James T. Lightwood, *The Music of the Methodist Hymn Book* (London: The Epworth Press, 1935), p. xix. See also *The Methodist Hymnal*, p. vii.

Practical Points

The members of an average congregation participate in the singing of hymns to the extent that they know and enjoy the tunes. When a hymn is mentioned to the average churchgoer, he usually responds in relation to the music he recalls. Consequently much hymn singing takes place in which mouths are open and loud noises are made, but the sentiments and thoughts of the texts are largely overlooked. Such thoughtless singing is often lethal to genuine worship.

Use of the Worship Folder

One way to help make the words of hymns meaningful to worshipers is to utilize their worship folders (also known as service bulletins). Hymns used at various points in public worship can be labeled by type or predominant mood and sentiment. Examples:

Hymn of Praise: "Praise the Lord, ye (O) heavens, adore him" (B11, L540, M42)

Hymn of Pentitence: "I lay my sins on Jesus (L305)

Hymn of Affirmation: "Jesus shall reign" (B282, L530, M472)

Hymn of Consecration: "Just as I am, thine own to be" (B243, M169)

When not overused, this practice can draw the people's attention to the basic mood or function of a particular hymn and thus aid them in singing it more meaningfully.

Moreover, since the meaning of hymns is often obscured by arranging their texts between the staves of musical notation on the hymnal page, printing the words as poems in the worship folder can enhance the meaning even of familiar hymns.[7] Attendants arriving early for worship can be encouraged to read and meditate on the words in the folder in preparation for the singing that will follow later.

If not overdone, hymnological information can also be helpful when included in the service folder. If sources are indicated, the name of the author (the devotional poet) should not be overlooked; the tune name and its composer could also be supplied. Examples:

Hymn 262: "Savior, again to thy dear name," John Ellerton; ELLERS—E. J. Hopkins

Hymn 367: "Father of mercies, in thy Word," Anne Steele; TALLIS'S ORDINAL—Thomas Tallis

Some hymnals also give dates of composition and/or the vital statistics of the author and composer; but this is so much excess baggage unless care is taken on occasion to explain the significance of the names, the sources, tune titles, abbreviations, and other information that is listed.

[7]See Erik Routley, "On the Display of Hymn Texts," *The Hymn*, 30 (January 1979), 16-20.

Verbal Introduction of Hymns

Progress can be made in soliciting the intelligent participation of the congregation in hymn singing by the manner in which hymns are announced in the service of worship. It is to be remembered that hymns are primarily expressive in purpose. They may often find their place in the worship order as responses to that which precedes them. In a thoughtfully planned order of service they can grow out of conditions of feeling that may have been brought about through other items or movements of worship.

Therefore in "free" services, where no fixed order exists, a few words of ascription or scriptural reminder could appropriately lead to the opening hymn of praise in order to give it an obvious reason for being. For example:

"Great is the Lord, and greatly to be praised!" (Ps. 48:1).

or

"Oh that men would praise the Lord for his goodness and for his wonderful works to the children of men!" (Ps. 107:8).

after which the instrumentalist would introduce the tune of a hymn such as:

Hymn 21: "O come, loud anthems let us sing"

or

Hymn 55: "Praise to the Lord the Almighty, the King of creation" (M55, B10, L543).

From time to time, the congregation might be told briefly why it is to sing a particular hymn at a particular moment. Because hymns are often considered as a kind of background activity or filler, many worshipers have little idea why they are singing a particular hymn at a given moment.

An occasional hymn commentary by the worship leader can focus the attention of the people on some reasons they may have for singing a particular hymn. For example:

"Had I a thousand tongues, I would praise God with them all!"
Thus exclaimed Peter Böhler, the Moravian preacher who was quite influential in the conversion of Charles Wesley. In 1739 near the anniversary day of his conversion, Charles, recalling Böhler's exuberant words, exclaimed:

"O for a thousand tongues to sing
My great Redeemer's praise,
The glories of my God and King,
The triumphs of his grace!"

Undoubtedly this is one of the most fervent and wholehearted of all our praise songs; it helps us recall the joy of our own salvation. Lacking a thousand tongues, let us freely use the one tongue we have to sing our "great Redeemer's praise!"

Hymn 559: "O for a thousand tongues to sing"

"Spoken modulations" can also be quite effective. Following prayer, an imaginative and creative leader will sense ways to move appropriately into the hymn that follows. For example:
"Let us continue in the spirit of prayer, as we speak to God in the words of the hymn, "Jesus, thou joy of loving hearts."
Hymn 329: "Jesus, thou joy of loving hearts"
Following Scripture, the simple quoting of the opening line or two of the hymn to be sung will help the congregation to regard it as their response to the Word of God read and shared. Hymns must be carefully selected for such "spoken modulations" if this device is to be of maximum value.

Certainly the tunes must be familiar and acceptable to those who sing them, but hymn singing must be much more than a mere pleasant musical pastime. Hymns have no real reason for being if they are regarded simply as *libretti* for the music. It is the worship leader's opportunity and sacred responsibility by whatever means he can command in introducing hymns to focus the congregations's attention on the words of prayer, affirmation, adoration, etc., for which the music is the effective medium.

Instrumental Introduction and Interpretation

Meaningful verbal introduction of hymns will be ineffectual without the sensitive introduction and interpretation of the hymn tunes by the organist, pianist, or other instrumentalist. Instrumentalists are the real leaders of the congregation in accompanied hymn singing. They should realize and magnify the privilege and responsibility of such leadership. The goal of organists should be to play in such ways that the people are encouraged to sing with purpose and enthusiasm. This means that while playing, they give attention to the texts as well as the tunes.

It is fundamentally important that instrumentalists perform notes and rhythms accurately and impregnate every hymn with musical feeling and vitality. In addition, there must be the imaginative interpretation of the mood of hymns, with thought given to matters of tempo, tone color (organ), articulation, volume, and phrasing. Whether organists actually sing along or not, they should play as if they were singing, in order to encourage the congregation to phrase together and to sing intelligently the words of the individual stanzas. Though they must avoid sudden or unexpected changes in registration or volume, organists who are aware of variations in textual sentiment can vary their playing accordingly.

For example, two familiar Christmas hymns: "Joy to the world" (ANTIOCH, B88, L39, M392) and "O little town of Bethlehem" (ST. LOUIS, B85, L41, M381) would certainly be introduced and interpreted through contrasting kinds of registration, tempo, and volume. Moreover, the third stanza of the latter hymn beginning:

© 1980 Charles Massey, Jr.

John G. Whittier

"How silently, how silently the wondrous gift is given" would be treated by the imaginative organist in somewhat more subdued fashion than the preceding stanzas. Following the text closely in either of these hymns will also shield the player from the embarrassment of beginning to perform a fifth stanza where none exists!

There are many other details of hymn playing, including treatment of ritards, modulations, free accompaniments, handling of the beginning and endings of phrases, accoustical matters, etc., which are beyond our purpose to treat.[8] Suffice it to say that a good instrumentalist will interpret the texts of hymns in such a manner that the people will want to sing with the spirit and with understanding.

"Liturgical Epigrams"

One writer on the subject of the use of hymns in worship has commented on "a certain decorative zeal" that many churches yield to "in adding interesting non-liturgical bits"[9] to the service. Indeed, as already noted, all too often hymns are interpolated in the service with no defined purpose. They appear to be just so much "bric-a-brac" placed there to serve some nonworship function such as affording musical pleasure to a certain segment of the choir or congregation or taking up time that could otherwise be profitably given over to silence.

Yet there is a place at certain points in the service for the use of short hymns or single stanzas of hymns used as "liturgical epigrams." Choirs too often usurp the prerogatives of the congregation in the singing of responses and other service music.

If the climax of worship is the commitment of life in dedication, how can this be better symbolized than in the offering? And if music is to accompany the self-offering of life at the moment of the presentation of the gifts, how can it be better done than by the singing participation of the entire worshiping group (congregation aided by the choir)?

The hymnbook contains a mine of "liturgical" responses for the congregation. First stanzas from hymns of consecration and/or stewardship can be appropriately employed as *offertory responses*:

"All things are thine, no gift have we" (M347)
"We give thee but thine own" (M181, L410)
"Lord of all good, our gifts we bring you now" (L411)
"Savior, thy dying love thou gavest me" (B418, M177)
"As men (saints) of old their first fruits brought" (L404, M511)
"As with gladness men of old" (Stanza 3) (L82, M397)

---

[8]See the bibliography for suggested sources dealing with matters of hymn playing.
[9]Northcott, *Hymns in Christian Worship*, p. 40.

Congregational *calls to worship* may be found in abundance:
"Come, we (ye) that love the Lord" (B505, M5)
"God himself is (present) with us" (B16, L249, M788)
"Ye (You) servants of God" (B292, L252, M409)
"All people that on earth do dwell" (B17, E21, L245, M21)
"Praise the Lord" (E8, refrain only)
"You we praise as God" (Antiphon I and final Alleluias only, E18)
"Praise the Lord with joyful cry" (E100)
There are numerous first stanzas of certain hymns that can serve as calls or *responses to Scripture:*
"Break thou (now) the bread of life" (B138, L235, M369)
"Father of mercies, in your (thy) Word" (L240, M367)
"O Word of God incarnate" (B140, L231, M372)
"Lord, keep us steadfast in your word" (L230)
"O God of light, your (thy) Word" (L237, M371)
"Thanks to God" (E103)
"My dear Redeemer and my Lord" (E37)
Some hymns are very suitable as *invocations:*
"Open now the gates of beauty" (L250, M13)
"Come, thou almighty king" (B2, L522, M3) (Stanza 1 or entire hymn)
"Lord Jesus Christ, be present now" (L253, M784)
"Come, thou Fount of every blessing" (B12, 13, L499, M93)
"Blessed Jesus, at thy word" (M257)
"Come, Holy Ghost, our souls inspire" (E16, L472, 473)
First stanzas of many prayer hymns are appropriate as calls or *responses to prayer:*
"Lord, teach us how to pray aright" (L438)
"O gracious father of mankind" (M260)
"I need thee every hour" (B379, M265)
"Prayer is the soul's sincere desire" (B400, M252) (final stanza)
"What a friend we have in Jesus" (B403, L439, M261)
Some hymns that can be used as *benedictions* or responses to closing prayers are:
"Lord, dismiss us with your (thy) blessings" (L259, M165)
"Savior, again to thy (your) dear name" (B65, M236, L262)
"May the grace of Christ our Savior" (M334)
"God be with you till we meet again" (B261, M539, 540)
"Blest be the tie that binds" (B256, L370, M306)
"Lord, as we rise" (E87)
The term "liturgical epigram" may more appropriately apply to *portions* of stanzas of hymns that may be used as interludes or responses in moving to and

from various elements of worship. For example, following the pastoral prayer:

O come to my heart, Lord Jesus
There is room in my heart for thee
—"Thou didst leave thy throne"
Here's my heart, O take and seal it
Seal it for thy courts above.
—"Come, thou fount of every blessing"
Take my life and let it be
Consecrated, Lord, to thee
—"Take my life and let it be consecrated"
O come to us, abide with us,
Our Lord Emmanuel.
—"O little town of Bethlehem"

Moreover, parts of hymns may be used instead of spoken sentences of prayer or thanksgiving in litanies. Example:

Our Father, for your holy Word by which we can live useful lives to glorify your name . . .

Christ our God to thee we raise
This our hymn of grateful praise.
—"For the beauty of the earth"

For the great love for all the world made known in your Son, Jesus Christ, through whom we have eternal life . . .

Christ our God to thee we raise
This our hymn of grateful praise.

For our church which teaches your truth throughout the world and ministers to its great heart hunger and spiritual need . . .

Christ our God to thee we raise
This our hymn of grateful praise.

For the privilege of serving in your kingdom and of reaching out, by your grace, to help one another and all mankind . . .

Christ our God to thee we raise
This our hymn of grateful praise. Amen.

Following the bendiction, some fragment of a hymn used previously in the service or in keeping with the theme of the season or sermon could be used:

Rejoice, rejoice, rejoice
give thanks and sing!
—"Rejoice, ye (you) pure in heart"
O give me grace to follow
My master and my friend.
—"O Jesus, I have promised"
Take from our souls the strain and stress

And let our ordered lives confess
The beauty of thy peace.
—"Dear Lord and Father of mankind"

Hymns belong to the people. Through them is voiced the people's prayer and praise, their eternal faith and hope. Memorable snatches of hymnic expression can be carried by the people to help and to bless as they depart from the service, singing inwardly.

Alternation Practices

A gentle but often effective stimulus to a responsible involvement of the congregation in hymn singing is available in the application of the old principle of alternation (*alternatim*). Alternation singing is an ancient practice extending back to the performance of the Hebrew psalms in temple worship. The parallel structure of psalm verses made antiphonal chanting between two groups a natural mode of performance. *Alternatim* as a term was applied as early as the twelfth century to alternating plain chant (probably by the entire clerical choir) and polyphony (by a group of more skilled soloists).[10]

Alternation practices among choirs, soloists, congregation, organ, and other instruments in sixteenth- and seventeenth-century Germany served the practical purpose of getting everyone meaningfully through the many, many stanzas of numerous Lutheran chorales. Today the alternation principle can be applied to many practices having as their aim the bringing of zest, variety, and inspiration to the normal *tutti* singing of hymns.

There are at least two categories of alternation. One kind, the more usual and traditional, pertains to the various performers in hymn singing. The other kind refers to the manner or medium of hymn performance.

Alternation as to Performers

Under this category the various stanzas of hymns may be alternately performed in the following ways:

1. Congregation with organ versus organ alone

This gives the congregational voices a recurring breather, relieving constant singing but keeping the flow and continuity of the hymn, provided that the organist "plays the words" skillfully. For the organist who possesses the skill of improvisation, this is an opportunity for the interpretation of the texts. For those organists without these skills, well-written hymn "preludes" and chorale improvisations are available.[11]

2. Congregation with choir versus choir alone

---

[10]See "Alternation practice" in Carl Shalk, (ed.), *Key Words in Church Music* (St. Louis: Concordia Publishing House, 1978), pp. 15-17.
[11]Consult the bibliography for published collections of hymn arrangements.

After a congregation has gained confidence in singing a particular hymn, it could well function alone in alternation with the choir. Singing *with* the congregation rather than *for* them is the first responsibility of the choir.

3. Choir *versus* choir *versus* congregation

If more than one choir is present, there can be antiphonal singing between them or between soloists and *tutti*. However, lest the congregation become mere auditor, a three-way alternation (Choir A—congregation—Choir B—congregation, etc.) could be arranged.

4. Congregation *versus* congregation

A congregation can be divided into two (or more) units in a number of different ways: men *versus* women; those on one side of the sanctuary *versus* those on the other side; lower congregation (downstairs) *versus* upper congregation (balconies); adults *versus* children/youth; combined (massed) choirs *versus* congregation, etc.

Many hymns and gospel songs by their poetic structure lend themselves suitably to alternation singing in one or more of the ways suggested:

1. Question-answer hymns may be sung antiphonally:
   "What child is this" (L40, M385)
   "Watchman, tell us of the night" (M358)
   "Art thou weary, art thou languid?" (M99)
   "Peace, perfect peace" (M229)
   "Ask ye what great thing I know" (B60, M124)
   "Where is this stupendous stranger" (E28)

2. Gospel songs, refrain-type hymns, and those provided with antiphons are all suitable for responsorial or antiphonal singing:
   "All creatures of our God and king" (B9, L527, M60)
   "When morning gilds the skies" (B44, L545, 546, M91)
   "Come, Christians, join to sing" (B61, M77)
   "You we praise as God" (E18)
   "Glorious the day when Christ was born" (E63)
   "Divided our pathways" (E59)
   "We do not know how to pray" (E110)
   "We praise thee, O God" (B263)
   "Let all the world in every corner sing" (B24, M10)

3. Contemporary psalm settings with their antiphons lend themselves to this treatment naturally:
   "My shepherd is the Lord" (E5)   Psalm 23
   "How good to offer thanks" (E6) Psalm 92
   "Praise the Lord" (E8)   Psalm 150

Alternation as to Manner and Medium

The other kind of *alternatim* results when the principle is extended in application to the mode or medium of performance. When imaginatively used, this can lead to varied methods of congregational participation:

1. Alternation of Scripture read with hymn stanzas sung.

This is particularly effective with metrical psalms, where the original verse(s) for each stanza can be read preceding its singing.

Example:　"Unto the hills I lift mine eyes" (M57)

or

"Unto the hills around do I lift up" (L445)

Reading:　Psalm 121; verses 1 and 2
Singing:　Stanza 1
Reading:　Psalm 121: verses 3, 4
Singing:　Stanza 2
Reading:　Psalm 121: verses 5, 6
Singing　　Stanza 3
Reading:　Psalm 121: verses 7, 8
Singing:　Stanza 4

2. Alternation by singing and speaking stanzas of a hymn.

A three- or five-stanza hymn usually works best in this method.

Examples:　"Alas and did my Savior bleed" (B113, L98, M415) *or* "Nature with open volume stands" (E39)

Stanza 1:　sung
Stanza 2:　spoken
Stanza 3:　sung
Stanza 4:　spoken
Stanza 5:　sung

"We believe in one true God" (B29, M463) *or* "We all believe in one true God" (L374)

Stanza 1:　sung
Stanza 2:　spoken
Stanza 3:　sung

3. Alternation of unison with singing in harmony.

Not to be overlooked are the early reasons for *alternatim*—simple congregational unison (even unaccompanied at times) and the polyphony (by the choir). Examples:

"Jesus, priceless treasure" (L457, M220)

Stanza 1:　unison
Stanza 2:　parts
Stanza 3:　unison

"Stand up and bless the Lord" (B26, M16)

Stanza 1: unison
Stanza 2: harmony
Stanza 3: unison
Stanza 4: harmony
Stanza 5: unison

Some hymnals provide for this kind of treatment in their notation and arrangement of music for the individual stanzas. Example:

"For all the saints" (L174)

Stanzas 1, 2, 3: unison
Stanzas 4, 5, 6: harmony
Stanzas 7, 8: unison

4. Alternation of modes.

Change from major to minor or vice versa is not to be done capriciously but rather employed when the text can be illuminated by this kind of alternation. Examples:

"Come, Holy Spirit, heavenly Dove" (B134, MEAR; M134, GRÄFENBERG or BALERMA)

Stanza 1: major
Stanza 2:
(3 and 4) minor
Last stanza: major

"Amazing grace! how sweet the sound" (B165, L448, M92)

Stanzas 1 and 2: major
Stanzas 3 (4): minor
Last Stanza: major

5. Alternation of tunes.

If thoughtfully planned, there can be an alternation of hymn tunes in the progress of singing the stanzas of a hymn. Examples:

"O Thou to whose all searching sight" (B470, M213)

Stanza 1: KEDRON (E-major)
Stanza 2: DUKE STREET
Stanza 3: KEDRON
Stanza 4: DUKE STREET

"How firm a foundation" (B383, L507, M48)

Stanza 1: ADESTE FIDELES (A♭-major)
Stanza 2: FOUNDATION
Stanza 3: ADESTE FIDELES
Stanza 4: FOUNDATION

"My hope is built on nothing less" (B337, L293-94, M222)

Stanza 1:   SOLID ROCK (F-major)
Stanza 2, 3: MELITA (C-major)
Stanza 4:   SOLID ROCK

The last example illustrates the fact that there can be textual reasons for selecting certain tunes for particular stanzas. MELITA was originally set by its composer, J. B. Dykes to William Whiting's "Almighty Father, strong to save"—the Navy Hymn. Therefore this tune usually calls to mind for many people the sea, along with concern for those who may be in peril upon it. It is thus appropriate especially for the middle two stanzas of "My hope is built" with their references to "high and stormy gale" and "raging flood." Moreover MELITA is a very expressive setting for the words of the chorus with its sturdy rising chromatic line for "On Christ the solid rock I stand" and the falling melodic line to the low tonic with the words "all other ground is sinking sand."[12] Here is also an example of alternation in keys. The two keys work together well, with C as the common tone for both tunes (the dominant of F-major—SOLID ROCK and the tonic of C-major—MELITA).

6. Alternation of hymns

Using stanzas of different hymns with the same tune is rare and not to be employed where the unity of thought of a hymn may thereby be disturbed. However, sometimes a medley of hymns on one tune can be used if their "message" can logically fit a common theme. Example:

Theme: "Praise the God of Our Salvation"
Tune: HYFRYDOL
"Come, Thou long expected Jesus" (Stanza 1)
"Praise the Lord! ye heavens adore him" (Stanza 2)
"I will sing the wondrous story" (Stanza 1)
"Jesus! What a friend of sinners" (Stanza 1)

7. Alternation with the use of descant.

A variation in the unison-polyphony alternation is the use of the descant part. This high soaring counter melody works well with the high voices (often also solo instruments) singing against the unison of the congregation and choir on the principal melody. Care must be taken to train the congregation to continue singing on those stanzas to which the descant is added. Without such training, individuals in the congregation will tone down or even stop their own singing in order to hear the descant. The purpose of the descant is to bring zest and vitality to the singing of all, not to entertain the congregation. The device, however, should be employed in moderation. Its use may best be reserved for especially festive and celebrative occasions.

---

[12]These affinities in text and tune could have been some of the reasons for the choice of MELITA as a second tune for "My hope is built on nothing less" at L294.

Special Services

The hymn can be a most effective vehicle of ministry in certain special times of worship such as weddings and funerals. Both these occasions are intended as services of public worship, even though this is a point sometimes difficult for families who are intimately involved in such services to grasp. They often tend to look upon these services as being private affairs rather than as worship to the Lord and in company with the larger Christian family.

The Christian Wedding Service should be directed toward God in Christ rather than the bride. The object of attention in a Christian wedding is the God in whose heart the marriage has been formed and whose presence blesses it. Although other types of music may be appropriately performed at weddings, the hymns directed toward God (sung by all the wedding party as well as by the congregation) can also be a simple but beautiful expression of loving support for the couple being married. Hymns of praise are suitable, such as:

"Now thank we all our God" (B234, L533, M49)

"Love divine, all loves excelling" (B58, L315, M283)

"Praise, my soul, the king of heaven" (B8, L549, M66)

These and other majestic hymns are sometimes played for the processional and recessional rather than marchlike (sometimes secular in association) music. Hymns like:

"Joyful, joyful we adore thee" (B31, L551, M38)

"Praise to the Lord, the Almighty" (B10, L543, M55)

"Praise the Lord, ye heavens adore him" (B11, M42)

are far more desirable than certain secular solo selections that are often sensuous and sentimental. The wedding should not be a spectacle to be witnessed by the congregation as audience. Rather it is a drama of worship in which all the people are even for a brief time, singing God's praises. Praise is an appropriate expression of the joy and thanksgiving which is engendered by such occasions.

The Christian Funeral too can be a service of divine worship, not a mournful surrender to death. The role of the hymn in the funeral service is to strengthen faith and express the good news of resurrection. The declaration of confidence and trust expressed in the singing of great hymns can be an eloquent Christian testimony to those attending who may be unbelievers. Generally speaking, the favorite hymns of the deceased or of a relative should be used only if they contain strong positive expression of Christian faith. The hymns for the funeral can function in several ways:

1. To express thanks and adoration to God:

"The God of Abraham praise" (B25, L544)

"Praise to the living God" (M30)

"Immortal, Invisible God only wise" (B32, L526, M27)
"Guide me, O Thou great Jehovah" (B202, L343, M271)
"For all the saints" (B144, L174, M536)
2. To give comfort to the living:
"A mighty fortress is our God" (B37, L228, M20)
"If you will only let God guide you" (B203, L453, M210)
"Sun of my soul, thou Savior dear" (M502)
"My faith looks up to Thee" (B382, L479, M143)
3. To strengthen resolve for continued living:
"O Master, let me walk with thee (You)" (B369, L492, M170)
"I know not what the future hath" (B492, M290)
"O God, our help in ages past" (B223, L320, M28)
"God of grace and God of glory" (B265, L415, M470)
While it is true that the death of a loved one is a saddening occasion and a sobering reminder of one's mortality, yet Christians view death as the door to eternal life made possible by Christ's victory over death. The hymns sung and played in the Christian funeral service should therefore be those reflecting Easter and the resurrection.[13]

Hymn Services

Many of the goals envisaged for the thoughtful selection and meaningful use of hymns in public worship may be achieved in the context of the hymn service, a worship service designed primarily for congregational participation in hymn singing. It may involve a choir and/or other performing individuals or groups, but the emphasis is upon the congregation as performers.

The hymn service may sometimes be designated a hymn festival. This term usually implies the involvement of more than one congregation and is of a celebrative or commemorative nature. Hymn festivals, particularly those observing some great church or hymnic anniversary or honoring some outstanding figure in church or hymnic history, are greatly to be encouraged. The ecumenicity of the hymnal can be dramatized by festivals which are planned to transcend denominational, cultural and racial barriers. The cause of Christian neighborliness has been greatly strengthened in such endeavors.

However, community-wide festivals should not displace nor lessen the emphasis on more modest hymn services planned (perhaps on a regular basis) for local congregational worship. Such services can be infinite in variety of content.[14] As to type they may be classified in at least three ways:[15]

[13]Consult the bibliography for suggestions and materials for the selection and use of hymns in the wedding and funeral.
[14]See the discussion of hymn sings in Chap. 12, The Hymn in Education.
[15]See Austin C. Lovelace, "Hymn Festivals" Paper XXXI of the Hymn Society of America (Springfield, O.: HSA, 1979).

1. *Topical*—a service arranged according to some hymnic classification not necessarily unified in theme. This could be a service in which the hymns bear a common relationship such as, those of one author or composer (commemorative anniversary services for James Montgomery, Ralph Vaughan Williams, John G. Whittier, Lowell Mason), or of those from one nation or ethnic group (British hymns, black hymns), or those translated from one language (Greek hymns, German hymns), or those of one sect or denomination (Methodist hymns, Presbyterian hymns), or those of certain periods of general or Christian history (Reformation hymns, eighteenth-century hymns), or those unified by some characteristic of their authors/composers (hymns by women, hymns by famous poets), or those of certain tune types (metrical psalms, carols). These are a few suggestions for topical hymn services.[16]

2. *Thematic*—a service with a unifying devotional theme often based either on some religious teaching or concept or on some liturgical form or piece of devotional literature or holy Scripture. Some examples follow:

Theological Concept or Christan Virtue
  1. The Cosmic Christ
  2. The Christian Life
  3. The Trinity
  4. The Cross
  5. The Church
  6. Faith, Hope, Love
  7. Discipleship and Service
  8. The Church Year

Scriptural Form or Passage
  1. The Lord's Prayer
  2. The Beatitudes
  3. The Ten Commandments
  4. Isaiah 6:1-8
  5. Psalm 23
  6. Colossians 3:16-17
  7. John 3:16
  8. Galatians 5:22-23

Traditional Worship Form or Theological (Liturgical) Formulations
  1. "Te Deum Laudamus"
  2. Apostle's Creed
  3. Prayer of St. Francis

---

[16]See Appendix for bibliography on hymn services. Many of the sources listed there offer valuable practical suggestions for planning hymn services. Such points to insure effectiveness and success should be carefully considered.

4. Lord's Prayer

5. Church Covenant

The thematic type of service lends itself more readily than the topical type to the use of hymns in a devotional sequence for the purpose of interpreting and expressing worship moods. However the topical service can also be a time of divine worship if the planners are careful to give the congregation reasons for its expressions of prayer and praise to God through the hymns in a manner already discussed.

It is also possible to have a hymn service which combines the topical and thematic elements.[17] For example:

1. Tractarian Hymnody and the Christian Year

   The topic: Hymns written by those connected with the Tractarian (High Church) Movement in nineteenth-century England

   The theme: The church (liturgical) year

2. Baptist Hymns and the Church Covenant

   The topic: Hymns by Baptists

   The theme: The church covenant

3. Wesleyan Hymns and the Lord's Prayer

   The topic: Hymns by the Wesleys

   The theme: The model prayer of our Lord

4. Luther's Hymns and Christian Doctrine

   The topic: The Hymns of Martin Luther

   The Theme: Hymns as vehicles of Christain doctrine

Demonstrative—a service with more didactic intentions. It may be conceived of as a kind of hymn study session or congregational rehearsal in which the leader assumes a more informal role as instructor and inspirer rather than as worship leader. The purpose is either to give more direct attention to the practical matters of improving congregational singing or simply to promote fellowship through singing. It can have either topical or thematic aspects but would ordinarily be more flexible and spontaneous than the other two types. Often it might be called a Hymn *Sing.*

A "Sing" could be gathered about such themes or topics as the following:

Hymn Meters

Hymn Patterns

Hymn Tune Names

Hymn Interpretations

Hymns and Psalms

Alternatim praxis

John Wesley's Singing Rules

[17]See Appendix for a suggested hymn service based on the worship pattern exemplified by the experience of Isaiah (Isa. 6:1-8) and using the hymns of Isaac Watts. This service can also illustrate the *alternatim* principle in a variety of ways.

The last suggestion is a reminder of Wesley's final rule for singing which aptly sums up the major concerns of this chapter: "Above all, *sing spiritually.* Have an eye to God in every word you sing. Aim at pleasing him more than yourself, or any other creature. In order to do this, attend strictly to the sense of what you sing, and see that your heart is not carried away with the sound, but offered to God continually; so shall your singing be such as the Lord will approve here, and reward you when He cometh in the clouds of heaven."[18]

Questions for Study/Projects for Action

1. Looking at the Topical Index in your hymnal, under what headings would you find hymns appropriate for the dialogical pattern of worship? List other hymns for each of the following:
    1. God's greatness, holiness, and power
    2. Human sinfulness and confession
    3. God's mercy and forgiveness
    4. God's call to discipleship
    5. Personal commitment, dedication, and consecration
2. If you worship within a tradition that does not give particular observance to the church year, consult a hymnal such as *The Lutheran Book of Worship* to study the index entitled "Hymns for the Church Year," pp. 929-31 in order to make a list of hymns appropriate for Advent, Lent, Pentecost.[19]
3. Make a file of service bulletins from various churches to discover:
    1. The number of hymns selected in a service
    2. The kinds of hymns chosen
    3. The ways hymns are labeled (if at all)
    4. The manner in which hymns are used
How may one become more sensitive to the worship uses of particular hymns?
4. List some ways that a musical worship leader can aid a congregation to sing hymns as genuine expressions of prayer and praise.
5. What are the practical reasons why the organist/pianist is an important leader of congregational hymn singing?
6. Think of three ways in which parts of these hymns (a stanza or a phrase) may be used as "liturgical epigrams":
    "Lead on, O King eternal" (B420, L495, M478)
    "O come, O come, Emmanuel" (B78, L34, M354)
    "My country, tis of thee" (B511, L566, M547)
    "Open my eyes, that I may see" (B358, M267)
7. Sketch one possible *alternatim* treatment for each of these hymns:
    "Jesus, Thou (O Jesus) joy of loving hearts" (B72, L356, M329)

---

[18]Austin C. Lovelace and William C. Rice, *Music and Worship in the Church* (Nashville: Abingdon Press, 1960; revised and enlarged edition, 1976), 157, but easily found in other places. See *The Methodist Hymnal*, viii.
[19]Another source for hymn selection is to be found in the Lectionary of the *Methodist Book of Worship.* For further reading on the meanings of the church seasons a book like William F. Dunkle, Jr., *Values in the Church Year* (Nashville: Abingdon Press, 1959) will be helpful. The bibliography contains other sources.

"When peace like a river" (B339, L346)
"Rock of Ages, cleft for me" (B163, L327, M120)
"Jesus, in Thy dying woes" (L112, 113)
"Jesus, with Thy church abide" (B241, M311)
"The Lord will come and not be slow" (B128, L318, M468)

8. Think of one suitable integrating subject for one each of the three kinds of hymn service treated in this chapter: Topical, Thematic, and Demonstrative; select at least five hymns that could appropriately be a part of each.

9. Sketch in detail a one hour's hymn service, using one of the integrating subjects chosen above.

12
The Hymn in Education

Some Values in the Teaching of Hymns

"If a hymn is worth singing, it is worth studying seriously in concert or privately"[1]

While much of the church's attention has been focused upon teaching the Bible (and rightly so), teaching of the hymnal has yet to become a significant part of the educational program of most congregations. Why should a church teach hymns?

One basic reason is that hymns are a means of communicating the message of the church. Some hymns are paraphrases of Scripture and others are based on specific Scripture verses.[2] Hymns also effectively convey the church's theology.[3] While listening to a sermon is usually a passive experience, hymn singing involves the congregation in active participation. Furthermore, hymns are sung over and over again, year after year. They teach effectively through repetition. Moreover, their melodies tend to linger long in the memory, carrying the thoughts connected with them into the mind and heart.

Hymns should also be taught for their value in helping a congregation or an individual to worship. Sometimes when worshipers lack words to express their feelings, they find them expressed meaningfully in the words of a hymn. In celebrating the birth of Christ or his resurrection, they are helped to express their worship through joyful hymns and carols. In the somber meditations upon the sufferings of Christ on the cross one finds hymns which communicate these sacred events with poignant power.

For example, those who are at a loss for words to utter their profound wonder concerning Christ's sacrifice may find their feelings expressed in certain hymns. A medieval poet's reaction to the crucifixion is embodied in "O sacred Head, now wounded" (B105, L117, M418):

> What language shall I borrow
>   To thank thee, dearest Friend,
> For this thy dying sorrow,
>   Thy pity without end?
> O make me thine forever,
>   And should I fainting be,
> Lord, let me never, never
>   Outlive my love to thee.

[1]David Hugh Jones, "Comments of a Hymnal Editor," *The Hymn* 29,4 (October 1978), 227.
[2]See chap. 3, The Hymn and Scripture.
[3]See chap. 4, The Hymn and Theology.

The pioneer English hymnist Isaac Watts expressed his feelings concerning the death of Christ in "When I survey the wondrous cross" (B111, L482, M435):

See, from his head, his hands, his feet,
Sorrow and love flow mingled down;
Did e'er such love and sorrow meet,
Or thorns compose so rich a crown?
Were the whole realm of nature mine,
That were a present far too small;
Love so amazing, so divine,
Demands my soul, my life, my all.

An anonymous Afro-American reacted to the cross of Christ with the following words (B108, L92, M436):

Were you there when they crucified my Lord?
Were you there when they crucified my Lord?
Oh! Sometimes it causes me to tremble, tremble, tremble.
Were you there when they crucified my Lord?

Hymns have value in providing instruction in Christian living. Both Baptist and Methodist hymnals have major headings entitled "The Christian Life" and the Lutheran hymnal has a similar heading, "The Life of Faith." For example, hymns can effectively teach that the Christian life involves a commitment to active service. Notice the action words in these hymn titles: "Rise up, O men of God" (B268, M174),[4] "Rescue the perishing" (B283, M175), and "Go, tell it on the mountain" (B82, L70, M404).[5]

The teaching of hymns is an avenue for passing on the heritage of the church. One cannot study hymnody without encountering such giants in the history of the Christian church as Ambrose of Milan, John of Damascus, Francis of Assisi, Martin Luther, John Calvin, John Wesley, John Mason Neale, and Harry Emerson Fosdick. In addition to Christian biography and the general sweep of church history, one learns a significant portion of the church's devotional poetry through hymnody. Through a study of hymns one can also learn about poetic form and style, including meter, rhyme, and the various poetic devices.[6] Much of the musical heritage of the church is encountered in hymnology (the practical study of and about hymns). Such forms as plainsong, chorale, psalm tune, and gospel hymn relate to interesting

---

[4]At L383 this hymn has been replaced by Norman O. Forness' "Rise up, O saints of God!."
[5]See Harry Eskew, "Hymns in the Church's Teaching Ministry," *The Theological Educator*, 8,2 (Spring 1978), 86-97.
[6]See chap. 1, The Hymn and Literature.

segments of the church's heritage.[7] Furthermore, a knowledge of hymnody illuminates the larger forms of church music which are related to hymns. To take just one example, a knowledge of Luther's Easter hymn *Christ Lag In Todesbanden* ("Christ Jesus lay in death's strong bonds," L134, M438) greatly enhances the meaning one finds in Bach's Easter cantata (BWV 4) based on this hymn.

Thus through hymn instruction one is able to teach the message of the church, to help persons worship, to provide guidance in Christian living, and to present the vast heritage of the church, including knowledge of outstanding leaders in its history and a significant portion of its devotional literature and music.

Hymns in the Church's Educational Program

Where Hymns Are Used

Hymn singing in most churches is not limited to the central worship services. This activity takes place in many of the church's organizations as well. Church organizations which can make good use of hymns include the Sunday School, graded choirs, mission study and action groups, and senior citizen groups. In addition, special educational courses, such as church membership or catechetical classes and Vacation Bible Schools, can make effective use of hymns. Each of the church organizations whose programs can allow for hymn singing provide excellent opportunities for the church music leader to enhance the effectiveness of this experience educationally.

Hymns in the Curriculum

The curriculum of each of the church's educational organizations can be effectively supported by appropriate hymns. For example, a Sunday School lesson dealing with Psalm 72 could make use of "Jesus shall reign" (B282, L530, M472). However, the fullest opportunity for singing hymns and teaching hymnology is provided through the graded choir program.

The importance of children's learning good hymns has often been emphasized. The favorite hymns of adults are frequently those they learned when young. Children, because they can do so with ease, should be encouraged to memorize hymns. Hymn study sheets are an excellent aid in teaching hymns,[8] as illustrated by the Choristers Guild hymn study sheet for "This is my Father's world."

[7]See chap. 2, The Hymn and Music.
[8]The hymn study sheets published by the Choristers Guild (P.O. Box 38188, Dallas, TX 75238) have study materials on one side, as in "This is my Father's world," and the words and music of the hymn on the reverse side for easy reference. These hymn study sheets are designed to fit in a three-ring binder. As of this writing, some eighty-five hymns for children are included in this series.

This Is My Father's World

When Jesus talked with his disciples, he often told them that God was his Father and also their Father. Dr. Maltbie Babcock had this same feeling about God and often expressed it, not only in sermons (for he was a minister), but also in poetry. Dr. Babcock loved God's outdoors—he often said he was "going out to see my Father's world." It was a natural thing then, for him to write a poem in which he said, "This is my Father's world." The three stanzas of our hymn are taken from a much longer poem called "Thoughts for Everyday Living."

How many of the beautiful objects of nature mentioned in the hymn can you count? _____. Have you ever heard or seen some of the things about which Dr. Babcock wrote? _____. If we listen, it is possible to hear many sounds when we are out in the country, in the woods, by a lake, that we cannot hear in the hustle and bustle of the city.

Have you ever listened to the rustling of the leaves in the woods when the wind blows? _____, when someone walks through them? _____. Have you listened carefully to the "caroling of the birds"? _____.

Many hundreds of years ago people thought that the various planets and stars sent out sounds, each one having a different pitch. It was from this ancient belief that Dr. Babcock found the phrase "and 'round me rings the music of the spheres." The spheres are his reference to the round planets out in space, for a sphere is a round ball. Can you imagine wonderful music being sent out from all the planets and bodies away out there in space? Wouldn't it be a terrifically great musical sound?

The tune called TERRA BEATA is thought to be taken from an old English melody that Mr. Franklin Sheppard's mother had sung to him when he was a little boy. There is an old English tune called RUSPER that is very similar and has phrases or parts of the melody exactly like the tune we sing to the words of "This is My Father's World." The words *Terra beata* mean *happy* or *blessed earth* in Latin.

Franklin Sheppard was a businessman but was also a good musician and deeply interested in his church life. He was one of the persons who helped edit and publish one of the Presbyterian hymnals many years ago. He also served as organist in the church in which he was confirmed as a boy. All through his life he was deeply interested in the musical life of his church and denomination.

Several Bible references help to show Dr. Babcock's thinking and deep interpretation of the Bible in his hymn. They are:

Genesis 1:1-2
Psalm 24:1
Matthew 10:29-31

Hymns and hymn tunes should be included in every church's graded choir curriculum. Kindergarten children can be prepared to learn hymns through exposure to hymn tunes, such as TERRA PATRIS ("This is my Father's world," B155, L554; TERRA BEATA, M45, DUKE STREET ("Jesus shall reign," B282, L530, M472), and HYFRYDOL ("Praise the Lord! ye heavens adore him," B11, M42; "Alleluia! Sing to Jesus," L158). Children in grades one, two, and three can learn to sing "Praise God from whom all blessings flow" (B6,7: L564; M809), "Holy, holy, holy, Lord God Almighty" (B1, L165, M26), and "Fairest Lord Jesus" (B48, M79; "Beautiful Savior," L518). Children in these early grades can begin to use the hymnal and to learn about authors and composers of hymns and hymn tunes. Children in choirs for grades four, five, and six can learn more hymnology and additional hymns, such as "Now thank we all our God" (B234, L533, 534: M49), "All creatures of our God and King" (B9, L527, M60), and "For the beauty of the earth" (B54, L561, M35). One plan that involves the systematic integration of hymns into the children's choir curriculum consists of two three-year hymn cycles, one three-year cycle for grades one through three, and another for grades four through six.[9]

100 Hymns for Children and Youth

The following list of 100 hymns is suggestive of the hymnic wealth available for the Christian education of children and youth. This list is not meant to be a "canon," for there are many other excellent hymns that may be used in the church's teaching ministry.

Although this list is divided into three age groupings, these divisions are not rigid. For example, some hymns in the second group (for fourth, fifth, and sixth graders) may be quite appropriate for third graders. Children in the early grades can be taught "Holy, holy, holy, Lord God Almighty" and other hymns of like complexity, but it is often wise for them to learn one stanza rather than attempting to master all stanzas. Children need not understand the full meaning of a hymn in order to benefit from it. As they grow, they will grow in their understanding of the hymns they have been taught.

---

[9]This plan is being followed by the Church Music Department of the Southern Baptist Sunday School Board (127 Ninth Ave., N., Nashville, TN 37234) and is incorporated in their periodicals: *Music Makers* (grades 1-3), *Youth Musician* (grades 4-6), and *The Music Leader* (for leaders of children's choirs).

Hymns for which study sheets are available from the Choristers Guild (see footnote 8) are marked with an asterisk (*).

20 Hymns for Grades 1-3 (ages 6-8)

*1. "All praise to thee, my God, this night" (TALLIS' CANON, L278, M493)
*2. "All glory, laud, and honor" (ST. THEODULPH, B39, L108, M424)
*3. "All things bright and beautiful" (ROYAL OAK, M34)
*4. "Away in a manger" (MUELLER, B80, L67, M384)
*5. "Come, Christians, join to sing" (MADRID, B61; SPANISH HYMN, M77)
*6. "Come, thou long-expected Jesus" (HYFRYDOL, B79, M360; JEFFERSON, L30)
*7. "Fairest Lord Jesus" (CRUSADERS' HYMN or ST. ELIZABETH or SCHOENSTER HERR JESU, B48, M79; "Beautiful Savior," L518)
*8. "Go, tell it on the mountain" (GO TELL IT, B82, L70, M404)
 9. "Holy, holy, holy, Lord God Almighty" (NICAEA, B1, L165, M26)
 10. "Joy to the world" (ANTIOCH, B88, L39, M392; JOY, E36)
 11. "O come, all ye faithful" (ADESTE FIDELES, B81, L45, M386)
*12. "O little town of Bethlehem" (ST. LOUIS, B85, L41, M381)
*13. "O sing a song of Bethlehem" (KINGSFOLD, B99)
*14. "Praise God, from whom all blessings flow" (OLD 100TH, B6,7; L564,565; M809)
 15. "Savior, like a shepherd lead us" (BRADBURY, B213, M121; HER VIL TIES, L481)
 16. "Savior, teach me day by day" (INNOCENTS, B291; ORIENTIS PARTIBUS, M162)
 17. "Sing to the Lord of harvest" (NORTHAVEN, B232; WIE LIEBLICH IST DER MAIEN, L412)
*18. "Take my life and let it be consecrated" (HENDON, B373; "Take my life that I may be," PATMOS, L406; MESSIAH, M187)
*19. "This is my Father's world" (TERRA PATRIS or TERRA BEATA, B155, L554, M45; MERCER STREET, E108)
 20. "This is the day the Lord hath made" (ARLINGTON, B68)

40 Hymns for Grades 4-6 (ages 9-11)

*21. "A mighty fortress is our God" (EIN' FESTE BURG, B37, E25, L228, 229, M20)
*22. "All creatures of our God and King" (LASST UNS ERFREUEN, B9, L527, M60)
*23. "As with gladness men of old" (DIX, L82, M397)
*24. "Christ the Lord is risen today" (EASTER HYMN, B114, M439; ORIENTIS PARTIBUS, L130)
*25. "Come, thou Almighty King" (ITALIAN HYMN, B2, L522, M3)

*26. "Come, ye thankful people, come" (St. George's Windsor, B233; M522; "Come, you thankful people, come," L407)

*27. "Day is dying in the west" (Chautauqua, M503)

*28. "Faith of our fathers" (St. Catherine, B143, L500, M151)

*29. "For the beauty of the earth" (Dix, B54, L561, M35)

30. "God moves in a mysterious way" (Dundee, B439, M215; Bangor, L483; London New, E41)

31. "God of our fathers" (National Hymn, B149, L567, M552)

*32. "Good Christian men, rejoice" (In dulci jubilo, B90; M391; "Good Christian friends, rejoice," L55)

33. "Hark! the herald angels sing" (Mendelssohn, B83, L60, M388)

*34. "He who would valiant be" (St. Dunstan's, B384, M155; "All who would valiant be," L498)

*35. "How firm a foundation" (Foundation, B383, L507, M48)

*36. "I sing the almighty power of God" (Forest Green, B154, M37)

*37. "In Christ there is no east or west" (Mckee, B258, L359; St. Peter, M192; No East Or West, E86)

*38. "Jesus shall reign" (Duke Street, B282, L530, M472)

*39. "Joyful, joyful, we adore thee" (Hymn To Joy, B31, L551, M38)

*40. "Let all the world in every corner sing" (All The World, B24, M10)

*41. "Let us break bread together" (Break Bread, B252, L212, M330)

*42. "Let us with a gladsome mind" (Monkland, B27; Williams Bay, L521; Innocents, M61)

43. "Lord, I want to be a Christian" (I Want To Be a Christian, B322, M286)

*44. "Now thank we all our God" (Nun Danket, B234, L533, 534, M49)

45. "O beautiful, for spacious skies" (Materna, B508, M543)

*46. "O come, O come, Emmanuel" (Veni Emmanuel, B78, L34, M354)

*47. "Praise the Lord! Ye heavens adore him" (Hyfrydol, B11; Austria, M42; "Praise the Lord, O heavens adore him," L540)

*48. "Praise to the Lord, the Almighty" (Lobe Den Herren, B10, L543, M55)

*49. "Rejoice, the Lord is King" (Darwall, B120, M483; Gopsal, E32; Laus Regis, L171)

*50. "Rise up, O men of God" (St. Thomas, B268, Festal-Song, M174)

*51. "Sing praise to God who reigns above" (Mit Freuden zart, B22, M4; "Sing praise to God, the highest good," Lobt Gott den Herren, ihr, L542)

52. "Stand up, stand up for Jesus" (Webb, B391, L389, M248)

*53. "The church's one foundation" (Aurelia, B236, L369, M297)

54. "The day of resurrection" (Herzlich tut mich erfreuen, L141; Lancashire, M437)

*55. "The God of Abraham praise" (LEONI or YIGDAL, B25, L544; "Praise to the living God," M30)

*56. "The Lord's my shepherd, I'll not want" (CRIMOND, B341; BROTHER JAMES' AIR, L451; EVAN, M68)

57. "We would see Jesus; lo! his star is shining" (MORA PROCTER, B98; CUSHMAN, M90)

58. "We've a story to tell to the nations" (MESSAGE, B281, M410)

59. "When morning gilds the skies" (LAUDES DOMINI, B44, L546, M91)

60. "While shepherds watched their flocks by night" (WINCHESTER OLD, B97, M394)

40 Hymns for Youth (ages 12 up)

61. "Ah, holy Jesus, how hast thou offended" (HERZLIEBSTER JESU, L123, M412)

62. "Amazing grace! how sweet the sound" (AMAZING GRACE or NEW BRITAIN, B165, L448, M92)

63. "All hail the power of Jesus' name" (CORONATION, B40, L328, M71)

*64. "Be thou my vision" (SLANE, B212, M256)

65. "Breathe on me, Breath of God" (TRENTHAM, B317, M133; DURHAM, L488)

*66. "Built on the Rock the church doth stand" (KIRKEN or KIRKEN DEN ER ET GAMMELT HUS, B235; "Built on a rock, the Church shall stand," L365)

67. "Christ is the world's true light" (DARMSTADT, B274; SURETTE, M408)

68. "Come, you faithful, raise the strain" (GAUDEAMUS PARITER, L132; ST. KEVIN, M446)

69. "Crown him with many crowns" (DIADEMATA, B52, L170, M455)

*70. "For all the saints" (SINE NOMINE, B144, L174, M536)

71. "God is my strong salvation" (WEDLOCK, B343, M211)

72. "God of grace and God of glory" (CWM RHONDDA, B265, L415, M470; MANNHEIM, E116)

73. "Great is thy faithfulness" (FAITHFULNESS, B216)

74. "Guide me, O thou great Jehovah" (CWM RHONDDA, B202, M271; "Guide me ever, great Redeemer," L343)

*75. "Hope of the world" (O PERFECT LOVE, B364; DONNE SECOURS, L493; VICAR, M161)

76. "I know not why God's wondrous grace" (EL NATHAN, B344)

*77. "If you will only let God guide you" (NEUMARK or WER NUR DEN LIEBEN GOTT, B203; "If you but trust in God to guide you," L453; "If thou but suffer God to guide thee," M210)

*78. "Immortal, invisible, God only wise" (ST. DENIO, B32, L526, M27)

79. "In heavenly love abiding" (NYLAND, B204, M230)

80. "Jesus, thou joy of loving hearts" (QUEBEC, B72; ROCKINGHAM (MASON), M329; WALTON, "O Jesus, joy of loving hearts," L356)
81. "Jesus, thy boundless love to me" (ST. CATHERINE, B326, M259; RYBURN, L336)
82. "Jesus, we want to meet" (NIGERIA, E65, M487)
83. "Lead on, O King Eternal" (LANCASHIRE, B420, L495, M478)
*84. "Lo, how a rose is growing" (ES IST EIN ROS, L58)
85. "Lord, as we rise to leave this shell of worship" (WANSBECK, E87)
*86. "Love divine, all loves excelling" (BEECHER, B58, M283; HYFRYDOL, L315)
87. "My hope is built on nothing less" (SOLID ROCK, B337, L293, M222)
88. "My song is love unknown" (ROBERTSON, B486; RHOSYMEDRE, L94)
89. "O for a thousand tongues to sing" (AZMON, B69, L559, M1)
*90. "O God, our help in ages past" (ST. ANNE, B223, L320, M28)
91. "O Master, let me walk with thee" (MARYTON, B369, M170; "O Master, let me walk with you," L492)
92. "O worship the King" (LYONS, B30, M473; HANOVER, L548)
93. "O sacred Head, now wounded" (PASSION CHORALE or HERZLICH TUT MICH VERLANGEN, B105, L116, 117, M418)
*94. "Of the Father's love begotten" (DIVINUM MYSTERIUM, B62, L42, M357)
*95. "Once to every man and nation" (EBENEZER, B385, M242)
96. "The bread of life for all men broken" (SHENG EN, B250, M317)
*97. "The King of love my Shepherd is" (DOMINUS REGIT ME, B215, M67; ST. COLUMBA, L456)
98. "What wondrous love is this" (WONDROUS LOVE, B106, E46, L385, M432)
*99. "Were you there when they crucified my Lord" (WERE YOU THERE, B108, L92, M436)
100. "When in our music God is glorified"[10] (FREDERICKTOWN, L555)

Teaching Unfamiliar Hymns

The Starting Point

Teaching hymns to a congregation involves first of all a certain knowledge of their hymn-singing repertory: which hymns they know and sing well. A list of the hymns the congregation knows may be made in several ways: (1) utilizing a hymn survey form, (2) surveying old church bulletins, or (3) interviewing persons who have been longtime members of the church. The use of this list of the congregation's hymns should serve as a starting point for

[10]Fred Pratt Green's original first line is "When in man's music God is glorified."

planning hymns to be used in worship and for introducing unfamiliar hymns.

How a Hymn Is Learned

The trained musician who takes music reading for granted may tend to forget that most of the persons in a typical church cannot read music. Most worshipers learn hymns by rote: by hearing their melodies over and over again. Giving the congregation ample opportunities to hear a new hymn sung or played is important in helping create a readiness to learn it. Most persons are not automatically ready to learn new hymns. In fact, most people in our churches probably prefer to sing the hymns they already know and are comfortable with.

Arousing Interest

Through church bulletins, newsletters, and posters, as well as the spoken word, the music leader or pastor can help create a readiness to learn new hymns. Arousing interest in learning a hymn may be accomplished in several ways:

1. Relating a new hymn to a particular theme of worship. For example, a service of worship emphasizing the Bible would be an ideal occasion to introduce hymns on the Scriptures, such as "O Word of God, incarnate" (B140, L231, M372).

2. Emphasizing the central message of the hymn text and how it relates to the beliefs and aspirations of the congregation. For example, the central message of Georgia Harkness's "Hope of the world" (B364, L493, M161) is that Christians have found their hope in Christ, who is the hope of all humanity.

3. Stressing the scriptural integrity of the hymn. Some hymnals have an index of scriptural bases of hymns.[11] Other hymnals list related Scriptures above each hymn.[12] A helpful resource is Donald A. Spencer's *Hymn and Scripture Selection Guide* (Valley Forge, PA: Judson Press, 1977). When a congregation is aware, for example, that the servant poem of Philippians 2 is the basis of F. Bland Tucker's "All praise to thee" (B43, M74), they will probably have more interest in learning this hymn.[13]

4. Recalling an interesting fact concerning the hymn's origin. The story of John Wesley's contacts with German-speaking Moravians on his transatlantic voyage to Georgia will help to arouse interest in his hymn translation from the

[11]See *Baptist Hymnal* (1975), p. 544; *The Methodist Hymnal*, 847.
[12]See *Hymns for the Living Church*, ed. Donald P. Hustad (Carol Stream, IL: Hope Publishing Co., 1974).
[13]See numerous other relationships between hymns and Scripture in chap. 3, The Hymn and Scripture.

German of Paul Gerhardt, "Jesus, thy boundless love to me" (B326, L336, M259).

A Positive Experience

Learning a new hymn should be a positive experience, an experience so pleasant that the congregation will want to repeat it. Careful preparation is important for a good hymn-learning experience. The instrumentalists and choirs should be thoroughly familiarized with the hymn to be introduced. The sureness of the choir in singing the hymn helps to erase the uncertainties felt by the congregation and bolsters their confidence in setting out into new territory.

The suggestions for introducing new hymns above can be adapted to formal or informal gatherings. Learning new hymns can be an integral part of the major weekly worship service when the largest number of persons are present if handled with care and dignity.

The Value of Repetition

Since most people learn hymns by rote, they must have opportunity to hear a melody before they can be expected to sing it with a reasonable degree of confidence. The instrumental introduction to a new hymn should include the entire hymn tune and should be played in such a way as to emphasize the melody. Beyond this, another opportunity to hear the tune can be provided by having the choir sing the first stanza in unison after which the congregation can join the choir on the remaining stanzas. The new hymn can also be presented instrumentally and chorally. The organist, pianist, and other instrumentalists may perform a piece based on the hymn tune as a prelude, offertory, or postlude. The choir can sing an anthem, a call to worship, or an introit based on the hymn tune while it is being taught to the congregation.

Once a new hymn has been introduced and sung by the congregation it needs to be repeated before it is forgotten. It is unrealistic to expect worshipers to sing a new hymn once and then to sing it again with ease six months or a year later. Keeping records[14] is invaluable in determining when a particular hymn has been sung and in planning for its repetition. Through repeated use a hymn once unknown and unsung can become a vital vehicle for worship.

Hymn Rehearsals and Sings

The learning of new hymns for most congregations takes place during regularly scheduled services of worship. Because of the limited time available and the desire not to use service time for hymn learning, some leaders prefer to schedule rehearsal time immediately before the beginning of worship or at a

---

[14]"Hymnal Plan Work Sheets" for recording hymns used from *Baptist Hymnal* (1975) are included in the annual publication, *Music Program Plan Book* (Nashville: Convention Press).

separate gathering, such as on a Sunday evening or at a midweek service.

Many of the same methods used in teaching music in choir rehearsals can be used effectively for teaching new hymns to a congregation. Although shorter hymns may be taught by playing and singing them over once, many longer hymn tunes need a line-by-line method. In teaching a hymn like "At the name of Jesus" (KING'S WESTON, B363, L179, M76) one can first call attention to the scriptural basis found in the servant poem of Philippians 2:5-11. Then the entire hymn melody could be played, perhaps without the harmony. Although all four lines of Vaughan Williams's tune are different, it might be helpful to point out that the rhythms of the first three scores are practically identical and that their three melodic phrases begin low and rise. After singing these phrases for the people, one could demonstrate the contrast of the final phrase in which the rhythm is different and the melody begins high and falls. Because each phrase of KING'S WESTON is different (including different initial pitches) it is important to learn each one separately. When the individual phrases are learned, the entire hymn can be sung, the accompanist playing only the melody in unison or octaves. Then the remaining stanzas can be sung, reinforcing the learning of the melody through repetition.[15]

While a hymn rehearsal may be devoted entirely to learning one or more unfamiliar hymns, a hymn sing provides an opportunity to introduce some new hymns sandwiched between old favorites. One church music leader used a quarterly (fifth Sunday) hymn sing to teach new hymns by devoting each sing to a particular topic, such as "Consecration and Dedication Hymns," "Hymns of the Great Revivals," and "A Survey of Hymns in their Historical Progression."[16] In a hymn sing on "The Christian Hope," for example, the relatively new hymn "Hope of the world" (B364, L493, M161) can be sandwiched between two more familiar hymns and related to Scripture as follows:

"Let thy steadfast love, O Lord, be upon us, even as we hope in thee" (Ps. 33:22, RSV).

"O God, our help in ages past," ST. ANNE

"God so loved the world that he gave his only Son, that whoever believes in him should not perish but have eternal life" (John 3:16, RSV).

"Hope of the world," VICAR, O PERFECT LOVE, DONNE SECOURS

"For they drank from the supernatural Rock which followed them, and the Rock was Christ" (1 Cor. 10:4, RSV).

"My hope is built on nothing less," SOLID ROCK, MELITA

---

[15]See James R. Sydnor, *The Hymn and Congregational Singing* (Richmond: John Knox Press, 1960), pp. 159-60, for a teaching plan of which this is an adaptation.

[16]See Paul M. Hall, "Hymn Rehearsals and Public Worship," *The Church Musician* 16,6 (June 1965), 13. See also chap. 11, The Hymn and Worship.

W. B. Bradbury

Hymn of the Month Plan

The most widely used scheme for learning new hymns is the Hymn of the Month Plan. Under this plan a congregation is exposed to a particular hymn through varied means several times during a month. For example, a hymn could be presented in four successive Sundays, first as an organ prelude[17] then as a choral selection, thirdly as a congregational hymn with the choir singing the first stanza, and finally it could be sung entirely in normal fashion by the congregation. In addition to its use in formal worship, the hymn of the month can be used in the graded choir program and in the Sunday School. Background and interpretive information[18] on the hymn of the month can be included in the church newsletter or as an insert in the church bulletin.

For some denominations (Lutherans for example), the hymn of the month can be selected from the *Hymns of the Week*,[19] a list suggesting a chief hymn for each day of worship based on the Scripture readings of a three-year cycle of lessons. In the *Lutheran Book of Worship* a list of "Hymns for the Church Year" (pp. 929-31) also relates to the three-year lectionary.

Hymn Study Classes

One of the most effective ways of teaching unfamiliar hymns is through a special class in hymnology. During the several hours of time normally available in such a class one is able to give more detailed attention to individual hymns and perhaps to study enough hymns to illustrate the entire history of hymnody from the early church to the present century.

A hymn study class also offers time to engage in a careful study of the hymnal, including its organization and various indexes. A class meeting in the weeks before Christmas could concentrate on hymns for Advent and Christmas. Class sessions might be devoted to hymns related to a church's own denominational heritage. Some denominations provide textbooks and other materials suitable for hymn study classes.

---

[17]Chorale preludes on hymns for the month for Lutherans are listed in the *Journal of Church Music* and also in *A Guide to Music for the Church Year*. 4th ed. (Minneapolis: Augsburg Publishing House, 1974). For Episcopalians, there is an index listing "Organ Works Based on Tunes in the *Hymnal 1940*" in *The Hymnal 1940 Companion*, 3rd rev. ed. (New York: Church Pension Fund, 1951), pp. 609-689. A reference work listing preludes by composer and by hymn tune name is Jean Slater Edson, *Organ Preludes*. 2 vols. Metuchen, N.J.: Scarecrow Press, 1970. Supplement, 1974.

[18]This information for the Southern Baptist Hymn of the Month is published in *The Church Musician*, monthly of the Church Music Department, Baptist Sunday School Board, Nashville.

[19]See the pamphlet *Hymns of the Week*, Series A of the Three Year Cycle of Lessons, prepared by Frederick H. Telschow (Valparaiso, IN: The Lutheran Society for Worship, Music and the Arts, Valparaiso University, 1974).

Hymns in the Home

In the days of Luther and Calvin the hymnal figured prominently in the homes and daily lives of Christian families. Although this is still the case with some Evangelicals of Latin America and in some other areas, the hymnal unfortunately for most American churchgoers is only a part of the church furniture to be used when at church. Consequently "As regards hymnody the congregation is very much where it would be in knowledge of scripture if there were no Bibles except those in the pulpit or the lectern."[20]

How can the families of the church be encouraged to sing hymns in their homes? First of all, each family member old enough to read could have his own hymnal. The hymns learned in church could also be a part of family worship. Devotional materials for family worship could suggest appropriate hymns for singing at home. Although some families will be fortunate enough to have a member who can accompany them on the piano, organ, guitar, or autoharp, good hymn singing can be done without accompaniment. Excellent recordings are available to assist families in singing hymns.

Several suggestions for encouraging family hymn singing have been made by James R. Sydnor:[21]

1. The church office can keep a supply of hymnals to be sold to members.

2. A list of suggested uses of hymns in the home can be published in the church bulletin.

3. Children can be provided music appreciation and training (e.g., recordings, private music study, and membership in a children's choir) which will result in improved hymn singing.

4. Parents may request piano teachers to include hymn playing in the private music studies of their children.

5. A hymn stanza frequently can be used as a table grace (e.g., the Doxology, "For the beauty of the earth," "Now thank we all our God").

6. Parents can use an evening hymn as they tuck their children into bed.

7. Families can enjoy informal hymn singing, either by themselves or with invited friends.

The congregation whose families sing hymns at home will realize a greater vitality of singing in Sunday worship. Furthermore, family hymn singing will be a unifying force in helping build a stronger family life.

Questions for Thought and Discussion, Projects for Action

1. Why do people retain more theology from the hymns they sing than through the sermons they hear?

---

[20]Louis F. Benson, *The Hymnody of the Christian Church*. Reprint of the original 1927 edition (Richmond: John Knox Press, 1956), p. 275.

[21]*The Hymn and Congregational Singing*, p. 139. This helpful book is unfortunately out of print.

2. Name some specific ways in which hymns provide instruction in Christian living and cite specific hymns which do this.

3. What aspects of the church's heritage can be learned through the teaching of hymns and their backgrounds?

4. Which organizations in your church make use of hymns? In what ways can the use of hymns in these organizations be made more effective? Are there additional church organizations which could be making more effective use of hymns? Formulate a plan for an effective use of hymn singing in one of your church's organizations.

5. At what ages should children learn hymns and hymn tunes? Develop a hymn curriculum for children of one age grouping in your congregation.

6. What resources are available for teaching hymns and hymn tunes to children? Cite some appropriate hymns for (1) younger elementary grade children, (2) older elementary grade children, and (3) youth.

7. How do most people learn hymns? What does this imply for teaching new hymns?

8. What are some ways of arousing interest in learning new hymns?

9. Can hymns be effectively taught without distracting from the dignity of a formal worship service? Why or why not?

10. Why is it important to keep a record of hymns sung?

11. What methods could one use to teach the following hymns:

"Of the Father's love begotten" (Divinum mysterium, B62, L42, M357), "What wondrous love is this, O my soul, O my soul" (Wondrous Love, B106, L385, M432), and "He who would valiant be" (St. Dunstan's, B384, M155; "All who would valiant be," L498)?

12. Is the Hymn of the Month or some other plan being used to teach new hymns systematically to your congregation? Evaluate the effectiveness of hymn learning in your church.

13. In what ways can one encourage hymn singing within the families of the church? Formulate a plan for encouraging hymn singing within the families of your congregation during Advent, Lent, or another season observed as a time of spiritual emphasis by your congregation.

13
The Hymn in Ministry

Ministry, however defined, carries the basic meaning of service. The Christian enters into a distinctive ministry, the ministry of Jesus Christ. The nature of Christian ministry has been determined by Christ's "life, death, and resurrection and by the work of his Spirit in the shaping of the apostolic ministry."[1] There is thus a biblical basis for ministry that is applicable to every Christian and is not restricted to the vocational ministry. Christian ministry, in this sense, may be interpreted as an active, positive response to the gospel of Jesus Christ by serving human needs: food for the hungry, companionship for the lonely, hope for the depressed, and assurance for the anxious given in the name of Christ. Ministry, by nature including a "minister" and the one "ministered to," involves responsive concern for the individual in all domains of life.

In one sense, the hymn functions in ministry whenever it is used. Thus the last three chapters dealing with the hymn in proclamation, worship, and education are dealing with forms of ministry. In this chapter, however, the focus will be on the hymn as it relates to Christian social service.

Hymns Encourage Ministry

Hymns serve as a stimulus to ministry, exhorting us to minister and urging us beyond ourselves. Whittier simply and eloquently describes the interaction necessary for ministry: "O brother man, fold to thy heart thy brother" (WELWYN, M199). Love of God and serving Christ through serving others are inextricably tied together in Jesus' teachings: "Whenever you did this for one of the least important of these brothers of mine, you did it for me!" (Matt. 25:40, TEV).

Godfrey Thring's prayer for caring concern toward all persons in "O God of mercy, God of light" (JUST AS I AM, L425) is based on the tenet that love of God finds expression in one's relationship to other persons:

Teach us the lesson Jesus taught
To feel for those his blood has bought
That ev'ry deed and word and thought
    May work a work for you.

For all are kindred, far and wide,
Since Jesus Christ for all has died;

[1] James D. Smart, *The Rebirth of Ministry* (Philadelphia: The Westminster Press, 1960), p. 20.

259

Grant us the will, and grace provide
To love them all in you.

In sickness, sorrow, want, or care,
Each other's burdens help us share;
May we, where help is needed, there
Give help as though to you.

Milburn Price in "O Lord, who came to earth to show" (FOREST GREEN,
B309) stresses the biblical injunction to minister, citing the example provided
by Jesus:

O Lord, who came to earth to show
Thy way of truth and love,
Who ministered to varied needs
With grace sent from above,
Equip us now to likewise go,
And thus fulfill thy word
Compelling us to minister:
Give us thy love, O Lord.[2]

Fred Pratt Green's "When the church of Jesus" (KING'S WESTON, B319)
acknowledges the tendency to allow the loftiness of worship to prevent the
church from seeing the need for ministry to others:

When the church of Jesus
Shuts its outer door,
Lest the roar of traffic
Drown the voice of prayer:
May our prayers, Lord, make us
Ten times more aware
That the world we banish
Is our Christian care.

If our hearts are lifted
Where devotion soars
High above this hungry
Suff'ring world of ours:
Lest our hymns should drug us
To forget its needs,
Forge our Christian worship
Into Christian deeds.

[2]© 1969 The Hymn Society of America. Used by permission.

Lest the gifts we offer,
  Money, talents, time,
Serve to salve our conscience
  To our secret shame:
Lord, reprove, inspire us
  By the way you give;
Teach us, dying Savior,
  How true Christians live.[3]

Hymns Express Specific Ministry

Hymns explore and define areas of ministry. They plant seeds that may germinate in active ministry. Hymns sometimes spring from the writer's response to a need and the ensuing recognition that the task requires more than one person's labors.

"Rescue the perishing" (RESCUE, B283, M175) grew out of Fanny Crosby's involvement with the homeless in New York City. The immediacy of their needs is communicated by ungarnished imperatives: "Rescue the perishing," "Care for the dying," and "Lift up the fallen." The urgency of human need requires ministry that is compassionate and timely.

Specific needs pointed out in hymns are needs of the sick, the handicapped (blind, deaf, and lame), the homeless, the lonely, the adolescent, and the aged. Frequently a number of these human conditions are grouped together. Albert Bayly in his "Lord, whose love through humble service" (BEACH SPRING, L423; BEECHER, M479) holds up Christ's example of ministry and enumerates the opportunities for active response—response that is an outgrowth of worship:

Lord, whose love in humble service
  Bore the weight of human need,
Who upon the cross, forsaken,
  Worked your mercy's perfect deed:
We, your servants, bring the worship
  Not of voice alone, but heart;
Consecrating to your purpose
  Ev'ry gift which you impart.

Still your children wander homeless;
  Still the hungry cry for bread;
Still the captives long for freedom;
  Still in grief we mourn our dead.
As you, Lord, in deep compassion

---

[3] ©Oxford University Press. Used by Permission.

Healed the sick and freed the soul,
By your Spirit send your power
    To our world to make it whole.

As we worship, grant us vision,
    Till your love's revealing light
In its height and depth and greatness
    Dawns upon our quickened sight,
Making known the needs and burdens
    Your compassion bids us bear,
Stirring us to ardent service,
    Your abundant life to share.[4]

Fred Pratt Green focuses on the poor in the second stanza of "The Church of Christ in every age" (WAREHAM, L433):

Across the world, across the street,
    The victims of injustice cry
For shelter and for bread to eat,
    And never live before they die.[5]

Hymns sometimes get very specific in enumerating the ills of mankind. Edward H. Plumtre's "Your hand, O Lord, in days of old" (OLD 107TH, L431) cites some of the conditions to which Jesus ministered and prays for those presently in need of healing and for those engaged in the ministry of healing:

Your hand, O Lord, in days of old
    Was strong to heal and save;
It triumphed o'er disease and death,
    O'er darkness and the grave.
To you they came, the blind, the dumb,
    The palsied and the lame,
The lepers in their misery,
    The sick with fevered frame.

And lo, your touch brought life and health,
    Gave speech and strength and sight;
And youth renewed and frenzy calmed
    Revealed you, Lord of light.
And now, O Lord, be near to bless,
    Almighty as before,

[4]© 1961 Albert F. Bayly. Used by permission.*
[5]© Oxford University Press. Used by permission.*

In crowded street, by beds of pain,
    As by Gennes'ret's shore.

Oh, be our great deliv'rer still,
    The Lord of life and death;
Restore and quicken, soothe and bless,
    With your life-giving breath.
To hands that work and eyes that see
    Give wisdom's healing pow'r,
That whole and sick and weak and strong
    May praise you evermore.

Fred Kaan looks beyond the plight of the hungry to unharvested fields and produce withheld from markets, and reminds us once again that our duty is to those in need beyond the bounds of nationality. The scope of ministry includes the world in his "Now join we to praise the Creator" (SHARING, E92):

Now join we to praise the Creator,
    Our voices in worship and song;
We stand to recall with thanksgiving
    That to Him all seasons belong.
We thank you, O God, for your goodness,
    For the joy and abundance of crops,
For food that is stored in the cupboards,
    For all we can buy in the shops.

But also of need and starvation
    We sing with concern and despair,
Of skills that are used for destruction,
    Of land that is burnt and laid bare.
We cry for the plight of the hungry
    While harvests are left in the field,
For orchards neglected and wasting,
    For produce from markets withheld.

The song grows in depth and in wideness;
    The earth and the people are one.
There can be no thanks without giving,
    No words without deeds that are done.
Then teach us, O Lord of the harvest,
    To be humble in all that we claim,
To share what we have with the nations,
    To care for the world in your name.[6]

[6] © 1968 Galliard Ld. Used by permission of Galaxy Music Corporation.

Among the hymns that encourage ministry are those that point out places of ministry. The compassion of the Christ who wept over the city of Jerusalem is the basis for the prayer Frank Mason North voices in "Where cross the crowded ways of life" (GERMANY or WALTON, B311, L429, M204). The second stanza describes the plight of a city in need of ministry:

> In haunts of wretchedness and need,
> On shadow'd thresholds dark with fears,
> From paths where hide the lures of greed,
> We catch the vision of thy tears.

Thomas C. Clark in his "Where restless crowds are thronging" (LLANGLOFFAN, L430) lists a number of places that opportunities to minister may be found: "along the city ways," "homes where kindness falters," "in busy streets of barter," and "in lonely thoroughfare." In addition to the city, Edward M. Blumenfeld in his "The Son of God, our Christ" (SURSUM CORDA, L434) mentions "in town" and "on the soil." Other hymns of recent decades mention the inner city, the suburbs, the ghetto, the prison, the slum, the mine, the field, and the marketplace.

Hymns Speak to Persons in Need

Hymns not only proclaim the necessity of ministry in the lives of Christians and illustrate specific needs in specific places, but hymns themselves may minister by speaking to people in need. Just as verses of Scripture speak to particular human circumstances, hymns can be applied to specific life situations. This is reflected in some of the categories used in topical indexes of hymnals: Assurance, Calmness, Consolation, Courage, Faith, Hope, Humility, Joy, etc. Stories abound in which hymns have played significant roles in the lives of people, and in times of need have been a source of strength.

President Woodrow Wilson, during the dark days after America entered World War I, found strength in the singing of a hymn. His biographer has described how Wilson, while cruising on the Potomac on a Sunday afternoon in June of 1917 with a Princeton classmate, suggested that they sing a favorite hymn of their undergraduate days:

> When peace, like a river, attendeth my way,
> When sorrows like sea billows roll;
> Whatever my lot, thou hast taught me to say,
> It is well, it is well with my soul. (B339, L346)[7]

Not only in time of war but also in the facing of death, hymns have provided

[7]Arthur Walworth, *Woodrow Wilson* 2nd ed. rev. vol. 2 (Boston: Houghton Mifflin Co., 1965), p. 123.

a note of joy and victory in anticipation of eternal life. The founder of Methodism, John Wesley, at the age of eighty-eight and near death, sang to those in his sickroom Watts's "I'll praise my Maker while 'I've breath" (OLD 113TH, M9). In the fourth stanza of "What wondrous love is this" (WONDROUS LOVE, B106, L385, M432—this stanza not included) the anonymous hymn writer vows to sing on, even after death: "and when from death I'm free, I'll sing and joyful be, And thro' eternity I'll sing on, I'll sing on" (lines 3-4). The positive declarations found in the fourth stanza of Lyte's "Abide with me" (EVENTIDE, B217—this stanza omitted, L272, M289) contribute to the frequent use of this hymn in times of death:

> I fear no foe, with thee at hand to bless;
> Ills have no weight, and tears no bitterness.
> Where is death's sting? Where, grave, thy victory?
> I triumph still, if thou abide with me.

Hymns can provide messages of comfort to the bereaved. Note the words addressed to the grieving in the third stanza of Johann J. Schütz's "Sing praise to God who reigns above" (MIT FREUDEN ZART, B22, M4; LOBT GOTT DEN HERREN, IHR, L542—a different translation):

> The Lord is never far away
>   But, thro' all grief distressing,
> An ever present help and stay,
>   Our peace and joy and blessing,
> As with a mother's tender hand
> He leads his own, his chosen band:
>   To God all praise and glory!

A hymn that offers consolation in all four of its stanzas is Charles Wesley's "Thou hidden source of calm repose" (ST. PETERSBURG, M89). The emphasis in its first stanza is on the all-sufficiency of God:

> Thou hidden source of calm repose,
>   Thou all-sufficient love divine,
> My help and refuge from my foes,
>   Secure I am if thou art mine;
> And lo! from sin and grief and shame,
> I hide me, Jesus, in thy name.

Jesus was poor in terms of material possessions and spent his ministry largely among the poor—the supreme example that worth is not to be measured in terms of wealth. It is no surprise, then, that Christian hymns would contain messages of encouragement and hope to those who live in poverty. God's providence is underscored in the gospel hymn "God will take care of you" (GOD CARES, B219, M207) by Civilla D. Martin:

> Be not dismay'd whate'er betide,
>   God will take care of you;
> Beneath his wings of love abide,
>   God will take care of you.

Refrain:
>   God will take care of you,
>   Through ev'ry day,
>   o'er all the way;
>   He will take care of you,
>   God will take care of you.

"Amazing grace" (AMAZING GRACE or NEW BRITAIN, B165, M92, L448; stanzas 1, 3, 4) has stepped outside the limits of the church service to minister to people of many stations, ages, races, and lands. It offers hope and security.

> Amazing grace! how sweet the sound,
>   That saved a wretch like me!
> I once was lost, but now am found,
>   Was blind, but now I see.

> Through many dangers, toils, and snares,
>   I have already come;
> 'Tis grace hath brought me safe thus far,
>   And grace will lead me home.

> The Lord has promised good to me,
>   His word my hope secures;
> He will my shield and portion be
>   As long as life endures.

Hymns can minister to children, youth, and adults. Their importance in the Christian nurture of children and youth and in family life has been emphasized in chapter 12.[8] Parents, especially during the years of rearing a family, will find encouragement in certain hymn texts. Most hymnals have a group of hymns dealing with the family as well as others that speak to parenting. One of the finest hymns on the family is F. Bland Tucker's "Our Father, by whose name" (RHOSYMEDRE, L357), a prayer to Father, Son, and Holy Spirit:

> Our Father, by whose name
>   All parenthood is known;

[8]See the list of "100 Hymns for Children and Youth," p. 248-51, and "Hymns in the Home," p. 257.

In love divine you claim
Each fam'ly as your own.
Bless mothers, fathers, guarding well,
With constant love as sentinel,
The homes in which your people dwell.

O Christ, yourself a child
Within an earthly home,
With heart still undefiled
To full adulthood come:
Our children bless in ev'ry place
That they may all behold your face
And knowing you may grow in grace.

O Holy Spirit, bind
Our hearts in unity
And teach us how to find
The love from self set free;
In all our hearts such love increase
That ev'ry home, by this release,
May be the dwelling-place of peace.[9]

The elderly make up a greater percentage of the American population than ever before. Many senior citizens face conditions previously mentioned: poverty, sickness, and loneliness; hymns related to these circumstances can provide for them a needed ministry. In 1976 a group of ten hymns celebrating the later years of life and the meaning of aging was published. It included "O Lord our God, whom all through life we praise"[10] by Frances Winters, a retired college teacher in Hattiesburg, Mississippi. In the third stanza her hymn refers to the problems of fear, doubt, bereavement, and illness commonly faced by senior adults. These problems, however, are overshadowed by praise (stanza 1), thankfulness (stanza 2), and hope (stanza 4):

O Lord our God, whom all through life we praise,
As year by year days add to numbered days,
With each we prove the wonder of Thy ways,
While still adoring, each new song we raise.

With thankful hearts Thy goodness we confess,
Our Guide and Help in gladness and distress.
For life, light, love, Thy holy name we bless;

9© 1940 The Church Pension Fund. Used by permission.
10 *10 New Hymns on Aging and the Later Years* (Springfield, Ohio: The Hymn Society of America; Washington, D.C.: National Retired Teachers Association and American Association of Retired Persons, 1976), p. 12.

Accept the gratitude our hearts express.

O God, be near in loneliness and need;
From fear and doubting may our minds be freed.
When losses come, Thy consolation speed;
For strength and healing love, O Lord, we plead.

Our hope is founded in Thy saving grace.
New hope abides to share love every place;
And hope to serve yet spurs our slowing pace,
Till, hope fulfilled, we see Thee face to face.[11]

Some Forms of Ministry Involving Hymns

In addition to regular worship services, the Sunday School, and other church programs that minister to the congregation in general, there are other forms of ministry in which hymns can be effective. The activities mentioned in this section are illustrative of the numerous types of ministry[12] in which a creative leader can find fruitful ways to utilize hymns.

In special worship services. In addition to usual worship services, many churches conduct worship in hospitals, nursing homes, prisons, and in missions for the homeless. In some instances worship in these places is conducted by a chaplain. The collection *Hymns of Hope and Healing (A Chapel Hymnal)*, compiled and edited by Barbara E. Goward, R.M.T., is an interdenominational Protestant hymnal for use in hospitals. Because of its unusual ministry, this hymnal has an introductory word that explains why certain hymns were omitted:

"Today, religious thinkers realize that the old threatening aspects of religion can often be destructive to the spirit. We have omitted the emphasis on man's unworthiness, God's fearful vengeance, and happiness to be found only in heaven. There is, however, allowance for the confession of error, necessarily followed by the assurance of Divine forgiveness and understanding.

"Generally speaking, we here offer a service hymnal in which every selection will be in accord with the efforts of the minister and the hospital staff toward constructive support of the spirit and a positive approach to rehabilitation."[13]

Joe Pinson, a music therapist in Texas, has written hymns specifically to fit a particular group of persons. He has written hymns for a choir of mentally retarded persons in a language and musical style suited to their capabilities. These hymns are used in this school's chapel services. He also edits *New Songs*

---

[11] © 1976 The Hymn Society of America. Used by permission.*
[12] Many forms of recent Christian ministry are discussed in William M. Pinson, Jr., *The Local Church in Ministry* (Nashville: Broadman Press, 1973).
[13] Cincinnati: The Willis Music Company, 1960 (p. iv).

Ira D. Sankey

for God's People, a periodical offering new music for institutional use.[14] The following is the first stanza of "King of Kings,"[15] one of the hymns Pinson has written to be sung by retarded persons:

When Christ was born so long ago;
His holy name he did not know.
But God the Father helped him grow
    To be the King of Kings.

Refrain:

King of Kings; Lord of Lords;
Born on a bed of hay.
King of Kings;
Lord of Lords;
Live in my heart today.[16]

Other settings for worship conducted away from the church for particular groups include those in resort areas, in summer camps, in retreats, and some designed for migrant workers. In certain areas churches sponsor worship and Sunday School for nonnative English-speakers in their native language. In each case, hymns appropriate to the group can provide a significant ministry.

In forms for the deaf and blind. Those who are handicapped in hearing or seeing can experience hymns through special means of communication. The deaf can visually hear the texts of hymns throught sign language rendered simultaneously during congregational singing. Two hymnals with adaptation in language for signing are *Sing Praises,*[17] and *Sing unto the Lord—A Hymnal for the Deaf.*[18]

For those who are visually handicapped but who can read large print, large print editions of some hymnals are available, such as *Baptist Hymnal* 1975. For the blind many hymnals have been published in Braille,[19] including the *Presbyterian Hymnbook,* the *Service Book and Hymnal* and *Lutheran Book of Worship, The Book of Hymns* (United Methodist, later title for *The Methodist Hymnal* 1964), and *Baptist Hymnal* 1975.[20] Hymns are also widely

---

[14]Joe Pinson, "Writing Hymns for Mentally Retarded Persons," *The Hymn* 30, 1 (January 1979), 21-25.
[15]*New Songs for God's People* 3 (September 1978), 19. Information on this periodical can be secured from *New Songs for God's People,* P.O. Box 491, Denton, TX 76201.
[16]© 1978 by Joe Pinson. Used by permission.*
[17]Nashville: Broadman Press, 1976.
[18]By E. Theo Delaney and Clark Bailey. St. Louis: Commission on Worship and Board for Missions, The Lutheran Church, Missouri Synod, 1969.
[19]J. Vincent Higginson, "Hymns for the Blind," *The Hymn* 3, 4 (October 1952), 116-18.
[20]These are among the hymnals in Braille or large print available on two-month loan from the Music Section, National Library Service for the Blind and Physically Handicapped, The Library of Congress, Washington, DC 20542. (A list of hymnals available for loan may be requested from this address.)

available on recordings which can be used by the blind, including both long-playing phonodiscs and cassette tapes. The convenience of cassette tapes has opened up other possibilities for ministry involving the use of hymns.

On cassette tape. For members of a congregation who are homebound, church services, including hymns, can be provided on cassette tapes. This same ministry can be provided for a congregation's military personnel and college students away from home. Cassette tapes of hymns can also be useful for ministry to a nursing home or prison when an accompanist and/or musical instrument is unavailable. Sometimes a group of hymns on cassette tape can be "tailor-made" to fit a particular person or set of circumstances.

Homebound individuals, for example, can be provided a cassette tape of some of their favorite hymns. A bereaved person can find help in a group of hymns of faith, hope, and consolation. Cassette tapes of hymns and other worship materials can be used to assist families in worship in the home.

Hymn singing events. In addition to the congregational hymn sing[21] and the third type of hymn service,[22] hymns can function in informal ways in other contexts. One event which can involve music and hymn singing is an art festival, an event in which artists from within and without a church are invited to show their work. Such a festival may include paintings, sculpture, crafts, drama, and other creative arts. Hymns written by members of the church or community can be sung.

Many churches now have clubs for senior adults which sponsor various activities involving fellowship, service, and recreation. Hymn singing, especially of selections that are well known, can be meaningful to senior citizens organizations.

Christmas carol sings. In the weeks before Christmas, hymns on the birth of Christ are heard on radio, television, and in shopping centers. Although the public may be saturated with Christmas music through the media, churches have an opportunity to provide a ministry by means of live music at this season. In New Orleans in the mid-1970's, for example, the local federation of churches established a ministry in which numerous church and school choirs and instrumentalists sang carols during the noon hour in lobbies of downtown office buildings for several days during the week before Christmas. In many suburban shopping malls live Christmas music is welcomed. Even though the motivation of the management may be primarily commercial, the opportunity to minister through songs of the season is nonetheless available. The custom of informal caroling by church groups, especially of children and youth, is widespread. Caroling often provides a ministry to the homebound. It can be done informally by neighbors who attend different churches and provides a bond of fellowship in sharing the good news of Christmas.

[21]See chap. 12, The Hymn in Education.
[22]See chap. 11, The Hymn in Worship.

In this chapter and in the three preceding ones the hymn has been treated in relation to the church's ministry in terms of social service and in the related tasks of proclamation, worship, and education. The potential of hymnody in the mission of the church needs to be more widely recognized. Intelligence, imagination, sensitivity, and skill in the use of hymns in the church contribute to the fulfillment of its mission. The resolve of the apostle Paul remains an appropriate resolution for today's hymn singers: "I will sing with the spirit, and I will sing with the understanding also" (1 Cor. 14:15).

Questions for Thought and Discussion, Projects for Action

1. List some hymns that encourage ministry in general. How well are these hymns known to your congregation?

2. Cite hymns that encourage Christians to minister to the following categories of persons in need: the poor, the sick and handicapped, the lonely, the sorrowful.

3. In what ways are hymns made available to the handicapped of sight and hearing?

4. List hymns which might speak to you in times of depression. What difficulties would a therapist encounter in selecting hymns for healing?

5. As a class project, list all the hymns pertaining to ministry within your denominational hymnal. Are there any generalizations that can be drawn concerning their origins? How adequate is this hymnal in terms of hymns on the subject of Christian ministry? What hymns pertaining to ministry would you like to see added?

6. Plan a worship service using hymns based on ministry.

7. Prepare a two-minute informal talk on hymns that have ministered to you or to someone you know.

8. Make a cassette or tape of hymns for a person experiencing grief in the death of a family member.

9. Plan a Thanksgiving hymn celebration for use in a shopping mall.

Appendix 1

A SERVICE OF WORSHIP IN SONG
(Featuring the Hymns of Isaac Watts)

IN COMMEMORATION OF
THE THREE HUNDREDTH ANNIVERSARY OF THE BIRTH OF

ISAAC WATTS (1674-1748)

Planned for congregation, organ, and male choir (chorale)

THE ORDER OF SERVICE
Organ Voluntary: Prelude on HAMBURG   PAUL BUNJES
Congregational Rehearsal
Prelude to Worship: "An Appreciation of Isaac Watts, Hymn Writer"

THE SERVICE OF WORSHIP
Contemplating God and His Mighty Works
Call to Worship:
Spoken: "Let all our powers be joined
           His glorious name to raise;
           Pleasure and love fill every mind
           And every voice be praise."

Sung: "Lord of the worlds above,   DARWELL
           How pleasant and how fair
           The dwellings of Thy love,
           Thine earthly temples are!
           To Thine abode my heart aspires
           With warm desires to see my God."

Scriptural Modulation: Psalm 90:1-2 (TEV)
Hymn: "O God, Our Help in Ages Past"   ST. ANNE
              (Congregation will rise with chorale to sing.)

Stanza 1:   Sung by congregation and chorale
Stanza 2:   *Spoken by congregation alone*
Stanza 3:   Sung by congregation and chorale
Stanza 4:   A substitute stanza sung by chorale alone:
            "Time, like an ever-rolling stream,
            Bears all her sons away;
            They fly forgotten as a dream
            Dies at the opening day."
Stanza 5:   Sung *in unison* by congregation and chorale
                              (with trumpet descant)

Sensing Our Humanity and Confessing Our Sin and Need
Spoken Modulation
Prayer Hymn: "Come, Holy Spirit, Heavenly Dove"   Balerma
                 (Congregation will remain seated.)

Stanza 1:   Sung by congregation and chorale
Stanza 2:   *Sung by chorale alone* (in minor key)
Stanza 3:   Sung by congregation and chorale (minor)
Stanza 4:   Sung by congregation and chorale (major)

Receiving Power and Comfort from God's Word
Spoken Modulation
Antiphonal Scripture Reading: "God the Ruler of the World"   Psalm 98 (TEV)
                 (Congregation will read *italicized* words.)

Sing a new song to the Lord: he has done wonderful things!
By his own power and holy strength he has won the victory.
The Lord announced his victory;
he made his saving power known to the nations.
He kept his promise to the people of Israel,
with loyalty and constant love for them.
All people everywhere have seen the victory of our God!
Sing for joy to the Lord, all the earth;
praise him with songs and shouts of joy!
Roar, sea, and all creatures in you;
sing, earth, and all who live on you!
Clap your hands, you rivers;
You hills, sing together with joy before the Lord,
because he comes to rule the earth!
He will rule all the peoples of the world with justice and fairness.
Spoken Modulation
Hymn: "Joy to the World! the Lord is Come"   Antioch
                 (Congregation will rise with chorale to sing.)
Introduction: Sung alone by the chorale
Stanza 1:   Sung by congregation and chorale
Stanza 2:   *Spoken by the chorale alone*
Stanza 3:   *Spoken by congregation* and chorale
Stanza 4:   *Sung by congregation in unison*
                 (Descant by the chorale)

Rededicating Our Lips to God's Praise: Our Lives to God's Work
Spoken Modulation
Hymn: "When I Survey the Wondrous Cross"   Hamburg
                 (Congregation will remain seated.)
Stanza 1:   Sung by congregation and chorale
Stanza 2:   Sung by congregation and chorale
Stanza 3:   *Solo* (in minor key)
Stanza 4:   Sung by congregation and chorale (major)
Spoken Modulation
Antiphonal Hymn: "From All that Dwell Below the Skies"   Lasst uns erfreuen
                 (Congregation will rise with chorale to sing *only italicized words.*)

From all that dwell below the skies
Let the Creator's praise arise:
Alleluia! *Alleluia!*
Let the Redemer's Name be sung
Through every land, in every tongue.
Alleluia! *Alleluia!*
Alleluia! *Alleluia!*
ALLELUIA!
Eternal are Thy mercies, Lord;
Eternal truth attends Thy word:
Alleluia! *Alleluia!*
Thy praise shall sound from shore to shore,
Till suns shall rise and set no more.
Alleluia! *Alleluia!*
Alleluia! *Alleluia!*
ALLELUIA! AMEN!
Bendiction and Ascription of Praise
Organ Postlude: Postlude on St. Anne   John Palmer Smith

Appendix 2

Hymn Analysis Checklist*

I. Literary Structure
   A. Meter (e.g., C.M.; 87.87.)
   B. Poetic Feet (e.g., iambic tetrameter)
   C. Rhyme Scheme (e.g., abab)
   D. Poetic Devices and Figures of Speech (See Lovelace, *The Anatomy of Hymnody* and chapter 1 above)
   E. Organization (e.g., literary patterns, e.g., itemization)
II. Thought Content
   A. Scriptural Background (If applicable, give scriptural references.)
   B. Theological Teaching (Relate specific phrases to doctrines expressed.)
   C. Direction (God-ward; in-ward; toward people)
   D. Prose Summary (In a few sentences, give a summary or prose paraphrase of the main ideas.) (See chapter 4 above)
   E. Organization (e.g., thought patterns, e.g., paradox)
III. Musical Characteristics
   A. Phrase Structure (repetitions; through-composed)
   B. Melodic Movement (step or skip; up or down; types of intervals)
   C. Harmony (basic chords; altered chords; modulations)
   D. Meter (e.g., simple; compound)
   E. Rhythm (e.g., straightforward; dotted; syncopated)
   F. Counterpoint (e.g., relation of bass line to melodic line)
   G. Form (e.g., AAB) (See chapter 2 above.)
IV. Evaluative Questions
   A. Words
      1. Are the thoughts expressed theologically sound?
      2. Does the hymn dwell on thoughts of God, or on the mood of the singer?
      3. Are the ideas expressed within the understanding of the average member of your congregation?
      4. What words, terms, names, phrases, if any, might need explanation?
      5. Does the poetry possess simplicity and beauty?
      6. Do the thoughts express spiritual reality? Would they apply to your congregation as a whole?
      7. Are the thoughts expressed relevant? Do they avoid well-worn hymnic clichés?
   B. Music
      1. Does it enhance the significance of the text?
      2. Would it be within the capability of those who must sing it? (e.g., range; tessitura; melodic leaps; rhythmic contrasts).
   C. Usage
      1. For what occasions would it be appropriate? (e.g., formal worship; church school; evangelistic service)
      2. With what age groups would it be suitable? (e.g., elementary, middle school; high school; adults)

3. If unfamiliar to your congregation, how could it be introduced? (e.g., method of presentation; connection with a particular occasion)
4. If already familiar, how could you bring fresh meaning and excitement to its use?

*For study suggestions in further depth, see Nancy White Thomas, "A Guide to Hymn Study," *The Hymn* 15 (July 1964), 69-82.

Bibliography

General Works

Benson, Louis F. *The English Hymn.* New York: George H. Doran Co., 1915; reprint ed., Richmond: John Knox Press, 1962.

_____. *The Hymnody of the Christian Church.* New York: George H. Doran Co., 1927; reprint ed., Richmond: John Knox Press, 1956.

Blume, Friedrich, ed. *Protestant Church Music: A History.* New York: W. W. Norton & Co., 1974.

Davidson, James R. *A Dictionary of Protestant Church Music.* Metuchen, N.J.: The Scarecrow Press, 1975.

Diehl, Katherine S. *Hymns and Tunes—An Index.* Metuchen, N. J.: The Scarecrow Press, 1966.

Douglas, Winfred. *Church Music in History and Practice: Studies in the Praise of God.* Revised with additional material by Leonard Ellinwood. New York: Charles Scribner's Sons, 1961.

Julian, John. *A Dictionary of Hymnology.* 2nd. ed. rev., London: John Murray, 1915; reprint in 2 vols., New York: Dover Publications, 1957.

Patrick, Millar. *The Story of the Church's Song.* Revised ed. by James R. Sydnor. Richmond: John Knox Press, 1962.

Reynolds, William J. and Price, Milburn. *A Joyful Sound.* 2nd. ed. of *A Survey of Christian Hymnody.* New York: Holt, Rinehart, and Winston, 1978.

Routley, Erik. *Hymns and Human Life.* London: John Murray, 1952.

_____. *The Music of Christian Hymnody.* London: Independent Press, 1957.

Ryden, Ernest E. *The Story of Christian Hymnody.* Rock Island, Ill.: Augustana Press, 1959.

Schalk, Carl, ed. *Key Words in Church Music.* St. Louis: Concordia Publishing House, 1978.

Stevenson, Robert. *Patterns of Protestant Church Music.* Durham, N.C.: Duke University Press, 1953.

The Hymn and Literature

Baker, Frank, ed. *Representative Verse of Charles Wesley.* Nashville: Abingdon Press, 1963.

Bayly, Albert F. "Writing Hymns for our Times," *The Hymn* 20 (January 1969), 22-27.

Benson, Louis F. "The Relation of the Hymn to Literature," Lecture III in *The Hymnody of the Christian Church* (New York: George H. Doran Co. 1927; reprint ed. Richmond, VA: John Knox Press, 1956), 99-138.

Bett, Henry. "The Methodist Hymns and English Literature," Chapter I in *The Hymns of Methodism.* 3rd edition, rev. and enlarged. (London: The Epworth Press, 1945), 9-12.

Briggs, George Wallace. "The Making of a Hymn," *The Hymn* 7 (April 1956), 53-57.

Caird, V.M. "The Hymn as a Literary Form," *Bulletin of the Hymn Society of Great Britain and Ireland* 38 (January 1974), 1-9.

Dearmer, Percy. "Introduction," *Songs of Praise Discussed* A Handbook to the Best-known Hymns and to others Recently Introduced. (London: Oxford University Press, 1952), ix-xxv.

Flew, R. Newton. *The Hymns of Charles Wesley: A Study of their Structure.* London: The Epworth Press, 1953.

Gregory, A. S. *Praises with Understanding.* London: Epworth Press, 1936; 2nd ed. rev. 1949.

Grindal, Gracia. "Language: A Lost Craft Among Hymn Writers," *The Hymn* 27 (April 1976), 43-8.

Haas, Alfred B. "American Poets as Hymn Writers," *The Hymn* 2 (January 1951), 13-18.

Hewlett, Michael. "Thoughts about words," *Bulletin of the Hymn Society of Great Britain and Ireland* 115 (Spring 1969): 11-14. Reprinted in *The Hymn* 20 (July 1969) 89-92.

Holmes, John Haynes. "What Makes a Good Hymn?" *Christian Century* 59 (June 10, 1942), 755-7.

Ingram, Tom and Newton, Douglas. *Hymns as Poetry.* London: Constable and Company, Ltd., 1956.

Lofthouse, W. F. "What makes a good hymn?" *The Congregational Quarterly* 31 (October 1953), 344-51.

Lovelace, Austin C. *The Anatomy of Hymnody.* Nashville: Abingdon Press, 1965.

Manning, Bernard. *The Hymns of Wesley and Watts.* London: Epworth Press, 1942.

Merryweather, Frank B. "Poetry and Hymns," *The Hymn* 5 (October 1954), 111-15.

Nicolson, Norman. "Bad Poetry or Good Light Verse?" *Bulletin of the Hymn Society of Great Britain and Ireland* 101 (Autumn 1964), 220-4.

Osborne, William, "Hymns for Today," *The Hymn* 20 (October 1969), 115-18,123.

Pratt Green, Fred. "Hymn Writers Today," *Bulletin of the Hymn Society of Great Britain and Ireland* 120 (January 1971), 122-24. Reprinted in *The Hymn* 22 (October 1971) 118-20.

Reeves, Jeremiah B. *The Hymn in History and Literature* or *(The Hymn as Literature).* New York: The Century Company, 1924.

Routley, Erik R. "What Remains for the Modern Hymn Writer to do?" *Bulletin of the Hymn Society of Great Britain and Ireland* 66 (January 1954), 148-53.

Sears, Donald A. "The Rise of the English Hymn," *Journal of Church Music* 13 (February 1971), 10-15.

Thomas, Nancy White. *A Guide to Hymn Study.* Springfield, Ohio: The Hymn Society of America, 1964.

Vallins, G. H. "Christian Hymns as Literature," *London Quarterly and Holborn Review* 180 (October 1955), 255-59.

Wren, Brian. " 'Genesis' of a Hymn," *Bulletin of the Hymn Society of Great Britain and Ireland* 143 (September 1978), 39-45.

_____. "Making Your Own Hymn," *Bulletin of the Hymn Society of Great Britain and Ireland* 142 (May 1978), 21-24.

Zimmermann, Heinz Werner. "Word and Tone in Modern Hymnody," *The Hymn* 24 (April 1973), 44-55.

The Hymn and Music

Best, Harold M. "Hymn Tune Writing," *The Hymn* 28 (October 1977), 183-85.

Bridges, Robert. "A Practical Discourse on Some Principles of Hymn Singing," *The Journal of Theological Studies* 1 (October 1899), 40-63.

Brown, Ray Francis. "Appraising 20th Century Hymn Tunes," *The Hymn* 3 (April 1952), 37-44, 63.

Calhoun, Philo C. "Selection of Hymn Tunes—One More Word," *The Hymn* 3 (July 1952), 79-80, 94.

Davidson, James Robert. *A Dictionary of Protestant Church Music*. See especially Anglican Chant; Carol; Chorale; Gospel Song; Hymn Tune; Plainsong; Psalmody, Metrical; Spiritual. Metuchen, New Jersey: The Scarecrow Press, 1975.

Frere, W. H. "Introduction," *Hymns Ancient and Modern* (Historical Edition). London: William Clowes and Sons, Ltd., 1909.

Frost, Maurice. *English and Scottish Psalm and Hymn-tunes*. London: S.P.C.K. 1953.

_____. *Historical Companion to Hymns Ancient and Modern*. London: William Clowes and Sons, Ltd. 1962.

George, Graham. "Hymn Tunes—The Old Vexed Question," *Journal of Church Music* 12 (October 1970), 4-7; (November 1970), 10-11.

Groom, Lester H. "Protestants and Plainsong," *Music Ministry* 1 (April 1969), 6-10.

Harvard Dictionary of Music, ed. Willi Apel, 2nd ed. rev. Cambridge, Massachusetts: Belknap Press of Harvard University Press, 1969. See especially Carol, Chorale, Melody.

Horn, Henry E: "The Hymn and Its Tunes," *O Sing unto the Lord*. (Philadelphia: The Muhlenberg, Press, 1956), 54-66.

Hutchings, Arthur J. B. "Dykes' Tunes," *The Hymn* 12 (July 1961), 69-76.

Liemohn, Edwin. *The Chorale*. Philadelphia: The Muhlenberg Press, 1953.

Lightwood, James T. *Hymn Tunes and Their Story*. London: Charles Kelly, 1906.

_____. *The Music of the Methodist Hymn Book*. London: Epworth Press, 1936. Rev. 1956.

Lovelace, Austin. "A Survey of Tunes," *Companion to the Hymnal,* a Handbook to the 1964 Methodist Hymnal, ed., Emory Stevens Bucke. (Nashville: Abingdon Press, 1970), 41-51.

McCutchan, Robert G. *Hymn Tune Names*. Nashville: Abingdon Press, 1957.

Marks, Harvey B. "The Musical Setting of Hymns," *The Rise and Growth of English Hymnody*. (New York: Fleming H. Revell Co., 1937), 250-270.

Patrick, Millar. *Four Centuries of Scottish Psalmody*. London: Oxford University Press, 1949.

_____. "Music in Hymnody," Occasional Paper No. 3 of the Hymn Society of Great Britain and Ireland. July, 1945.

Pocknee, C. E. *The French Diocesan Melodies*. London: Faith Press, 1954.

Pratt, Waldo Selden. *The Music of the French Psalter of 1562*. New York: Columbia University Press, 1939.

Riedel, Johannes. *The Lutheran Chorale—Its Basic Traditions*. Minneapolis, Augsburg Press, 1967.

Routley, Erik. Hymn Tunes: *An Historical Outline*. Study Notes, No. 5. Croydon: The Royal School of Church Music n.d.

_____. *The English Carol*. London: Herbert Jenkins, 1958.

_____. *The Music of Christian Hymnody*. London: Independent Press, 1957.

Sanders, Robert L. "Judgment Criteria in Hymn-Tunes," Address before the Hymn Society of America, Springfield, Ohio. The Hymn Society of America, 1948.

Schalk, Carl (ed.). *Key Words in Church Music.* St. Louis: Concordia Publishing House, 1978. See especially Cantional, Cantional Style; Carol; Chant, Anglican; Chant, Gregorian; Chorale; Gospel Song; Hymnody.

Stevens, Denis. *Plainsong Hymns and Sequences.* Study Notes, No. 12. Croydon: The Royal School of Church Music, n.d.

Stulken-Ekwo, Marilyn. "Contemporary Hymn Tunes: A Look at Some New Tunes in the Lutheran Book of Worship," *Journal of Church Music* 20, 2 (February 1978), 7-11.

Sydnor, James R. "The Music of Hymns," *The Hymn and Congregational Singing.* (Richmond: John Knox Press, 1960), pp. 31-42.

Taylor, Cyril. *The Way to Heaven's Door.* London: Epworth Press, 1957.

Zimmerman, Heinz Werner. "Word and Tone in Modern Hymnody," *The Hymn* 24, 2 (April 1973), 44-55.

The Hymn and Scripture

Bailey, Albert E. *The Gospel in Hymns.* New York: Charles Scribner's Sons, 1950. (Hudson River Publications)

Bayly, Albert. "Hymn Writing for our Times," *Bulletin of the Hymn Society of Great Britain and Ireland* 113 (Summer 1968), 211-20.

Benson, Louis F. "The Relation of the Hymn to Holy Scripture," Lecture II in *The Hymnody of the Christian Church* (Richmond: John Knox Press, 1956), 57-95.

Bett, Henry. "The Hymns and the Scriptures," Chapter VI in *The Hymns of Methodism* (London: The Epworth Press. 3rd rev. ed. 1945), 71-97.

Brandon, George. "Services of Songs and Bible Readings," *The Hymn* 26 (July 1975), 85-89.

Bushong, Ann Brooke. *A Guide to the Lectionary.* New York: The Seabury Press, 1978. Hymn List, pp. 202-205.

Leaver, Robin. "The Hymns and the Old Testament," *Bulletin of the Hymn Society of Great Britain and Ireland* 141 (January 1978), 14-16.

Pfatteicher, Helen E. "Psalms for the Congregation," *Journal of Church Music* 10 (April 1968), 12-14.

Routley, Erik R. "An 'Honest to God' Controversy, 1866," *The Hymn* 18 (January 1967), 11-15, 18-19.

_____. "Charles Wesley and Matthew Henry," *Bulletin of the Hymn Society of Great Britain and Ireland* 3 (Autum 1954):193-9.

_____. *Hymns Today and Tomorrow.* Nashville: Abingdon Press, 1964.

_____. "The Hymns of Philip Doddridge" in *Philip Doddridge: His Contribution to English Religion.* Edited by Geoffrey F. Nuttall. London: Independent Press, 1951.

Shero, Lucius Rogers. "Familiar hymns from the Hebrew and their Translations," *The Hymn* 13 (April, October 1962) and 14 (April 1965).

Spencer, Donald A. *Hymn and Scripture Selection Guide.* Valley Forge, PA: Judson Press, 1977.

The Hymn and Theology

Balleine, G. R. *Sing with Understanding, some hymn problems unravelled.* London: Independent Press, 1954.

Benson, Louis F. *The Hymnody of the Christian Church.* Richmond: John Knox Press, 1956.

Braun, H. Myron. "Yes, Heresies in Hymns," *Music Ministry* 10 (September 1977), 1, 31-32.

Buszin, Walter E. "Theology and Church Music as Bearers of the *Verbum Dei,*" *The Musical Heritage of the Church VI.* edited by Theodore Hoelty-Nickel (St. Louis: Concordia Publishing House, 1963), pp. 17-31.

Campbell, Duncan. "Introduction," *Hymns and Hymn-Makers.* (London: A. and C. Black, 1912), xv-xxvii.

Dewar, Lindsay. "Hymns and Theology," *Bulletin of the Hymn Society of Great Britain and Ireland* 30 (January 1945), 4-6.

Foelsch, Charles B. "Let's not lose the 'Category of the Holy,' " *The Hymn* 24 (October 1973), 109-11.

Foreman, Kenneth J. "Theology and the Hymnal," *Presbyterian Outlook.* (January 26, 1953), 4-5.

Giles, William Brewster. "Christian Theology and Hymnody," *The Hymn* 14 (January 1963), 9-12.

Gregory, A. S. "Hymns and the Faith," Chapter III in *Praises with Understanding.* Second edition (revised and enlarged). London: The Epworth Press, 1949, pp. 57-85.

Hall, Raymond. "Hymns for This Age," *The Hymn* 27 (April 1976), 62-63.

Hendricks, William L. "The New Hymnal—Its Theological Dimension," *The Church Musician* 26 (March 1975), 7-11.

Houghton, Edward. "Poetry and Piety in Charles Wesley's Hymns," *The Hymn* 6 (July 1955), 77-86.

Jones, Kenneth O. "Hymns and Theology," *The Hymn* 12 (April 1961), 36.

Langford, Norman F. "Church Hymnody as a Repository of Doctrine," *Religion in Life* 25 (Summer 1956), 421-31.

_____. "Theological Problems for Hymnology," *The Hymn* 4 (April 1953), 45-51.

McElrath, Hugh T. "Praise and Worship," *The Review and Expositor* 62 (Summer 1965), 293-306.

_____. "We Proclaim our Beliefs Through Congregational Song" *The Church Musician* 16 (December 1965), 6-7.

Martin, George Currie. "Byways of Doctrine," Chapter XI in *The Church and the Hymn Writers* "The Living Church Series." (London: J. Clarke 1928), 223-39.

Moyer, Karl E. "Christmas Hymns—Are They Christian?" *Journal of Church Music* 12 (December 1970), 9-11.

Naumann, Martin J. "Hymnody: A Reflection on the Beginning, Middle, and End of Man's Destiny," *The Musical Heritage of the Church VI* edited by Theodore Hoelty-Nickel (St. Louis: Concordia Publishing House, 1963), pp. 32-37.

Parry, Kenneth L. *Christian Hymns.* London: SCM Press, 1956.

Payne, Ernest A. "The Theology of Isaac Watts as Illustrated in His Hymns," *Bulletin of the Hymn Society of Great Britain and Ireland* 45 (October, 1948): 49-58.

Pirner, Reuben G. "The Nature and Function of the Hymn in Christian Worship," *Church Music* 66-1, 5.

Rattenbury, John E. *The Evangelical Doctrines of Charles Wesley's Hymns.* London: The Epworth Press, 1941-42.

Reppen, Dennis. "Hymn Notes: O Sacred Head . . . Wounded," *Journal of Church Music* 20 (March 1978), 12-13.

Routley, Erik R. *Church Music and Theology.* Philadelphia: Muhlenberg Press, 1959.

_____. *Hymns and the Faith.* Greenwich, Connecticut: The Seabury Press, 1954.

_____. *Hymns Today and Tomorrow.* New York: Abingdon Press, 1964.

_____. *Church Music and the Christian Faith.* Carol Stream, Ill. Agape, 1978.

Stählin, Wilhelm. "The Church Hymn and Theology," *Response* 1 (Pentecost 1959), 22-30.
Thomas, Nancy White. "Hymns Draw Out and Point Up Meaning," *The Hymn* 13 (January 1962), 24-27.

Early Church and Pre-Reformation Traditions

Apel, Willi. *Gregorian Chant.* Bloomington: Indiana University Press, 1958.
Binder, A. W. *Biblical Chant.* New York: Philosophical Library, 1959.
Britt, Dom Matthew, ed. *The Hymns of the Breviary and Missal.* New York: Benziger Brothers, 1948.
Bullough, John F. "Notker Balbulus and the Origin of the Sequence," *The Hymn* 16 (January 1965), 13-16; 24.
The Catholic Encyclopedia, 1913 ed. S. v. "Hymnody and Hymnology" by Clemens Blume.
Cumming, Charles G. *The Assyrian and Hebrew Hymns of Praise.* New York: Columbia University Press, 1934.
Duffield, Samuel W. *The Latin Hymn Writers and Their Hymns.* Ed. R.E. Thompson. New York: Funk and Wagnalls Co., 1889.
Encyclopedia of Religion and Ethics. S. v. "Hymns (Greek Christian)," by A. Baumstark.
Gerrison, R. Benjamin. "Ode to the Grecian Hymn," *The Hymn* 11 (October 1960), 105-109.
Higginson, J. Vincent. "A Thirteenth Century Anniversary" (The Contributions of Saint Thomas Aquinas and Saint Bonaventure to Hymnody), *The Hymn* 26 (July 1975), 80-84.
_____. "Revival of Gregorian Chant: Its Influence on English Hymnody," Papers of the Hymn Society of America XV; 1949.
The Interpreters Dictionary of the Bible, 1962 ed. S. v. "Music" by Eric Werner.
Johansen, John H. "Hymnody in the Early Church," *The Hymn* 25 (April 1974), 45-53.
_____. "Te Deum Laudamus," *Journal of Church Music* 10 (April 1968), 2-3, 32.
Jones, Douglas. "The Background and Character of the Lukan Psalms," *Journal of Theological Studies.* N.S. 19 (April 1968), 19-50.
Julian, John. *A Dictionary of Hymnology* 2 vols. New York: Dover Publications, 1957. Reprint of the Second Revised Edition, 1907. Articles on "Greek Hymnody," Latin Hymnody," "Sequence," "Carols."
Lamb J. A. *The Psalms in Christian Worship.* London: Faith Press, 1962.
Lang, Paul Henry. *Music in Western Civilization.* New York: W. W. Norton and Co., 1941.
Messenger, Ruth E. *The Medieval Latin Hymn.* Washington: Capital Press, 1953.
_____. "Christian Hymns in the First Three Centuries," Papers of the Hymn Society of America, IX, 1932.
_____. "Latin Hymns of the Middle Ages," Papers of the Hymn Society of America, XIV, 1948.
_____. "The Praise of the Virgin in Early Latin Hymns," Papers of the Hymn Society of America, III, 1932.
_____. "Rabanus Maurus," *The Hymn* 16 (April 1965), 44-48.

_____. "Vernacular Hymnody of the Late Middle Ages," *The Hymn* 16 (July 1965), 80-86.

Moule, C.F.D. *Worship in the New Testament.* Richmond: John Knox Press, 1961.

Neale, John Mason. *Collected Hymns, Sequences, and Carols.* London: Hodder and Stoughton, 1914.

Pierik, Marie. *The Song of the Church.* New York: Longmans, Green and Co., 1947.

Pocknee, C. E. "Gloria in Excelsis," *Bulletin of the Hymn Society of Great Britain and Ireland* 6 (April 1965), 14-16.

_____. "Three Latin Hymns: Te Deum Laudamus, Gloria Laus et Honor, Veni Creator Spiritus," *Bulletin of the Hymn Society of Great Britain and Ireland* 6 (April 1966), 61-65.

_____. "Veni, Veni, Emmanuel," *Bulletin of the Hymn Society of Great Britain and Ireland* 7 (Spring 1970), 65-69.

Raby, F. J. E. "The Poem 'Dulcis IESU Memoria,' " *Bulletin of the Hymn Society of Great Britain and Ireland* 33 (October 1945), 1-6.

_____. "The Hymn 'Adoro Devote, Latens Veritas,' " *Bulletin of the Hymn Society of Great Britain and Ireland* 23 (April 1943), 1-3.

_____. *A History of Christian-Latin Poetry from the Beginnings to the Close of the Middle Ages.* Second ed. London: Oxford University Press, 1953.

Reese, Gustave. *Music in the Middle Ages.* New York: W. W. Norton and Co., 1940.

Routley, Erik. *The Church and Music.* London: Duckworth and Co., Ltd., 1950.

Sanders, J. T. *The New Testament Christological Hymns; Their Historical Religious Background.* Cambridge: Cambridge University Press, 1971.

Wellesz, Egon. *Byzantine Music and Hymnography.* Second ed. Oxford: Clarendon Press, 1961.

_____. ed. *Ancient and Oriental Music.* Vol. I, *The New Oxford History of Music.* London: Oxford University Press, 1957.

Werner, Eric. *The Sacred Bridge.* New York: Columbia University Press, 1959.

Reformation Traditions
A. The Chorale

Aaberg, J.C. *Hymns and Hymn Writers of Denmark.* Des Moines, Iowa: The Committee on Publication of the Danish Evangelical Lutheran Church in America, 1945.

Bäumker, Wilhelm. *Das katholische deutsche Kirchenlied.* 4 vols. Freiburg: Herdersche Verlagshandlung, 1883-1911. Reprint ed. Hildesheim: Georg Olms, 1962.

Blankenburg, Walter. "The Music of the Bohemian Brethren" in *Protestant Church Music: A History* by Friedrich Blume, pp. 591-607. New York: W. W. Norton Co., 1974.

Blume, Friedrich. "The Age of Confessionalism," in *Protestant Church Music: A History,* pp. 125-315. New York: W. W. Norton & Co., 1974.

_____. "The Period of the Reformation" (rev. by Ludwig Finscher), in *Protestant Church Music: A History,* pp. 1-123. New York: W. W. Norton & Co., 1974.

Buszin, Walter E. "Johann Crüger: On the Tercentenary of His Death," *Response in Worship—Music—The Arts* 4(1962), 89-97.

_____. "Luther on Music," *Musical Quarterly* 32 (January 1946), 8-97.

Cantate Domino. New Edition. [4th ed.] Kassel, Germany: Published by Bärenreiter Verlag for the World Council of Churches, 1974.

Erickson, J. Irving. *Twice-Born Hymns,* Chicago: Covenant Press, 1976.

Evangelisches Kirchengesangbuch, Edition for the Lutheran Church in Bavaria. Munich: Evang. Presserverband für Bayern e. V., 1957.

Feder, Georg. "Decline and Restoration," in *Protestant Church Music: A History* by Friedrich Blume, pp. 317-404. New York: W. W. Norton & Co., 1974.

Frostenson, Anders (ed.) and Fred Kaan (tr.). *Songs and Hymns from Sweden.* London: Stainer & Bell, Ltd., 1976.

Gennrich, F. (ed.). *Troubadours, Trouveres, Minne and Meistersinger.* v.2 of *Anthology of Music,* ed. K. G. Fellerer. Cologne, Germany: Arno Volk Verlag, 1960.

Giessler, John H. "Bicentennial of Gregor's Hymnal 1778," *The Hymn* 29 (October 1978), 211-13.

————. "Musical Ministers of the Moravian Church," *The Hymn* 29 (January 1978), 6-14, 28.

Hewitt, Theodore Brown. *Paul Gerhardt as a Hymn Writer and His Influence on English Hymnody.* New Haven: Yale University Press, 1918; Reprint ed. with a new afterword and updated bibliography, St. Louis: Concordia Publishing House, 1976.

Hymnal and Liturgies of the Moravian Church. Bethlehem, Pa. and Winston-Salem, N.C.: The Moravian Church in America, 1969.

Jenny, Markus. "The Hymns of Zwingli and Luther: a Comparison," *Cantors at the Crossroads.* Ed. Johannes Riedel, pp. 45-63. St. Louis: Concordia Publishing House, 1966.

Leupold, Ulrich S., ed. *Liturgy and Hymns.* Vol. 53 of *Luther's Works.* Philadelphia: Fortress Press, 1964.

Liemohn, Edwin. *The Chorale Through Four Hundred Years of Musical Development as a Congregational Hymn.* Philadelphia: Muhlenberg Press, 1953.

Moore, Sydney H. *Sursum Corda, Being Studies of Some German Hymn Writers.* London: Independent Press, 1956.

Reed, Luther D. *Luther and Congregational Song.* Papers of The Hymn Society of America, XII, 1947.

Riedel, Johannes. *The Lutheran Chorale, Its Basic Traditions.* Minneapolis: Augsburg Publishing House, 1967.

Schousboe, Torben. "Protestant Church Music in Scandinavia" in *Protestant Church Music: A History* by Friedrich Blume, pp. 609-636. New York: W. W. Norton & Co., 1974.

Zahn, Johannes. *Die Melodien der deutschen evangelischen Kirchenlieder.* 6 vols. Gütersloh: Bertelsmann, 1889-1893. Reprint ed. Hildesheim: Georg Olms, 1962.

B. Metrical Psalmody

Bible Songs. Due West, S.C.: Executive Board, Associate Reformed Presbyterian Church, 1930, 7th ed., 1975.

Blankenburg, Walter. "Church Music in Reformed Europe," in *Protestant Church Music: A History* by Friedrich Blume, pp. 509-590. New York: W. W. Norton Co., 1974.

The Book of Psalms for Singing. Pittsburgh: Board of Education and Publication, Reformed Presbyterian Church of North America, 1973, 2nd ed., 1975.

Douen, E. O. *Clement Marot et le Psautier Huguenot.* Paris: L'Imprimerie Nationale, 1878-1879.

Frost, Maurice. *English and Scottish Psalm and Hymn Tunes* c. 1543-1677. London: SPCK; London, New York: Oxford University Press, 1953.

Haraszti, Zoltan. *The Enigma of the Bay Psalm Book*. Chicago: University of Chicago Press, 1956.

_____. (ed.). *The Bay Psalm Book. A Facsimile Reprint of the First Edition of 1640*. Chicago: University of Chicago Press, n.d. *[1956]*.

Hohmann, Walter. *"The Greiter Melody and Variants,"* The Hymn 12 (April 1961), 47-51.

Lowens, Irving. "The Bay Psalm Book in 17th Century New England," in *Music and Musicians in Early America*, pp. 25-38. New York: W. W. Norton, 1964.

Patrick, Millar. *Four Centuries of Scottish Psalmody*. London: Oxford University Press, 1949.

Pidoux, Pierre. *Le Psautier Huguenot du XVIe Siecle*. 2 vols. Basel: Edition Bärenreiter, 1962.

Pratt, Waldo S. *The Music of the Pilgrims*. Boston: Oliver Ditson Co., 1921. Reprint edition. New York: AMS Press, 1966.

_____. *The Music of the French Psalter of 1562*. New York: Columbia University Press, 1939; Reprint ed., New York: AMS Press, 1966.

_____. *The Significance of the Old French Psalter Begun by Clement Marot in 1532*. Papers of the Hymn Society of America, IV, 1933.

Prothero, Rowland E. *The Psalms in Human Life*. London: Thomas Nelson & Sons, 1903.

Reese, Gustave. *Music in the Renaissance*. Rev. ed. New York: W. W. Norton & Co., 1959.

Roan, Eugene. "Claude Goudimel: French Composer," *The Hymn* 19 (July 1968), 86-89.

Smith, Carlton Sprague, "The 1774 Psalm Book of the Reformed Protestant Dutch Church in New York City," *Musical Quarterly* 34 (January 1948), 84-96.

The Scottish Psalter. London: Oxford University Press, 1929.

Terry, Richard (ed.) *Calvin's First Psalter (1539)*. London: Ernest Benn, 1932.

British Traditions

Allinger, Helen. "William Henry Monk," *The Hymn* 12 (April 1961), 37-41, 51.

Anglican Hymn Book. London: Church Book Room, Ltd., 1965.

Baker, Frank and Williams, George W. *John Wesley's First Hymnbook: A Collection of Psalms and Hymns*. Charleston: Dalcho Historical Society, 1964.

Baker, Frank, ed. *Representative Verse of Charles Wesley*. London: The Epworth Press, 1962.

The Baptist Hymn Book. London: Psalms and Hymns Trust, 1962.

Batchelder, Robert C. "Ralph Vaughan Williams, 1872-1958," *The Hymn* 10 (July 1959), 87-90.

Bayly, Albert F. *Again, I Say Rejoice*. Privately printed by author: 3 Church Lane, Springfield, Chelmsford, Essex, CM155F, England, 1967.

_____. *Rejoice Always*. Privately printed by author: 3 Church Lane, Springfield, Chelmsford, Essex, CM155F, England, 1971.

_____. *Rejoice in God*. Privately printed by author: 3 Church Lane, Springfield, Chelmsford, Essex, CM155F, England, 1977.

_____. *Rejoice, O People*. Privately printed by author, 3 Church Lane, Springfield, Chelmsford, Essex, CM155F, England, 1950.

Beaumont, Geoffrey. *Eleven Hymn Tunes*. London: Josef Weinberger, Ltd., 1957.

_____. *More 20th Century Hymn Tunes*. London: Josef Weinberger, 1962.

_____. *Thirty 20th Century Hymn Tunes.* London: Josef Weinberger, 1960.
Benson, Louis F. *The Hymns of John Bunyan.* Papers of the Hymn Society of America, I., 1930.
Bett, Henry. *The Hymns of Methodism in their Literary Relations.* Revised edition. London: The Epworth Press, 1945.
Bishop, Selma L. *Isaac Watts Hymns and Spiritual Songs.* A Study in Early Eighteenth Century Language Changes. London: The Faith Press, 1962.
Brant, Cyr de. "Chope's Christmas Carols," *The Hymn* 23 (October 1972), 105-10.
_____. "Edward J. Hopkins: Hymn Tune Composer," *The Hymn* 19 (April 1968), 54-9.
Bridges, Robert, ed. *The Yattendon Hymnal.* Oxford: Clarendon Press, 1899.
Bristol, Lee Hastings, Jr. "A Dutch Congregationalist in Switzerland," *The Hymn* 22 (July 1971), 83-85.
_____. "Sullivan, Hymn Tune Composer," *The Hymn* 18 (October 1967), 101-103.
The BBC Hymn Book. London: Oxford University Press, 1951.
Brunton, Grace. "Horatius Bonar, Minister and Hymnist, 1808-1889," *The Hymn* 9 (October 1958), 101-5, 125.
_____. "John Ellerton, 1826-93," *The Hymn* 12 (October 1961), 101-106, 112.
_____. "Reginald Heber, Bishop of Calcutta," *The Hymn* II (April 1960), 37-44.
Bunn, Leslie H. "Richard Baxter Speaks to Our Time," *The Hymn* 9 (July 1958), 79-82.
_____. "Hymns Ancient and Modern," *The Hymn* 12 (January 1961), 5-12.
_____. "Why Julian Needs Revision" (a review of British hymnic trends in the first half of the 20th century). *The Hymn* 7 (January 1956), 5-8,17.
Cairns, William T. "Richard Baxter, Hymn Writer," *Bulletin of the Hymn Society of Great Britain and Ireland* 24 (July 1943), 1-6.
The Cambridge Hymnal. Cambridge: Cambridge University Press, 1967.
Carter, Sydney. *Songs of Sydney Carter in the Present Tense.* London: Galliard, Ltd., 1969.
Clarke, William Kemp Lowther. *A Hundred Years of Hymns Ancient and Modern.* London: William Clowes and Sons, Ltd., 1960.
Cohn, Wayne H. "Ralph Vaughan Williams and Hymnody," *The Hymn* 19 (July 1968), 81-5.
A Collection of Tunes set to music as they are commonly sung at the Foundery. Facsimile reprint. London: T. Woolmer, n.d.
Congregational Praise. London: Independent Press, 1951.
Davis, Arthur P. *Isaac Watts.* London: Independent Press, 1943.
Dearmer, Percy, ed. *The English Hymnal With Tunes.* New ed. London: Oxford University Press, 1933.
_____. Ralph Vaughan Williams and Martin Shaw. *The Oxford Book of Carols.* London: The Oxford University Press, 1964.
_____. *Songs of Praise.* Enlarged ed. London: Oxford University Press, 1931.
_____. *Songs of Praise Discussed.* London: Oxford University Press, 1933.
England, Martha Winburn and Sparrow, John. *Hymns Unbidden.* New York: New York Public Library, 1966.
English Praise. London: Oxford University Press, 1975.
Escott, Harry. "The Influence of Richard Baxter on English Hymnody," *The Hymn* 3 (October 1952), 105-9, 118.

_____. *Isaac Watts, Hymnographer: A study of the Beginnings, Development and Philosophy of the English Hymn.* London: Independent Press, Lt., 1962.

Finlay, Kenneth G. "A Scot Considers the English Hymn Tune, 1900-1950," *The Hymn* 6 (October 1955), 117-123.

Flanigan, Alexander. "Cecil Frances Alexander," *The Hymn* 5 (April 1954), 37-42, 59.

_____. "Thomas Kelly, 1769-1855," *The Hymn* 6 (April 1955), 59-64.

Flew, Newton. *The Hymns of Charles Wesley: A Study of Their Structure.* London: The Epworth Press, 1953.

Fountain, David. *Isaac Watts Remembered.* Worthing: Henry E. Walter, Ltd., 1974.

Fox, Adam. *English Hymns and Hymn Writers.* London: William Collins Sons and Co., Ltd., 1947.

Frost, Maurice. "The Tunes Associated with Hymn Singing in the Lifetime of the Wesleys," *Bulletin of the Hymn Society of Great Britain and Ireland* 4 (Winter 1957/8), 118-26.

_____. *English and Scottish Psalm and Hymn Tunes c. 1543-1677.* New York: Oxford University Press, 1953.

_____. ed., *Historical Companion to Hymns Ancient and Modern.* London: William Clowes and Sons, Ltd., 1962.

Gospel Song Book. London: Geoffrey Chapman, 1970.

Gregory, Arthur E. *The Hymnbook of the Modern Church.* London: Charles E. K. Kelly, n.d.

Haas, Alfred Burton. *Charles Wesley.* New York: Papers of the Hymn Society of America, XXII, 1957.

Herbert, George. *The Temple. Sacred Poems and Private Ejaculations.* London: n.p. 1667.

Higginson, J. Vincent. "English Carols—Survival and Revival," *The Hymn* 23 (October 1972), 101-5.

_____. "William Henry Havergal, 1793-1870," *The Hymn* 20 (January 1969), 9-16, 21.

_____. "Daniel Sedgwick: Pioneer of English Hymnology," *The Hymn* 4 (July 1953), 77-80.

_____. "Richard Redhead, Organist and Composer, 1820-1901," *The Hymn* 21 (April 1970), 37-42.

_____. "Edward Perronet," *The Hymn* 18 (October 1967), 105-13.

_____. "John Keble and Hymnody," *The Hymn* 17 (July 1966), 85-90.

_____. "John Mason Neale and 19th Century Hymnody, His Work and Influence," *The Hymn* 16 (October 1965), 100-27.

_____. "Sir George 'J. Elvey, 1816-1893," *The Hymn* 18 (January 1967), 5-10.

Hodges, H. A. "Williams Pantycelyn," *Bulletin of the Hymn Society of Great Britain and Ireland* 8 (February, 1976), 145-52; 8 (June, 1976), 161-66.

Holbrook, Arthur S. "American Associations of James Montgomery," *The Hymn* 5 (July 1954):73-78.

Hope, Norman Victor. "Isaac Watts and His Contribution to English Hymnody," Papers of the Hymn Society of American, No. XIII, 1947.

Horder, Garrett. *The Hymn Lover.* An Account of the Rise and Growth of English Hymnody. Third edition, Revised. London: J. Curwen, and Sons, Ltd. 1901.

Housman, Henry. *John Ellerton.* Being a Collection of His Writings on Hymnology. London: S.P.C.K. 1896.

Hughes, Anselm, ed. *Early Medieval Music up to 1300. New Oxford History of Music,* Vol. II. London: Oxford University Press, 1954.

Hutchings, Arthur. "J. B. Duke's Tunes," *The Hymn* 12 (July 1961), 69-76.

Hymns and Songs. London: Methodist Publishing House, 1969.

Hymns Ancient and Modern Revised. London: William Clowes and Sons, Ltd., 1950.

Hymn Tunes Composed by Joseph Barnby. London: Novello, Ewer and Co., 1897.

Hymn Tunes Composed by J. B. Dykes. London: Novello and Co., n.d.

Hymn Tunes Composed by John Stainer. London: Novello and Co., 1900.

Hymn Tunes Composed by Arthur Sullivan. London: Novello and Co., 1902.

The Hymnal 1940 of the Protestant Episcopal Church in the United States of America. New York: The Church Pension Fund, 1943.

Jefferson, H.A.L. *Hymns in Christian Worship.* London: Rockliff, 1950.

Johansen, John H. "The Christian Psalmist," *The Hymn* 22 (April 1971), 51-53.

_____. "Frances Ridley Havergal, 1836-1879: Poetess of Consecretion," *The Hymn* 7 (April 1956), 41-48.

_____. "John Cennick, 1718-1755 Moravian Evangelist and Hymn Writer," *The Hymn* 6 (July 1955), 87-97.

_____. *The Olney Hymns.* New York: Papers of the Hymn Society of America, XX, 1956.

Kaan, Fred. *Break Not the Circle.* Carol Stream, IL: Agape, 1975.

_____. *Pilgrim Praise.* London: Galliard, 1972.

_____. "Saturday Night and Sunday Morning," *The Hymn* 27 (October 1970), 100-108.

Knight, George Litch. "Philip Doddridge's Hymns," *The Hymn* 2 (October 1951), 11-16.

_____. "William Cowper as a Hymn Writer," *The Hymn* 1 (October 1950), 5-12,20.

Leaver, Robin A. *Catherine Winkworth: The Influence of Her Translations on English Hymody.* St. Louis: Concordia Publishing House, 1978.

Lock, William. "Six Hymns from Olney," *Journal of Church Music* 17 (November, 1975), 8-10.

_____. "John Newton and the Olney Hymns," *Journal of Church Music* (October 1962), 2-5.

Lough, A. B. *The Influence of John Mason Neale.* London: S.P.C.K., 1962.

_____. *John Mason Neale—Priest Extraordinary.* Devon, England, 1976.

Martin, Hugh, ed. *The Baptist Hymn Book Companion* (Revised edition, R. W. Thomson, ed.) London: Psalms and Hymns Trust, 1967.

_____. *Puritanism and Richard Baxter.* London: SCM Press, Ltd., 1954.

_____. *They Wrote Our Hymns.* London: SCM Press, 1961. Napierville, Illinois: Alec R. Allenson, Inc. 1961.

Messenger, Ruth E. "John Mason Neale, Translator," *The Hymn* 2 (October 1951), 5-10,24.

Micklem, Caryl. "Pilgrim Praise—A Review," *Bulletin of the Hymn Society of Great Britain and Ireland* 7 (January 1973), 235-38.

New Catholic Hymnal. New York: St. Martin's Press, 1971.

New Church Praise. Edinburgh: The Saint Andrew Press, 1975.

Newton, John and Cowper, William. *Olney Hymns in Three Books.* London: W. Oliver, 1779.

Nuttall, Geoffrey F., ed. *Philip Doddridge 1702-51: His Contribution to English Religion.* London: Independent Press, 1951.

100 Hymns for Today. London: William Clowes and Sons, Ltd., 1969.

Parker, Edna. *The Hymns and Hymn Tunes Found in the English Metrical Psalters.* New York: Coleman-Ross Company, 1966.

_____. *Early English Hymns: An Index.* Metuchen, New Jersey: Scarecrow Press, 1972.

Parry, K. L. and Routley, Erik. *Companion to Congregational Praise.* London: Independent Press, 1953.

Pfatteicher, Helen E. "The Hymn Tunes of Mendelssohn," *The Hymn* 4 (October 1960), 110-13.

Phillips, C. S. *Hymnody Past and Present.* New York: The Macmillan Company, 1937.

Pocknee, Cyril E. *The French Diocesan Hymns and Their Melodies.* New York: Morehouse-Gorham Co., Inc. 1954.

Praise for Today. London: Psalms and Hymns Trust, 1974.

Praise the Lord. London: Geoffrey Chapman Publishers, 1972. Reprinted, 1973.

Pratt Green, Fred. *26 Hymns.* London: The Epworth Press, 1971.

Purcell, William. *Onward Christian Soldier; A Life of Sabine Baring-Gould, Parson, Squire, Novelist, Antiquary, 1834-1924.* New York: Longmans, Green and Co., Inc., 1957.

Rattenbury, John E. *The Eucharistic Hymns of John and Charles Wesley.* London: The Epworth Press, 1948.

_____. *Wesley's Legacy to the World.* London: The Epworth Press, 1928.

Reilly, Joseph J. "The Hymns of John Henry Newman," *The Hymn* 2 (January 1951), 5-10, 20.

Rippon, John. *A Selection of the Hymns from the Best Authors.* 15th ed. London: W. W. Woodward, 1813.

_____. *A Selection of Psalm and Hymn Tunes from the Best Authors.* 13th ed. London: n.d. (1810).

Rogal, Samuel J. "John Bunyan and Congregational Song," *The Hymn* 28 (July 1977), 118-25.

Ronander, Albert C. "Christmas Carols New and Old," *The Hymn* 21 (October 1970), 103-110, 122.

_____. "The Hymnody of Congregationalism" (Isaac Watt's Hymns). *The Hymn* 8 (January 1957), 5-14.

Routley, Erik. *Eternal Light.* New York: Carl Fischer, 1971.

_____. "Hymn Writers of the New English Rennaissance," *The Hymn* 28 (January 1977), 6-10.

_____. *I'll Praise My Maker.* London: Independent Press, Ltd., 1951.

_____. *The English Carol.* London: Barrie and Jenkins, 1958.

_____. "James Montgomery in the Church of Today," *Bulletin of the Hymn Society of Great Britain and Ireland.* 7 (Spring 1971), 129-32.

_____. *A Short History of English Church Music.* London: Mowbray's, 1977.

_____. *The Musical Wesleys.* London: Herbert Jenkins, 1968.

_____. "Percy Dearmer: 20th Century Hymnologist" *The Hymn* 19 (July 1968), 74-80.

Taylor, Cyril. "Pilgrim's Way," A Review of *Eternal Light.* Bulletin of the Hymn Society of Great Britain and Ireland. (April 1972), 199-202.

Telford, John. *The Methodist Hymn-book Illustrated in History and Experience.* London: The Epworth Press, 7th ed., 1959.

Temperly, Nicholas. "The Anglican Communion Hymn," A Series of Four Articles. *The Hymn* 30 (January 1979), 7-15; (April 1979), 93-101,105; (July 1979), 178-86; (October 1979), 243-51.

Turner, Maxine. "Joseph Addison's Five Hymns," *The Hymn* 23 (April 1972), 40-41.

Watts, Isaac. *Horae Lyricae*. 2nd ed., London: J. Humfreys, 1709.
_____. *Hymns and Spiritual Songs*. Coventry: M. Luckman, 1785.
_____. *The Psalms of David Imitated in the Language of the New Testament and Applied to the Christian State and Worship*. Coventry: M. Luckman, 1785.
Wesley, John. *A Collection of Hymns for the Use of the People Called Methodists*. London: J. Mason [1779].
Westermeyer, Paul. "The Hymnal Noted: Theological and Musical Intersection," *Church Music*. 73-2; pp. 1-9.
Williamson, Malcolm. *12 New Hymn Tunes*. London: Joseph Weinberger, Ltd., 1962.
_____. *16 Hymns and Processionals*. Carol Stream: Agape, 1975.
Wither, George. *Songs and Hymns of the Church*. London: J. R. Smith, 1856.
Woodward, G. R. ed., *Piae Cantiones*, London: The Plainsong and Mediaeval Music Society, 1910.
_____. ed., *Songs of Syon*. London: Schott and Co., 1910.
Worship the Lord. Oakville, Ont.: Harmuse Publications, 1977.
Young, Carlton R. Review of *New Church Praise*, *The Hymn* 28 (January 1977), 28-30.
Young, Robert H. "The History of Baptist Hymnody in England from 1612 to 1800." D.M.A. dissertation, University of Southern California, 1959.

American Traditions
Alexander, Helen C. and Maclean, J. Kennedy. *Charles M. Alexander*. London: Marshall Brothers Ltd., 1920.
Allen, William Allen, Ware, Charles P., and Garrison, Lucy McKim, eds. *Slave Songs of the United States*. New York, 1867. Reprint. New York: Peter Smith, 1951. Rev. ed. New York: Oak Publications, 1965.
Andrews, Edward D. *The Gift to Be Simple. Songs, Dances and Rituals of the American Shakers*. New York: J. J. Augustin, 1940.
Appel, Richard G. *The Music of the Bay Psalm Book 9th Edition (1698)*. New York: Institute for Studies in American Music Monographs Number 5, 1975.
_____. "Philip Schaff, Pioneer American Hymnologist," *The Hymn* 14 (January 1963), 5-7.
Batastini, Robert J., Hustad, Donald P., Lovelace, Austin C., and Taylor, Cyril V. "The CEH List: Four Diverse Appraisals," *The Hymn* 29 (April 1978), 83-90.
Battles, Ford Lewis and Simmons, Morgan. "The Consultation on Ecumenical Hymnody," *The Hymn* 28 (April 1977), 67-68, 87.
Beary, Shirley. "Stylistic Traits of Southern Shape-Note Gospel Songs," *The Hymn* 30 (January 1979), 26-33, 35.
Benson, Louis F. *The English Hymn*. New York: George H. Doran, 1915. Reprint ed., Richmond: John Knox Press, 1962.
Brandon, George. "Some Classic Tunes in Lowell Mason's Collections," *The Hymn* 18 (July 1967), 78-79.
Bristol, Lee Hastings, Jr. "Thomas Hastings, 1784-1872," *The Hymn* 10 (October 1959), 105-110.
Britton, Allan P. "Theoretical Introductions in American Tune-Books to 1800," Ph.D. dissertation, University of Michigan, 1949.
Buchanan, Anabel Morris. (ed.). *Folk Hymns of America*. New York: J. Fischer and Brother, 1938.
Chase, Gilbert. *America's Music: From the Pilgrims to the Present*. Rev. ed. New York: McGraw-Hill, 1966.

Clark, Linda. "God of Grace and God of Glory: A Very Urgent Personal Prayer," *The Hymn* 29 (October 1978), 206-210, 213.
Cobb, Buell E., Jr. *The Sacred Harp: A Tradition and Its Music.* Athens: University of Georgia Press, 1978.
Davisson, Ananias. *Kentucky Harmony.* Harrisonburg, Va., 1816. Reprint with a new introduction by Irving Lowens. Minneapolis: Augsburg Press, 1976.
Downey, James Cecil. "The Music of American Revivalism." Ph.D. dissertation, Tulane University, 1968.
Ellinwood, Leonard. *The History of American Church Music.* New York: Morehouse-Gorham Co., 1953.
_____. *To Praise God: The Life and Work of Charles Winfred Douglas.* Papers of The Hymn Society of America, XXIII, 1958.
Emurian, Ernest K. *Forty True Stories of Famous Gospel Songs.* Natick, Mass.: W.A. Wilde Co., 1959.
Eskew, Harry. "Shape-Note Hymnody in the Shenandoah Valley, 1816-1860." Ph.D. dissertation, Tulane University, 1966.
_____. "William Walker, 1809-1875: Popular Southern Hymnist," *The Hymn* 15 (January 1964), 5-13.
Epstein, Dena J. *Sinful Tunes and Spirituals.* Urbana: University of Illinois Press, 1977.
Fleming, Jo Lee. "James D. Vaughan, Music Publisher, Lawrenceburg, Tennessee, 1912-1964." S.M.D., dissertation, Union Theological Seminary, 1972.
Foote, Arthur, 2nd. *Henry Wilder Foote, Hymnologist.* Papers of The Hymn Society of America, XXVI, 1968.
Foote, Henry Wilder. *An Account of the Bay Psalm Book.* Papers of The Hymn Society of America, VII, 1940.
_____. *Recent American Hymnody.* Papers of The Hymn Society of America, XVII, 1952.
_____. *Three Centuries of American Hymnody.* Cambridge, Mass.: Harvard University Press, 1940. Reprint. ed. Hamden, Conn.: The Shoe String Press, 1961.
Gray, Gladys E. "Mary Artemisia Lathbury," *The Hymn* 14 (April 1963), 37-46.
Hall, Jacob Henry. *Biography of Gospel Song and Hymn Writers.* New York: Fleming H. Revell Co., 1914. Reprint ed. New York: AMS Press, 1971.
Hammond, Paul. "The Hymnody of the Second Great Awakening," *The Hymn* 29 (January 1978), 19-28.
Higginson, J. Vincent. *Hymnody in the American Indian Missions.* Papers of The Hymn Society of America, XVIII, 1954.
_____. "Notes on Lowell Mason's Hymn Tunes," *The Hymn* 18 (April 1967), 37-42.
_____. "Phillips Brooks and Sunday School Music," *The Hymn* 19 (April 1968), 37-43.
Hill, Richard S. "Not So Far Away in a Manger. Forty-one Settings of an American Carol," *Notes* 2nd ser. 3 (December 1945), 12-36.
Hitchcock, H. Wiley. *Music in the United States: A Historical Introduction.* 2nd ed. Englewood Cliffs, N.J.: Prentice-Hall, Inc., 1974.
Holden, Edith and Knight, George Litch. "Brick Church's Role in American Hymnody," *The Hymn* 3 (July 1952), 73-78.
Horn, Dorothy D. *Sing to Me of Heaven: A Study of Folk and Early American Materials in Three Old Harp Books.* Gainesville: University of Florida Press, 1970.

"Hymns and Tunes Recommended for Ecumenical Use," *The Hymn* 28 (October 1977), 192-209.

Jackson, George Pullen. *Another Sheaf of White Spirituals.* Gainesville: University of Florida Press, 1952.

_____. *Down-East Spirituals and Others.* 2nd ed. Locust Valley, N.Y.: J.J. Augustin, 1953.

_____. *Spiritual Folk-Songs of Early America: Two Hundred and Fifty Tunes and Texts.* New York: J.J. Augustin, 1937. Reprint. New York: Dover Publications, 1975.

_____. *White and Negro Spirituals.* New York: J. J. Augustin, 1943. Reprint ed. New York: J. J. Augustin, 1975.

_____. *White Spirituals in the Southern Uplands.* Chapel Hill: University of North Carolina Press, 1933. Reprint eds. Hatboro, Pa.: Folklore Associates, 1964. New York: Dover Publications, 1965.

Jefferson, Helen G. "Samuel Longfellow," *The Hymn* 9 (July 1958), 69-73.

Johnson, Charles A. *The Frontier Camp Meeting: Religion's Harvest Time.* Dallas: Southern Methodist University Press, 1955.

Kidder, David H. "John Greenleaf Whittier's Contribution to American Hymnody," *The Hymn* 8 (October 1957), 105-111.

Knight, George Litch. "Maltbie Davenport Babcock, D.D., a Centenary Appreciation," *The Hymn* 9 (April 1958), 37-44.

Loftis, Deborah C. "The Hymns of Georgia Harkness," *The Hymn* 28 (October 1977), 186-91.

McCormick, David. "Oliver Holden, 1764-1844," *The Hymn* 14 (July 1963), 69-77,79.

McCurry, John G. *The Social Harp.* Hart County, Ga. (printed at Philadelphia, Pa.), 1855. Reprint edited by Daniel W. Patterson and John F. Garst. Athens: University of Georgia Press, 1973.

McCutchan, Helen Cowles. *Born to Music. The Ministry of Robert Guy McCutchan.* Papers of The Hymn Society of America, XXVIII, 1972.

McKay, David P. and Crawford, Richard. *William Billings of Boston.* Princeton: Princeton University Press, 1975.

McLoughlin, William G. *Billy Sunday Was His Real Name.* Chicago: University of Chicago Press, 1955.

_____. *Modern Revivalism.* New York: The Roland Press Co., 1959.

Marrocco, W. Thomas and Gleason, Harold (eds.). *Music in America: An Anthology from the Landing of the Pilgrims to the Close of the Civil War 1620-1865.* New York: W. W. Norton & Co., 1964.

Mason, Henry Lowell. *Hymn Tunes of Lowell Mason. A Bibliography.* Cambridge, MA: Harvard University Press, 1944.

_____. *Lowell Mason: An Appreciation of His Life and Work.* Papers of The Hymn Society of America, VIII, 1941.

Metcalf, Frank J. *American Writers and Compilers of Sacred Music.* Cincinnati: Abingdon Press, 1925. Repr. 1967, Russell & Russell.

Music, David W. "A New Source for the Tune 'All Is Well,' " *The Hymn* 29 (April 1978), 76-82.

Noyes, Morgan P. *Louis F. Benson, Hymnologist.* Papers of The Hymn Society of America, XIX, 1955.

Osborne, Stanley L. "Recent Canadian Hymnody," *The Hymn* 29 (July 1978), 134-40.

Porter, Ellen Jane. *Two Early American Tunes: Fraternal Twins?* Papers of The Hymn Society of America, XXX, 1975.
Reid, William W. "The Hymns of Oliver Wendell Holmes," *The Hymn* 10 (July 1959), 69-78.
_____. "Frank Mason North—An Appreciation," *The Hymn* 1 (April 1950), 5-10,14.
_____. *Sing with Spirit and Understanding, the Story of the Hymn Society of America.* New York: Hymn Society of America, 1962.
_____. *Sing with Spirit and Understanding: The Story of the Hymn Society of America 1962-1972.* New York: The Hymn Society of America, 1972.
Rodeheaver, Homer. *Twenty Years with Billy Sunday.* Winona Lake, Ind.: Rodeheaver Hall-Mack, 1936.
Ruffin, Bernard. *Fanny Crosby.* Philadelphia: United Church Press, 1976.
Sallee, James. *A History of Evangelistic Hymnody.* Grand Rapids, Mich.: Baker Book House, 1978.
Sankey, Ira D., *et al. Gospel Hymns Nos. 1-6 Complete.* New York and Chicago, 1894. Reprint ed. New York: Da Capo Press, 1972.
_____. *My Life and the Story of the Gospel Hymns and of Sacred Songs and Solos,* with an introduction by Theodore L. Cuyler. Philadelphia: The Sunday School Times Co., 1907.
Scholes, Percy A. *The Puritans and Music in England and New England.* London: Oxford University Press, 1934.
Southern, Eileen. *The Music of Black Americans: A History.* New York: W. W. Norton, 1971.
Stansbury, George W. "The Music of the Billy Graham Crusades 1947-1970: An Analysis and Evaluation." D.M.A. dissertation, Southern Baptist Theological Seminary, 1971.
Stebbins, George C. *Reminiscences and Gospel Hymn Stories.* With an introduction by Charles H. Gabriel. New York: George H. Doran Co., 1924.
Stevenson, Robert. *Protestant Church Music in America.* New York: W. W. Norton & Co., 1966.
Sydnor, James R. "Twentieth Century Hymnody in the United States," *Addresses at the International Hymnological Conference.* New York: The Hymn Society of America, 1962, pp. 28-41.
Tucker, F. Bland. "Reflections of a Hymn Writer," *The Hymn* 30 (April 1979), 115-16.
Tufts, John. *An Introduction to the Singing of Psalm Tunes.* 5th ed. Boston, 1721. Reprint with an introduction by Irving Lowens. Philadelphia: Printed for Musical Americana by Albert Saifer, Publisher, 1954.
Underwood, Byron E. "Bishop John Freeman Young, Translator of 'Stille Nacht,' " *The Hymn* 8 (October 1957), 123-30.
Walker, William. *The Southern Harmony.* Rev. ed. Spartanburg, S.C. (printed at Philadelphia, Pa.), 1854. Reprint with an introduction by Glenn C. Wilcox. Los Angeles: Pro Musicamericana, 1966. (Available from Box 649, Murray, KY 42071).
White, B. F. and King, E. J. *The Original Sacred Harp.* Cullman, Ala.: Sacred Harp Publishing Co., 1971. (Available from P.O. Box 185, Bremen, GA 30110).
_____. *The Sacred Harp.* 3rd ed. Hamilton, Ga. (printed at Philadelphia, Pa.). Reprint ed. with "The Story of the Sacred Harp 1844-1944" by George Pullen Jackson and a postscript by William J. Reynolds. Nashville: Broadman Press, 1968.
Work, John W. "The Negro Spiritual," *Addresses at the International Hymnological Conference.* New York: The Hymn Society of America, 1962, pp. 17-27.

Wyeth, John. *Wyeth's Repository of Sacred Music, Part Second.* 2nd ed. Harrisburg, Pa., 1820. Reprint ed. with an introduction by Irving Lowens. New York: Da Capo Press, 1964.

Yoder, Don. *Pennsylvania Spirituals.* Lancaster, Pa.: Pennsylvania Folk Life Society, 1961.

Zellner, John F., III. "Robert Lowry: Early American Hymn Writer," *The Hymn* 26 (October 1975), 117-24, and 27 (January 1976), 15-21.

American Denominational Hymnody

Binder, A. W. "History of American Jewish Hymnody," *The Hymn* 14 (October 1963), 101-107; 15 (January 1964), 23-26.

Burrage, Henry S. *Baptist Hymn Writers and Their Hymns.* Portland, Me.: Brown, Thurston and Co., 1888.

Brandon, George. "The Hymnody of the Disciples of Christ in the U.S.A.," *The Hymn* 15 (January 1964), 15-22.

Cornwall, J. Spencer. *Stories of Our Mormon Hymns.* Salt Lake City: Deseret Book Co., 1961.

DeLaney, E. Theodore. "Prairie Hymnody—Lutherans: 1820-1970," *The Hymn* 23 (October 1972), 119-24; 24 (January 1973), 23-28.

The Development of Lutheran Hymnody in America. Articles reprinted from *The Encyclopedia of the Lutheran Church,* edited by Julius Bodensieck, for The Lutheran World Federation. Minneapolis: Augsburg Publishing House, 1967.

Foote, Henry W. *Catalogue of American Unitarian Hymn Writers and Hymns.* New York: Compiled for The Hymn Society of America, 1959.

_____. *Catalogue of American Universalist Hymn Writers and Hymns.* New York: Compiled for The Hymn Society of America, 1959.

Giesler, John H. "Musical Ministers of the Moravian Church," *The Hymn* 29 (January 1978), 6-14,28.

Hall, Roger. "Shaker Hymnody," *The Hymn* 27 (January 1976), 22-29.

Higginson, J. Vincent. *Handbook for American Catholic Hymnals.* Springfield, Ohio: The Hymn Society of America, 1976.

"The Hymnal of the Protestant Episcopal Church in the U.S.A." in *The Hymnal 1940 Companion.* 3rd, rev. ed. New York: The Church Pension Fund, 1951, pp. xix-xxvii.

The Mennonite Encyclopedia. s.v. "Hymnology of the American Mennonites," by Harold S. Bender.

New Catholic Encyclopedia. s.v. "Hymnology," by J. Szövérffy.

_____. s.v. "Hymns and Hymnals," by M. M. Hueller, M. A. Bichsel, E. J. Selhorst.

Reynolds, William J. "Baptist Hymnody in America," Part One of *Companion to Baptist Hymnal.* Nashville: Broadman Press, 1975, pp. 5-23.

Schalk, Carl. "Hymnody, American Lutheran," in *Key Words in Church Music,* ed. Carl Schalk. St. Louis: Concordia Publishing House, 1978, pp. 222-31.

Smith, C. Howard. "Scandinavian Free Church Hymnody in America," *The Hymn* 29, 4 (October 1978), 228-37.

Van Burkalow, Anastasia. "Expanding Horizons: Two Hundred Years of American Methodist Hymnody," *The Hymn* 17, 3 (July 1966), 77-84,90.

Weber, William A. "The Hymnody of the Dutch Reformed Church America," *The Hymn* 26 (April 1975), 57-60.

Westendorf, Omer. "The State of Catholic Hymnody," *The Hymn* 28 (April 1977), 54-60.

Young, Carlton R. "A Survey of American Methodist Hymnbooks," in *Companion to the Hymnal: A Handbook to the 1964 Methodist Hymnal*, ed. Emory Stevens Bucke. Nashville: Abingdon Press, 1970, pp. 54-61.

Cultural Perspectives

Adams, Charles G. "Some Aspects of Black Worship," *Andover Newton Quarterly* 11 (January 1971), 124-38; *Music Ministry* 5 (September 1972), 2-9; *Journal of Church Music* 15 (February 1973), 2-9,16.

International Encyclopedia of the Social Sciences. s.v. "Culture: Cultural Relativism," by David Bidley.

Cantato Domino New Edition (4th ed.). Kassel, Germany: Published by Bärenreiter Verlag for the World Council of Churches, 1974.

E.A.C.C. Hymnal, Daniel T. Niles (general ed.) and John M. Kelly (music ed.). Tokyo: East Asia Christian Conference, 1964. (Distributed by AVACO, 22 Midorigaoka-machi, Shibuya-ku, Tokyo, Japan)

Fleming, Jo Lee. "James D. Vaughan, Music Publisher, Lawrenceburg, Tennessee, 1912-1964." D.S.M. dissertation, Union Theological Seminary, 1971.

Goines, Leonard. "Music of Africa South of the Sahara," *Music Educators Journal* 59 (October 1972), 46-51. (Issue reprinted as *Music in World Cultures*, available from the Music Educators National Conference, 1201 16th St., N.W., Washington, D. C. 20036.)

Hohmann, Rupert Earl. "The Church Music of the Old Order Amish in the United States." Ph.D. dissertation, Northwestern University, 1959.

Herskovits, Melville J. *Cultural Anthropology*. New York: Alfred A. Knopf, 1958.

Hymns of Universal Praise. Shanghai, 1936. (An interdenominational Chinese hymnal.)

Isaacs, Frank C. "The Gymanfa Ganu in America," *The Hymn* 14 (April 1963), 47-52.

Jackson, George Pullen. *White and Negro Spirituals*. New York: J. J. Augustin, 1944. Reprint ed., New York: Da Capo Press, 1975.

Joyner, Jane Linville. "Black Music in a White Church," *Music Ministry* 8 (February 1976), 2-5.

Laster, James H. "The Persian Tunebook: A Dream Fulfilled," *The Hymn* 30 (April 1979), 78-88.

Luff, Alan. "Welsh Hymn Melodies: Their Present and Future Use in English Hymn Books," *Bulletin*, The Hymn Society of Great Britain and Ireland, 4 (Spring 1970), 76-77.

McAlpine, Pauline Smith. *Japanese Hymns in English*. Nagoya, Japan: Tsubobue Sha, 1975.

McKellar, Hugh D. "The Lord's Song in a Strange Land: Music in the Ethnic Churches of Toronto," *The Hymn* 29 (October 1978), 217-21.

Malm, William P. *Music Cultures of the Pacific, the Near East and Asia*. Englewood Cliffs, N.J.: Prentice-Hall, Inc., 1967.

Merriam, Alan P. *The Anthropology of Music*. Evanston, Ill.: Northwestern University Press, 1964.

Nettl, Bruno. *Folk and Traditional Music of the Western Continents*. Englewood Cliffs, N.J.: Prentice-Hall, Inc., 1965.

Nketia, J. H. Kwabena. *The Music of Africa*. New York: W. W. Norton and Co., 1974.

Olson, Howard S. (ed.). *Lead Us, Lord: A Collection of African Hymns*. Minneapolis: Augsburg Publishing House, 1977.

Picken, Laurence. "The Music of Far Eastern Asia. 1. China" in *New Oxford History of Music* v. 1, *Ancient and Oriental Music*, pp. 82-134. London, New York and Toronto: Oxford University Press, 1957.

Ressler, Martin E. "Hymnbooks Used by the Old Order Amish," *The Hymn* 28 (January 1977), 11-16.

Southern, Eileen. *The Music of Black Americans: A History.* New York: W. W. Norton and Co., 1971.

Weman, Henry. *African Music and the Church in Africa.* Uppsala, Sweden: Ab Lundequistska Bokhandeln, 1960.

Wiant, Bliss. *The Music of China.* Hong Kong: Chung Chi Publications, 1965.

Williams, Robert R. "Some Aspects of Welsh Hymnody," *The Hymn* 4 (January 1953), 5-11.

Yoder, Paul M. (ed.) *Four Hundred Years with the Ausbund.* Scottdale, PA: Herald Press, 1964.

York, Terry W. "Lining-Out in Congregational Singing," *The Hymn* 28 (July 1977), 110-113.

The Hymn in Proclamation

Barrows, Cliff. "Musical Evangelism," *Decision* 3 (December 1962), 12-13.

Cleall, Charles. "An Interlude on Evangelism and Music," in *The Selection and Training of Mixed Choirs in Churches.* London: Independent Press Ltd., 1960, pp. 57-73.

Davies, J. G. *Worship and Mission.* New York: Association Press, 1967.

Elmer, Richard M. "Modern Evangelism and Church Music," *The Hymn* 7 (January 1956), 13-17.

Gold, Charles E. "The Gospel Song: Contemporary Opinion," *The Hymn* 9 (July 1958), 69-73.

Hille, Waldemar. "Evaluating Gospel Songs," *The Hymn* 3 (January 1952), 15-18.

Hull, William E. "Make a Joyful Noise unto the Lord," *The Church Musician* 28 (July 1977), 12-13, 24.

Hustad, Donald P. *Church Music in the Evangelical Tradition.* Carol Stream: Hope Publishing Co., 1980.

_____. "Music and the Church's Outreach," *Review and Expositor* 69 (spring 1972), 177-185.

Kerr, Phil. *Music in Evangelism.* 4th ed. Glendale, CA: Gospel Music Publishers, 1939, 1954.

Lacour, Lawrence. "Music in Evangelism," *Music Ministry* 4 (August 1964), 2-4,14.

McKissick, Marvin. "The Function of Music in American Revivals Since 1875," *The Hymn* 9 (October 1958), 107-117.

Proclamation: Aids for Interpreting the Lessons of the Church Year (a series of 25 books). Philadelphia: Fortress Press, 1974.

Sallee, James. *A History of Evangelistic Hymnody.* Grand Rapids, MI: Baker Book House, 1978.

Smyth, Richard Renwick. "A Sermon in Song—The Word Proclaimed by John Wesley; The Response to This Word Confessed in Song by Charles Wesley," *The Hymn* 15 (April 1964), 47-52.

Webber, F. R. "The Gospel in the Great Hymns," *Christianity Today* 4 (August 29, 1960), 6-8.

Westerman, R. Scott. "The Term 'Gospel Hymn,' " *The Hymn* 9 (April 1958), 61-62.

Wilson, John F. "Music in Evangelism," in *An Introduction to Church Music.* Chicago: Moody Press, 1965, pp. 51-64.

The Hymn in Worship

Arnold, Corliss R. "Hymns of Advent, Christmas and Epiphany," *The Hymn* 5 (October 1954), 121-27.

Babcock, Richard M. "The Liturgical Year in Six Contemporary Protestant Hymnals," *The Hymn* 12 (October 1961), 113-19.

Brand, Eugene L. "Congregational Song: the Popular Music of the Church," *Church Music* 68-1: 1-10.

Braun, H. Myron. "Blow up the Trumpet," *Music Ministry* 8 (November 1975), 1, 40.

_____. "The Closing Hymn," *The Hymn* 5 (July 1954), 90-94.

_____. "Love That Hymnal," *Music Ministry* 9 (May 1977), 1, 32.

_____. "Total Hymnody for the Eighties," *Music Ministry* 10 (October 1977), 7-8, 29.

_____. "Who's Out of Date?" *Music Ministry* 8 (June 1976) 1, 32.

Buchner, John F. "Alternation in Hymn Singing," *Journal of Church Music* 18 (December 1976) 7-9.

Cammerer, Richard R. "The Congregational Hymn as the Living Voice of the Gospel," in *The Musical Heritage of the Church,* Vol. V, Theo. Hoelty-Nickel, ed. Valparaiso: Concordia Publishing House, 1959, pp. 166-77.

Davies, Horton. *Worship and Theology in England from Watts and Wesley to Maurice, 1690-1850.* Princeton: Princeton University Press, 1961.

Dunstan, Alan. "Hymnody in Christian Worship" in *The Study of Liturgy.* New York: Oxford University Press, 1978. pp. 454-65.

_____. *These Are the Hymns.* London: Society for the Preservation of Christian Knowledge, 1973.

Egge, Mandus. "Let There Be a Surprise," *Journal of Church Music* 13 (July-August 1971), 2-6.

Gealy, Fred D. "What Shall We Sing?" *The Hymn* 14 (July 1963), 80-82.

Gillman, Frederick J. "Reality in Worship," Occasional Paper #2. The Hymn Society of Great Britain and Ireland, October 1939.

Gray, G. F. S. *Hymns and Worship.* London: S. P. C. K., 1961.

Gregory, A. S. "The Hymn in Christian Liturgy," *Bulletin of the Hymn Society of Great Britain and Ireland* 7 (April 1939), 6-7.

Heaton, Charles Huddleston. "How About a Prelude of Hymns?" *Journal of Church Music* 19 (November 1977), 3.

Hiebert, Clarence. "The Selection and Use of the Sermon Hymn," *The Hymn* 5 (April 1954), 51-53.

Hoon, Paul Waitman. *The Integrity of Worship:* Ecumenical and Pastoral Studies in Liturgical Theology. Nashville: Abingdon Press, 1971.

Horn, Henry E. *O Sing Unto the Lord.* Philadelphia: The Muhlenberg Press, 1956.

Johansen, John H. "Come, Christians, Join to Sing," *The Hymn* 21 (October 1970), 116-20.

Knight, George Litch. "The Creative Use of Hymns in Worship," *Union Seminary Quarterly Review* 7 (June, 1952), 21-26.

Leaver, Robin A. *The Liturgy and Music.* Nottingham: Grove Books, 1976.

Lock, William. "Now and Then," *Journal of Church Music* 14 (February 1972), 10-11.

Lorah, Theodore R. Jr. "The Use of Amens," *Journal of Church Music* 18 (September 1976), 5-7.

Lovelace, Austin C. *Hymn Festivals.* Papers of The Hymn Society of America, XXXI, 1979.

————and Rice, William C. *Music and Worship in the Church.* Revised and enlarged ed. New York and Nashville: Abingdon Press, 1976.

McCaleb, Jimmy. "Creative Worship," *The Church Musician* 27 (January 1976), 4-7.

————. "Exciting Congregational Singing," *The Church Musician* 27 (September 1976), 6-8.

McDormand, Thomas Bruce. *The Art of Building Worship Services.* Nashville: Broadman Press, 1942. "Making the most of hymns," pp. 25-54.

Manning, Bernard L. *The Hymns of Wesley and Watts.* London: Epworth Press, 1942.

Miller, Edward O. "Hymns in Aid of Worship," *The Hymn* 10 (July 1959), 79-80.

Miller, L. David. "Do It Yourself Descants," *Journal of Church Music* 16 (November 1974), 2-7.

Moeser, James. "Why and How Do We Celebrate?" *The Hymn* 26 (July 1975), 92-94.

Northcott, Cecil. *Hymns in Christian Worship.* Richmond: John Knox Press, 1964.

Messenger, Ruth E. "Hymnology: Handmaiden of Worship," *The Hymn* 6 (April 1955), 64-67.

Moyer, J. Edward. *The Voice of His Praise.* Nashville: Graded Press, 1965, pp. 64-125.

Murphy, Donald L. *The Hymn Chart Manual.* Mt. Airy, MD: Genesis Enterprises, 1977.

Noyes, Morgan Phelps. "Hymn as Aids to Devotion," *The Hymn* 5 (January 1954), 5-12.

Parker, Alice. *Creative Hymn Singing.* Chapel Hill: Hinshaw Music, Inc., 1976.

Patrick, Millar. "Congregational Song," *The Hymn* 3 (January 1952), 5-9.

Pirner, Reuben G. "The Nature and Function of the Hymn in Christian Worship," *Church Music* 66-1: 1-5.

Pratt, Waldo Selden. *Musical Ministries in the Church* New York: Fleming H. Revell Co., 1902. "Hymns and Hymn-singing," pp. 45-82.

Robbins, Howard Chandler. "The Place of Hymns in Public Worship," in *Addresses at the Twentieth Anniversary of the Hymn Society of America,* Paper X, 1943.

Rogers, James A. "John Wesley Can Help Improve the Hymn Singing in Your Church," *Music Ministry* 8 (March, 1976), 28,31.

Routley, Erik. *Hymns Today and Tomorrow.* Nashville: Abingdon Press, 1964.

————. *Music Leadership in the Church.* Nashville: Abingdon Press, 1967. "The Art of Worship," pp. 106-20.

————. *Music, Sacred and Profane.* Occasional Writings on Music 1950-58. London: Independent Press, 1960.

————. "On Congregational Singing—The Next Chapter," *Bulletin of the Hymn Society of Great Britain and Ireland* 120 (January, 1971), 113-22.

————. *Words, Music, and the Church.* Nashville: Abingdon Press, 1968.

Shealy, William R. "Towards a More Transitional Hymnody," *The Hymn* 24 (October, 1973), 112-18.

Smith, H. Augustine. *Lyric Religion: The Romance of Immortal Hymns.* New York: D. Appleton-Century Company, 1931.

Sydnor, James Rawlings. *The Hymn and Congregational Singing.* Richmond: John Knox Press, 1960.

Waggoner, Richard D. "A Reason to Sing," *Music Ministry* 9 (November 1976), 8-9,27.

Whitehead, William. "Making Hymns Meaningful Experiences," *Journal of Church Music* 19 (November 1977), 2-3.

York, David. "Hymn Singing—*Now,*" *The Hymn* 22 (April 1971), 42-43.
Young, Carlton R. "The Changing Shape of Parish Music," *Church Music* 67-2: 16-24.

The Hymn and Funeral Services

A Manual for the Funeral. New York and Nashville: Abingdon Press, 1962.
Biddle, Perry H. Jr. "Music for the Christian Funeral," *Music Ministry* 8 (February 1976), 6-7.
Knight, George Litch, William W. Reid, Jr. and Gerald E. Hedges. "Symposium: The Funeral Service and Hymns," *The Hymn* 10 (April 1959), 39-48.
Mulder, Robert G. "Honor the Dead—Respect the Living," *Journal of Church Music* 15 (November 1973), 11-12.
Music for Church Funerals. Greenwich: The Seabury Press, 1952.
Music for Funerals. The Joint Commission on Church Music. New York: H. W. Gray Co., 1963.
Snell, Frederick A. *Music for Church Funerals and Memorial Services.* Philadelphia: Fortress Press, 1966.

The Hymn and Weddings

Braun, H. Myron. "Here Comes the Bride," *The Hymn* 24 (July, 1973), 85-87.
Carlson, J. Bert. "A Pastoral View of Music for a Christian Wedding," *Journal of Church Music,* 19 (June 1977), 2-5.
Contemporary Worship 3—The Marriage Service. St. Louis: Concordia Publishing House, 1972.
Ellinwood, Leonard. "Congregational Participation for Weddings Urged," *Diapason* (July, 1957).
Epley, Linda Morrison and Epley, William Arnold. *Music and Your Wedding.* Nashville: The Sunday School Board of the Southern Baptist Convention, 1972.
Fryxell, Regina H. *Wedding Music.* Rock Island, Ill: Augustana Press, 1961.
Handbook of Church Music for Weddings. Chicago: Office for Divine Worship, the Archdiocese of Chicago, 1977.
Halter, Carl. "Special Services," in *The Practice of Sacred Music.* (St. Louis: Concordia Publishing House, 1955), 50-51.
Lovelace, Austin C. "Music at Weddings, Funerals," *The Baptist Program* (November 1964).
McDonald, Robert. "Weddings," *The Church Musician* 28 (June 1977), 8-13.
Music for Church Weddings. Greenwich: The Seabury Press, 1953.
Rotermund, Donald. "The Marriage Service . . . and the Role of the Congregation," *Church Music* 74-1: 17-19.

Hymn Playing

Anderson, Margaret Sihler. *A Guide to Effective Hymn Playing.* Minneapolis: Augsburg Publishing House, 1964.
Clokey, Joseph C. "The Organist in the Small Church," "Congregational Singing in the Small Church," "Hints for the Organist" in *In Every Corner Sing.* New York: Morehouse-Gorham Co., 1945.
Gehring, Philip. "The Role of the Organ in Congregational Song," *Journal of Church Music* 12 (April 1970), 2-5.

Greenlee, Anita. "Introducing Hymns for the Service," *Journal of Church Music* 14 (November 1972), 7-13.

Halter, Carl. "The Playing of Hymns" in *The Practice of Sacred Music*. St. Louis: Concordia Publishing Co., 1955, pp. 30-36.

Hinkle, Donald. "Practical Suggestions for Improved Hymn Playing," *Journal of Church Music* 16 (November 1974), 9-11; *Journal of Church Music* 16 (December 1974), 5-8.

Kettring, Donald D. "Two Years a Pew Sitter," *Journal of Church Music* 16 (May 1974), 4-5; *Journal of Church Music* 16 (June 1974), 9-11.

_____. "Organ Interludes in Worship," *Journal of Church Music* 10 (May 1968), 8-11.

_____. "Reflections," *Journal of Church Music* 19 (April 1977), 13-15.

Krapf, Gerhard. *Liturgical Organ Playing*. Minneapolis: Augsburg Publishing House, 1964.

Leaf, Robert. "Organists: How to Improve Your Hymn Accompanying," *Journal of Church Music* 18 (April 1976), 14-16,46.

Litterst, Richard W. "Hymn Playing," *The Hymn* 13 (April 1962), 45-47,57.

Lovelace, Austin C. "Free Harmonizations for the Organ," *Journal of Church Music* 19 (April 1977), 17-20.

_____. *The Organist and Hymn Playing*. Nashville: Abingdon Press, 1962.

Pratt, Waldo Selden. "The Organist's Relation to Hymn Tunes and Hymn Singing," *The Hymn* 6 (April 1955), 41-51.

Reynolds, William J. *Congregational Singing*. Nashville: Convention Press, 1975. "Tempos and Keys in Congregational Singing" and "Instrumental Accompaniment for Congregational Singing," pp. 7-40.

Ripper, Theodore W. "The Organist Can Stimulate or Stifle Congregational Song," *Music Ministry* 9 (September 1976), 5-7.

Routley, Erik. *An Organist's Companion to the Worshipbook* Vol. IX (Spring 1975) issue of *Reformed Liturgy and Music*—A Journal of Discipleship and Worship.

_____. "Can We Enjoy Hymns?" *Music Ministry* 9 (April 1977), 28-29.

_____. "The Organist and the Congregation" in *Church Music and the Christian Faith*. Carol Stream, Ill: Agape, 1978, pp. 121-28.

_____. *The Organist's Guide to Congregational Praise*. London: Independent Press, Ltd., 1957.

Scofield, Constance E. "Stand Up and Bless the Lord . . . a Look at Hymn Tune Introductions," *Journal of Church Music* 20 (November 1978), 8-9.

Sydnor, James Rawlings. "The Playing of Hymns" in *The Hymn and Congregational Singing* Richmond: John Knox Press, 1960, pp. 105-24.

Warder, Velma. "The Organist in Church," *Journal of Church Music* 16 (April 1974), 8-11.

Wetzler, Robert. "Organists—Please Read the Words!" *Journal of Church Music* 20 (April 1978), 5-7.

Hymn Introductions and Harmonizations

Beck, Theodore. *Forty-Seven Hymn Intonations*. St. Louis: Concordia Publishing House, 1971.

Bender, Jan. *Twenty Hymn Introductions*. St. Louis: Concordia Publishing House, 1974.

_____. *Twenty-four Hymn Introductions*. St. Louis: Concordia Publishing House, 1974.

Cassler, G. Winston. *Organ Descants for Selected Hymn Tunes*. Minneapolis: Augsburg Publishing House, 1972.

Ferguson, John. *Ten Hymn Tune Harmonizations*. Cleveland: Ludwig Music Co., 1975.

Free Organ Accompaniments to Festival Hymns. Minneapolis: Augsburg Publishing House, 1963.

Hustad, Donald. *Organ-Piano Accompaniments for Congregational Hymns*. Carol Stream, Ill.: Hope Publishing Co., 1974.

_____. *Organ-Piano Accompaniments for Congregational Singing*. Nashville: Broadman Press, 1975.

Johnson, David N. *Deck Thyself, My Soul, with Gladness: Organ Music for Communion and General Use*. Minneapolis: Augsburg Publishing House, 1968.

_____. *Free Harmonizations of Twelve Hymn Tunes*. Minneapolis: Augsburg Publishing House, 1964.

_____. *Free Hymn Accompaniments for Manuals*, Books I and II. Minneapolis: Augsburg Publishing House, 1966.

Manz, Paul. *Ten Short Intonations on Well-Known Hymns*. Minneapolis: Augsburg Publishing House, 1970.

Noble, T. Tertius. *Fifty Free Organ Accompaniments to Well-Known Hymn Tunes*. Glen Rock, NJ.: J. Fischer, 1949.

_____. *Free Organ Accompaniments to One Hundred Well-Known Hymn Tunes*. Glen Rock, NJ.: J. Fischer, 1946.

Rohlig, Harald. *55 Hymn Intonations*. New York: Abingdon Press, 1962.

Thiman, Eric. *Varied Accompaniments to Thirty-Four Well-Known Hymn Tunes for Unison Singing*. London: Oxford University Press, 1937.

_____. *Varied Harmonizations of Favorite Hymn Tunes*. Melville, NY.: H. W. Gray, 1955.

Wood, Dale. *New Settings of Twenty Well-Known Hymn Tunes*. Minneapolis: Augsburg Publishing House, 1968.

Hymn Festivals and Hymn Services

Bays, Alice A. *Worship Programs in the Fine Arts*. Nashville: Abingdon-Cokesbury Press, 1940.

The Church Musician 1950-   Nashville: The Sunday School Board of the Southern Baptist Convention. (Special hymn services of varied kinds in most monthly issues.)

Coon, Zula Evelyn. *Worship Services from the Hymns*. Westwood, NJ.: Fleming H. Revell Co., 1958.

_____. *O Worship the King*. Nashville: Broadman Press, 1951.

Curry, Louise H. and Chester M. Wetzel. *Worship Services Using the Arts*. Philadelphia: The Westminster Press, 1961.

Emurian, Ernest K. *Popular Programs Based on Hymn Stories*. (Reprint of *Hymn Festivals*, 1961). Grand Rapids: Baker Book House, 1972.

Heaton, Charles Huddleston. *A Guidebook to Worship Services of Sacred Music*. St. Louis: The Bethany Press, 1962. "Hymn Festivals," pp. 44-52.

Jensen, Donald F. "Behold, I make all things new!" a Hymn Service. *Music Ministry* 1 (September 1968), 3-5.

Knickel, David A. "Hymn Festivals, U.S.A.," *The Hymn* 8 (April 1957), 50-52; *The*

Hymn 9 (April 1958), 53-58; *The Hymn* 10 (July 1959): 91-94; *The Hymn* 11 (October 1960), 117-22.

Kruschwitz, Robert B. "The Program of Hymn Interpretation," *The Hymn* 24 (October 1973), 119-21.

Lovelace, Austin C. *Hymn Festivals.* Papers of the Hymn Society of America, XXXI, Ohio, 1979.

McDormand, Thomas Bruce. "Making the Most of Hymns" in *The Art of Building Worship Services.* Nashville: Broadman Press, 1942.

Moen, Kathryn Ulvilden. "Hymn Festivals," in Egge, Mandus A. and Moede, Janet. *Hymns—How to Sing Them.* Minneapolis: Augsburg Publishing House, 1966, pp. 25-28.

Moyer, J. Edward. "Hymn Services" in *The Voice of His Praise.* Nashville: Graded Press, 1965, pp. 120-125.

Pfatteicher, Helen E. "Man's Yearning for Freedom" (A hymn festival with a reader), *The Hymn* 21 (January 1970), 21-26.

Simmons, Morgan F. "Hymn Festivals, U.S.A.," *The Hymn* 12 (July 1961), 83-87; *The Hymn* 13 (July 1962), 86-91.

Sydnor, James Rawlings. "Hymn Services and Festivals," in *The Hymn and Congregational Singing.* Richmond: John Knox Press, 1960, pp. 163-70.

Whittlesey, Federal Lee. *A Comprehensive Program of Church Music.* Philadelphia: The Westminster Press, 1957.

_____. "Some Suggested Topics for Hymn Services," *The Hymn* 9 (July 1958), 83-85.

The Hymn in Education

Baker, Philip E. "Existential Hymn Singing," *Music Ministry* 8 (February, 1976), 28-29,31.

Benson, Louis F. *The Hymnody of the Christian Church.* New York: George H. Doran Co., 1927; reprint ed., Richmond: John Knox Press, 1956.

Braun, H. Myron. "Do we still teach hymns?" *Music Ministry* 8 (September, 1975), 1,40.

_____. "The Minister of Music as Teacher," *Music Ministry* 1 (April 1969), 40.

_____. "Our Goal is Music for Worship," *New Christian Advocate* 2 (October 1958), 42-45.

Buchner, John F. "Church Music is for the Congregation, Too," *Journal of Church Music* 16 (March 1974), 5-7.

Cheesman, Virginia. "Young People Learn Church Music" *International Journal Of Religious Education* 35 (December 1958), 18-20.

Darnell, Grace Leeds. "How to Teach a Hymn—And Why," *The Hymn* 2 (April 1951), 11-13.

Demarest, Alison (ed.). *The Canyon Hymnal for Boys and Girls.* Leader's Edition. East Orange, N.J.: Canyon Press, 1958. (Available from E. C. Kerby Ltd., 198 Davenport Road, Toronto, Canada.)

Egge, Mandus A. and Janet Moede. *Hymns—How to Sing Them.* Minneapolis: Augsburg Publishing House, 1966.

Eskew, Harry. "Hymns in the Church's Teaching Ministry," *The Theological Educator* 8 (Spring 1978), 86-97.

Hackney, Vivian and Key, Jimmy. *Hymns to Know and Sing.* Nashville: Convention Press, 1973.

Haeussler, Armin. "The Struggle for Better Hymnody," in *Cantors at the Crossroads.*

St. Louis: Concordia Publishing House, 1967, pp. 163-84.
Hall, Paul M. "Hymn Rehearsals and Public Worship," *The Church Musician* 16 (June 1965), 12-14.
Hicks, Roger W. "A Total Concept: Choirs, Leaders, Congregations United in Music." *Music Ministry* 1 (May 1969), 2-5.
Horn, Henry E. *O Sing Unto the Lord: Music in the Lutheran Church.* Philadelphia: Muhlenberg Press, 1956.
Hunnicutt, Judy. "Using Hymns with Children's Choirs," *The Hymn* 30 (January 1979), 34-35.
Hymn Study Series. Dallas: Choristers Guild, n.d. (a series of hymn study sheets). (Order from Choristers Guild, P.O. Box 38188, Dallas, TX 75238.)
Key, Glennella. "Experiences with Hymnody" Chapter 8 of *Guiding Fours and Fives in Musical Experiences* Nashville: Convention Press, 1972.
Kintner, Robert J. "A New Approach to Hymn Learning," *Journal of Church Music* 13 (April 1971), 9-11.
Morsch, Vivian Sharp. *The Use of Music in Christian Education.* Philadelphia: The Westminster Press, 1956.
Moyer, J. Edward. *The Voice of His Praise: A New Appreciation of Hymnody.* Nashville: Graded Press, 1965.
Rogers, James A. "Traditional First Church and the Pre-Service Hymn Sing," *Music Ministry* 9 (December 1976), 28.
Spencer, Robert A. *Hymn and Scripture Selection Guide.* Valley Forge, Pa.: Judson Press, 1977.
Sydnor, James R. *The Hymn and Congregational Singing.* Richmond: John Knox Press, 1960.
_____. "Teaching Hymnology," *The Hymn* 29 (July 1978): 152-54, 163.
Tamper, E. E. "From Boredom to Inspiration," *Music Ministry* 9 (June 1977), 25.
Thomas, Edith Lovell. *Music in Christian Education.* New York and Nashville: Published for the Cooperative Publication Association by Abingdon Press, 1953.
West, Diane. "Using the Hymnal in the Confirmation Class," *Music Ministry* 8 (December 1975), 7-8.
Woodward, Betty. *The Singing Book.* Nashville: Convention Press, 1975.
Wilson, John F. "Music in Christian Education" in *An Introduction to Church Music.* Chicago: Moody Press, 1965, pp. 39-50.

The Hymn in Ministry

DeLaney, E. Theo. and Bailey, Clark. *Sing Unto the Lord—A Hymnal for the Deaf.* St. Louis: Commission on Worship and Board for Missions, The Lutheran Church, Missouri Synod, 1969.
Gee, H. L. *Hymns That Came to Life.* London: The Epworth Press, 1954.
Goward, Barbara E. *Hymns of Hope and Healing.* Cincinnati: The Willis Music Co., 1960.
Haas, Alfred B. "The Therapeutic Value of Hymns," *Pastoral Psychology* 1 (December 1950), 39-42.
Higginson, J. Vincent. "Hymns for the Blind," *The Hymn* 3 (October 1952), 116-18.
McElrath, Hugh T. "Hymns of Concern," *The Church Musician* 18 (October 1967), 4-6.
Merrill, William P. "The Religious Value of Hymns," Paper II of the Hymn Society of

America. New York: The Hymn Society, 1931.

Pinson, Joe. "Writing Hymns for Mentally Retarded Persons," *The Hymn* 30 (January 1979), 21-25.

Pinson, William M., Jr. *The Local Church in Ministry.* Nashville: Broadman Press, 1973.

Reid, William W., Jr. "The Social Note in Christmas and Easter Hymns," *The Hymn* 19 (April 1968), 44-48.

Rice, Cathy. *Music with the Deaf.* Murfreesboro, TN.: The Bill Rice Ranch, n.d.

Sing Praise, Hymnal for the Deaf. Nashville: Broadman Press, 1975.

Smart, James D. *The Rebirth of Ministry.* Philadelphia: The Westminster Press, 1960.

Stickney, Doris Brenner. "Songs in the Night," *Journal of Church Music* 14 (November 1972), 5-6.

Ten New Hymns on Aging and the Later Years. Springfield, Ohio: The Hymn Society of America; Washington, D.C.: National Retired Teachers Association and American Association of Retired Persons, 1976.

Tomiak, Walter M. and Calvert, Robert H. "Guidelines for a Hymn Sing in a Nursing Home," *The Hymn* 26 (April 1975), 39-40.

Turnbull, Agnes Sligh. "There's Healing in Hymns," *Christian Herald* 76 (November 1953), 64-66,70-71.

White, Emma Jane, ed. *Let's Do More with Persons with Disabilities.* Nashville: Local Church Education, Board of Discipleship of the United Methodist Church, 1973.

Index

316

318

Old Order Amish, 196-7
Old Testament, 209. See also Bible, Bible references.
Old Version, 107, 110
Olearius, Johannes, 95
Olivers, Thomas, 128
Olney Hymns (1779), 129, 136
Oratorio, 100, 169
Organ (organist), 95, 103, 178, 183, 199, 219, 227, 232, 241, 253, 257
Original Sacred Harp, Denson Revision (1971 ed.), 164, 165
Orthodox Christians, 206
Osborne, Stanley L., 192
Our Hymnody (1937), 185
Our Own Hymnbook (1866), 142
Owens, Priscilla, 179
The Oxford Book of Carols (1928), 145
Oxford Movement, 61, 74, 93, 126, 133, 136ff., 240, 242

Palestrina, 81
Palm Sunday, 84, 138, 223
Palmer, Ray, 86, 170, 171
Palmer, Sir Roundell, 142
A Panorama of Christian Hymnody (1979), 154
Papacy, 84
Paraclete, 85
Paraphrase of Scripture, 45ff.
The Paris Breviary (1736), 90
Parker, Archbishop Matthew, 107
Parry, Sir Hubert, 143
Particular Baptist, 117
Paschal Lamb, 58
Passion of Christ, 94, 100
Passion Sunday, 83
Passover, 78
Pastor, 219, 224, 231
Patrick, Millar, 109, 152, 153
Patriotic, 150, 170, 171-2, 173, 175, 187
Patterns of thought, 64ff.
    Objective-subjective, 65
    Paradox and contrast, 66
    Hebrew, 67
Pauline hymn fragments, 73
Peace, 137, 189
The Pedagogue (*ca.* 200), 75, (*The Tutor* or *The Instructor,* ca. 200), 75
Pennsylvania, 158, 160, 161, 165, 178, 179, 184, 185, 196, 199
Pentatonic scale, 27, 160, 162, 164, 181, 202, 204
Pentecost, 86, 122, 213-4, 223
Pentecostal denominations, 182
The People's Mass Book (1964, eds. to 1976), 188
Perronet, Edward, 128
Persian, 206
Peterson, John W., 182

Petri, Theodoric, 92
Phelps, Sylvanus D., 170, 171
Philadelphia, 112, 158, 171, 172, 175, 177, 183
Phillips, Philip, 178
Piae Cantiones (1582), 92, 141
Piano (pianist), 177, 180, 182, 199, 241, 253, 257
Pierpoint, Folliett Sandford, 138
Pietism, 96-7, 98, 121, 122, 126
Pilgrims, 110
Pilgrim's Progress (1684), 116
Philippine, 206
Pilsbury, Amos, 162
Pindar, 81
Pinson, Joe, 268, 270
Plainsong (or Gregorian Chant), 35-6, 45, 81, 144, 169, 232, 244
Playford, John, 108
Pliny the Younger, 74
Plumptre, Edward Hayes, 49, 138, 262
Pollard, Adelaide A., 179
Pollock, Thomas Benson, 138
Poetic devices, 18ff., 244
    Alliteration, 19
    Anadiplosis, 19
    Anaphora, 19
    Antithesis, 20
    Apostrophe, 22
    Chiasmus, 19, 124
    Climax, 22
    Hyperbole, 20
    Metaphor, 20
    Paradox, 19, 66
    Personification, 20
    Simile, 20
    Tautology, 22
Poetic meter, 16-17, 33, 120, 124, 200, 240
    Ambrosian, 80, 82
    Classical, 75
    Common, 16, 120
    Double common, 107
    Long, 16, 80, 120
    Sapphic, 83, 93
    Short, 16, 120
Poetry, 13ff., 115, 124, 131, 244
Poland, 97
Pop-style, 103, 147, 152
Portuguese, 184
Postlude, 253
Pratt, Waldo Selden, 105, 110, 185
Praxis pietatis melica (1644), 95
Prentiss, Elizabeth P., 172, 177
Prayer, responses to, 230
Prelude, 253
Presbyterian, 169, 172, 179, 182, 185, 186, 187, 239
Price, Carl F., 67
Primitive Baptist, 195
Primitive Methodist, 188

Sunday, 138, 150
Sunday school, 176-7, 184, 245, 268
Sunday, William (Billy), 180
*Sursum Corda, Being Studies of Some
German Hymn Writers* (1956), 93
Sweden, 92, 102, 104
Sweney, John R., 179
Swiss-American, 196
Switzerland, 104-6, 185, 210
Sydnor, James R., 254, 257
Syncopation, 42, 103, 198
Synesius of Cyrene, 75, 79
Syria, 171

Table grace, 93, 127, 257
Tag line, 24, 165
Tallis, Thomas, 81, 107, 225
Tanzania, 201
Tate, Nahum, 22, 48, 109, 118
Taylor, Cyril V., 146
Taylor, Sarah E., 188
Teaching hymns, 251-6, 258
Television, 271
Ten New Hymns on the Bible (1952), 188
Tennessee, 181
The Temple (1633), 115
Tennyson, Alfred, Lord, 14, 18, 24, 143
Tersteegen, Gerhard, 97
Teschner, Melchior, 92
Tessitura, 28
Testimony, 216, 237
Texas, 181
Text and tune matching, 43-4, 140, 186
Texture, musical, 33
Thailand, 206
Thanksgiving (See also Harvest), 93, 150,
187, 201, 231, 237, 272
Theological controversy, 59
Theology, 59ff., 200, 243, 257
Arian, 61, 79, 80
Armenian, 125
Calvinist, 120-1, 127, 129, 130, 132
Fundamentalist, 182
Gnostic, 61, 75
Liberal, 144
Therapist, music, 268, 270
Theodore of the Studium, 78
Theodulph of Orleans, 83, 84, 92
Thiman, Eric H., 146
Third World countries, 191, 193, 205
Thirty Years' War, 92-4
Thomas of Celano, 87
Thompson, Mary Ann, 171
Thring, Godfrey, 138
Thrupp, Dorothy A., 46
Tindley, Charles A., 183, 184
Tisserand, Jean, 89
Toplady, Augustus, 52, 63, 64, 130, 133,
136

Torry, Reuben A., 180
Towner, Daniel B., 179
Tractarian. See Oxford Movement.
Trajan, Emperor, 74
Translators, 103-4, 122, 139, 145, 169-70,
171
Trautwein, Dieter, 103
Trinitarian, 61, 78-9
Trinity, 80, 149
Trinity Sunday, 213
Trinitytide, 223
Trochaic, 16-17, 33, 44
Trombone, 180
Trope, 86-7
Trumpet, 179
Tucker, F. Bland, 49, 76, 85, 188, 252, 266
Tufts, John, 155
Tune. See Hymn tune.
Tunebook, 155-68
Tweedy, Henry H., 63, 188
Twells, Henry, 49
Twentieth-century Church Light Music
Group, 147, 152
Twentieth-Century Folk Mass (1956), 147

Unaccompanied, 196, 199
Unison, 43, 234, 236
Unitarian, 173
Unitas Fratrum. See Moravian.
United Church of Canada, 191-2
United Presbyterian, 112
United Reform, 150
United States Harmony (1799), 162
Urban. See City.
Utah, 172

Vacation Bible School, 245
Valentinian, Emperor, 80
Van Dyke, Henry, 62, 186
[James D.] Vaughan Music Company, 181
Verbal introductions of hymns, 226-7
Verse, differentiated from stanza, 13
Verdi, 81
Virgil, 81
Victorian era, 38, 133ff., 153
Victorian part-song tune, 38, 139-40
Virginia, 161, 162, 164, 181
Virginia Harmony (1831), 162
Vulpius, Melchior, 92

Wade, John Francis, 90
Wales, 39, 122, 127, 128, 131, 146, 198-200
Walker, William, 39, 161, 164, 167
Walking bass, 43
Wallin, Johan Oolf, 102
Walton, Izaak, 115
Waring, Anna Laetitia, 135
Warren, George W., 172
Washington, George, 112

Waters, Moir A. J., 191
Watts, Isaac, 65, 67, 68, 110, 112, 116, 118, 119, 120, 121, 126, 129, 132, 133, 136, 141, 153, 162, 224, 265
Watts, school of, 119-20
Webb, George J., 170
Wedding, 138, 186, 206, 237
Welsh folk tune, 39, 127, 146
Welsh-American, 199
Weman, Henry, 200, 201
Wesley, Charles, 19, 53, 60, 63, 64, 66, 121-8, 130, 131, 133, 136, 141, 153, 226, 265
Wesley, John, 63, 97, 98, 112, 121-8, 130, 133, 136, 240, 244, 265
Wesley, Samuel Sebastian, 140
Westendorf, Omer, 188
White, B. F., 161
White spiritual, 42, 167-8
Whitefield, George, 126, 127, 128, 130, 136
Whiting, William, 139, 236
Whitsunday, 122
Whittier, John Greenleaf, 15, 60, 67, 70, 144, 172, 239
Whittle, Daniel W., 67, 178, 179
The Whole Book of Psalmes, collected into English Metre, (completed 1562), 107; (1677), 108
Wiant, Bliss, 202
William III, 109
Williams, Ralph Vaughan, 81, 143, 144, 145, 239, 254
Williams, William, 48, 127, 199
Williamson, Malcolm, 152
Willis, Richard S., 171
Wilson, John, 152
Wilson, Woodrow, 264
Winters, Frances, 267
Wither, George, 114, 118
Witness, 208-9, 217
Wolcott, Samuel, 171
Woodford, J. R., 87
Woodward, George R., 143, 144
Worcester, Samuel, 112
Words, Music, and the Church (1968), 154
Wordsworth, Christopher, 138
Wordsworth, William, 131, 153
World Council of Churches, 187, 189, 206
World Student Christian Federation, 205
World War I, 186
Worship, 150, 154, 194, 208, 217, 219-42, 243-4, 245, 252-3, 257, 268, 272
Worship folder, 225, 251-2, 257
Wren, Brian, 150, 152
Wyeth, John, 160, 162

Xavier, Francis, 90

Yattendon Hymnal (1899), 143
Yoruba, 206

Young, Carlton R., iii, iv, 41
Young, Geoffrey W., 104
Young Men's Christian Association, 178
Youth, 233, 247, 250-1, 271
Yugoslavia, 80

Zimmerman, Heinz Werner, 103
Zinzendorf, Count, 97, 98
Zion, 54, 55, 56
Zondervan Publishing House, 182
Zundel, John, 171